The
Heart's
Eye

The Heart's Eye

Emotional Influences in Perception and Attention

Edited by

Paula M. Niedenthal
Department of Psychology
Indiana University
Bloomington, Indiana

Shinobu Kitayama
Department of Psychology
University of Oregon
Eugene, Oregon
and
Kyoto University
Kyoto, Japan

 Academic Press
A Division of Harcourt Brace & Company

San Diego   New York   Boston   London   Sydney   Tokyo   Toronto

This book is printed on acid-free paper. ∞

Copyright © 1994 by ACADEMIC PRESS, INC.
All Rights Reserved.
No part of this publication may be reproduced or transmitted in any form or by any
means, electronic or mechanical, including photocopy, recording, or any information
storage and retrieval system, without permission in writing from the publisher.

Academic Press, Inc.
525 B Street, Suite 1900, San Diego, California 92101-4495

United Kingdom Edition published by
Academic Press Limited
24–28 Oval Road, London NW1 7DX

Library of Congress Cataloging-in Publication Data

The heart's eye : emotional influences in perception and attention /
  edited by Paula M. Niedenthal, Shinobu Kitayama.
      p.   cm.
  Includes bibliographical references and index.
  ISBN 0-12-410560-2
  1. Emotions.   2. Perception.   3. Attention.   I. Niedenthal, Paula
M.   II. Kitayama, Shinobu.
  BF531.H378   1994
  152.4 --dc20   93-23395
                                                            CIP

PRINTED IN THE UNITED STATES OF AMERICA
94 95 96 97 98 99   BC   9 8 7 6 5 4 3 2 1

For our parents, Morris and Corrine Niedenthal,
and Ryoyu and Hideko Kitayama

Contents

Consciousness and Automatic Evaluation
Felicia Pratto

Comments on Unconscious Processing: Finding Emotion in the Cognitive Stream
Marcia K. Johnson and Carolyn Weisz

Section II Emotion and Attention

Motivating the Focus of Attention
Douglas Derryberry and Don M. Tucker

Attitudes, Perception, and Attention
Russell H. Fazio, David R. Roskos-Ewoldsen, and Martha C. Powell

Contributors

Numbers in parentheses indicate the pages on which the authors' contributions begin.

Jerome Bruner (269), New York University, New York City, New York 10012

Douglas Derryberry (167), Department of Psychology, Oregon State University, Corvallis, Oregon 97331

Christine Madeleine Du Bois (23), The Johns Hopkins University, Baltimore, Maryland 21217

Howard Egeth (245), Department of Psychology, The Johns Hopkins University, Baltimore, Maryland 21218

Russell H. Fazio (197), Department of Psychology, Indiana University, Bloomington, Indiana 47405

Anthony G. Greenwald (67), Department of Psychology, University of Washington, Seattle, Washington 98195

Christine H. Hansen (217), Department of Psychology, Oakland University, Rochester, Michigan 48309

Ranald D. Hansen (217), Department of Psychology, Oakland University, Rochester, Michigan 48309

Susan Howard (41), Department of Psychology, University of Oregon, Eugene, Oregon 97403

Marcia K. Johnson (145), Department of Psychology, Princeton University, Princeton, New Jersey 08544

Douglas E. Jones (87), Department of Psychology, The Johns Hopkins University, Baltimore, Maryland 21218

Shinobu Kitayama (1, 41), Department of Psychology, University of Oregon, Eugene, Oregon 97403, and Kyoto University, Kyoto, Japan

Mark R. Klinger (67), Department of Psychology, University of Arkansas, Fayetteville, Arkansas 72701

Paula M. Niedenthal (1, 87), Department of Psychology, Indiana University, Bloomington, Indiana 47405

Martha C. Powell (197), Department of Psychology, University of Colorado, Boulder, Colorado 80309

Felicia Pratto (115), Department of Psychology, Stanford University, Stanford, California 94305

David R. Roskos-Ewoldsen (197), Department of Psychology, University of Alabama, Tuscaloosa, Alabama 35487

Marc B. Setterlund (87), Department of Psychology, Concordia College, Moorhead, Minnesota 56560

Don M. Tucker (167), Department of Psychology, University of Oregon, Eugene, Oregon 97403

Israel Waynbaum[1] (23), Paris, France

Carolyn Weisz (145), Department of Psychology, Princeton University, Princeton, New Jersey 08544

R. B. Zajonc (17), Department of Psychology, University of Michigan, Ann Arbor, Michigan 48109

[1] *Deceased.*

Preface

The editors of this volume once informally interviewed people about the accuracy of their perception and found that most people admitted that there had been occasions on which their eyes seemed to fail them. While on some of these occasions people were exposed to well-known perceptual illusions (e.g., demonstrated in a psychology class), on many other occasions the perceiver was experiencing a strong emotion. Fear was a predominant emotion in people's stories about distorted perception. Two individuals reported that they thought they had seen a bear (during a fearful state) when, in fact, they saw a small dog in one incident, and a normal-sized man in the other. Love was also a frequently mentioned emotion, with both subjective qualities (e.g., attractiveness) and objective qualities (e.g., hair and eye color) being subject to perceptual distortion during strong emotion. As these examples imply, the possibility that emotions mediate perception in an early and fundamental way is important, not only to basic models of perception and attention, but also for specific concerns in psychology, such as eyewitness testimony, detection of deceit, and stereotyping.

The chapters contained in this volume all address the possibility that affect exerts early influences in the processes that are involved in transforming sensations into internal representations of words and objects. The chapters that compose the first section of the volume focus on the possibility that emotions influence automatic processes in perception. The chapters by Waynbaum, Klinger and Greenwald, Pratto, and Niedenthal and colleagues focus specifically on visual perception. Kitayama also reports the results of experiments on auditory perception. Chapters in this section discuss whether emotion alters perceptual thresholds for certain types of stimuli, how the emotional content and emotional tone of spoken communication interact, and how much cognitive processing is required for perceivers to make judgments about the affective meaning of visual stimuli.

The chapters that compose the second section examine the influences of emotional state, as well as the affective connotation of stimulus events, in processes of visual attention. This section is noteworthy in that the chapters report research examining the processing of pictures (attitude objects), words, human faces, and spatial location. Chapters in this section discuss whether affect influences the direction and breadth of attention, and whether individuals allocate attention to positive and negative stimuli with equal probability and efficiency. Each of the two sections closes with a discussion authored by an expert in the field of perception and attention. We believe that the volume takes psychology as a field some distance in answering two major questions: Does emotion play an important and distinctive role in low-level cognitive processes? And, finally, who cares if it does?

We have many people to thank for their roles in producing this volume. We thank Robert Zajonc for fielding our occasional frantic phone calls, for suggesting that the Waynbaum chapter be translated from the French for publication in our book, for evaluating the English translation, and for agreeing to write an introduction to the chapter at the last possible minute. Christine M. Du Bois was the competent and sensitive translator of the Waynbaum chapter. She put far more effort into understanding the terminology of Waynbaum's time than we could ever have hoped.

We also thank our colleagues and students at The Johns Hopkins University, Indiana University, and the University of Oregon for their feedback, criticism, advice, and encouragement. These people include Asher Cohen, Howard Egeth, Russell Fazio, Igor Gavanski, Jamin Halberstadt, Robert Peterson, Michael Posner, Myron Rothbart, and Marc Setterlund.

Howard Egeth suggested the title of this book, and we thank him for it.

Finally, we thank several funding agencies for support of the research we report in our respective chapters and for support of the preparation of the book. These include National Science Foundation Grants BNS-8919755 and DBS-921019 and National Institute of Mental Health Grant MH44811 to Paula M. Niedenthal, and NSF Grant BNS-901054 and NIMH Grant MH50117 to Shinobu Kitayama.

Introduction

Shinobu Kitayama
University of Oregon and Kyoto University

Paula M. Niedenthal
Indiana University

One of us once taught an undergraduate psychology course in which we discussed the ideas of the New Look in perception. As Bruner so eloquently explains in the concluding chapter of this volume, the overarching goal of the New Look was to address the possibility that emotional states and emotional traits influence basic processes of attention and perception. After teaching this class on the New Look, we ran into a colleague, a perception and attention researcher, and told him, enthusiastically, that the topic of our just-completed lecture was the New Look in perception. The colleague looked quizzical and asked, "What is the New Look in perception?"

The New Look in the 1950s

The New Look in perception, a set of loosely related programs of perception research conducted in the 1940s and 1950s, was represented by a number of researchers who argued that the emotional meaning of a stimulus could be responded to (as indicated by an emotional reaction in the perceiver) before the stimulus was consciously perceived, and that the reaction could determine the content or form of the resulting conscious percept. For example, because of their value, positive stimuli—or stimuli previously associated with reward—were hypothesized to be dominant or "figural" in the perceptual field (Schafer & Murphy, 1943; Jackson, 1954; Smith & Hochberg, 1954). The physical attributes of positive or valued stimuli were also proposed to be enhanced (e.g., larger, brighter, louder), compared to those of negative stimuli, in conscious perception (e.g., Bruner & Goodman, 1947); negative information was thought to be perceptually defended against under many conditions (Bruner & Postman, 1947; McGinnies, 1949).

Although the ideas were intriguing and clearly important, theoretical and empirical problems prevented the work conducted during the New Look from having a significant impact on theories of perception. One problem was that models of perception at the time regarded perception as an all-or-none phenomenon and, thus, did not allow for the possibility that conscious perception may be a final product of distinct stages of processing or mental operations performed on an impinging stimulus. Not surprisingly, there was little place for the involvement of emotional reactions in perception and virtually no place for the idea of nonconscious (or preattentive) processing prior to the resolution of a conscious percept. Another problem was that empirical and quantitative methods were not yet sophisticated enough to address serious methodological criticisms. For example, many of the findings in this literature were interpretable in terms of biases in verbal or motor responses. Thus, they were dismissed as irrelevant in addressing perceptual processes. Finally, some of the "New Lookers" were grounded in psychoanalytic theory. Thus, the question "Does emotion influence perception?" was sometimes posed as a question of unconscious, and largely sexual, motivation: "Do unconscious, sexual drives elicited by evocative stimuli distort conscious perception?" This focus, anathema to many experimentalists, necessarily limited the impact of the New Look on theories of perception and attention.

Cognition without Emotion

The New Look of the 1950s was lost in the subsequent "cognitive revolution," as rather dramatically illustrated by our conversation with a perception researcher–colleague. The core agendas of the New Look simply could not compete with the ones compelled by the Zeitgeist. The cognitive project was premised on an image of the person as a rational actor, resembling a serial computer, that is capable of receiving stimuli, analyzing, comprehending them, and acting according to the ensuing cognitive representation of those stimuli. With this emphasis on the rational, systematic, or logically permissible computations that constitute cognitive processing, considerable progress was achieved in our understanding of, for example, learning and memory of verbal, referential communications such as words and descriptive sentences. In a similar vein, social psychologists learned a great deal about, for instance, how specific pieces of information about a person are encoded and integrated to yield a coherent personality impression or to draw attributional inferences.

If the metaphor of the person as computerlike, systematic information processor helped define certain "core" problems such as learning, memory, impression formation, and attribution, and advance the scientific knowledge in those areas, it also veiled or impeded others. For the present purposes, it is noteworthy that within the cognitive paradigm, emotion, motivation, or whatever else relates to or results from the person's actual interaction with the external environment, whether it be ecological, social, or cultural, represented no more than error variance. Emotion and motivation were regarded as epiphenomena that inflate the variance in virtually every dependent measure, ranging from simple motor response to complex learning and were, therefore, to be carefully controlled or otherwise to be partialled out of the resulting data. No wonder emotion and motivation were effectively ousted from the content domain of cognitive psychology.

The same enthusiasm to explain seemingly emotional or motivational effects as a somewhat convoluted or otherwise trivial consequence or concomitant of systematic cognitive information processing was also evident in social psychology. It was fashionable during the cognitive revolution to attribute evidently motivational effects such as self-serving bias to cognitive factors (e.g., Miller & Ross, 1975). Although the Zeitgeist produced a number of fruitful insights and important empirical findings (e.g., Nisbett & Ross, 1980), it also effectively masked potentially powerful contributions of motivation or emotion, as eloquently pointed out by Zajonc (1980).

New Functionalism and the Role of Emotion

Times have changed. Emotion and motivation have come back to the center stage of psychological inquiry. This trend is evident in every subarea of psychology, including cognitive psychology (e.g., Bower, 1981), social psychology (e.g., Clark & Fiske, 1982; Isen, 1984; Zajonc, 1980), neuroscience (e.g., LeDoux, 1989), clinical psychology (Gotlib, McLachlan, & Katz, 1988; MacLeod & Mathews, 1988), developmental psychology (Harris, 1989; Izard, 1993), and neuropsychology (Van Lancker, 1991).

One major catalyst for this change, we think, was an acute realization that even though the processes of the mind can be described in terms of rational, computerlike operations, the processes have nonetheless been shaped by their effectiveness in adapting to the biological, ecological, social, and cul-

tural environments. In the fields of cognitive and social psychology in particular, researchers have, in large numbers, begun to realize a limit imposed by
the narrow focus on mental operations and mechanisms that used to be
quite fashionable and, in some way, highly respectable in these fields. It is in
this context that, we believe, an emphasis on functionalism returned (e.g.,
Anderson & Milson, 1989; Bruner, this volume; Neisser, 1982; Snyder, 1992).
Such an approach poses and addresses the following sorts of questions:
What are the adaptive functions of the mental operations and mechanisms
we study? How are they recruited in everyday life to perform biologically,
socially, and culturally meaningful tasks of the human organism? What are
the ecological factors that both constrain and afford perception (Gibson,
1979)? What kind of social or cultural processes would modulate perception,
cognition, or memory, with what consequences on the person and the social
interaction in which she participates? Functional considerations can greatly
improve our understanding of basic mechanisms themselves.

By function we mean a role any given mechanism can serve within a
broader system in which the mechanism operates as its part. Functions
therefore refer to actions of the mechanism vis-à-vis the "real world" in
which it is embedded. Not surprisingly, then, the currently re-emerging functionalist perspective has revived *naturalism* of a sort in various branches of
psychology (e.g., Neisser, 1982, in memory research). Further, functions inevitably entail an assortment of "hot" factors—reward, punishment, hope,
threat, goal-oriented action, reaction to a success or failure to attain the
goal, evaluation by others, concerns about such evaluation, and so forth.

From this perspective, theoretical and empirical inquiries into emotion
are essential and indispensable to make sense of the very workings of
cognitive mechanisms themselves. The emphasis on adaptation and functions of mental processes implicated in emotion can be easily discerned in
a couple of the chapters in this volume (e.g., Derryberry & Tucker; Hansen
& Hansen; Pratto; Fazio, Roskos-Ewoldsen, & Powell). Further, functions of
any given mechanism can be defined only with respect to a particular setting
in which the mechanism is allowed to operate, whether the setting is ecological, social, or cultural. It is not coincidental, therefore, that many of
these investigators have begun to take a systematic approach to nonverbal,
ecologically more valid vehicles of emotional communication such as facial expression (Hansen & Hansen; Niedenthal, Setterlund, & Jones), voice
tone (Kitayama & Howard), and graphic images of attitudinal objects (Fazio
et al.).

Nonverbal signals of emotion may carry information that uniquely conveys adaptationally significant information in a way verbal information cannot; in general, they may be quicker in speed, simpler in processing operations involved, and more unequivocal in the responses afforded or required.
It would also seem likely that at least some of the distinct characteristics of

the nonverbal emotional signals are selected, acquired, and hardwired into the psychological information processing system through the evolutionary process, as suggested by both the Hansen and Hansen and the Derryberry and Tucker chapters. Accordingly, they are a reasonable place to start exploring the functional, adaptational nature of emotion, motivation, and their interface with systematic cognitive processing.

The return of functionalism along with its concomitant naturalism in psychology has necessitated taking a newer look at the New Look and, more generally, seriously reconsidering the effects of emotion and motivation, and incorporating them into theories of mental processes. It is with this currently reemerging functionalist perspective on emotion that we conceived this volume, which Bruner (this volume) calls part of the "new" New Look and Greenwald has called the New Look 3 (Greenwald, 1992). By way of introducing the volume, we discuss below a couple of features unique to the currently emerging "new" New Look, followed by some clarifications about definitional issues. Finally, we give a brief overview of the chapters.

Emotion, Perception, and Attention

The current volume consists of 13 chapters, which together suggest an emerging theme in the current psychological thinking on two issues: (1) the emotion–cognition interface—the question of how emotion interacts with other mental processes such as perception and cognition; and (2) nonconscious processing—the question of how and when mental processes proceed without the awareness of the individual (i.e., occur automatically) or are initiated by events of which the individual is not aware (i.e., by implicitly or subliminally perceived information).

By focusing on perception and attention, the current volume seeks to make a unique contribution. A number of influential and important contributions can be found on the role of emotion in more deliberate, and often slower, processes such as judgment and decision making (e.g., Clark & Fiske, 1982; Forgas, 1991). In contrast to these processes, both perception and, to a large extent, what William James (1890/1983) called involuntary attention are more instantaneous, automatic, and out of one's deliberate control and effort. Analyzing emotional influence in conscious and nonconscious perception as well as in the regulation of attention, therefore, amounts to posing questions about the organization of emotional and cognitive processes at the most elementary level of mental operations. Needless to say, delineating emotional influence at this level presents fascinating theoretical and empirical challenges for cognitive, social, and clinical psychologists alike. This precisely is one major reason for the current enthusiasm on the topic shared in the field.

Defining Emotion

The authors of this volume share an interest in emotional influences in perception and attention. Their ideas about where the emotion comes from, the types of feelings they are interested in, and the processes of perception and attention that they believe are affected vary, however. In order to provide something of a common language for the readers of this volume, we attempt to define key terms such as emotion, motivation, affect, and mood, and to associate the definitions with different authors.

We see emotion as a set of adaptive functions of acting or responding to stimuli, that are both prewired or "prepared" by biological evolution and yet at the same time, shaped, elaborated, and finely "configured" by learning—especially by social and cultural learning. Emotion, then, is seen as a psychological processing structure of action readiness with which to perceive, attend, and respond to biologically, personally, and/or culturally significant stimuli. Emotion consists of myriad component processes organized into some fuzzy sets according to the functional relationship between the organism or the self and its biological or cultural environment (e.g., Ortony & Turner, 1991; Buck, 1988). Some components involve cognitive and lexical processing as suggested by recent cognitive appraisal theorists of emotion (e.g., Ellsworth, 1991); other components involve autonomic, efferent, and somatic activations (Smith & DeVito, 1984). Clearly, many of these components are interconnected. Recent advances in neuroscience indicate that the brain substrates involved in the processing of emotion are highly integrated with those that participate in memory, learning, and other cognitive processes (see Steinmetz, 1993, for an overview).

Above and beyond this general definition of emotion, researchers vary considerably in emphasis, and some of them use different, albeit related, terms for it accordingly. Depending on their major emphases, the contributions to this volume can be divided into the following four groups. Although in actuality the groups overlap in some obvious ways, the divisions are offered here as a heuristic frame with which to understand the scope of the current volume.

1. Emotion as a biological function of adaptation. Consistent with a definition of emotion offered by Davidson and Cacioppo (1992), as a "self-organizing, integrative state that is coherent across several response systems," Hansen and Hansen emphasize the biologically hardwired processes of emotion and its information processing structure. Adopting a similar biological view of emotion, Derryberry and Tucker highlight the goal-oriented function of emotion, for which they use the notion of *motivation*. They use the term, emotion, somewhat narrowly to refer to a subjective concomitant of the motivation so defined.

2. Emotion as evaluation. Some other contributors to this volume are

more psychological in their approach to emotion. Thus, Pratto and Klinger and Greenwald study the evaluative–informational function of emotion. Many would agree that this is the central element of emotion, captured by a number of classic dimensions of "good–bad," "approach–avoidance," "like–dislike," and the like. But because evaluation is just one of many components of emotion just noted, Kitayama and Howard use the term *affect* to narrowly refer to the evaluative dimension of emotion and distinguish it from emotion itself. Affect so defined is also central in social attitudes, as made evident by Fazio et al. in their chapter on an emotional basis of attitude.

3. Emotion as categorical states. When emotional states are fairly enduring and have no specific objects to which the emotion is directed, they are called *moods*. By contrast, there appear to be a small number of primary emotions (e.g., Ekman, 1984; Izard, 1993; Tomkins, 1962) that are acute, structurally distinct, and have specific eliciting conditions. Consistent with researchers who study conceptual emotion knowledge (Shaver, Schwartz, Kirson, & O'Connor, 1987) and brain substrates of emotion (Gray, 1991), Niedenthal et al. argue that these categorical states, such as joy, sadness, and fear, have unique information processing effects, organizing memory in a more categorical way. A paper written at the turn of this century by a French physician, Israel Waynbaum, which is included here with an introduction by Robert Zajonc, seem to share this view of emotion.

4. Emotion as activation. Finally, another important aspect of emotion is its energizing or amplifying capacity or what has traditionally been called *arousal*. The emphasis on arousal is evident in a number of influential papers in the history of psychology of emotion including Schachter (1964). It is reflected in the notion of amplification described by Kitayama and Howard. In a related vein, Egeth discusses both promises and problems of this notion in his review of the literature on the effects of arousal in eyewitness testimony. Finally, Derryberry and Tucker differentiate this unidimensional, admittedly oversimplified notion of arousal into two qualitatively distinct kinds of arousal, called *phasic arousal* and *tonic activation*.

Perception and Attention

The present volume is organized into two sections, the first on emotion and perception, the second on emotion and attention. Perception and attention are not strictly separate. They are indeed highly overlapping. However, this does not mean that the division of chapters was made in an arbitrary way. The specific effects, experimental tasks, and cognitive mechanisms implicated differ systematically.

Perception is the transformation of sensations caused by an impinging stimulus into an internal representation of that stimulus. There are many component processes that mediate the transformation. And attention mediates perception when it is aligned with the mental pathway corresponding to the perceived event. However, the perceptual phenomena described in chapters in the first section are largely ones in which the mechanism of attention does not, or, in some case, does not exclusively, play a role.

Some chapters are concerned with affect in nonconscious perception (e.g., Klinger & Greenwald; Pratto). In work of this sort, the issue is whether implicit or explicit measures of affect indicate that the emotional meaning of a stimulus is extracted prior to the conscious detection or recognition of the stimulus. Other work addresses the idea that emotions have automatic effects in early perceptual processes that cause individuals to perceive certain events more efficiently than other events (Kitayama & Howard; Niedenthal et al.; Waynbaum).

One mechanism implicated in much of this work is that of spreading activation. Spreading activation involves the *automatic* transfer of excitation between interconnected elements of the cognitive processing system. In such models, for example, preliminary nonconscious processing of the visual (or auditory) field primes corresponding perceptual pathways, thereby making some representations more likely than others to organize perception or bias responses. Internal sources of activation include emotional state and, relatedly, arousal. Kitayama and Howard suggest, for example, that emotional arousal can amplify activation of perceptual pathways that have been previously excited.

Tasks that allow the researcher to measure the efficiency or ease with which a perceiver can detect a stimulus are most often used in the examination of automatic activation in perception. In theory, the tasks involve measurement of the facilitation in the ease of perception of a primed, compared to a nonprimed, stimulus. In practice, of course, subjects communicate perceptibility with a motor response. Consequently, a problem with such tasks is that it is difficult to separate the facilitation of a perceptual response from that of a motor response.

Attention is held to be a limited capacity mechanism that mediates conscious awareness of internal and external events. Events that are the focus of attention receive the benefit of conscious processing. Processing "costs" accrue when attention has been allocated to certain events but processing of different events is required for some task (Posner, 1978). One of the classic paradigms for studying the allocation of visual and auditory attention is the Stroop task in which interference with conscious attention by automatic processes such as access to the semantic meaning of words can be observed. Several of the authors of the chapters contained in this volume have used the Stroop task to examine the effects of negative and positive information on the allocation of visual attention (e.g., Hansen & Hansen; Pratto).

Others, including Fazio and his colleagues and Derryberry and Tucker have used a variety of other tasks to assess the role of affect and motivation in attention. These include both learning and incidental learning tasks that provide evidence of the relative allocation of attentional resources among multiple objects in the visual field, and visual search and identification tasks that reveal the disruption of attention to a task by the incidental presence of other objects or changes in motivation.

Recently, technological advances have made the measurement of eye movements (saccade) more accessible to the researchers. Thus, tasks that involve change in the allocation of visual attention are also frequently used in this area (Hansen & Hansen).

Overview

The first section of this book is composed of chapters that report empirical research that has been inspired by the idea that emotion influences, even establishes, the "perceptual readiness" of a perceiver. One can imagine, for example, that when experiencing a particular emotion—a transient one, such as a happy state, or a chronic one, such as trait anxiety—an individual sees certain stimuli and ignores others. Perhaps those stimuli that support or are consistent with the feelings (stimuli that have made one happy, or anxious in the past) are more likely to be consciously seen. Laypersons refer to this phenomenon in daily conversation when they say that someone who is happy is "looking at life through rose-colored glasses." In these chapters, a variety of different models are presented to account for this and related phenomena.

The second chapter in the section is rather unusual and we are excited to include it. The paper was written more than 80 years ago by a French physician, Israel Waynbaum, and it is published here for the first time in English translation. Waynbaum, a contemporary of Darwin, was a largely unknown, but innovative and provocative, emotions theorist. His work was uncovered by Robert Zajonc and his collaborators (particularly Pamela Adelmann) in their efforts to research the involvement of facial efference in the subjective experience of emotion. The paper that we chose to include in this volume directly addresses the possibility that emotion guides perception. More specifically, the theory holds that emotional perception is basic perception, and the process is altered by learning and cognitive development. As Zajonc notes in his introduction to the chapter, Waynbaum anticipates many of the theoretical constructs that are central in our current psychological theorizing on emotion and cognition, including the ideas that repeated exposure influences preference (the mere exposure effect); that expectations and other top-down processes can guide perception; and that empathy plays an important role in the perception of others' emotions.

In the second chapter, Kitayama and Howard discuss emotional regulation of both perception and comprehension. In their work on perception, they take another look at one core problem of the New Look, namely, perceptibility of emotionally charged stimuli. Their data indicate that the emotional significance of a briefly shown stimulus does influence—either improve or impair—the accuracy of the conscious percept independent of response bias. Based on these data, the authors propose that early cognitive and emotional activations interact with each other preconsciously to regulate conscious attention, thereby modifying the perceptibility of the impinging stimulus. Their work also addresses influences of emotional vocal quality in comprehension of speech communications.

Niedenthal, Setterlund, and Jones examine emotion congruence in perception. This is the idea that emotional states influence the perceptual system such that emotion-congruent events are perceived more efficiently than are other events. They report experiments that demonstrate such an effect, and propose that emotion congruence in perception operates in terms of discrete emotional states such as joy, sadness, and anger, rather than a commonly postulated dimension of pleasantness. They also make an important theoretical point that the power of emotional influence in cognition is derived from the fact that emotion categories are connected to a variety of bodily responses. Emotional experience, therefore, is bound to be embodied, accompanied by spontaneous, immediate, and "natural" reaction of the body.

The chapter by Klinger and Greenwald is concerned with the subliminal mere exposure effect; the phenomenon that the repeated exposure of subliminal stimuli can yield increases in preference for such stimuli. In a series of experiments, Klinger and Greenwald show that this effect obtains for pleasant stimuli but not for unpleasant stimuli. Repeated exposure of unpleasant subliminal stimuli appears to yield decreases in preference. A consideration of this "affect-polarization" result and findings of other recent research (Mandler, Jacoby) suggest to the authors a two-stage process by which perceivers develop implicit memories for subliminal stimuli and later can be induced to attribute feelings of familiarity to contextually relevant factors.

Pratto also examines the automatic and largely nonconscious aspect of emotional activation. She presents experimental evidence to suggest that the emotional valence of stimuli is apprehended automatically and inevitably. Like Kitayama and Howard (and Hansen & Hansen, see below), Pratto argues that one function of automatic evaluation is the regulation of conscious attention. The results of some of her recent work suggest that nonconscious evaluation of external events allows the perceiver to direct conscious attention to that which is most significant in the environment, namely, threatening stimuli.

The first section of the book concludes with a commentary by Johnson and Weisz. They raise a number of interesting points that must be seriously considered in further research. They ask, for example, whether and to what extent the "front-end" psychological processing—including automatically activated emotion—is spontaneous or rigid, and independent of the current motives and goal structure of the perceiver or characteristics of the task environment such as the nature of stimulus array used in a given study. As an alternative to the idea of the front-end emotion as entirely automatic and context independent, they suggest an "opportunistic" model whereby whether or not emotion is computed and how quickly may all depend on these and other contextual variables. They also raise a critical question of how separate emotion is from cognition. Is emotion a special type of meaning, or may emotion be better conceptualized as functionally distinct from semantic meaning?

The second section includes chapters that consider the idea that emotional stimuli in the environment influence how perceivers allocate their attentional resources. Many stimulus events are inherently emotion arousing or carry strong evaluative meaning. Spiders and suddenly looming figures, for example, are strongly negative events, at least when they occur naturally. Emotionally significant events may be more likely than neutral or mundane events to capture attention.

In their pioneering work on attention-capturing potential of angry faces, Hansen and Hansen have demonstrated that angry faces capture attention automatically and, perhaps, even before they are consciously categorized as such. In this chapter, Hansen and Hansen outline, from both cognitive and functional perspectives, why the perceiver should process facial displays of emotion automatically, and why attention should be allocated to threatening faces in particular. In addition, they describe a series of new experiments in which attention is monitored with eye movement recording and emotional responding is monitored with electromyographic recording. These experiments provide further evidence for the idea that facial displays of emotion automatically elicit congruent affective responses in perceivers, and that attention is allocated to emotional faces that display anger more often than by faces that display positive emotion.

A similar fruitful mixture of cognitive tasks with physiological measures can also be found in the next chapter by Derryberry and Tucker. Drawing on the cognitive literature that has posited direction and breadth as major, functionally independent aspects of attention, these researchers present a detailed review of behavioral manifestations and neurological substrates of the integrated workings of motivation and cognition, and attention. They point out that adaptation of the organism in any environment is made possible through a delicate balance between a selective focusing of attention on a currently significant stimulus and a broader search for potentially significant stimuli. Various discrete emotions vary in the specific balance between the two attentional functions they entail.

Fazio, Roskos-Ewoldsen, and Powell address similar issues of attention in the domain of attitude, which has traditionally been the central construct in social psychology. A number of proposals have been made regarding some distinct functions of attitude, but until recently little work was conducted to address how those functions are enabled by the underlying cognitive, emotional, and attentional mechanisms. The work described in their chapter represents a ground-breaking examination of this issue. Specifically, in their work Fazio and collaborators have demonstrated that some attitudes can serve to regulate attention. It appears that objects toward which individuals hold highly accessible attitudes—attitudes that Fazio argues are most likely to be automatically activated—are more likely to be noticed and later recalled than are other objects presented in the same visual display.

Finally, another social domain in which emotion can have an obviously significant effect is addressed by Egeth. He carefully examines a variety of claims made in the literature about effects of emotion on eyewitness testimony. He rightly pointed out that many of these claims are often one-sided and cannot be complete by themselves. He concludes his chapter by making a number of suggestions for future research in this area.

To complete the intellectual loop where it began in the New Look of the 1950s, the book closes with a discussion chapter by Jerome Bruner. The chapter is composed of three parts: a historical overview (which he initially warned one of us he definitely would not write!), an autobiographical note in which he reviews his own work and outlines the biases that he has retained throughout the years as well as those that he has discarded, and, finally, careful scrutiny of the chapters contained in the book. It is in the last section that he gives us all a run for our money. All we can say is: Thanks, Jerry!

References

Anderson, J. R., & Milson, R. (1989). Human memory: An adaptive perspective. *Psychological Review, 96*, 703–719.

Bower, G. H. (1981). Mood and memory. *American Psychologist, 36*, 129–148.

Bruner, J. S., & Goodman, C. C. (1947). Value and need as organizing factors in perception. *Journal of Abnormal and Social Psychology, 42*, 33–44.

Bruner, J. S., & Postman, L. (1947). Emotional selectivity in perception and reaction. *Journal of Personality, 16*, 69–77.

Buck, R. (1988). *Human motivation and emotion* (2nd ed.). New York: Wiley.

Clark, M. S., & Fiske, S. T. (1982). *Affect and cognition: The 17th annual Carnegie symposium on cognition.* Hillsdale, NJ: Erlbaum.

Davidson, R. J., & Cacioppo, J. T. (1992). New developments in the scientific study of emotion: An introduction to the special section. *Psychological Science, 3*, 21–22.

Ekman, P. (1984). Expression and the nature of emotion. In K. Scherer & P. Ekman (eds.), *Approaches to emotion* (pp. 319–343). Hillsdale, NJ: Erlbaum.

Ellsworth, P. C. (1991). Some implications of cognitive appraisal theories of emotion. In K. T. Strongman (ed.), *International Review of Studies on Emotion*. Chicester, England: John Wiley and Sons.

Forgas, J. (1991). *Affect and social judgment*. Oxford: Pergamon Press.

Gibson, J. J. (1979). *Ecological approach to visual perception*. Boston: Houghton Mifflin.

Gotlib, I. H., McLachlan, A. L., & Katz, A. N. (1988). Biases in visual attention in depressed and nondepressed individuals. *Cognition and Emotion*, 2, 185–200.

Gray, J. A. (1991). The neuropsychology of temperament. In J. Strelau & A. Angleitner (eds.), *Explorations in temperament. International perspectives on theory and measurement* (pp. 105–128). New York: Plenum Press.

Greenwald, A. G. (1992). New look 3: Unconscious cognition reclaimed. *American Psychologist*, 47, 766–779.

Harris, P. L. (1989). *Children and emotion: The development of psychological understanding*. New York: Basil Blackwell.

Isen, A. M. (1984). Toward understanding the role of affect in cognition. In R. S. Wyer & T. K. Srull (eds.), *Handbook of social cognition* (Vol. 3). Hillsdale, NJ: Erlbaum.

Izard, C. E. (1993). Four systems for emotion activation: Cognitive and noncognitive processes. *Psychological Review*, 100, 68–90.

Jackson, D. N. (1954). A further examination of the role of autism in a visual figure–ground relationship. *Journal of Psychology*, 38, 339–357.

James, W. (1983). *The principles of psychology*. Cambridge, MA: Harvard University Press. (Originally published, 1890.)

LeDoux, J. E. (1989). Cognitive–emotional interactions in the brain. *Cognition and Emotion*, 3, 267–289.

McGinnies, E. M. (1949). Emotionality and perceptual defense. *Psychological Review*, 56, 471–482.

MacLeod, C., & Mathews, A. (1988). Anxiety and the allocation of attention to threat. *The Quarterly Journal of Experimental Psychology*, 40A, 653–670.

Miller, D. T., & Ross, M. (1975). Self-serving attributional bias: fact or fiction? *Psychological Bulletin*, 82, 213–225.

Neisser, U. (1982). *Memory observed*. San Francisco: W. H. Freeman.

Nisbett, R. E., & Ross, L. (1980). *Human inference: Strategies and shortcomings in social judgment*. Englewood Cliffs, NJ: Prentice-Hall.

Ortony, A., & Turner, T. J. (1990). What's basic about basic emotions? *Psychological Review*, 97, 315–337.

Posner, M. I. (1978). *Chronometric explorations of mind*. New York: Oxford University Press.

Schachter, S. (1964). The interaction of cognitive and physiological determinants of emotional state. In L. Berkowitz (ed.), *Advances in experimental social psychology* (Vol. 1, pp. 49–80). New York: Academic Press.

Schafer, R., & Murphy, G. (1943). The role of autism in a visual figure–ground relationships. *Journal of Experimental Psychology*, 32, 335–343.

Shaver, P., Schwartz, J., Kirson, D., & O'Connor, C. (1987). Emotion knowledge: Further exploration of a prototype approach. *Journal of Personality and Social Psychology*, 52, 1061–1086.

Smith, D. E., & Hochberg, J. E. (1954). The "autistic" effect of punishment on figure–ground perception. *American Psychology*, 7, 243–244.

Smith, O., & DeVito, J. (1984). Central neural integration for the control of autonomic responses associated with emotion. *Annual Review of Neuroscience*, 7, 43–65.

Snyder, M. (1992). Motivational explanation of behavioral confirmation. In M. Zanna (ed.), *Advances in experimental social psychology* (Vol. 25). San Diego, CA: Academic Press.

Steinmetz, J. E. (1993). Brain substrates of emotion and temperament. In J. E. Bates & T. D. Wachs (eds.), *Temperament: Individual differences at the interface of biology and behavior.* Washington, D.C. American Psychological Association.

Tomkins, S. S. (1962). *Affect, imagery, and consciousness* (Vol. 1). New York: Springer.

Van Lancker, D. (1991). Personal relevance and the human right-hemisphere. *Brain and Cognition*, 17, 64–92.

Zajonc, R. B. (1980). Feeling and thinking: Preferences need no inferences. *American Psychologist*, 35, 151–175.

Emotion and Perception

An Early Insight into the Affect–Perception Interface

R. B. Zajonc
University of Michigan

The following chapter entitled "The Affective Qualities of Perception" (AQP) was written 85 years ago. It has seen no citations in the American literature, and it is most unlikely that there were any in other literatures. It is offered to the psychological community for the first time in English. Its author, Israel Waynbaum, a French physician, is as unknown as the article. His other work has lain in obscurity for nearly eight decades. No references to AQP or to Waynbaum will be found between 1907 and 1985. Yet those who read it now will find it engaging, important, and timely. It is a sad testimony to our scholarship that only now we are becoming acquainted with it.

Waynbaum was a Russian immigrant who came to France at 18 years of age, went to medical school in Paris, and after his studies established private practice in one of the best arrondissements of the city (the 16th). There are exactly three publications of Waynbaum's that I was able to find, including the present one translated ably by Christine M. DuBois. Besides AQP there is a book (Waynbaum, 1907) published the same year as AQP, with

The Heart's Eye: Emotional Influences in Perception and Attention
Copyright © 1994 by Academic Press, Inc. All rights of reproduction in any form reserved.

which I became familiar by accident a few years ago and came to admire. The book proposed a revolutionary theory of emotional expression (Zajonc, 1985) now fueling a new development in the study of the interface between biological and subjective strata in emotion (Zajonc, Inglehart, & Murphy, 1989). Published a year earlier, there is also a short anticipatory resumé of the book (Waynbaum, 1906). That is all that remains of Waynbaum's intellectual contributions. There would have possibly been other publications had Waynbaum lived at a different time and in a different intellectual community.

Waynbaum had no lab, had no background in the physiology of emotions, and he was not in the network of the French workers on emotion that featured Dumas, Piéron, and Ribot as leaders of that field. He was definitely an outsider—academically, socially, and ethnically—and he was treated as such. When he presented an outline of his ideas to the Academy, he was immediately and summarily dismissed for his lack of credentials (Waynbaum, 1906). It is true that his ideas about emotional expression were novel and even bizarre, one might say. And it is true also that he invoked some conjectures about the neurophysiology of the emotions that were questionable. But he came up with a totally original and productive view of emotional expression: he offered the hypothesis that facial expression had as its original and primary function the regulation of blood flow to the brain. He noted that blood supplied to the head is carried by the main carotid artery, which is split at the neck into two branches, the external carotid supplying the face and skull and the internal carotid supplying the brain. Since the brain requires a constant and invariant blood supply, Waynbaum was puzzled by the fact that the brain had to share its blood supply with the face. Why wasn't arterial blood routed to the brain independently and directly? Waynbaum cleverly resolved the puzzle by proposing that the configuration allowed the external carotid that carried blood to the face and skull to serve as a safety valve that protected the brain from extreme fluctuations in blood supply. If there was insufficient blood going to the brain, then the internal carotid, because of its common source with the external branch, could "borrow" blood from the external carotid. Since blood supply to the face and skull are much less critical than blood supply to the brain, facial tissues could suffer a temporary anemia, shunting some blood to the brain. If, on the other hand, there was a threat of hyperemia, facial and skull vessels could without any threat of damage absorb the surplus. Facial pallor and blushing are manifestation of relocation of blood away and toward the face. For Waynbaum, the relocation was a matter of muscular action of the face such as that occurring in emotional expressions. Facial muscles can press against the bony structure of the face, and thus act as tourniquets on the branches of the facial artery, or they can relax and thus redirect blood supply.

The muscular action of the face is what we now know and understand as emotional expression, but that function was a secondary one, according to

Waynbaum. The function of facial action *as* expression evolved because it was fairly well correlated with internal states and could thereby broadcast this information among conspecifics. But it did not evolve because its primary adaptive value was communication of internal states. For Waynbaum also asserted that the changes in blood flow to the brain had hedonic consequences: anemia was a source of negative feelings, whereas hyperemia was positive.

Waynbaum's vascular theory of emotional expression was not an attempt to specify the Cartesian dualism. Yet within some limits, the question of how subjective states derive from bodily processes was answered by his vascular theory of emotional expression. There was still the question of how the person becomes aware of hedonic feelings that are created by the variations in blood supply to the brain. These hedonic states had to be considered in the realm of *res limits*, whereas their source in the vascular process belonged to the realm of *res extensa*. Somehow the biological process had to turn into a mental process, and if the pineal gland was not the organ of the biopsychological interface, then where and what was that interface?

Waynbaum's AQP paper together with his book on physiognomy (on which he relies in AQP) can well be viewed as a landmark in the intellectual approach to the emotions that originates in Greek philosophy. For Waynbaum removed some of the mystery from the biopsychological interface by specifying and articulating some of the component processes on both the biological and the psychological side of the interface, thus making the gap smaller than it had ever been.

Mind and body were opposite realms, and life was a struggle between the animal and evil forces of passion and the mind with which humans were endowed mainly to harness these evil forces. The seven deadly sins were the sins of passion—avarice, envy, gluttony, indolence, ire, lechery, and pride. It was reason and prudence that would protect the soul from the "weaknesses" of the body. The moral and psychological dualism of passion and reason still reign over many domains of our social, political, and cultural life. The laws distinguish quite clearly between a crime of passion and a premeditated murder. We still regard a crime of passion partly excusable because it is presumed to have been committed spontaneously and outside the perpetrator's control over his or her actions. There is no responsibility if there is no mind to ward off the "animal" impulses. That is why murder by poison is almost always regarded as a crime committed deliberately, that is with *deliberation*, with "evil aforethought."

The classical view of mind–body dualism was that of a zero-sum game. Mind and body combine to dominate action, and the more the mind participates in the process, the less the body can contribute. But Waynbaum rises above the zero-sum dualism to claim that affect and cognition are engaged in a zero-sum game in only some circumstances. He says that "*in certain cases* [italics mine] these [affective] properties are antagonistic to the cognitive elements" (AQP, p. 2). An instance where affect and cognition are not in a zero-sum game is in music where both affect and cognition are mutually promoted, for when we learn to understand and become more familiar with a novel composition, our initially negative affect weakens and eventually changes into positive.

He also represents cognition as capable of modifying an incipient affective reaction. He views the individual changing with experience such that as his or her knowledge of the world accumulates, there are less surprises and less causes for strong reactions of fear or anger. And as the individual becomes *"prescient"* the grounds for evocation of affect become fewer.

Waynbaum was a child of the nineteenth century and although he was fairly free of the intellectual biases of his time, he obviously carried many social prejudices. His view that women were more emotional and "less able to inhibit the perceptional–emotional wave" was the common view of the time. But Waynbaum did not close the books on the predisposition of women to emotion at the cost of reason, even though he accepted it as innate. He says that "the more [women] dedicate themselves to their cognitive development, the more they will have the good fortune to rid themselves of their often troublesome, hereditary perceptive emotionality" (AQP, p. 8). This is patronizing, to be sure, but consider the social atmosphere of the year in which it was written.

Many modern ideas are to be found in Waynbaum's AQP paper. His analysis of how affect can influence perception is as acceptable and as vulnerable as any account today. The view that affect and perception are independent even though both can be elicited by the same stimulus is equally up-to-date. There is a clear assertion that affect relies on a cognitive appraisal, which grows in efficiency and sophistication with experience. The idea about the spreading of affect and its contagious properties predates LeBon. There is a clear statement how affect changes as a result of repeated exposure (AQP, p. 18). There is a strong idea about the role of affect in the maintenance of social relationships to which he ascribes a dominant role. "Most of our social relations are based on a principle of affective reflectivity in perception" (AQP, p. 14). Here in the discussion of fashion, he again waxes Victorian and misogynist. His discussion of music appreciation does not entirely shun the view of intrinsic physical qualities. He asserts that we love best that music that comes closest to reflecting human affect. Thus, we love the cello because it is like the male larynx and enjoy the violin because it resembles a female soprano.

One has to excuse Waynbaum's neurophysiology, for it is based on the knowledge existing at the turn of the century. He was offering his neurophysiological ideas mainly on a speculative basis, speaking of them as tentative and quite imperfect (AQP, p. 5). His neurophysiology served mainly to represent better the content of his ideas.

Waynbaum's ideas for AQP had no impact on subsequent psychology. Dumas (1932), who wrote extensively about the emotions and who knew Waynbaum's work, ignores AQP entirely. It is good, therefore, for the editors of this volume to allow space for an old and unknown work whose ideas are as timely today as others in this volume.

References

Dumas, G. (1932). *Nouveau traité de psychologie.* (Vol. 2) Paris: Alcan.

Waynbaum, I. (1906). Communication a la Société de Psychologie. *Journal de la Psychologie Normale et Pathologique,* 3, 467–475.

Waynbaum, I. (1907). *La physionomie humaine: Son mécanisme et son rôle social.* Paris: Alcan.

Zajonc, R. B. (1985). Emotion and facial efference: A theory reclaimed. *Science,* 228, 15–21.

Zajonc, R. B., Inglehart, M., & Murphy, S. T. (1989). Feeling and facial efference: Implications of the vascular theory of emotion. *Psychological Review,* 96, 395–416.

The Affective Qualities of Perception*

Israel Waynbaum
Translated from the French by
Christine Madeleine Du Bois
The Johns Hopkins University

I

How does the outer world impinge upon us? What psychic states are provoked within us when one of our perceptive senses brings us an impression of the world? Why is the inner result of a given perception sometimes an emotion, more or less vivid, and sometimes only a state of cognition? This is the subject briefly presented here.

The critical psychic act connecting us to the outer world is *perception*. Perception transmits external impressions to us and conveys them to our consciousness. There it generates different but equivalent reactions. Thus, if we wish to know how the external world reaches us and what is produced after its arrival, we must understand all the properties of perception.

*This article was originally published in 1907 in the Journal de la Psychologie Normale et Pathologique, 4, 289–311.

When we speak of perception, what we first have in mind is the localization of our different sensations. Seen thus, this psychic act seems to generate only cognitive states of consciousness. These states are linked either to a sensation's localization or to its specific character. For example, if I am touched by a hot object, thanks to my perception I become conscious of the type of sensation—in this case, heat. I also immediately recognize what part of my body was touched, as well as the source emitting the heat. If I hear a noise, immediately I classify the auditory sensation as belonging to this or that object. At first, then, the essential elements of perception seem purely *cognitive*.

By extension, other cognitive elements can also be evoked by perception. Thanks to the synthetic power of each sense, the experience of a single sensation causes a bursting into consciousness[1] of all those attributes indissolubly linked to an object's materiality. The appearance of this orange, for example, makes me immediately aware not only of its form, color, and position in space, but also of its texture, delicate aroma, and flavor. These notions more or less form the total attributes of the outer object. They can all instantly be elaborated by perception. Elaboration is made possible by our different interconnecting central pathways, which are accustomed to being activated in concert. For any given object, they are constantly traversed in the same pattern.

The physioanatomical model for the process of perception can be outlined as follows: the external excitation of peripheral neurons in the perceiving organ travels straight toward the organ's central neurons. From there it radiates via ascending pathways toward the cortical layers. From those layers, the excitation radiates again, this time via all the higher interconnecting central pathways that are habitually linked to each other. This process occurs so that all the elements of cognition about an outer object, the full retinue of cognitive clichés, will immediately be put into the forefront of consciousness—all because of a single sensation. Such are the cognitive qualities of perception—the only perceptual qualities that are widely known, and the only ones that we generally pay attention to.

II

We have just seen that the mental product of perception is a state of cognition. We almost always acknowledge cognition as the final result of perception: by means of perception we recognize something; we become conscious of it. This seems to be perception's exclusive role.

We are now going to show that perception also possesses affective properties, and that in certain cases these properties are antagonistic to the

---

[1]Tr. note: French: *irruption dans le cerveau*

cognitive elements, or are masked by them. Hence, the inner result of a perception can be an emotion rather than a cognitive state. Although there are fewer distinct types of affective perceptions than cognitive ones, the former do not occur any less frequently than the latter. It is thus very important to understand them.

We should note first that there are two categories of perception with affective qualities. We will examine each in turn.

1. In the first category, perception becomes affective because it brings us a mass of stimuli or sensations that either overwhelm our ambient cognitive state or else contradict that state.

2. In the second category, which occurs just as frequently, perception acquires an affective stamp because the emotional element is contained in the perception, is carried by it, or comes from the outer world.

Let us start by examining the first group of emotional perceptions. If the usual conscious result of a perception is a cognitive state, it is because generally perception does nothing more than make us aware of things that are *expected* or *known in advance*. In the great majority of cases, we are *prescient* of the cognition that perception elicits in us. The perception only quickens or puts in the forefront of consciousness something that was more deeply buried or that existed in an unconscious state. Thus, for example, in this room where I work everything is perfectly familiar to me. Whether I turn my head to the right or left, up, or behind me, everything is known to me. Immediately I classify the noises from the outer world; it is unlikely that one of these perceptions could cause me any emotion. Everything that strikes one of my senses will follow an ascending path toward the cortical layers. There it will only confirm my more or less conscious prior knowledge—my *prescience*—of my surroundings. Hence, during a variable but potentially long period, I will experience only *cognitive* perceptions.

But if something *unforeseen, unexpected*, strikes me, the perception's result will no longer be the same. I will inevitably be shaken by an emotional shock of greater or lesser intensity. Suppose, for instance, that in this room where I thought myself entirely alone, without my realizing it someone arrives from behind me and touches me—even very lightly—or else reveals his or her presence in some other manner, such as making a noise or an unexpected movement. It is almost absolutely certain that my fright will be severe, that I will be shaken from head to foot by a wave of emotion. These facts are commonplace and occur too often in daily life to warrant further elaboration with examples. Quite frequently we can be affected by sudden and unexpected impressions that come from outside us. Despite their apparent triviality and insignificance, these impressions cause us to experience more or less violent emotions because we were not at all *prepared* to receive them. In such cases perception becomes purely affective or emotional.

The anatomical explanation for this perceptive affectivity arises from the following fact: all the central nuclei of the perceptive organs are connected by large anastomoses to the ensemble of central nuclei from which emanate the nerves of our principal vital organs. These latter nuclei are situated on the floor of the fourth ventricle, at the level of Varolius's bridge. Together they are usually designated as the general center of the emotions. The excitation of some or all of these nuclei produces organic disturbances of varying intensity, which in psychic life transform themselves into equivalent emotions.

If I see, or if I hear something *unexpected* or *unusual*, there is nothing above the perception (as represented in the accompanying diagram) to receive the impression. The first effect of the perceptive wave is thus to generate an emotion, thanks to the perception's anastomotic pathway. Hence we see that in certain cases a perception can elicit an emotion. In other words, we possess a true interconnecting, central, perceptual–emotional pathway whose direction is fairly horizontal when compared with the ascending cortical pathway.

Properly speaking, here perception is composed of two time periods: first, emotionality engendered by the absence of cognitive representations; and second, recognition of the external impression, or inhibition of emotionality. But these two purely theoretical periods follow each other so rapidly that we can simply label the phenomenon an affective perception.

III

To clarify what has been said, and for a better understanding of how the outer world impinges on us, I will attempt to represent the process in the abbreviated diagram (Figure 1). In the diagram, we see the course of an external impression from the time it arrives, via the peripheral neurons, until its expansion in the higher cortical layers. The figure also shows the possibility of bifurcation at the level of the horizontal pathway; this occurs when the perception does not correspond to any equivalent cognitive representation.

The solid arrows indicate the habitual direction of perception toward the cortical layers. By contrast, the dotted arrows indicate the horizontal course toward the emotion center, in cases when there is an absence of cognitive representation. Of course, the direction of the arrows could be reversed, since each of these different, interconnecting central pathways could also be traversed in the opposite direction. Everyone knows that an emotional state acts upon a person's psychic state and can even engender perceptive hallucinations.

Imperfect as it may be, the diagram does show that any perception can easily bring forth emotional states. The diagram also quickly makes us aware

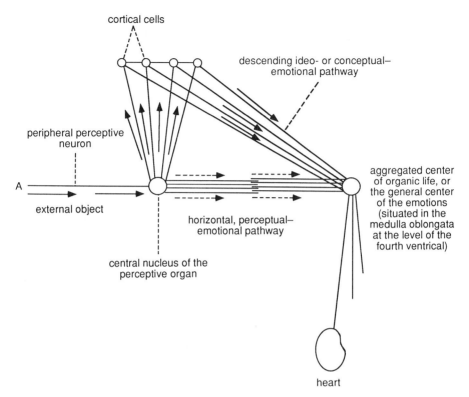

Figure 1 The course of an external impression, from peripheral neurons to the emotion center.

of the antagonism that must exist between perception's cognitive and affective elements. The more imperfect our prior knowledge, the more we will be vulnerable to experiencing an intense emotion as the consequence of a perception. If we block some of the cortical cells from participating in the cellular pageant that each perception surely evokes in our brains, then we will feel tiny emotional flutters occasioned by the flow of the perceptive wave toward the affective pathways.

It is also evident from the diagram that interconnecting, perceptual–emotional central pathways link the perceptive organs with the general center of the emotions. Similarly, central ideoemotional or conceptual–emotional pathways connect central ideas or concepts to that same emotion center. The emotion center is thus connected to the passage between the outer world and the higher cognitive layers, as is appropriate to its role as a center of life. Each world—the inner and the outer—can play the emotion center's keyboard and activate it. If it impinges abruptly, the outer world by itself is capable of profoundly disturbing the emotion center, provided that the outer impression has not been foreseen, preclassified, coordinated, or recognized and dominated by an inner, cognitive equivalent.

We will later examine the ideo- or conceptual–emotional pathway, which furnishes an important share of our affective perceptions. First, however, we will pause for a moment to explicate the class of affective perceptions generated exclusively by the greater or lesser absence of prior knowledge. It will be instructive to consider some cases in which the affective qualities of such perceptions manifest themselves clearly.

IV

With infants, who are devoid of much prior knowledge, almost every perception follows the perceptual–emotional pathway. Hence, as the baby examines whatever insignificant object that falls into his hands, at every moment he will have a source of continuous emotions. We know what pleasure and joy children receive first of all from their toys, which they touch and turn around and around again in all directions in order to establish cognition, that is, representations equivalent to all these apparitions from the outer world. The pure affectivity of these infantile perceptions is so obvious that it is unnecessary to detail it further. Soon, however, once cognition has been fully elaborated for each object, children become sophisticated, and their perceptions follow the ascending pathway. For those objects at least, the horizontal path atrophies. The child finds no more delight in those items. He loses interest in them; he passes on to others. One can say that for a long time perception in children is almost always affective; thus the child's exclamations, leaps, and exuberant movements upon experiencing a perception that would leave us nearly indifferent.

We should note parenthetically that everyone misunderstands the true nature of this perceptive affectivity in children. Hence several authors, for example, Darwin and Perez, interpret the precocious appearance of an infantile smile as sympathy.[2] However, a smile is only an external expression. I am certain that the child's smile at the age of nine or twelve months, which according to those authors signals the beginnings of that elevated senti-

---

[2]Tr. note: The French word *sympathie* can include both English "sympathy" and "empathy." The word is consistently translated as "sympathy" here, although in certain contexts the reader could appropriately understand Waynbaum to mean "empathy." In popular usage, the French do not distinguish sympathy from empathy, although a small circle of academics do use *empathie* as a technical term. According to the *Petit Robert* dictionary, *empathie* first appeared in the French language in 1903.

For a discussion of the English terms, see: Miller, P., and Eisenberg, N. (1988). The relation of empathy to aggressive and externalizing/antisocial behavior. *Psychological Bulletin*, 103, 324–344.

ment, does not in any way signify the existence in the child of such a complex emotion. If the child smiles at his parents or nanny so early, it is because he is learning to classify these individuals and to distinguish better and yet better among them. They are among the first objects that it is to his advantage to cognize well. He may also smile because he has a vague cognition about the future joys that his mother or nanny will bring him. He does not smile because of sympathy or affection—at least, not as we understand sympathy. In my opinion, for a long time a baby's smile is purely mechanical and perceptive. It does not at all possess the altruistic value that we ascribe to it. By stimulating reflex and illusion, his smile engenders in the parents a strong feeling that is, moreover, completely to his advantage.[3]

Thus, during our first years on earth, for a long time our perceptions remain affective. One can observe the same affectivity, for the same reasons, among all savage peoples. Such peoples are uncultivated and spend all their lives, so to speak, in an uncognized state quite similar to that of our childhoods.

In women perception often takes the perceptual–emotional path. It is generally held that women are more emotional and impressionable than men. Much of women's perceptive emotionality comes from a habitual lack of prior knowledge that would be able to inhibit the perceptual–emotional wave. The more women dedicate themselves to their cognitive development, the more they will have the good fortune to rid themselves of their often troublesome, hereditary perceptive emotionality.

Everything new and unknown will have a strong tendency to affect us and to evoke an emotion of variable intensity. This occurs because of the same principle, that when no cognitive representation exists, perception instead follows the horizontal pathway to transform itself into an emotion before generating cognition. From this phenomenon arises the pleasure of traveling; at such times we feel we are doubly alive, and everything new is beautiful and interesting. In a new country, at first we cannot stop exclaiming about things and admiring them. It is the period of affective perceptions. But after an indefinite period of time, all our cognitive representations have been elaborated. We become indifferent to the beauty of the scenery that we so admired in the beginning. We have adapted, as it were. We have become knowledgeable, and the place no longer charms us.

People try to create new affective perceptions with their clothing. From that proclivity springs the phenomenon of fashion, with all its tyranny and periodic changes. In the beginning, a novel fashion is all the rage. It surprises us—nearly moves us—as it draws our gaze. Everyone wants to keep up with fashion, since an out-of-style person fears ridicule. The masses champion a particular cut of cloth or shape for hats; by not submitting, a

---

[3]I developed this idea in detail in my book *La Physionomie Humaine* (Alcan, 1907).

person seriously runs the risk of appearing grotesque. But after a while people experience satiety. The styles are no longer striking; rather, they elicit purely cognitive sensations. It is time then to change the fashion, to create new affectivities by transforming the previous style. In considering all the frequently unhygienic annoyances caused by fashion, we should also bear in mind humanity's innately imitative tendencies.

Women especially excel in covering themselves with showy fabrics, beautiful colors, and brilliant jewelry in order to dazzle men. They envelop themselves in an affective atmosphere and create all sorts of optical illusions, thus falsifying their admirers' vision. Similarly, some people are dogged throughout their lives by a need for changes. Such people change their clothes, their homes, their furniture, their relationships, and even their affections. They are always searching out new things as sources of affective perceptions.

Idiosyncratically, many people develop a true permeability of the interconnecting, central perceptual–emotional pathway. Such individuals are generally designated as having an impressionable character. It is also said that their sensibilities are extremely delicate, but I think it wrong to impute this hyperexcitability exclusively to their sensibilities. What contributes more than anything else to making these people so excitable, so impressionable, is the ease with which their emotion centers are activated. Each perception, no matter how insignificant—a doorbell ringing, for example, or a somewhat disagreeable sight—causes them an emotion rather than a cognition. It is, thus, a matter of a genuine emotional idiosyncrasy caused by the special permeability of the horizontal, perceptual–emotional pathway. Moreover, this perceptive affectivity responds to fluctuations in the individual's overall health. It is not rare to find that the special affectivity disappears when general health no longer leaves anything to be desired. In passing, we should note too that certain neurasthenics suffer in a unique way from this morbid impressionability, which is none other than a form of affective perception.

If an external stimulus is out of the ordinary—if it bears little or no resemblance to the stimuli that a particular sensory organ is accustomed to conveying—then that sensory organ will bring us an affective perception. Thus, seeing a beautiful bed of flowers immediately causes us to smile. The handsome array of colors, of pretty hues, fascinates us and commands our attention. It causes us a sudden emotion because it is not part of our usual knowledge. We are not used to receiving that kind of visual impression. Likewise, when not in banal encounters, the sense of touch often affords us thrilling perceptions. If we touch the soft, smooth skin of an infant, despite ourselves we experience an emotional tremor. Certain fabrics—and the velvet of a peach—attract our fingers and hold them there, all the while eliciting gentle waves of affect within us.

We will stop enumerating cases in which perception becomes manifestly affective either due to excessive stimuli from the outer world, or else due to the disharmony between the outer sensation and our previous cognitive state. The intention here was only to give a few typical, everyday illustrations of this type of affective perception; it was not to provide a complete list.

What concerns us now is to formulate the logical conclusions that can be distilled from the aforementioned cases. The conclusions can be expressed as follows: we all possess an interconnecting, horizontal, central perceptual–emotional pathway, which enables each perception to engender emotions. The more this pathway is traversed, however, the more it tends to disappear, be dulled, or atrophy. Dulling occurs because as perception generates cognition, it travels directly up the ascending pathway rather than first reverberating in the medulla oblongata. Since humans are almost always prescient, perception routinely loses its affective qualities and more frequently addresses the cognitive elements directly. But if cognition is the least bit lacking, the affective elements of perception will reappear. *The affectivity of perception is therefore inversely related to prior knowledge.*

Such is the first type of affective perceptions, which acquire their special quality because the inner cognitive state does not perfectly correspond to the mass of external sensations. Let us now turn to the second type of affective perceptions.

V

From the start we have noted a second, equally prevalent category of cases—those in which perception acquires an affective quality because the emotional element is contained in the perception, is carried by it, or comes from the outer world. It is important to examine this class of perceptions carefully. This category differs completely from the first, even though it, too, generates emotionality in us. The mechanism here is quite distinct; it comes about precisely because of the ideoemotional pathway mentioned above.

In daily life, certain frequent perceptions elicit in us a special affectivity we call *sympathy.* Truly, we must thoroughly grasp that all the emotional states caused by sympathy arise from the external affective element. This element is contained and transported by a certain class of perceptions such that every stirring of sympathy is nothing more than an *affective perception sui generis.*

Everyone knows what is meant by sympathy when the term is correctly used. As the word's etymology adequately indicates, it means to suffer or to feel together. According to Mr. Ribot,[4] sympathy "consists of the existence of

---

[4]Th. Ribot (1899). *Psychologie des sentiments.* Paris: F. Alcan.

identical dispositions in two or more individuals of the same or different species." Mr. Bain defines it thus: "What we understand by 'sympathy' is the tendency of an individual to harmonize him- or herself with the active or emotional states of others—these states having been revealed by certain modes of expression."

By virtue of the laws of sympathy, all sentiments externalized by an individual will generate echoes in the social environment, provided that the perceptive senses of the people in that environment are capable of picking up on the expression. This law, which is almost without exception, has become a psychological axiom. Quite correctly, everyone freely repeats that to see suffering causes one to suffer, and to see merriment makes one joyful. In short, we can easily see that we are talking about a particular type of affective perception. We are so constructed that we cannot *see* either the expression of a feeling, or a stand-in for it, without experiencing an emotional impact in return. Thus, it is because of affective perceptions that we are involved in all sorts of manifestations of sympathy.

Can we offer a physioanatomical explanation for this reflectivity of feelings? Why should all men tremble together at the sight of only one man's suffering? Why is affect so contagious, and what is it that evokes solidarity among men in merriment, just as in sadness or any other emotional state? Responding to these questions, Mr. Ribot says that "before it is moral or psychological, sympathy is biological; it is a property of life, of living matter." What he says is quite true. Yet we had best show the actual physioanatomical process that links men together by making every feeling expansive the moment it is revealed in a social environment.

To become aware of the contagiousness of feeling, of its automatic reflectivity, we need only refer to Figure 1. In this schema, I sketched an ideoemotional pathway, in contrast with the horizontal, or perceptual–emotional pathway that we have been discussing until now. Clearly, with all sympathetic emotions it is the existence of this descending, ideoemotional pathway that makes the organism's affective agitation possible and even obligatory.

I do not claim the discovery of this pathway. It has been widely known, and for a long time, that each idea, or each cortical component, has the capacity to act upon the general center of the emotions. In order to effect immediately changes in our bodies, often all we need do is think of something merry or sad. We then feel palpitations, we are short of breath, we blush, or we become pale. In these cases, too, the affective impulse travels down from the central idea via the same descending pathway. But here I most wish to highlight cases in which the affective element comes from the outside, from the external world. It is conveyed by the sense of perception, and as it travels along the same descending pathway it blindly engenders a sympathetic or reflexive emotion. This is the anatomical reason for the reflectivity of feelings. The reflectivity is, in the final analysis, a property or effect of a certain class of affective perceptions.[5]

VI

For a better understanding of what has just been said, let us now turn to an example. In the absolute silence of a still night, while in my room I suddenly hear distant, mournful crying outside. Immediately my heart is rent. It beats in unison with that of the sufferer—someone far from me and whom I cannot even see. I will not discuss here my later behavior, namely whether, pushed by my sympathetic wave of emotion, I will or will not go to the aid of the person I hear wailing. Instead, I will focus exclusively on the manner in which the emotion impinged upon me. Now there is no doubt that the emotion flooded into me via a single entrance, that is, by my sense of hearing. My perception of sound produced both the emotion and a cognitive notion of the external event.

As noted earlier, the role of each perceptive sense is to be synthetic, to elicit a genuine pageant in our cortical cells, and immediately to inform us of all the inextricably linked attributes of an object from the moment just one of those attributes presents itself. Well, in the case outlined above, I have just heard a plaintive sound. From that time, all the attributes of suffering should flood through me. The idea of suffering should be revived, having been put in the forefront by the external symbol that has reached me. But I will not really understand the suffering unless I too begin to suffer— unless my circulation, my breathing, and other important bodily functions are transformed accordingly. This process produces the reflectivity of all expressed and perceived feelings. Here the affective course *descends*, since the stimulus to the emotion center comes from the *higher* central element. Yet this higher element, which was activated by the external affective component, that is, by affect's symbol or substitute, is only responding to an impression from the environment.

I stated above that the mere sight of an orange is enough to elicit within us all of its inseparably linked attributes. We often even experience some salivation, as if we already had a foretaste of the pleasure of chewing. Here, in the case of a plaintive sound that strikes my ear, the same thing happens. The lament that I hear from far away, without even seeing the sufferer, carries within it the expression of suffering, that is, the symbol of or stand-in for it. If

---

[5] I wish to clarify here that each time I speak of sympathetic feelings, I refer only to *perceived* feelings in one or another of their expressions. Of course, everyone knows that one can also have *conceived* sympathetic emotions; but I will not deal with those here.

it becomes perceptible while traveling through the higher centers of my brain, this stand-in can, all by itself, animate within me the idea of suffering, with all the attendant bodily consequences. This process is why, necessarily and automatically, I must experience a certain emotionality that makes me feel sympathetic and in solidarity with the sufferer outside, despite my inability to see the person. Such is the course of sympathy. Such is the simple yet marvelous mechanism that makes all men sympathetic and creates solidarity among them.

By this frequent and ordinary, everyday example, we can clearly see that sympathy is nothing more than a kind of affective perception. The affect is imprinted onto sympathy by the element from the environment. The role of each perceptive sense is to be synthetic, to bring us up to date with the shortest delay possible of all that is happening around us, even when changes in our environment are conveyed to us by only the slightest signs and tiniest symbols. If an affective phenomenon occurs, immediately we are plunged into the same affectivity, *in order better to understand it*. Thus, sympathy becomes possible and even obligatory among men, since each perceptive sense has its own synthetic power and since there is a descending, ideoemotional pathway by which all central elements can act upon our general center of emotion.

It follows that if two senses together intervene in our lives, each brings its own, external, affective stand-in. Perception then increases in affectivity, and sympathy grows. If, instead of only hearing faraway moans, I can also *see* the sufferer, the mass of affective impressions brought to me by these two senses will be much greater. I will certainly manifest a more intense sympathy for a miserable person whom I both hear and see agonizing next to me.

All that we have said about suffering could just as well be applied to any other emotional state, since as everyone knows, all feelings have an expansive force, provided that they are perceptible to one or another of our senses. Thus, laughter is contagious, because to see the symbol of merriment awakens the idea of it, which in turn makes everyone truly more merry. Even to see someone yawn brings to mind the idea of boredom. This idea immediately expresses itself by the imitative, involuntary act of yawning in turn.

VII

Most of our social relations are based on a principle of affective reflectivity in perception. We have already seen that people willingly tolerate all the tyrannies of fashion and change in order to satisfy their need for affective stimulation. To this first type of perception, we must moreover add all those of the second type, with which people surround themselves just as willingly; they wish to sow affective reflexes in the people around them. Undeniably, a certain reflex is emitted by a military uniform, a priest's habit, a judge's robes, a doctor's top hat, an undertaker's sad outfit, and so on. When we see them, these symbols thoroughly concretize the inherent feelings exuded by these different social roles. Just at the sight of them, it would be quite rare for us not to experience a corresponding affective reflex. Thus, men are maintained in a sort of discipline, or automatic hierarchy, thanks to their different outfits and uniforms. Furthermore, society religiously preserves many of these outfits, despite their grotesque form and evident lack of utility. If, in addition to this affective symbolism of clothing, we also include the real symbolism that every man possesses in his gestures, voice, postures, or physiognomy, we see immediately how enormous a mass of reflective, affect-laden perceptions each man can generate around himself.

The art of *pleasing others* consists of nothing more than eliciting these sympathetic reflexes wherever there is a field of perception. Obviously, in this realm, too, people can draw upon all sorts of natural and artificial means in order to stimulate a positive affective perception in their peers. For example, when people see someone smiling, they come up to chat. A smile has the advantage of immediately inspiring merriment in those we encounter, as well as making a person who is laughing look more attractive. For two people conversing, the face is truly a living movie screen where one can read all sorts of expressions of altruistic feelings.

Women, of whom we have already spoken briefly, are especially adept at wrapping themselves in a halo of affective symbols, simulating various elevated and pure sentiments. These affective symbols often glitter and more successfully beguile men when there is actually a complete absence of genuine sentiment. Thus, certain morally perverse and notorious women manage to inspire wild passions—because they style their hair the way candid, fresh young women do, or because an expression of innocence, of ingenuousness, imparts them with a symbolic power that captivates their admirers. If their admirers' temperaments are the least bit affective—and sexual need plays a role here, too—they will forever see the object of their adulation as an angel or divinity. The sight of these seductresses, whether actual or in representations, awakens the very depths of their feelings about religion (or analogous experiences). Their intellects become completely clouded over. This is why one should never try to reason with a man in love, nor to dissipate his illusions. When time and the assuaging of sexual hunger have accomplished their work, the intellect will again take up its responsibilities. The man will then realize what reality lay behind those affective symbols of purity.

In a word, in the art of pleasing others one must know how to propagate sympathetic, affective perceptions around oneself. One must thoroughly grasp the science of affective symbolism and be skilled in playing this powerful keyboard. The effects will be nearly unfailing, because in all affective perceptions cognition is obscured. One will therefore always be more certain to fascinate and please everyone.

VIII

Naturally, all the senses have this property of transporting external affective elements to the higher brain centers and of thereby evoking sympathetic feelings. However, we must make special mention of the sense of hearing. In certain cases, this sense actually transmits to us an uninterrupted series of perceptions that are exceptionally rich in external affective elements. This transmission has the gift of automatically plunging us into the state of sympathetic emotion previously discussed. Such cases particularly occur whenever we hear music.

The captivating charm and sublime art of music, its magical power to move and overcome us, consists precisely in its abundance of affective elements. Our ears can immediately interpret these elements with great sensitivity. I will readily define music as an art in which admirable use is made of all the natural and especially the artificial means invented by human genius to excite our auditory, sympathetic affectivity. In the final analysis, music can be reduced to a series of affective symbols—vocal or instrumental, combined, arranged, and more or less differentiated and expressed. Music is designed to stir up within us, via the sense of hearing, a sympathetic affectivity. The correspondence of this affectivity to the music will, of course, depend on each individual's capacity for understanding, as well as the extent to which he or she has a trained ear. Each musical work, if it is worthy of the name, has only one aim: to imitate as much as possible the innumerable human sentiments, with all their nuances, in order to generate within us a sympathetic, matching affectivity.

Everything about music carries the seal, the stamp, of affect. I will go even further: this affectivity must be anthropomorphic or anthropocentric in order to become musical. Apart from a certain quantitative and qualitative combination of aerial vibrations, sound has nothing *musical* or *harmonious* about it. It is merely crude, amorphous noise. Moreover, if the vibrations occur faster than a certain speed, their harmony is lost. They become strident, shrill, and disagreeable to us. Instead, the vibrations must in some cases accelerate their rhythm, and in others slow it down. The final result will once again be musical. Why is this so? Where does this new attribute, "*musical*" or "*harmonious*," come from? Why is it ascribed to a series of intermingled aerial vibrations? Since already this mingled sound resembles something human, it exists within the range of possible human affects. The resemblance transforms the sound, and we begin to find it euphonic and musical. Already it begins to excite our sympathetic, auditory affectivity.

A pure, richly harmonic sound, made by any instrument, is beautiful and enraptures our souls; but two sounds, when combined to produce a chord, heighten our affectivity and immerse us in greater ecstasy. The increase occurs because with a chord, the richness of the external affective elements is greater than with a single note. The sympathetic stimulation becomes more intense. Naturally, these combinations of sounds must also abide by certain laws. Probably these laws merely echo the serial nature of our own feelings, or else the sequentiality of certain external resonances linked to our affective states. Otherwise, the incoherent multiplication of sounds—even sounds that are musical when heard one at a time—would run the risk of producing a cacophony repulsive to our ears.

Indeed, everyone knows how much we prefer those instruments that most faithfully reproduce human feeling and the human voice. This is why we so love to hear the violin, and even more so the cello: one could say that within its cavity, this last instrument truly contains a male larynx. By their pastoral sounds, the oboe and tenor oboe immediately evoke vague recollections within us of idyllic landscapes and scented fields where we love to linger. In their high notes, the clarinet, the flute, and even the violin easily bring to mind the female soprano, which faintly arouses our sexual affectivity. Here we see what an ocean of affectivity swirls within us—how much we must become organically transformed—when we listen to an entire, full orchestra in which all these harmonious elements are intensified and multiplied.

When it becomes affective, the human voice is altogether different from the voice we use in ordinary circumstances. Inflamed with passion, the voice vibrates. It carries far then; it possesses tremendous qualities of social expansion, due to the aforementioned affective perceptions generated around it. Any affective state has repercussions on phonetic innervation and thereby transforms the voice. But if this affective state attains the strength of a passion, the voice undergoes a complete change. It becomes an enormously powerful affective substitute, with considerable effects on the auditory senses of those in the social environment.

Accordingly, when skillfully played, certain stringed instruments, such as the violin and cello, have the remarkable ability to translate the voice of passion. All the while these instruments also imbue the sound with their special tonalities. The passion becomes enveloped by something invisible and superhuman. It is common knowledge that violin and cello virtuosos rhythmically quiver their fingers in order to intensify the expressivity of their instruments' sounds. Without these vibrations, the sound is not as sweet or affective. All great artists work toward perfection in this technical aspect of performance. They wish to identify the sound of their stringed instrument with the equally vibrating, trembling voice of human passion.

For this reason, the piano is such a forbidding, fruitless instrument, hated and feared even by many music lovers. The piano's nearly mechanical registering of a melody can proffer no more than the skeleton—the outline, the faint, colorless shadow—of a feeling. It cannot bring forth the essence or soul, which is precisely what engenders sympathetic reflectivity. Few virtuoso pianists can attain the flawlessness of a Rubinstein or a Liszt, so as to manage the instrument according to their wishes and make it express all the affectivity that a piece contains.

We should also point out that human singing charms us so much because in song the voice inevitably becomes affective. Indeed, all singers strive for the maximum number of impassioned vocal vibrations. Some human voices have an affective, harmonious tone even in their natural states; there is no need for song. These melodious voices immerse everyone who listens to them into a sympathetic, reflective affectivity. Such voices have the gift of predisposing everyone in the speaker's favor. There are also repugnant voices, which have negative reflective qualities. As a general rule, the more an instrument or even a human voice contains combined affective elements, the more splendid its expansive effect.

What now of the many emotional treasures that a genius composer amasses within a piece in order to move us, to subjugate us, and to turn us into his plaything? Clearly affectivity is limited here only by the composer's sensitivity and by the relative richness of his affective conceptions. Whether of the Italian masters, or of a Beethoven, Gounod, or Wagner, in such music the affectivity has always been symbolized, externalized, and concretized in order to create echoes everywhere there is a human heart to feel and a brain to understand.

In general, music has all the more affective influence on us when, in addition to the mass of affective and sympathetic perceptions that it normally affords, we also experience numerous affective perceptions of the first type—those that follow the horizontal, perceptual–emotional pathway. Obviously, hearing a fine orchestra is not an everyday perception. It goes beyond the sum of our common prior knowledge and thus must engender a special affectivity. The two types of affectivity are added together, enhancing the effect.

No one can deny that all serious musical works profit from being heard several times. With each new hearing, we appraise them better. The affectivity they generate becomes deeper and less chaotic, all the while becoming more intellectual. This process is easy to grasp: upon first hearing, a classical piece, for instance, a Beethoven symphony, crushes us. It generates a chaos of feelings. Yet, as we listen, a few central elements are being cognitively elaborated. Later, an embryonic memory remains. Upon a second hearing, these central elements are revived by the repetition, which gives us our first sense of satisfaction. Moreover, the affectivity is channeled, having already become attached to some cognitive elements. The piece does not crush us as much, and we begin better to appreciate the *affective nuances*. With each new hearing, the cognitive element is consolidated. Yet if the work is truly profound and serious, as for example with Beethoven's Fifth Symphony, then there is still ample room left for affectivity. After a certain number of hearings, our memory is completely organized; the whole sequence of harmonious sounds is retained in order. However, our pleasure is just as great when we listen to the work anew. We wish precisely to revive the central elements that we had elaborated during all our affective moments. In short, a truly musical work acts upon us just like a good book or good friend: the more we know them, the more we love them, and the more we need to see or think about them, because more and more both our brains and our hearts belong to them.

We thus see the exceptional affective richness contained in music. One could say that this art rests on a material substratum of affect. There is no justification for calling a tone "musical" unless it carries within itself some resemblance to or symbolism of affect. When these symbols are arranged, coordinated, and combined in a tune or melody, they constitute the expression of a more powerful, more organized feeling. Once expressed, this phenomenon is faithfully registered by our sense of hearing. Then in traveling via the two emotional pathways previously discussed—especially the descending pathway—the perception automatically awakens new affectivities within us. Such is the specific character of perceptions generated by music, and such is the almost exclusively affective role that our sense of hearing plays when we attend the performance of a musical work.

Obviously, I could write more about all the affective elements that music contains, but in a brief overview I cannot pretend to exhaust such a vast subject. My only intention here has been to highlight the exceptional affective richness of the perceptions engendered by music, as well as their special mode of transmission and their similarity to the other affective and sympathetic perceptions discussed above. I trust that what little has been said has been enough to convince the reader.

Conclusions

I shall now summarize what I have tried to demonstrate in this article.

When we speak of perceptions, we must never forget that many have affective properties. Although less extensive than cognitive perceptions, affective perceptions nonetheless occupy an important place in our psychic life. Their role is itself subdivided into two quite distinct types. The first consists of perceptions that become affective because of a lack of knowledge about them, or because of an incomplete adaptation to the environment. By contrast, the second type generates affectivity within us merely by transmitting an affective element that comes from the outer world. Hence, what distinguishes the two types is their composition, or very substance, as well as the pathway for transmitting affectivity. The first type is, in and of itself, devoid of all affective elements; but it travels via the horizontal, perceptual–emotional pathway and therefore produces an emotional jolt. The second type is just the opposite: often it abounds richly in affectivity, and it follows the descending, or ideoemotional, pathway to generate an emotion.

The first type comes from the outer world and goes straight toward the emotion center; there is nothing above it to receive or inhibit it. The second, by contrast, beings by heading toward the higher brain centers—centers that contain an equivalent to the perception. From there the perception descends toward the emotion center.

We have already summarized above our conclusions concerning the first type of affective perceptions. Let us recall here also the conclusions that can be drawn from study of the second type.

What we generally, commonly call "sympathy" is nothing other than a particular form of affective perception, one in which the emotional element comes straight from the outer world. It comes in the form of some sort of substitute, just as any other cognitive element would come. Since the role of each perceptive sense is essentially to be synthetic, our affectivity is immediately aroused by this affective input from the external world. This process is what elicits the obligatory reflectivity of feelings and puts all men in consensus with each other. Music is simply an uninterrupted emanation of such affective, sympathetic perceptions. These perceptions surely also have a reflective effect on all human sensibilities, provided that their symbolism is compatible with an individual's cognitive and perceptive capacities.

By indicating the subjective effects that perception generates, we have also tried to reconstruct a kind of schema for perception's course among our differing critical brain centers. From this schema, it clearly follows that the outer world can act upon the emotion center via two different pathways. One path is perceptual–emotional and rather horizontal; the other, ideoemotional and descending. It is good to bear in mind that while this latter pathway belongs to the inner world, it can also be indirectly influenced by the world outside. Obviously, the external world can, at times, act upon our affectivity via both pathways. Then our emotion is all the greater.

Thus, our direct contact with the outer world often results in a cognition, but also sometimes in an emotion. A large proportion of our perceptions is purely cognitive, while other, slightly less frequent perceptions are thoroughly affective. Perceptive affectivity can, in turn, have either *noncognitive* or *reflective* origins.

Acknowledgments

The translator gratefully acknowledges the assistance of Laurence U. Buxbaum and Joseph Arditty.

Affective Regulation of Perception and Comprehension: Amplification and Semantic Priming

Shinobu Kitayama
University of Oregon and Kyoto University

Susan Howard
University of Oregon

Introduction

In recent years affect has reemerged as an issue of considerable significance in social psychology (e.g., Isen, 1984; Niedenthal & Showers, 1991;
Zajonc, 1980). Affect is a directive force "toward" or "against" a given object,
either actual or imagined. As such, it underlies virtually every human action
and cognition and, in particular, it is inseparably connected with social
perception and social interaction.[1] That is to say, it is importantly shaped

[1]We thus consider affect as a major component of *emotion*, which is taken here as a more
comprehensive psychological state encompassing not only affect but also myriad other processes including somatic, motor processes, cognitions regarding the nature of the pertinent
social situation, and overt or covert behaviors in coping with the situation (e.g., Scherer &
Ekman, 1984; Ellsworth, 1991; Frijda, 1986; Ortony & Turner, 1990). Another closely related
construct is *attitude*, which is also regarded as a more inclusive construct encompassing both
knowledge about and behavioral intentions toward the object (e.g., Fishbein & Ajzen, 1974). Yet,

and constructed through these social processes and, once generated, it in turn guides and organizes them. Of major theoretical interest, then, are the questions of how affective processes are interconnected with cognitive processes, and what types of causal influences affect has on cognition. More specifically, at what level (e.g., semantic or presemantic) will this interaction take place, and with what consequences (e.g., enhancement or impairment)?

In the literature on affective information processing, two sets of contrasting theoretical positions, and ensuing debates, have guided empirical research. One debate concerns the function of affect to either enhance or impair cognitive processing: Is affect benign or malicious? Some have supposed the primary function of affect to be interruption of cognitive processing (e.g., Simon, 1967), whereas others have believed it to be potentiation or enhancement of processing (e.g., Easterbrook, 1959). The other controversy has revolved around the "level" at which affective influence on cognition takes place: Is affect essentially semantic or "presemantic"? Some have maintained that affect can be usefully seen as one particular form of semantic information, say, as generalized "goodness" or "badness" (Bower, 1981). According to this view, affect is a special form of cognition and, as such, it regulates thinking or remembering by providing these cognitive processes with an additional, affective piece of information. Some other theorists, however, have considered affect as essentially presemantic (and possibly precognitive) activation. As such, it can influence cognition in a manner that is qualitatively distinct from semantic or cognitive influence (LeDoux, 1987; Zajonc, 1980).

As is often the case with prominent debates in the history of psychology, subsequent empirical research has suggested that the seemingly opposing views are in fact all correct, but only in part. As we shall see below, affect can either enhance or impair cognitive processing under different conditions and, furthermore, this affective influence in information processing can be mediated both semantically and pre- (or non-) semantically. Nevertheless, at present, we have yet to integrate the multifaceted aspects of affect within a comprehensive framework of information processing.

In this chapter, we review recent research on affective regulation of perception and comprehension, especially focusing on our own experimental work. First, we present two theoretical principles of affective regulation of cognition that can be identified in the literature, namely, amplification and semantic priming. *Amplification* refers to affect's function to energize some cognitive or behavioral responses. We believe that this function of affect can have pervasive influence on cognitive processes even before the affect is semantically encoded. Affect, however, can be semantically encoded as

---

many have assumed that affect is the central component of attitude (see Fazio, Roskos-Ewoldsen, & Powell, this volume).

"good," "bad," "happy," "sad," and the like; and, once so encoded, it can activate a variety of associated thoughts, images, and meanings. This more semantic or cognitive influence of affect is called *semantic priming*. After briefly reviewing evidence pertaining to these two functions of affect, we discuss two distinct ways in which affect regulates cognition. Affect will be shown to exert systematic influence on (1) immediate conscious perception and (2) comprehension of spoken communications.

Two Theoretical Principles: Amplification and Semantic Priming

Amplification

One widely postulated property of affect is arousal, or its ability to *amplify* a variety of psychological functions. Tomkins (1962, 1980) proposed that various basic emotions such as joy and anger can be described in terms of differential patterns of amplification of the nervous system. Although Tomkins's analysis may no longer seem feasible, arousal or the intensity dimension of affect has been shown to be essential in defining a variety of everyday vocabularies of emotion and concepts in general, and it is suggested that it is universal across cultures (Osgood, 1962; Russell, 1980). Another major dimension of affect identified in this literature is pleasantness.

The notion that affect energizes a variety of cognitive and behavioral responses can be traced back to the heyday of behaviorism. Several lines of research have strongly suggested that affect amplifies "dominant" cognitive as well as behavioral responses. This theme is central to a behavioral theory of learning proposed by Hull, Spence, and Taylor in the 1950s (cf. Spence, 1956). The assumption that an amplifying function is a major component of affect (Lindsley, 1951; Sternbach, 1966) is at the core of the Yerkes–Dodson's (1908) law and, further, has proved applicable to an analysis of social facilitation (Zajonc, 1965).

A number of studies, most notably by Lacey and Lacey (e.g., 1968), have suggested that the notion of generic, unidimensional arousal involving all aspects of the sympathetic nervous system and those of cortical processes does not do justice to the highly differentiated character of physiological arousal (Derryberry & Tucker, this volume). Yet, even today it remains still reasonable to postulate that at least *some* aspects of psychological processes are likely to be amplified by affect (Buck, 1988). The notion of affect as having an amplifying potential was incorporated into a perceptual framework by Easterbrook (1959). He proposed that affect limits the range of perceptual features that can be attended by the perceiver. Thus, stimuli located at the center of attentional focus can receive more attention and, therefore, the perception of these stimuli can be enhanced (Christianson & Loftus, 1991; Christianson, Loftus, Hoffman, & Loftus, 1991).

Semantic Priming

The second dominant theme in theories of affective information processing is semantic priming. It is assumed that affective activation can be semantically coded as, say, pleasant or unpleasant, happy or sad, good or bad, and so on, and represented in the form of corresponding nodes within an associative network of semantic memory (e.g., Bower, 1981; Blaney, 1986; Niedenthal, Sutterlund, & Jones, this volume). Once the semantic representation of affect is activated, the activation can spread to other ideas, thoughts, and images associated with it, thereby influencing the nature and the outcome of subsequent cognitive activities (Lang, 1984). One prominent phenomenon that seems to be mediated by this mechanism is a mood congruence effect (e.g., Blaney, 1986; Isen, Shalker, Clark, & Karp, 1978). This phenomenon is illustrated by the fact that individuals can encode and retrieve materials that are congruent with their current mood more effectively than those that are incongruent. Further, some attempts have recently been made to demonstrate similar effects in judgment and decision making (Isen, 1984; Johnson & Tversky, 1983; Mayer, Gaschke, Braverman, & Evans, 1992). Semantic priming effects of affect have also been demonstrated with more transient affective stimuli such as briefly presented words with affective connotations (e.g., Fazio, Sanbonmatsu, Powell, & Kardes, 1986; Greenwald, Klinger, & Lui, 1989); the processing of affective information is enhanced by a preceding word with equally valenced affective meanings and impaired by one with oppositely valanced affective meanings.

In sum, we have distinguished between two loci at which affect can interact with cognition. Relatively primitive, presemantic activation of affect can potentiate some responses. Simultaneously, however, the affective activation can be coded in terms of the corresponding semantic categories of affect. Once this semantic encoding occurs, the affect can prime related ideas in memory. In what follows, we use the two principles as a general framework within which more specific theoretical models are developed. Specifically, we examine two substantive domains: perception of affective stimuli and comprehension of spoken communications.

Affective Regulation of Perception

Will perceptibility of a briefly shown stimulus depend on affect associated with the stimulus itself? Historically, effects of affect in perception can be traced back to the literature on the "New Look" in perception in the 1950s

(Bruner, 1957). In one of the first experimental studies on the topic, McGinnies (1949) compared recognition threshold for sexually explicit, "taboo" words with that of affectively neutral words, and found the former to be considerably higher than the latter. He claimed that perception of a word was impaired by the affective connotation of the word itself. Critics, however, maintained that the finding could be explained most parsimoniously by postperceptual response bias such as reluctance or readiness to report a taboo word (Eriksen, 1963; Goldiamond, 1958; see Erdelyi, 1974, Dixon, 1980, for reviews). Three decades later, it appears that at least part of McGinnies's original finding was in fact perceptual. Several more recent studies have used methods that allow one to examine perceptual accuracy independent of postperceptual response bias. For instance, subjects may be asked to choose the item shown from a pair of equivalently valenced words. Research employing this and other similar procedures has demonstrated that the affective tone of a stimulus *does* influence perceptibility (e.g., Bootzin & Natsoulas, 1965; Dorfman, 1967).

The Amplification Model

Mechanisms underlying immediate conscious perception are necessarily preconscious. Thus, the effect of affect on immediate perception may serve as an important window through which to theorize on an interaction between affect and cognition in early perceptual processing (cf. Jacoby, Lindsay, & Toth, 1992; Kihlstrom, 1987, 1990). In our recent work we have asked what variables would mediate such effects of affect in perception, and suggested that an amplification function of affect can provide a reasonable account for the phenomenon (Kitayama, 1990, 1991, 1992a).

Specifically, the current cognitive literature suggests that an impinging stimulus is initially processed automatically and preconsciously (McClelland & Rumelhart, 1981; Posner, 1978), thus activating the perceptual information, or perceptual code, that represents the stimulus. The perceptual code corresponding to an impinging stimulus may be called the *target* code. Once the target perceptual code has been preconsciously activated, two additional processes come into play. First, although this activation can happen preconsciously (e.g., Bargh, Bond, Lombardi, & Tota, 1986; Carr & Dagenbach, 1990; Marcel, 1983a,b), it is sufficient to evoke some associated affective response (e.g., Dawson & Schell, 1982; Greenwald, 1992; Greenwald et al., 1989; Niedenthal, 1990; Tassinary, Orr, Wolford, Napps, & Lanzetta, 1984). Perhaps the target code thus activated preattentively summons affective circuits of the brain located in the limbic or subcortical regions (Derryberry & Tucker, this volume; Le Doux, 1989). Second, simultaneously with the elicitation of the associated affect, a set of additional cognitive processes that operate in more top-down and serial fashion, called *attentive processing*, is engaged. Attentive processing is selective, limited solely to the code to which it is directed. It, therefore, must first be directed to a target code and, once so directed, it furthers the processing of the information represented in the attended code to produce the conscious experience of this information and thus that of the impinging stimulus. Notice that conscious perception is not merely a function of sensory (i.e., externally caused) activation. The external activation must be combined with attentional (i.e., internally caused) activation to produce a full-fledged conscious percept.

According to this analysis, some affect associated with an impinging stimulus can be produced by the preconscious activation of the target code and, therefore, can be induced *before* attentive processing is fully engaged in the target code. There are two important implications of this hypothesis. First, the affect thus preconsciously induced may then influence the attentive processing used to produce the conscious perception of the stimulus. A number of researchers have assumed that attentive processing can vary in its "intensity" or in the amount of attentional resources that can be brought to bear on the processing of the attended information (see, e.g., Kahneman, 1973, Johnston & Dark, 1985, for reviews). Evidence indicates that one important determinant of the attention's "intensity" is affect. As briefly reviewed earlier, affect can *amplify* attentive processing.

The second implication stems from the hypothesis that attentive processing is qualitatively different from preattentive, automatic processing. Under certain conditions, attentive processing may not be applied to the target code. Obviously, the quality of the conscious perception of the impinging stimulus should depend on whether or not the attentive processing is applied to the target code. In conjunction with the amplifying function of preconsciously evoked affect, this analysis predicts that the preconsciously activated affect should either enhance or impair the final conscious perception, depending on the accuracy with which attentive processing is directed to the target code.

On one hand, if attentive processing is deployed to the target code, the evoked affect should amplify the attentive processing of this target code, causing the final conscious perception to be accurate and efficient. This beneficial effect of affect is called *affective enhancement*. On the other hand, attentive processing can be misdirected to one of potentially many perceptual codes that have nothing to do with the impinging stimulus (called *nontarget* codes), but that have retained some residual activation from prior experience. The possibility of attention misdirected to a nontarget code is especially likely in many perceptual experiments where stimuli are presented under impoverished viewing conditions. Once attentive processing is misdirected to a nontarget perceptual code, affect and ensuing amplification of attentive processing will augment the information represented in this nontarget perceptual code, activating invalid information and thus impairing the efficiency of correct perception. This impeding effect of affect is called *affective impairment*.

One implication of the above model (called the *amplification model* hereafter) is that an affective impairment effect should be most likely to occur when the presentation of a target stimulus is impoverished. Under these conditions, the activation of the target perceptual code will be weak. Under these conditions, even though this weak activation is enough to produce some affect and ensuing amplification of subsequent, attentive processing (see Greenwald, 1992, for a review), it will also make it difficult to locate that code, leading to a misengagement of attentive processing to other non-target codes. As a consequence, affect associated with the target code and ensuing amplification of attentive processing should augment invalid perceptual information and, consequently, it should impair the emerging conscious percept. The amplification model also implies that this impairment effect should disappear or even reverse itself once the difficulty in locating the target perceptual code is alleviated by some other means and, consequently, attention is directed to the target perceptual code. The major prediction of the amplification model, then, is that any variable that increases the activation of a target perceptual code relative to the activation of other, nontarget codes will increase the likelihood of affective enhancement and/or decrease the likelihood of affective impairment.

Evidence

Word length   Some prominent models of word recognition in the current cognitive literature (e.g., McClelland & Rumelhart, 1981) suggest that word length may systematically change the extent to which a target perceptual code is unequivalently or uniquely activated by a briefly presented word. According to these models, the initial, preattentive processing of a visual word stimulus proceeds in parallel, leading to simultaneous activation of its "parts." For the sake of clear exposition of the argument, these parts may be assumed to correspond to individual letters. Once the individual letters have been activated, they in turn impose significant constraints on the likely identity of the input, permitting only a limited number of English words as reasonable candidates for the input. All else being equal, as word length increases, a greater number of letters should be activated and the letter-level information should more strongly constrain the word-level identity. If so, an increase of word length should lead to more unequivocal and unique activation of the target code and, therefore, to accurate deployment of attention to the target perceptual code. As word length increases, there should be a greater chance of affective enhancement as opposed to affective impairment.

Support for this prediction was found in recent experiments, in which both word affect and word length were systematically manipulated within a fairly narrow range of word frequency (Kitayama, 1992a). Subjects were exposed to a 33-msec flash of a target word. The target was presented with a high level of contrast. In order to reduce the perceptibility of the target, it was immediately followed by a pattern mask. The subjects then chose the target word from a word pair. This procedure was designed to minimize the possibility of response bias. In one experiment, the word pair consisted of the target word and an equivalently valenced filler. In another experiment, a signal detection technique was used to control for response bias. Both the affective meaning of the targets (positive, negative, or neutral) and their length were systematically manipulated. It was found, in general, that the accuracy of perceptual identification was lower for affective words than for neutral words (affective impairment) if the words were relatively short (shorter than 6 letters); but the pattern tended to be reversed to show affective enhancement if they were relatively long (longer than 8 letters).[2]

Expectation   Another variable that could increase the likelihood of affective enhancement and reduce that of affective impairment is expectation. It has been shown in a number of studies on lexical priming that previous exposure to a target increases the activation of the corresponding perceptual code (e.g., Higgins & Bargh, 1987; Jacoby, 1983; Neely, 1977; Posner & Snyder, 1975). If so, in a perceptual identification task, the difficulty of locating a target perceptual code should be relieved by a correct expectation about the target word. Thus, affective enhancement will be more likely and affective impairment less likely in the presence of a valid expectation than in its absence. Our recent studies have provided support for this analysis (Kitayama, 1990, 1992a). In these experiments, subjects were presented with a brief flash of a word. They were then shown the word and another word and asked to choose between them the one that was flashed. Some subjects were given the pair prior to the flash of the target word as well to create an expectation. Generally, accuracy in word identification was lower for affective words than for neutral words in the absence of the expectation (impairment); once the expectation was given, however, affective words tended to be identified more accurately than neutral words (enhancement).

Further, the current prediction involving expectation provides a way to integrate inconsistent findings from the past literature on perceptual defense. We showed that these findings can be sorted out neatly once the extent to which subjects supposedly expected a valid target in each experi-

---

[2]Kitayama (1991) failed to find such an effect of word length. In this study, however, instead of using pattern mask, the contrast between the target and its background was degraded to reduce its perceptibility. It appears, then, that word length can modulate the effects of affect only when the contrast is sufficiently high to ensure strong stimulus input.

ment is taken into account. Some of the past studies used a procedure that inadvertently provided subjects with a clear expectation about a target stimulus (e.g., Chapman & Feather, 1972; Dorfman, 1967; Dorfman, Grossberg, & Kroeker, 1965), whereas others did not use any comparable procedure so that subjects had no valid expectation about target stimuli (e.g., Bootzin & Natsoulas, 1965; Broadbent & Gregory, 1967; Sales & Haber, 1968). A review of this literature showed that affective enhancement is a typical finding in the former group of studies, but affective impairment is more common in the latter (Kitayama, 1990).

It must be noted that in this perceptual identification paradigm we have found little difference between positive and negative affective stimuli (Broadbent & Gregory, 1967; Kitayama, 1990, 1991, 1992a). This finding is consistent with the amplification model, insofar as it can be reasonably assumed that amplification of attention can occur once the system has detected the significance of the impinging stimulus, which can be signaled by both positive and negative affective activations preconsciously induced at an early stage in the stimulus processing (LeDoux, 1989).

It is possible that the absence of any difference between positive and negative affect in the present conditions may be due to the fact that affect examined here is quite rudimentary, neither differentiated nor consciously recognized. After further stimulus processing, affect may be differentiated and, as a result, it may have valence-specific effects on attention. In line with this analysis, when stimuli are presented in optimal viewing conditions, it is typically negative affect that captures more attention (e.g., Kitayama, 1992b; Hansen & Hansen, this volume; Pratto, this volume; but also see Roskos-Ewoldsen & Fazio, 1992).

In sum, research reported here suggests that affect can be elicited early in stimulus processing and can influence perceptual identification. And at this early stage of processing, the major function of affect is to amplify subsequent attentive processing. In the rest of this chapter, we broaden the scope of our analysis and examine affective influence in comprehension of spoken communications. In comprehension, which involves far more elaborate cognitive operations, the amplification function of affect may operate hand in hand with another, more cognitive function of affect, namely, semantic priming.

Affective Regulation of Comprehension

Processing of Affective Speech

Speech can simultaneously convey two kinds of affect, that is, affect communicated by verbal content and affect expressed in vocal quality. For example, a sentence with positive meaning, "I love you," can be read in a positive, pleasant voice tone. The same sentence, however, can also be read in a negative, cynical voice tone. In many social interactions, especially among people who know each other well, what is important is not the content of the communication, but rather its vocal tone. As might be expected, a number of studies have demonstrated that vocal tone can modulate diverse social psychological processes, including impression formation (e.g., O'Sullivan, Ekman, Friesen, & Scherer, 1985), deception (e.g., DePaulo, Stone, & Lassiter, 1985; Ekman & Freisen, 1969; Zuckerman, Amidon, Bishop, & Pomerantz, 1982), self-fulfilling prophecy (e.g., Blanck, Rosenthal, & Vannicelli, 1986), and psychopathology (e.g., Bateson, Jackson, Haley, & Weakland, 1956). A great deal has been learned from this literature about, for example, conditions in which people can and cannot detect deception, or which nonverbal cues tend to dominate in personality impression formation.

Currently, however, we need to understand, in detail, how affect communicated by this nonverbal cue might regulate specific information processing mechanisms. In particular, the current literature on affective information processing, including our own work reviewed above (e.g., Bargh et al., 1986; Bower, 1981; Fazio et al., 1986; Greenwald et al., 1989; Kitayama, 1990, 1991, 1992a; Lang, 1984; Zajonc, 1980) has so far been concerned mostly with printed linguistic materials (but see Hansen & Hansen, 1988; Niedenthal, 1990, for notable exceptions). Because printed language is not the typical means of social interaction, implications of this literature for social psychological phenomena might be somewhat limited. Furthermore, by restricting the data base to printed language, the literature on affective information processing may have been unnecessarily narrow in scope. Because nonverbal signals of affect, unlike affective verbal content, can activate affective responses *before* semantic processing comes into play, an in-depth analysis of these signals from the current perspective might reveal some important, and hitherto unknown, modes of affective regulation of social cognition.

Processing of Vocal Quality and Verbal Content

Extant studies in this area have suggested that verbal content and vocal quality of speech are processed, at least initially, through relatively separate processing channels. A number of studies have examined brain lesion patients, and demonstrated that depending on the specific location of damage or lesion, one function can be lost with the other kept perfectly intact (see Tucker & Frederick, 1989, for a review). In general, an assault in the right hemisphere often causes difficulties in voice tone processing. These patients often fail to produce appropriate reactions to vocal expressions of affect. Yet, in many cases, they are still capable of understanding the literal meaning of the communication. Conversely, in patients with physical as-

saults in the left hemisphere, the lexical processing function is often se-
verely impaired or even lost. Even then, however, the capacity to react to
more nonverbal signals like voice tones is often spared.

Several researchers have used a dichotic listening task with normal subjects, and have shown that the processing of each is mediated by somewhat
different brain pathways (see, e.g., Buck, 1988, Springer & Deutsch, 1985, for
reviews). For example, Safer and Leventhal (1977) showed, consistent with
the studies with brain lesion patients, that the relative salience of the two
channels of speech (verbal content and vocal tone) depends on the ear to
which the speech is presented. That is to say, the verbal content tends to
dominate the subjective impression about the overall meaning of the
speech if it is presented in the right ear and thus projected first on the left
hemisphere, whereas the vocal tone tends to dominate the overall subjective impression if the speech is presented in the left ear and thus projected
first on the right hemisphere. Overall, these findings from both the patient
and the normal populations have indicated that sequential/linguistic processing (e.g., processing of verbal content) and more holistic/affective processing (e.g., processing of vocal tone) are performed primarily in the left
and the right hemispheres, respectively.

Yet, at the same time, the two forms of affective information can interact.
Even though the two may be processed relatively separately in early stages
of processing, they will soon have extensive contact with one another. At
present, however, little is known about the ways in which the two forms of
affect are encoded and represented, and precisely how they interact with
each other to yield a coherent perceptual impression. In order to fill in this
gap, we have explored an interaction between affective vocal tone and affective verbal content in speech perception by using a procedure Stroop (1935)
devised in his study of the perception of differently colored words.

Stroop Effect in Color Perception

A Stroop effect in color perception is perhaps one of the most studied
phenomena in psychology. The effect involves facilitation or impairment in
naming of ink color as a function of the congruence or incongruence of the
meaning of a printed word with the color of ink with which it is printed. The
original Stroop (1935) experiment used five words and their corresponding
ink colors: red, blue, green, brown, and purple. The combination of ink color
and color word was experimentally manipulated, and the subject was required either to name the ink color aloud, or to read the word aloud. In a
control condition the same words were printed in black ink. Results showed
that incongruent words interfered with color naming and, to a lesser extent,
congruent words facilitated color naming. Interestingly, congruence or incongruence of ink colors did not interfere with word naming. Modifications

of this technique have since been used to explore a variety of interference effects in cognitive and social psychology (see MacLeod, 1991, for a review).

Several related accounts have been proposed to explain the Stroop effect in color perception. Stroop's (1935) own interpretation of his experiment was closest to what is now called the relative speed-of-processing account. This explanation proposes that word meaning is processed more quickly than ink color and, as a result, there will be facilitation in color naming if the word meaning is congruous, but interference if the former is incongruous with the latter. Another, related view, the automaticity account, assumes that word meaning is activated more automatically than ink color. Note, however, that more controlled processing may be typically slower than less controlled, or more automatic, processing. Accordingly, for the present purposes, the relative speed explanation can be seen as a subtype of the automaticity account (see, e.g., Dunbar & MacLeod, 1984; Logan, 1989; Posner & Snyder, 1975).

More recently, both the automaticity and the relative speed explanations have been integrated within a more fully explanatory model, which is informed by the current connectionist thinking. Cohen, Dunbar, and McClelland (1990) have proposed that both ink color and word are processed in parallel. Information about each channel is therefore accumulated relatively separately over time until a threshold is reached. It is assumed that in everyday life individuals are more likely to encode word meanings rather than colors of ink used to print the words. As a result, a much denser, more redundant and robust, or "stronger" processing network must have developed for word meaning than for ink color. Thus, when words printed in different inks are presented, information about word meaning is developed more clearly and reliably (and perhaps more quickly) than information about ink color, causing an "intrusion" effect of word meaning information on ink color naming, but not vice versa. As reviewed by MacLeod (1991), this model seems capable of accommodating a number of findings, even those that pose problems to the first two, more traditional, accounts, and, as such, provides a reasonable conceptual guide for our study of an interaction between affective voice tone and affective verbal content.

Affective Stroop Effect in Comprehension of Spoken Words

Drawing on both the Stroop literature in color perception and the literature on affective information processing, we have recently examined an interaction between affect represented in the meaning of a spoken word and affect expressed in the voice tone of the speech. Following the Cohen et al. (1990) proposal in the original Stroop task, we hypothesized that an aspect of speech (verbal content or vocal tone) that was encodable more efficiently and reliably would influence the processing of the other, less efficiently encodable aspect. But the reverse might not necessarily be the case—that is, the less efficient aspect might not influence the processing of the more efficient aspect. To explore this possibility, we presented subjects with tape-recorded words, one at a time (Kitayama & Ferguson, 1992). Subjects were either to judge affective word meaning while ignoring voice tone or to judge affective voice tone while ignoring word meaning. Affective voice tone and affective word meaning were orthogonally manipulated. Thus, some words had a good meaning (e.g., LOVE) and were read in a positive, neutral, or negative tone of voice. Similarly, other words had a bad meaning (e.g., ANGER) and were read in the three voice tones.

The following steps were taken to develop the stimulus materials. A female undergraduate was trained to read words with different affective meanings in "free and melodic" sounds (positive tone), "monotonic" sounds (neutral tone), or "constricted and harsh" sounds (negative tone). To determine whether the voice tone was manipulated successfully, and independently of the word meanings, the tape recording of the spoken words was digitized and low-pass filtered at 400 Hz so that the meaning could no longer be discerned. A group of subjects, not used in the main studies, were presented with either the filtered tape recording or the original, nonfiltered recording and asked to judge the voice tone for each utterance on a rating scale defined by an affectively positive and a negative pole. The ratings from the filtered tape and those from the nonfiltered tape were highly correlated, but the latter were more extreme. Based on this data, utterances that had clearly pleasant, unpleasant, or neutral tones were selected. As might be predicted from previous research (e.g., Kaiser, 1962; Scherer, Ladd, & Silverman, 1984; see Frick, 1985, Scherer, 1986, for reviews), the judgment of affective voice tone turned out to be quite consistent and consensual, and it was entirely possible to manipulate affective voice tone even when the stimulus was as short as a single word. Further, the manipulation of voice tone proved to be independent of the affective word meaning. Finally, all the utterances were highly articulate.

First, we examined voice tone judgment. Subjects (N = 20) were instructed to ignore the meaning of the word and, instead, to judge whether the voice tone was pleasant or unpleasant. Only positive and negative voices were examined. They listened to each word and responded by pressing the appropriate one of two response keys as quickly as they could. Results were quite clear in a first half. In a second half, however, many of the effects simply disappeared because of, perhaps, habituation, practice in the task, or both. Here we will summarize the results from the first half. The crossover interaction between the affective meaning and the affective voice tone, evident in Figure 1A, proved to be highly significant. The accuracy in tone judgment was highest when the affective meaning of the stimulus word was congruent with the tone, whereas it was lowest when the meaning was

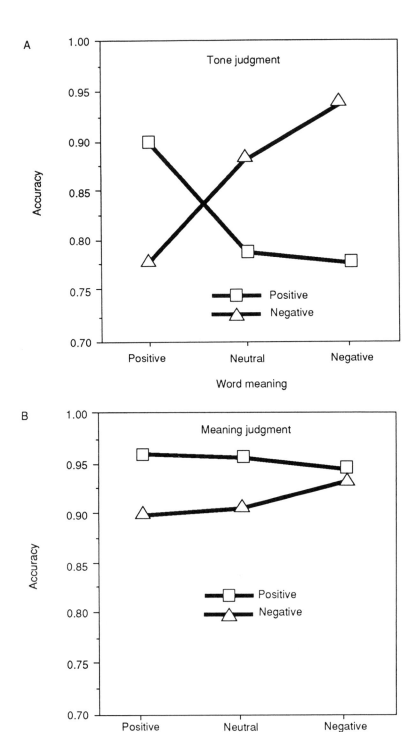

incongruent with the tone. The comparable pattern was observed in reaction time as well: reaction time was shortest when the affective meaning and the voice tone were congruent and it was longest when they were incongruent. These results suggest a varying degree of automaticity or redundancy of semantic encoding of meaning versus voice tone: at least under the present conditions, the encoding of the evaluative meaning of a word may be more automatic and redundant than the encoding of voice tone in evaluative terms.

This finding is consistent with the original Stroop effect, which suggests that the semantic encoding of word meaning is accomplished through highly dense and redundant, or simply quite "strong," processing networks—a conclusion congruent with a number of studies on semantic priming showing that word meaning can be activated automatically. This high extent of automaticity perhaps results because individuals routinely encode word meaning in everyday communications. In contrast, the associative connections between the spoken word and the internal representation of the meaning of its vocal tone might be neither redundant nor robust, or in other words, the connection might not be as "strong." Alternatively, in the present stimulus materials, the manipulation of vocal tone might have been relatively ambiguous. In either case, under the current conditions, word meaning judgment should be efficiently performed regardless of congruence/incongruence of affective vocal tone. The evaluative category (positive versus negative) of word meaning should become available more immediately and reliably than that of affective voice. This prediction was tested next.

Subjects (N = 18) were instructed to ignore the tone of voice and, instead, to judge whether the meaning of the word was pleasant or unpleasant. Only positive and negative words were tested. The result was consistent with the above analysis, showing no interaction between affective meaning and affective voice tone both in the analysis of accuracy (see Figure 1B) and in the analysis of reaction time. Finally, response latency was considerably shorter, and accuracy, higher, for the meaning judgment than for the tone judgment, thus lending support to the hypothesis that word meaning was more automatically and spontaneously encodable in terms of the corresponding affective meaning than was voice tone.

The asymmetry between the two judgmental tasks could happen if evaluative word meanings were more extreme than affective vocal tones. Our pilot judgmental data suggested that positive (nonfiltered) voices were indeed judged *less* positive than the evaluative meanings of the positive words

Figure 1 (A) Accuracy in voice tone judgment as a function of voice tone and word meaning. (B) Accuracy in word meaning judgment as a function of voice tone and word meaning. (From Kitayama & Ferguson, 1992.)

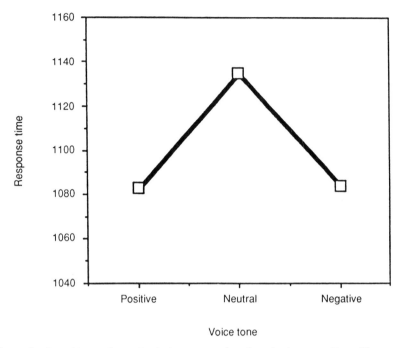

Figure 2   Speed in word meaning judgment as a function of voice tone. (From Kitayama & Ferguson, 1992.)

used here, but the negative (nonfiltered) voices were rated as negative as the evaluative meanings of the negative words. The above asymmetry between the tasks happened regardless of the valence of either the words or the voices and, therefore, the perceived extremity of affect cannot explain the entire pattern.[3]

In the analysis of reaction time for meaning judgment, there was a significant main effect of voice tone (see Figure 2). Regardless of the affective

[3]Nevertheless, some boundary conditions of the asymmetry demonstrated here must be carefully specified in future work. First, all the emotional words used here had unequivocal (i.e., extreme) evaluative meanings. Thus, the current findings do not preclude the possibility that emotional vocal tone can influence meaning judgment of words with ambiguous or less extreme evaluative meanings. Second, the utterances used here were highly articulate so that phonemes and, thus, the words themselves were easy to identify. It is possible that once utterances are degraded and made less articulate, emotional voice tone begins to bias the semantic encoding of word meaning. Finally, even though the voice tones used here were sufficiently extreme overall, they could have been made even more extreme and unequivocal. Once the voice tone manipulation is strengthened in this way, vocal tone may well influence the efficiency with which word meaning is judged. Indeed, our recent work (unpublished data, University of Oregon) has provided some preliminary data showing this in fact to be the case.

meaning of the words (positive or negative), meaning judgment was quicker when the tone was affective than when the tone was neutral. This may suggest that affective voice was, in fact, capable of eliciting affect and the induced affect *amplified* cognitive processes involved in the meaning judgment. As described above, there was no effect of the congruence or incongruence between meaning and voice tone in the meaning judgment. Thus, the amplifying effect of affective voice was obtained in the absence of any semantic interaction effect between voice tone and word meaning. Together, these results imply a dissociation between the two loci where affect regulates cognition. It would appear that an amplifying effect of affect can happen without any semantic encoding of the affect, whereas a semantic priming effect, that is, the effect due to congruence/incongruence in valence, comes into play once affect is categorized as positive or negative and so represented in semantic memory.

Affective Stroop Effect in Comprehension of Spoken Sentences

The above finding that affective voice tone has virtually no impact on the semantic encoding of verbal content might go against a common observation that the overall meaning of a social communication is often modulated by its vocal tone. Indeed, without such an effect of vocal tone, rich figurative meanings created in social communications, such as humor, cynicism, and irony, might seem entirely impossible. These linguistic phenomena strongly suggest that affective voice tone can powerfully bias the encoding of the meaning of social communications. This paradox of not confirming our common sense in the Kitayama and Ferguson study may be resolved, at least in part, if it is remembered that in this study single words were used as stimuli (see also Footnote 3). In actual social interactions, sentences are more common as means of communication than single words and, in addition, the sentences typical in social situations are bound to be highly ambiguous and polysemous. It is likely that sentence processing is less automatic, involving more deliberate cognitive operations, than word processing. Furthermore, sentences are necessarily longer than any single constituent words, requiring much more time to speak than does a single word. This means that there will be a greater chance for affective voice tone information to accumulate in sentence comprehension than in word comprehension. All in all, biasing effects of affective voice tone on comprehension may be uncovered once sentences are examined as stimuli.

We have recently addressed this possibility and obtained supportive evidence. Twenty-four pairs of sentences were prepared. Sentences in each pair were identical except for one or two critical words, which made the overall affective meaning of the sentences diametrically opposite (i.e., pleasant/positive or unpleasant/negative). Examples are given in Table 1. As in

***Table* 1   Sample Sentences Used in the Sentence Comprehension Study**

The landlord *lowered* the rent 50 dollars.
The landlord *raised* the rent 50 dollars.
The house was *nicely renovated* last month.
The house was *badly damaged* last month.
Our belongings were all *saved from* the flooding.
Our belongings were all *destroyed in* the flooding.
My uncle *got* a very good job.
My uncle *lost* a very good job.
The new neighbors turned out to be very *friendly.*
The new neighbors turned out to be very *nasty.*

the Kitayama and Ferguson study, a female undergraduate was trained to read all the sentences in one of three voice tones, namely, "free and melodic" sounds (positive tone), "monotonic" sounds (neutral tone), or "constricted and harsh" sounds (negative tone), and pilot data assured that the voice tone manipulation was both highly effective and independent of the verbal content.

Subjects (N = 47) were presented with one sentence at a time, and asked to judge the affective meaning of the sentence. They were explicitly told to *ignore* the vocal tone of the sentences. Both accuracy (Figure 3A) and response time (Figure 3B) showed a significant interaction between affective verbal content and affective voice tone. The effect was most pronounced when voice tone was pleasant. Under this condition accuracy was significantly higher, and response time significantly shorter for sentences with positive verbal content than for those with negative verbal content. This effect was slightly reversed when voice tone was neutral. Finally, when voice tone was negative, our initial prediction had no support: accuracy for sentences with negative verbal content was statistically no higher than the accuracy for sentences with positive verbal content; nor was response time significantly shorter for the former than for the latter. Hence, the semantic priming effect of voice tone was reliably observed only when the voice tone was positive. The reason of this asymmetry between positive and negative voices is not clear at present. Yet, this study provides the first demonstration that affective vocal quality can have a semantic priming effect on comprehension of verbal content.

Figure 3   (A) Accuracy in sentence comprehension as a function of verbal content (literal meaning) and voice tone. (B) Speed in sentence comprehension as a function of verbal content (literal meaning) and voice tone.

A   Sentence comprehension (accuracy)

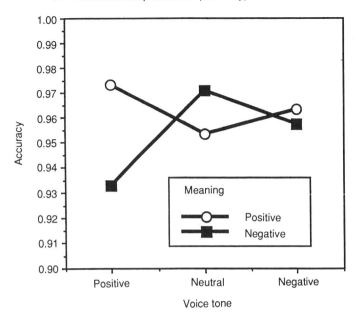

B   Sentence comprehension (response time)

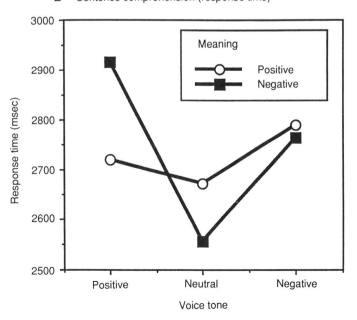

Another finding from this sentence comprehension study deserves mention. As is evident in Figure 3B, sentence comprehension took significantly more time if the sentences were spoken in affective voice tone than if they were spoken in neutral voice tone, whether the former was positive or negative. This effect of affective voice is diametrically opposite to the effect obtained in the Kitayama and Ferguson study (Figure 2), where we found that affective voice tone increases the speed of word comprehension. This pattern of findings is consistent with the amplification model discussed earlier, which proposes that preattentively evoked affect can amplify attentive processing directed to the most strongly activated (i.e., "dominant") perceptual code. Because the activation of constituent words is more pronounced (and thus "dominant") than that of the overall sentence, especially early in the comprehension process, affect evoked by voice tone may be expected to facilitate word comprehension but interfere with sentence comprehension.

Conclusions

In this chapter we have examined some systematic influences of affect on perception and comprehension. These effects can be integrated with two general principles, that is, amplification and semantic priming.

Amplification by affect comes into play early in processing. This aspect of affect is implicated in the effect of affective connotation of a stimulus on the perceptibility of the stimulus itself. In addition, affective voice tone amplifies subsequent cognitive processes even before the verbal content of the message is fully analyzed and comprehended, as indicated by the finding that affective vocal tone increases the speed of word recognition in the complete absence of any effect of the congruence of the tone with the meaning of the target word.

At the same time, affective stimuli can be semantically encoded, and once so encoded, they prime associated ideas, thoughts, and images. In the existing literature, affective connotations thus primed have been shown to influence affective or evaluative categorization of temporally and spatially contiguous events. The current research extended this literature and showed that semantic or affective priming effects can happen *within* a single stimulus event, depending on the relative automaticity of the processing of separable aspects of the event—in this case, verbal content and vocal quality. The aspect of an event that receives more automatic and reliable processing can bias the encoding of the other aspect. Thus, in word perception, verbal content biases the encoding of vocal quality; whereas in sentence comprehension, vocal quality biases the encoding of verbal content.

The work summarized here also suggests many open questions. Specifically, the effect of affective connotation in perception has so far been demonstrated with affective words as stimuli. Future work must examine other stimulus domains: Can similar effects occur with different stimuli such as human faces with affective expressions or graphic images of affect-provoking stimuli? What about auditory perception? Second, the processing of vocal tone should be extended to further clarify its role in the entire array of affective information processing. For example, future work may address the interconnections between the processing network for affective voice quality and that for affective face expression. Given the highly correlated nature of these two affective stimuli in everyday life and, perhaps, in evolutionary history, it would seem possible that they form a highly integrated processing structure. Further work on these issues may reveal the full extent of the dynamic influence of affect on cognition. We suggest that the two principles examined here, that is, amplification and semantic priming, can provide a useful theoretical framework for this endeavor.

Acknowledgments

This research was supported in part by a National Science Foundation grant (BNS 85-4286), a National Institute of Mental Health grant (1R01MH50117-01) and a research fund from the University of Oregon. We thank Paula Niedenthal for helpful comments on an earlier draft. Address correspondence to Shinobu Kitayama, Department of Psychology, Faculty of Integrated Human Studies, Kyoto University, Kyoto, 606-01 Japan.

References

Bargh, J. A., Bond, R. N., Lombardi, W. J., & Tota, M. E. (1986). The additive nature of chronic and temporary sources of construct accessibility. *Journal of Personality and Social Psychology*, 50, 869–878.

Bateson, G., Jackson, D., Haley, J., & Weakland, J. (1956). Toward a theory of schizophrenia. *Behavioral Science*, 1, 251–264.

Blanck, P. D., Rosenthal, R., & Vannicelli, M. (1986). Talking to and about patients: The therapist's tone of voice. In P. D. Blanck, R. Buck, & R. Rosenthal (eds.), *Nonverbal communications in clinical context* (pp. 99–143). University Park, PA: Pennsylvania State University Press.

Blaney, P. H. (1986). Affect and memory: A review. *Psychological Bulletin*, 99, 229–246.

Bootzin, R. R., & Natsoulas, T. (1965). Evidence for perceptual defense uncontaminated by response bias. *Journal of Personality and Social Psychology*, 5, 461–468.

Bower, G. H. (1981). Mood and memory. *American Psychologist*, 36, 129–148.

Broadbent, D. E., & Gregory, M. (1967). Perception of emotionally toned words. *Nature (London)*, 215, 581–584.

Bruner, J. (1957). On perceptual readiness. *Psychological Review*, 64, 123–152.

Buck, R. (1988). *Human motivation and emotion* (2nd ed.). New York: Wiley.

Carr, T. H., & Dagenbach, D. (1990). Semantic priming and repetition priming from masked words: Evidence for a center-surround attentional mechanism in perceptual recognition. *Journal of Experimental Psychology: Learning, Memory, and Cognition*, 16, 341–350.

Chapman, C. R., & Feather, B. W. (1972). Modification of perception by classical conditioning procedure. *Journal of Experimental Psychology, 93,* 338–342.

Christianson, S.-Å., & Loftus, E. F. (1991). Remembering emotional events: The fate of detailed information. *Cognition and Emotion, 5,* 81–108.

Christianson, S.-Å., Loftus, E. F., Hoffman, H., & Loftus, G. R. (1991). Eye fixations and memory for emotional events. *Journal of Experimental Psychology: Learning, Memory, and Cognition, 17,* 693–701.

Cohen, J. D., Dunbar, K., & McClelland, J. L. (1990). On the control of automatic processes: A parallel distributed processing account of the Stroop effect. *Psychological Review, 97,* 332–361.

Dawson, M. E., & Schell, A. M. (1982). Electrodermal responses to attended and nonattended significant stimuli during dichotic listening. *Journal of Experimental Psychology: Human Perception and Performance, 8,* 315–324.

DePaulo, B. M., Stone, J. I., & Lassiter, G. D. (1985). Deceiving and detecting deceit. In B. R. Schlenker (ed.), *The self and social life* (pp. 323–370). New York: McGraw Hill.

Dixon, N. F. (1980). *Preconscious processing.* New York: Wiley.

Dorfman, D. D. (1967). Recognition of taboo words as a function of a priori probability. *Journal of Personality and Social Psychology, 7,* 1–10.

Dorfman, D. D., Grossberg, J. M., & Kroeker, L. (1965). Recognition of taboo stimuli as a function of exposure time. *Journal of Personality and Social Psychology, 2,* 552–562.

Dunbar, K., & MacLeod, C. M. (1984). A horse race of a different color: Stroop interference patterns with transformed words. *Journal of Experimental Psychology: Human Perception and Performance, 10,* 622–639.

Easterbrook, J. A. (1959). The effect of emotion on cue utilization and the organization of behavior. *Psychological Review, 66,* 183–201.

Ekman, P., & Friesen, W. V. (1969). Nonverbal leakage and cues to deception. *Psychiatry, 32,* 88–106.

Ellsworth, P. C. (1991). Some implications of cognitive appraisal theories of emotion. In K. T. Strongman (ed.), *International Review of Studies on Emotion.* Chicester, England: John Wiley and Sons.

Erdelyi, M. H. (1974). A new look at the new look: Perceptual defense and vigilance. *Psychological Review, 81,* 1–25.

Eriksen, C. W. (1963). Perception and personality. In J. M. Wepman & R. W. Heine (eds.), *Concepts of personality.* Chicago: Aldine.

Fazio, R. H., Sanbonmatsu, D. M., Powell, M. C., & Kardes, F. R. (1986). On automatic activation of attitudes. *Journal of Personality and Social Psychology, 50,* 229–238.

Fishbein, M., & Ajzen, I. (1974). Attitudes toward objects as predictors of single and multiple behavioral criteria. *Psychological Review, 81,* 59–74.

Fishbein, M., & Ajzen, I. (1975). *Belief, attitude, intention, and behavior: An introduction to theory and research.* Reading, MA: Addison-Wesley.

Frick, R. W. (1985). Communicating emotion: The role of prosodic features. *Psychological Bulletin, 97,* 412–429.

Frijda, N. (1986). *The emotions.* New York: Cambridge University Press.

Goldiamond, I. (1958). Indicators of perception: I. Subliminal perception, subception, unconscious perception: An analysis in terms of psychophysical indicator methodology. *Psychological Bulletin, 55,* 373–411.

Greenwald, A. G. (1992). New look 3: Unconscious cognition reclaimed. *American Psychologist, 47,* 766–779.

Greenwald, A. G., Klinger, M. R., & Lui, T. J. (1989). Unconscious processing of dichoptically masked words. *Memory and Cognition, 17,* 35–47.

Hansen, C. H., & Hansen, R. D. (1988). Finding the face in the crowd: An anger superiority effect. *Journal of Personality and Social Psychology,* 54, 917–924.

Higgins, E. T., & Bargh, J. A. (1987). Social cognition and social perception. *Annual Review of Psychology,* 38, 369–425.

Isen, A. M. (1984). Toward understanding the role of affect in cognition. In R. S. Wyer & T. K. Srull (eds.), *Handbook of social cognition* (Vol. 3). Hillsdale, NJ: Erlbaum.

Isen, A. M., Shalker, T. E., Clark, M., & Karp, L. (1978). Affect, accessibility of material in memory, and behavior: A cognitive loop. *Journal of Personality and Social Psychology,* 36, 1–12.

Jacoby, L. (1983). Perceptual enhancement: Persistent effects of an experience. *Journal of Experimental Psychology: Learning, Memory, and Cognition,* 9, 21–38.

Jacoby, L., Lindsay, D. S., & Toth, J. P. (1992). Unconscious influences revealed. *American Psychologist,* 47, 802–809.

Johnson, E. J., & Tversky, A. (1983). Affect, generalization, and perception of risk. *Journal of Personality and Social Psychology,* 45, 20–31.

Johnston, W. A., & Dark, V. J. (1985). Selective attention. *Annual Review of Psychology,* 37, 43–75.

Kahneman, D. (1973). *Attention and effort.* Englewood Cliffs, NJ: Prentice-Hall.

Kaiser, L. (1962). Communication of affects by single vowels. *Synthese,* 14, 300–319.

Kihlstrom, J. F. (1987). The cognitive unconscious. *Science,* 238, 1445–1452.

Kihlstrom, J. F. (1990). The psychological unconscious. In L. A. Pervin (ed.), *Handbook of personality: Theory and research.* New York/London: Guilford Press.

Kitayama, S. (1990). Interaction between affect and cognition in word perception. *Journal of Personality and Social Psychology,* 58, 209–217.

Kitayama, S. (1991). Impairment of perception by positive and negative affect. *Cognition and Emotion,* 5, 255–274.

Kitayama, S. (1992a). Affect and perception: Some implications of the amplification model. Unpublished manuscript, University of Oregon.

Kitayama, S., & Ferguson, C. M. (1992). Emotional voice quality and emotional verbal content in speech perception: An exploration with a Stroop task. Technical Report No. 92-5. Institute of Cognitive & Decision Sciences. University of Oregon.

Lacey, J. I., & Lacey, B. C. (1968). Verification and extension of the principle of autonomic response stereotypy. *American Journal of Psychology,* 71, 50–73.

Lang, P. (1984). Cognition in emotion: Concept and action. In C. Izard, J. Kagan, & R. B. Zajonc (eds.), *Emotion, cognition, and behavior* (pp. 192–225). New York: Cambridge.

LeDoux, J. E. (1987). Emotion. In F. Plum (Ed.), *Handbook of physiology—The nervous system* (Vol. 5, pp. 419–459). Washington, DC: American Physiological Society.

Lindsley, D. B. (1951). Emotion. In S. S. Stevens (ed.), *Handbook of experimental psychology.* New York: Wiley.

Logan, G. D. (1989). Automaticity and cognitive control. In J. S. Uleman & J. A. Bargh (eds.) *Unintended thought.* New York: Guilford Press.

McClelland, J. L., & Rumelhart, D. E. (1981). An interactive activation model of context effects in letter perception: Part I. An account of basic findings. *Psychological Review,* 88, 375–407.

McGinnies, E. M. (1949). Emotionality and perceptual defense. *Psychological Review,* 56, 471–482.

MacLeod, C. M. (1991). Half century of research on the Stroop effect: An integrative review. *Psychological Bulletin,* 109, 163–203.

Marcel, A. J. (1983a). Conscious and unconscious perception: Experiments on visual masking and word recognition. *Cognitive Psychology,* 15, 197–237.

Marcel, A. J. (1983b). Conscious and unconscious perception: An approach to the relation between phenomenal experience and perceptual processes. *Cognitive Psychology,* 15, 238–300.

Mayer, J. D., Gaschke, Y. N., Braverman, D. L., & Evans, T. W. (1992). Mood-congruent judgment is a general effect. *Journal of Personality and Social Psychology,* 63, 119–132.

Neely, J. (1977). Semantic priming and retrieval from lexical memory: Roles of inhibitionless spreading activation and limited-capacity attention. *Journal of Experimental Psychology: General,* 106, 226–254.

Niedenthal, P. M. (1990). Implicit perception of affective information. *Journal of Experimental Social Psychology,* 26, 505–527.

Niedenthal, P. M., & Showers, C. J. (1991). The perception and processing of affective information and its influence on social judgment. In J. Forgas (ed.), *Affect and social judgment.* Oxford: Pergamon Press.

Ortony, A., & Turner, T. J. (1990). What's basic about basic emotions? *Psychological Review,* 97, 315–337.

Osgood, C. E. (1962). Studies on the generality of affective meaning systems. *American Psychologist,* 17, 10–28.

O'Sullivan, M., Ekman, P., Friesen, W., & Scherer, K. (1985). What you say and how you say it: The contribution of speech content and voice quality to judgments of others. *Journal of Personality and Social Psychology,* 48, 54–62.

Posner, M. I. (1978). *Chronometric explorations of mind.* New York: Oxford University Press.

Posner, M. I., & Snyder, C. R. R. (1975). Attention and cognitive control. In R. Solso (ed.), *Information processing and cognition: The Loyola Symposium.* Hillsdale, NJ: Erlbaum.

Roskos-Ewoldsen, D. R., & Fazio, R. H. (1992). On the orienting value of attitudes: Attitude accessibility as a determinant of an object's attraction of visual attention. *Journal of Personality and Social Psychology,* 63, 198–211.

Russell, J. A. (1980). A circumplex model of affect. *Journal of Personality and Social Psychology,* 39, 1161–1178.

Safer, M. A., & Leventhal, H. (1977). Ear differences in evaluating emotional tones of voice and verbal content. *Journal of Experimental Psychology: Human Perception and Performance,* 3, 75–82.

Sales, B. D., & Haber, R. (1968). A different look at perceptual defense for taboo words. *Perception & Psychophysics,* 3, 156–160.

Scherer, K. R. (1986). Vocal affect expression: A review and a model for future research. *Psychological Bulletin,* 99, 143–165.

Scherer, K. R., & Ekman, P. (eds.). (1984). *Approaches to emotion.* Hillsdale, NJ: Erlbaum.

Scherer, K. R., Ladd, D. R., & Silverman, K. E. A. (1984). Vocal cues to speaker affect: Testing two models. *Journal of Acoustical Society of America,* 76, 1346–1356.

Simon, H. A. (1967). Motivational and emotional controls of cognition. *Psychological Review,* 74, 29–39.

Spence, K. W. (1956). *Behavior theory and conditioning.* New Haven: Yale University Press.

Spinger, S. P., & Deutsch, G. (1985). *Left brain, right brain* (revised edition). New York: W. H. Freeman.

Sternbach, R. A. (1966). *Principles of psychophysiology.* New York: Academic Press.

Stroop, J. R. (1935). Studies of interference in serial verbal reactions. *Journal of Experimental Psychology,* 18, 643–662.

Tassinary, L. G., Orr, S. P., Wolford, G., Napps, S. E., & Lanzetta, J. T. (1984). The role of awareness in affective information processing: An exploration of the Zajonc hypothesis. *Bulletin of the Psychonomic Society,* 22, 489–491.

Tomkins, S. (1962). *Affect, imagery and consciousness, Vol. 1. The positive affect.* New York: Springer.

Tomkins, S. (1980). Affect as amplification: Some modification in theory. In R. Pluchik & H. Kellerman (eds.), *Emotion: Theory, research, and experience* (pp. 141–164). New York: Academic Press.

Tucker, D. M., & Frederick, S. (1989). Emotion and brain lateralization. In H. Wagner & A. Manstead (eds.), *Handbook of social psychophysiology* (pp. 27–70). New York: John Wiley.

Yerkes, R. M., & Dodson, J. D. (1908). The relation of strength of stimulus to rapidity of habit formation. *Journal of Comparative Neurology and Psychology*, 18, 459–482.

Zajonc, R. B. (1965). Social facilitation. *Science*, 149, 269–274.

Zajonc, R. B. (1980). Feeling and thinking: Preferences need no inferences. *American Psychologist*, 35, 151–175.

Zuckerman, M., Amidon, M. D., Bishop, S. E., & Pomerantz, S. D. (1982). Face and tone of voice in the communication of deception. *Journal of Personality and Social Psychology*, 32, 347–357.

Preferences Need No Inferences?: The Cognitive Basis of Unconscious Mere Exposure Effects

Mark R. Klinger
University of Arkansas

Anthony G. Greenwald
University of Washington

It is a critical question for cognitive theory and for theories of emotion to determine what is the minimal information process that is required for emotion. Can untransformed, pure sensory input directly generate emotional reactions? (Zajonc, 1984)

Over ten years ago, Zajonc (1980) resurrected interest in the unconscious nature of emotional experiences. At the time, this was a topic largely deemed appropriate only for students of psychodynamic approaches to the study of the mind. Zajonc's thesis was that "preferences need no inferences," that persons can have an emotional reaction to a stimulus without any corresponding cognitive reaction. Zajonc suggested that emotional responses may be produced by a system that is completely independent from cognitive processes. Zajonc's position contradicted information-processing theories of emotional experience. In information-processing theories, as typified by Lazarus (1982), emotion is thought to be the result of conscious, cognitive appraisal of a stimulus or situation.

It is important to clarify exactly what is meant by cognition in this chapter. Neisser (1967) defined cognition as encompassing "all processes by which the sensory input is transformed, reduced, elaborated, stored, recovered, and used." This definition seems to preclude an emotional response to a stimulus preceding all cognitive processes (unless one postulates that emotional processes physically occur in the eye of the beholder rather than in the mind of the beholder). To respond to a stimulus emotionally one must *use* the sensory input and one must *recover* stored information about past experiences. With this definition, it is quite unfair to characterize Zajonc as suggesting that stimuli are responded to emotionally without using sensory input. Instead, it is more proper to conceive of Zajonc's line of argumentation as suggesting that persons have conscious access to feelings toward a stimulus before having conscious access to nonemotional information about the stimulus. Following a suggestion by Mandler (1982), we prefer to rephrase Zajonc's statement that "preferences need no inferences" as "*conscious* preferences need no *conscious* inferences."

The principal empirical support for Zajonc's thesis came from results of several experiments on the subliminal mere exposure effect. He interpreted the effect as evidence that affective responses can be elicited by stimuli that have been repeatedly encountered, but that are not consciously detectable. However, there are also other interpretations of the subliminal mere exposure effect. In this chapter we review research on the mere exposure effect and subliminal mere exposure effect. We also consider the attempts to account for these findings in theory. Finally, we present a program of research that has strong implications for an explanation of this effect. In so doing we point to limitations of past theories of mere exposure and extend them to account for our recent findings.

The Mere Exposure Effect

The mere exposure effect is a remarkably simple phenomenon and is summarized by the statement that the more frequently a person is exposed to any external stimulus event, the more the person will come to like that stimulus. The effect was first described by Zajonc (1968; but see also Waynbaum, this volume). The procedure for a typical mere exposure experiment involves two phases, an exposure phase and a test phase. During the exposure phase, subjects are presented, either visually or auditorily, with a sequence of different members of a class of experimental stimuli. In most cases, the subject is given no particular processing goal during the exposure phase. The various stimuli are presented to the subjects different numbers of times. In previous research subjects have been exposed to Chinese ideographs, nonsense syllables, irregular geometric shapes, abstract paintings, pictures of human faces, and auditory tones.

Following the exposure phase, subjects enter a test phase in which they perform liking judgments on previously exposed and (often, but not always) novel stimuli of the same stimulus class. We use the terms novel stimuli and distractor stimuli interchangeably to refer to stimuli to which a subject is not exposed at all during the exposure phase. The mere exposure effect is observed when a relationship between number of exposures and liking is observed such that the more often a perceiver is exposed to an object, the more it is liked.

In a classic demonstration of this effect, Zajonc (1968) presented subjects with a series of Turkish ideographs. Each ideograph was presented between 1 and 25 times during the exposure phase. The presentation order of the ideographs was randomized. Subjects later rated on a Likert-type scale how much they liked each ideograph. Zajonc found a strong relationship between exposure and liking such that the items presented most often were the items that were also most liked.

Over the subsequent 20 years, the mere exposure effect has been found to be robust and general (see Bornstein, 1989, for a metaanalytic review of over 200 mere exposure experiments). Not only does the effect seem to generalize across stimuli and processing channels, it also generalizes to nonlaboratory settings. In an ingenious test of mere exposure, Zajonc and Rajecki (1969) bought advertising space in the student newspapers of two similar large universities. Over time, the researchers simply printed different 7-letter pronounceable nonsense syllables different numbers of times in the advertising space. Finally, they sent questionnaires to members of the student body of both universities. Respondents were asked to rate each of the nonsense syllables on a scale of pleasantness. Even though students did not appear to remember where they had seen the words, a mere exposure effect was obtained.

It is easier to obtain evidence of mere exposure than it is to account for it, however. Over the years, as data accumulate, a variety of theories have emerged to explain the exposure effect. The theories advanced include a response competition theory (Harrison, 1968), a two-factor learning/satiation theory (Berlyne, 1970), and an arousal model (Crandall, 1970). Reviews of the empirical support for these theories by Harrison (1977) and Stang (1974) suggest that support for all of the theories is inconclusive and inconsistent. Of even greater importance for the present concerns, results marshaled by Zajonc (1980) to support his claims of the primacy of affect are not easily explained by any of the theories as stated. It is these results to which we turn next.

Subliminal Mere Exposure

Kunst-Wilson and Zajonc (1980) demonstrated the mere exposure effect with stimuli that were presented so briefly during the exposure phase that subjects could not actually consciously perceive the stimuli, as evidenced by their later inability to discriminate the stimuli from distractor stimuli. In this research, Kunst-Wilson and Zajonc presented irregular renderings of randomly constructed octagons to subjects. Exposure duration, controlled by electronic shutter, was just 1 or 2 msec. Each octagon was presented to subjects five times. After the exposures, Kunst-Wilson and Zajonc presented pairs of octagons to subjects. One item in each pair was an octagon that had been previously seen and one was a novel octagon (the distractor). For every pair, subjects were instructed to answer two questions: Which octagon did you see in the first portion of the experiment? and Which octagon do you like better? Results showed that while the exposed octagons were accurately identified as having been previously seen only 48% of the time (no different from chance), they were nonetheless preferred over the distractors 60% of the time (significantly greater than chance). Because these results showed that subjects were processing emotional information (developing a preference) without processing cognitive information (developing a retrievable memory), Zajonc claimed that the mere exposure effect was an affective phenomenon involving little or no cognition and that, in general, affective reactions to stimuli can be processed by a system that is independent of cognition.

Replications and Alternative Explanations

The "subliminal" mere exposure effect has been replicated by several independent research laboratories (Bonanno & Stillings, 1986; Seamon, Brody, & Kauff, 1983; Bornstein, Leone, & Galley, 1987; Johnson, Kim, & Risse, 1985). Because of the apparent reliability and strength of the effect, it has achieved the status of being one of the most scientifically credible demonstrations of unconscious mental processes (Reingold & Merikle, 1988).

The researchers who have observed the effect have proposed a number of related explanations for it. Bonanno and Stillings (1986), for example, based their theory on the assumption that people intrinsically prefer familiar stimulus events over unfamiliar ones. They then argue that memories of a visual or auditory stimulus can be constructed even with brief exposures to the stimuli. The memory created is simple, containing only representations of the physical features of the exposed object (see Johnson & Weisz, this volume). Upon later exposure to the previously exposed stimulus, such as during the test phase of an experiment, the sensory input of the stimulus activates the memory established during the prior exposure. This matching of sensation to a memory mediates the feeling of familiarity. The feeling of familiarity produces liking.

Bonanno and Stillings (1986) found some support for this position in a replication of the Kunst-Wilson and Zajonc (1980) experiment. In the replication, they added a condition in which subjects judged which of two stimuli (a previously exposed one and a distractor) seemed more familiar. Their results replicated the finding that subjects like repeatedly exposed octagons more than novel octagons, even when the stimuli are presented at exposures too brief to support conscious perception. However, they also found that subjects found the exposed octagon more familiar than the novel ones at virtually identical rates as the liking judgment.

These data were interpreted as providing support for a two-process model of recognition memory posited by Mandler (1980). In Mandler's model, the act of recognition is composed of two sequential processes: a process in which a memory is activated and a sense of familiarity is established, and an identification process in which contextual (elaborative) information about the stimulus is retrieved. Thus, Bonanno and Stillings's (1986) results along with others (Seamon et al., 1983; Seamon, Marsh, & Brody, 1984) are consistent with the idea that subliminal perception of a stimulus is sufficient for the construction of a memory trace. When the previously exposed stimulus is subsequently reencountered, the memory is activated thereby causing the stimulus to seem familiar. However, the activated memory is not accompanied by enough contextual information for the individual to recall where and when they have seen the stimulus. For this reason, subjects in subliminal mere exposure experiments typically perform poorly on recognition judgments. In contemporary jargon, there is evidence of *implicit* memory for the perceptual event, but no evidence of *explicit* memory (Schacter, 1987).

Mandler, Nakamura, and Van Zandt (1987) extended these basic ideas in several ways. They argued that once activated, an implicit memory causes exposed objects to be perceived, not as more familiar, but as more *distinct*. Therefore, any quick judgment that might be made about the stimuli would reveal a bias toward the objects to which an individual has been exposed in the past. Support for this claim was observed in an exposure experiment in which during a test phase subjects were instructed to indicate either which of two shapes (one previously seen and one distractor) appeared brighter or which of two shapes appeared darker. Subjects who judged brightness reported perceiving the previously seen objects as brighter than the distractor and subjects who judged darkness judged those objects as darker than the distractors at a rate similar to preferring the previously seen shape in liking judgments. This result challenges the familiarity account of the mere exposure effect. That is, the result is at odds with the idea that repeated exposure leads to increased liking per se.

In the remainder of this chapter seven experiments are presented that test the memory-based models of the subliminal exposure effects. The data generally support such models but also indicate that they are somewhat incomplete. An elaborated memory-based model of unconscious exposure effects is presented.

Testing the Memory-Based Models of Subliminal Mere Exposure

This program of research began quite by accident. An attempt was made to replicate the subliminal mere exposure effect. What was found was a peculiar moderating effect of the subliminal mere exposures. Our subsequent research therefore necessarily focused on establishing the reliability of the interaction and explaining the interaction. The first three experiments are presented together, as they constitute exact replications of each other. Then, attempts to explain the results of these first three experiments are described, as are our efforts to extend the generality of these findings.

An Unexpected Finding

The three initial experiments used methods similar to those used by Kunst-Wilson and Zajonc (1980). In the experiments, subjects were exposed to irregular octagons five times each. The stimuli were presented on a computer monitor. The briefest period that an image could be displayed on the available computer monitors was 16.7 msec. This is substantially longer than the presentation durations used by previous researchers of subliminal mere exposure experiments. In those studies, electronic shutters were used to present slide stimuli for 1 or 2 msec. Therefore, in order to make the octagons subliminal, the stimuli were presented for 16.7 msec to the subject's left eye while a bright pattern of black and white blocks was presented to the subject's right eye. This type of dichoptic masking procedure is similar to that used in a variety of subliminal perception experiments using verbal stimuli (Marcel, 1983; Greenwald, Klinger, & Liu, 1989).

The octagons prepared for use in the experiments were first rated on attractiveness by pilot subjects. Based on these data, octagons were categorized as low, medium, and high in attractiveness and pairs of similarly attractive octagons were constructed. This was done in order to minimize reasons for preference of one octagon over another. One member of each pair was actually presented to subjects during the exposure phase of the experiments. During the test phase, subjects made forced-choice liking or recognition judgments between these equally attractive octagons.

Because the pattern of findings did not significantly differ across experiments, the data sets were combined. Results revealed that, first, across all three experiments, subjects were unable to discriminate the octagons they had seen during the exposure phase from distractor items. Subjects recognized the exposed octagons as having been seen during the exposure phase only 49.5% of the time, which did not differ from chance, so we were clearly successful in presenting the stimuli such that subjects could not later recognize them. Surprisingly, subjects showed no evidence of a mere exposure effect. Subjects preferred the exposed octagons over the distractors only 50.1% of the time, which also did not differ from chance. Second, a significant attractiveness-moderating effect was observed (see Figure 1A). Exposure increased preference for the exposed octagons that were high in attractiveness over the equally attractive distractors. Third, perhaps even more interesting, repeated exposure *decreased* liking for unattractive objects compared to the matched controls.

The experiment was replicated three times because the interaction between exposure and attractiveness was such a surprising result. Across the replications, the attractiveness-moderating effect was significant twice and was marginally significant once. This *exposure-polarization effect* obtained in these three experiments is at odds with Kunst-Wilson and Zajonc's (1980) contention that exposure increases liking for all stimuli. However, the finding that repeated subliminal exposures of attractive stimuli increase liking and repeated subliminal exposures of unattractive stimuli decreases liking is not a completely new finding. Brickman and colleagues observed a similar phenomenon (Brickman, Redfield, Harrison, & Crandall, 1972). Subjects in that experiment were exposed to abstract paintings that were prerated as either positive (appealing), neutral, or negative (unappealing). Each painting was exposed to a given subject from 1 to 10 times and each exposure lasted three seconds. The results parallel those just reported. Appealing paintings became more liked with exposure. Unappealing paintings became less liked with exposure. Unlike our first three experiments, in the Brickman et al. study, the stimuli were highly detectable.

In the third experiment an additional condition was therefore included in which octagons were presented for 16.7 msec but were not masked, so that subjects could clearly see and remember them. The condition was added to the experimental design for two reasons. First, we wanted to rule out the possibility that the exposure-polarization effect was caused by an idiosyncrasy of the octagons used. It was possible that we had constructed a set of stimuli in which it was impossible to obtain traditional mere exposure effects. By presenting the octagons at durations that allowed subjects to consciously detect them, we could experimentally ask whether the interaction observed in the first two studies was produced by features of the stimuli or the conditions of the presentations. Contrary to the results of Brickman et al. (1972), the typical mere exposure effect was observed in this condition (see Figure 1B). Exposure increased liking for both attractive and unattractive octagons. Based on this result, we concluded that the exposure-polarization effect, at least with more subtle stimuli, was a phenomenon of unconscious processing. In the remainder of the chapter, we outline a frame-

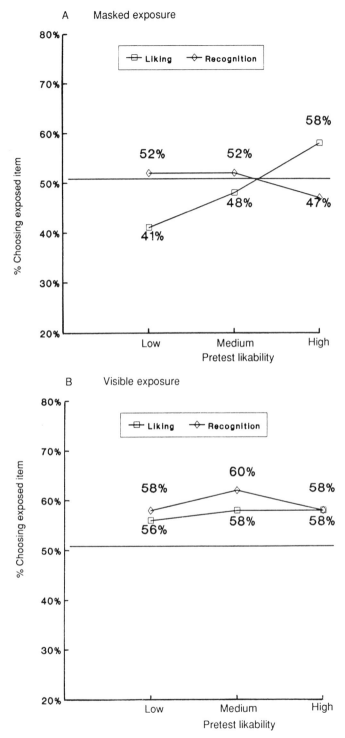

Figure 1 Proportion of exposed octagons chosen on liking and recognition judgments for masked and visible exposures. (A) Experiments 1–3 ($n = 175$); (B) Experiment 3 ($n = 61$).

work that accounts for the effects of repeated exposures to stimuli that cannot be recognized.

Application of a Memory Attribution Model

The theoretical model we propose builds upon explanations of subliminal mere exposure that invoke the idea of implicit memory associated with Bonanno and Stillings (1986), Seamon et al. (1983), and Mandler et al. (1987). As mentioned above, in this interpretation, the matching of sensory input to a memory trace produces subjective feelings of familiarity. Given the prior assumption that familiar objects are inherently preferred to unfamiliar objects, this explanation seems plausible. However, this explanation does not account for the exposure-polarization effect observed in our experiments; rather, it predicts increased liking with exposure for both attractive *and* unattractive octagons.

In the present view, the exposure-polarization effect observed in preferences for repeatedly exposed, unrecognizable objects is mediated by two psychological processes. The first process is the construction of a perceptual memory; a process similar to that described by Seamon et al. (1983) and Bonanno and Stillings (1986). Initial perception of a stimulus results in a basic perceptual memory of that stimulus. The memory represents only the physical characteristics of the stimulus that have actually been processed. Jacoby (1983) has demonstrated that when the perceptual features of a stimulus (such as typeface or color) are processed, those features are stored in memory. When processing is deeper, and the conceptual features (such as meaning or category membership) are perceived, those features of the stimulus are stored in memory. Presumably only physical, and not conceptual features of subliminally presented objects are encoded and stored in memory.

The second process that mediates exposure-polarization is an attribution process that responds to subtle feelings of familiarity. We refer to these as *memory attributions*. At the time of a test phase of repeated-exposure experiments, when a familiar object is encountered, we propose that individuals attempt to attribute the feelings of familiarity to something that makes sense to them. This theory is similar in structure to Schachter and Singer's (1962) theory of emotional experience. First, a general form of memory activation occurs. The activation initiates an attribution process aimed at using and understanding the activation. In Schachter and Singer's theory the general form of activation is arousal. Once a person is aroused, the person is held to draw inferences about why he or she is aroused. The attributions shape the nature of the arousal and recruit additional appropriate cognitions so that a specific emotion develops. In the present theory, a feeling of familiarity is activated (i.e., it results from a match between a percept and a perceptual memory). When a stimulus feels familiar, an attribution process is initiated that is aimed at explaining why the stimulus is familiar.

A comment needs to be made here about what is meant by the claim that subjects *make attributions* about the source of familiarity of exposed stimuli. Traditional attribution theories of social behavior (e.g., Jones and Davis, 1965; Kelley, 19670 viewed perceivers as naive scientists who rationally and deliberately weigh and balance information about other person's actions in order to draw conclusions about the characteristics of these other persons. Within the present memory attribution model, attributional processes are conceived of quite differently. Individuals are not seen as creatures who rationally and consciously weigh and balance reasons why stimuli seem to be or feel familiar. Rather, we suggest that memory attributions are quick and require little attention to perform (Jacoby, Woloshyn, & Kelley, 1989c). Jacoby has described memory attributions as unconscious inference processes (Jacoby, Kelley, & Dywan, 1989b).

This process can be illustrated by way of an example of a typical memory attribution experiment. Jacoby, Kelley, Brown, and Jasechko (1989a) conducted an experiment that demonstrated the importance of memory attributions to judgments of social stimuli. Subjects participated in two experimental tasks. In the first (exposure) task, subjects were instructed to study a long list of names (study list). Subjects were informed that all of the names on the study list had been drawn at random from a telephone directory. The implication was that all of the names on the study list were those of everyday residents of a garden variety city (i.e., that they were not famous people). In the second task, subjects were furnished with a second list of names (test list) and were asked to indicate whether each name on the list was that of a famous person or not. In fact, the list included names of the people that appeared on the study list (nonfamous ones) as well as names of famous people. One group of subjects performed the fame judgment task immediately following the exposure task (the memorable condition). The remaining subjects made the fame judgments on the following day (the nonmemorable condition).

The logic of these experiments was that if subjects consciously remembered the study list, they could then perform quite well on the fame judgments; that is, they would be more likely to call names from the study list "not famous" and all famous names, "famous." However, if subjects did not consciously remember the previous exposure, they could easily misattribute the feeling of familiarity and suspect that the study list names were actually familiar because in fact the people they named were famous. As expected, subjects in the nonmemorable condition tended to make just this error. They tended to call names of nonfamous people from the study list "famous." Subjects in the memorable condition did not make this type of error as frequently.

The interpretation of the result was a simple one. Jacoby and colleagues (1989a) reasoned that subjects compared the names on the test list with their memory of famous names. Presumably the chief characteristics of famous names are that they are *names* and that they are *familiar*. Because after previous exposure the names of nonfamous people on the study list possessed both of these features, the familiarity of those names was quickly and easily misattributed to the fact that the person was famous.

We suggest that memory attributions of the type that may be operating in subliminal mere exposure experiments are only slightly more complex. In those experiments, when subjects makes preference judgments, they can compare the perceived stimulus to memories of known, liked and known, disliked objects. When a person finds a match between a perceived object and a memory of a previously seen object, that object necessarily seems familiar. In the first three experiments reported here, the octagon stimuli could be compared to representations of prototypically pleasing shapes in memory. Presumably the central characteristics of liked geometric shapes are that they are *attractive* and that they are *familiar*. The central characteristics of disliked geometric shapes is that they are unattractive and familiar. Thus, as an attractive geometric shape becomes more familiar, that shape matches better the features of well-liked shapes in memory. This better match makes subjects more likely to attribute greater liking to the shape. As an unattractive shape becomes more familiar, that shape better matches the features of disliked shapes in memory, presumably causing subjects to attribute greater dislike to the shape.

Furthermore, we argue that the *context* in which a familiar stimulus is encountered will delineate the population of plausible attributions that will be made about it. For instance, in the context of performing fame judgments on lists of names, misattributions to famousness are likely because the goal of the task is to evaluate the likelihood of fame of each name. In the context of performing liking judgments, misattributions to liking and disliking are likely because the goal of the subject is to form a preference. As familiar objects are encountered outside of the laboratory, similarly, the context should delineate the possible attributions. For example, when a familiar man is encountered as one walks across campus, inferences that the man is a student that was previously in one's class or is a faculty member once met may be extremely likely because he is encountered in the university context. Inferences that the man is a famous movie star are unlikely. However, if the same familiar man is seen on television, the inference that he is a famous movie star may be quite likely. These are examples of how the context in which a familiar stimulus is perceived may determine what inferences are drawn.

Similarly, the *characteristics* of the stimulus affect which candidates are drawn from the pool of plausible attributions. The more similar the characteristics of a perceived stimulus are to the features of an attribution category, the more likely that attribution will be made. In the case of liking judgments, attractive, familiar objects match well with known, liked objects. Returning to the example of the familiar man encountered on campus, if the man is young, carrying a backpack, and wearing a fraternity shirt, all characteristics that match the features of the attribution category of "student," the man will likely be attributed to being a former student. However, if the familiar man encountered on campus has graying hair, is carrying a briefcase, and is wearing a sports jacket, the man will more likely be attributed to being a faculty member who was encountered somewhere previously.

It is important to remember that such attributional processes occur only if the source of the familiarity is not consciously available. If the source of familiarity is recalled, no attributional processes are necessary. We next describe four additional experiments that were designed to evaluate this theoretical model.

Tests of the Memory Attribution Model

The next two experiments were conducted to test the generality of the exposure-polarization effect and to establish its relation to memory attributions. The procedure used in these experiments was a variation of Jacoby et al.'s (1989a) famous-name method in which we added a manipulation of name memorability; subjects were assigned to a memorable or a non-memorable condition. In the experiments all subjects performed three tasks. First, subjects engaged in the exposure task in which they read a long study list of nonfamous names and reported the number of syllables in each name. The purpose of the syllable-counting task was to force subjects to silently pronounce each name (it is actually impossible to count syllables without pronunciation) so that a memory of each name containing both visual and phonetic features of the name was established. Neither the analysis of the visual features nor the production of the phonetic features was a demanding and elaborative task so that, presumably, subjects did not generate well-elaborated memory traces of the names.

Next, subjects in the nonmemorable condition performed a long distractor task in order to decrease explicit recollection of the names on the study list. Subjects in the memorable condition did not perform this task. Finally, all subjects were exposed to a test list of names that contained previously seen and novel names. In one experiment (Experiment 4), subjects judged how much they liked the names on the test list. In the other experiment (Experiment 5), subjects judged whether the names belonged to someone famous or not.

The study list in these experiments was composed of 60 names drawn randomly from a telephone directory. The names were rated on their attractiveness by pilot subjects. Pairs of names matched on attractiveness were then constructed. Among the most attractive names were names such as Charles Gordon, John Garrett, and Gary Covington. Among the least attractive names were names such as Earl Yock, John Gout, and Melford Flatten. Subjects were exposed to one member of each pair on the study list. The other member served as the not-exposed control and appeared on the test list.

The results obtained in the experiment involving the liking-dependent variable were similar to those obtained in the three octagon experiments described above. Subjects in the memorable condition liked the exposed (study list) names more than the novel names. This effect was not moderated by name attractiveness and served, therefore, as a replication of the typical mere exposure effect. However, the exposure effect in the nonmemorable condition was significantly moderated by name attractiveness (Figure 2). A large positive exposure effect was obtained for attractive names, and a small negative exposure effect was obtained for unattractive names.

Apparently, the exposure-polarization result found in the octagon experiments is general in that it replicated with a different class of stimuli and with a different exposure procedure. Also, the exposure-polarization effect was observed only when the exposed stimuli were not memorable. When the exposed stimuli were recognizable, the typical exposure effect of increased liking for all stimuli was obtained. Presumably this occurred because when making liking judgments, subjects compared each name with known, liked and known, disliked names. Familiar, attractive names matched the known, liked names better than unfamiliar, attractive names and were therefore preferred.

The results of the experiment (Experiment 5) in which the fame judgment was the dependent variable of interest were similar to those observed in the previous experiments. For subjects in the nonmemorable condition, the effect of exposure was moderated by stimulus attractiveness. Familiar names were differentially attributed to being famous depending on name attractiveness (Figure 3). Exposure increased misattributions of famousness for attractive names more than for unattractive names. The parallels between the memory attribution result and the liking result bolster our belief that memory attributions mediate the exposure-polarization results obtained in the previous experiments.

Furthermore, a similar result has recently been reported by Banaji and Greenwald (1993). Those researchers found that when male and female names were used in a fame-judgment experiment similar to Jacoby's, previously seen nonfamous *male* names were more likely to be called famous than were *female* names. Probabilistically speaking, famous people are more likely to be male than female. Thus, it is presumed that both familiar attractive names and familiar male names match the features of known famous names better than familiar unattractive names or familiar female names, which may

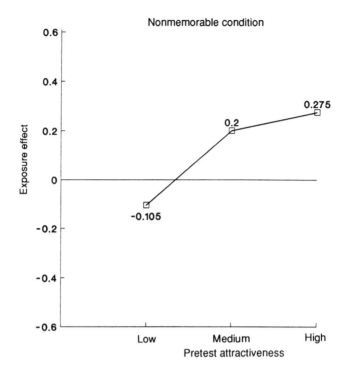

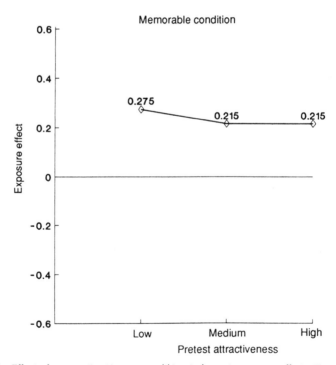

Figure 2 Effect of name attractiveness on liking judgment exposure effects. Experiment 4. Exposure effect = liking (exposed) − liking (not exposed).

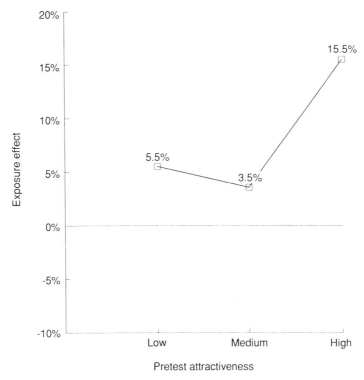

Figure 3 Effect of name attractiveness on fame judgment exposure effects. Experiment 5: nonmemorable condition. Exposure effect = % famous (exposed) − % famous (not exposed).

explain the greater rate of misattribution to famousness in the case of the former stimuli.

The goal of the final two experiments was to show that the match between the attributions made salient by the context of the test phase and the features of exposed stimuli is critical to the exposure-polarization effect. It was predicted that, as in the fame-judgment experiment, if the judgment task was a relatively positive judgment, attractive names would show a substantial exposure effect. However, if the test judgment was negative, then unattractive names would show a substantial exposure effect.

In Experiment 6, subjects judged whether names belonged to a famous senator or to a nonfamous individual, and in Experiment 7, subjects judged whether names belonged to a famous criminal or to a nonfamous individual. The experiments were otherwise identical to the previous fame-judgment experiment. It was expected that familiar attractive names would show a large exposure effect for the senator judgments (because senators' names are conceived of as being prototypically attractive and dignified sounding) and that familiar unattractive names would show a large exposure effect for the criminal judgments (because criminals' names are conceived of as being rather unpleasant). The results of the senator judgment experiment paralleled those obtained in the previous five experiments (Figure 4). Large exposure effects were obtained for attractive names, while no exposure effect was obtained for unattractive names. That is, subjects in the nonmemorable condition were more likely to call attractive names of nonfamous senators than were subjects in the memorable condition.

For the criminal judgment experiment, overall, exposure increased attributions of criminality. An interaction between exposure and attractiveness was observed that was exactly the opposite of that obtained in the previous studies. Large exposure effects were obtained for unattractive names, while no exposure effect was obtained for attractive names. Thus, subjects in the nonmemorable, but not the memorable, condition were more likely to assume that people with unattractive names were criminals, and less likely to assume that people with attractive names were criminals.

The results from these two experiments support the claim that exposure increases the familiarity of both attractive and unattractive names (otherwise exposure effects would not have been observed for each), but that the match between stimulus attractiveness and context is critical to the attributions made about why a stimulus appears familiar.

Conclusions

Drawing on evidence from mere exposure experiments, Zajonc (1980) argued that untransformed, pure sensory input can elicit new affective reactions toward the perceived stimulus with no intervening cognitive processes. He reasoned that because liking judgments can be influenced by exposure even when recognition is not, the only information encoded about the exposed stimulus is affective in nature. The series of experiments presented here suggest that the subliminal mere exposure effect can be obtained even if affective information is not encoded. That is, preferences for repeatedly exposed subliminal stimuli may not be a product of affective reactions to pure sensory input.

The theoretical model we present suggests that only perceptual features of a stimulus are encoded into memory automatically. When that stimulus is subsequently reencountered, the perceptual memory is activated. This acti-

Figure 4   Effect of name attractiveness on (A) Senator and (B) criminal fame-judgment exposure effects. Nonmemorable conditions. Exposure effect for (A) = % senator (exposed) − % senator (not exposed); exposure effect for (B) = % criminal (exposed) − % criminal (not exposed).

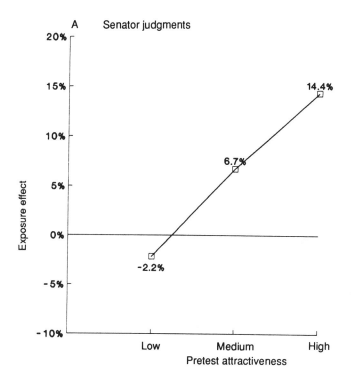

A   Senator judgments

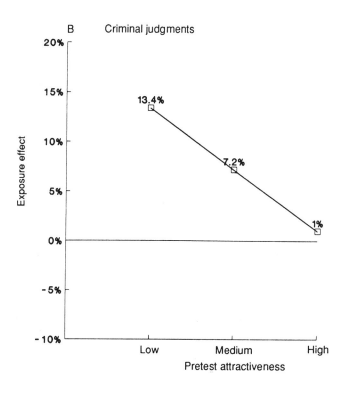

B   Criminal judgments

vation produces a feeling of familiarity. It is further suggested that attributions about familiar objects mediate the changes in affect caused by exposure. The changes in affect do not take place at the time of exposure, but, instead, occur at the time of the test, creating a change in interpretation of a stimulus because of its familiarity. This theory of the mere exposure effect does not require emotional processes that are independent of cognition. The theory does require that preferences for exposed but unrecognizable objects involve inferences. These inferences may occur automatically, but they are inferences nonetheless. Still, affect does play an important, albeit cognitively mediated, role in these exposure effects. In these experiments the aesthetics of objects (the attractiveness of both octagons and names) affected which attributions were drawn. Affective qualities of objects appear to be vitally important in determining what attributions are made about familiar objects.

References

Banaji, M. R., & Greenwald, A. G. (1993). Implicit stereotyping and prejudice. In M. P. Zanna & J. M. Olson (eds.), *The psychology of prejudice, the Ontario symposium* (Vol. 7). Hillsdale, NJ: Erlbaum.

Berlyne, D. E. (1970). Novelty, complexity, and hedonic value. *Perception and Psychophysics, 8,* 279–286.

Bonanno, G. A., & Stillings, N. A. (1986). Preference, familiarity and recognition after repeated brief exposures to random geometric shapes. *American Journal of Psychology, 99,* 403–415.

Bornstein, R. F. (1989). Exposure and affect: Overview and meta-analysis of research, 1968–1987. *Psychological Bulletin, 106,* 265–289.

Bornstein, R. F., Leone, D. R., & Galley, D. J. (1987). The generalizability of subliminal mere exposure effects: Influence of stimuli perceived without awareness on social behavior. *Journal of Personality and Social Psychology, 53,* 1070–1079.

Brickman, P., Redfield, J., Harrison, A. A., & Crandall, R. (1972). Drive and predisposition as factors in the attitudinal effects of mere exposure. *Journal of Experimental Social Psychology, 8,* 31–44.

Crandall, J. E. (1970). Preference and expectancy arousal. *Journal of General Psychology, 83,* 267–268.

Greenwald, A. G., Klinger, M. R., & Liu, T. J. (1989). Unconscious processing of dichoptically masked words. *Memory and Cognition, 17,* 35–47.

Harrison, A. A. (1968). Response competition, frequency, exploratory behavior, and liking. *Journal of Personality and Social Psychology, 9,* 363–368.

Harrison, A. A. (1977). Mere exposure. In L. Berkowitz (ed.), *Advances in experimental social psychology* (Vol. 10). New York: Academic Press.

Jacoby, L. L. (1983). Remembering the data: Analyzing interactive processes in reading. *Journal of Verbal Learning and Verbal Behavior, 22,* 485–508.

Jacoby, L. L., Kelley, C., Brown, J., & Jasechko, J. (1989a). Becoming famous overnight: Limits on the ability to avoid unconscious influences of the past. *Journal of Personality and Social Psychology, 56,* 326–338.

Jacoby, L. L., Kelley, C. M., & Dywan, J. (1989b). Memory attributions. In H. L. Roediger & F. I. M. Craik (eds.), *Varieties of memory and consciousness: Essays in honor of Endel Tulving.* Hillsdale, NJ: Erlbaum.

Jacoby, L. L., Woloshyn, V., & Kelley, C. M. (1989c). Becoming famous without being recognized: Unconscious influences of memory produced by dividing attention. *Journal of Experimental Psychology: General*, 118, 115–125.

Johnson, M. K., Kim, J. K., & Risse, G. (1985). Do alcoholic Korsakoff's syndrome patients acquire affective reactions? *Journal of Experimental Psychology: Learning, Memory, and Cognition*, 11, 22–36.

Jones, E. E., & Davis, K. E. (1965). From acts to dispositions: The attribution process in person perception. In L. Berkowitz (ed.), *Advances in experimental social psychology* (Vol. 2). New York: Academic Press.

Kelley, H. H. (1967). Attribution theory in social psychology. In D. L. Vine (ed.), *Nebraska symposium on motivation*. Lincoln, NE: University of Nebraska Press.

Klinger, M. R. (1991). Conscious and unconscious processing in the mere exposure effect. Unpublished doctoral dissertation. University of Washington.

Kunst-Wilson, W. R., & Zajonc, R. B. (1980). Affective discrimination of stimuli that cannot be recognized. *Science*, 207, 557–558.

Lazarus, R. S. (1982). Thoughts on the relations between emotion and cognition. *American Psychologist*, 37, 1019–1024.

Mandler, G. (1980). Recognizing: The judgment of previous occurrence. *Psychological Review*, 87, 252–271.

Mandler, G. (1982). The structure of value: Accounting for taste. In M. S. Clark & S. T. Fiske (eds.), *Affect and cognition*. Hillsdale, NJ: Erlbaum.

Mandler, G., Nakamura, Y., & Van Zandt, B. J. S. (1987). Nonspecific effects of exposure to stimuli that cannot be recognized. *Journal of Experimental Psychology: Learning, Memory, and Cognition*, 13, 646–648.

Marcel, A. J. (1983). Conscious and unconscious perception: Experiments in visual masking and word recognition. *Cognitive Psychology*, 15, 197–237.

Neisser, U. (1967). *Cognitive psychology*. New York: Appleton-Century-Crofts.

Reingold, E. M., & Merikle, P. M. (1988). Using direct and indirect measures to study perception without awareness. *Perception and Psychophysics*, 44, 563–575.

Schachter, S., & Singer, J. (1962). Cognitive, social, and physiological determinants of emotional states. *Psychological Review*, 69, 379–399.

Schacter, D. S. (1987). Implicit memory: History and current status. *Journal of Experimental Psychology: Learning, Memory, and Cognition*, 13, 501–518.

Seamon, J. G., Brody, N., & Kauff, D. M. (1983). Affective discrimination of stimuli that are not recognized: Effects of shadowing, masking, and cerebral laterality. *Journal of Experimental Psychology: Learning, Memory, and Cognition*, 9, 544–555.

Seamon, J. G., Marsh, R. L., & Brody, N. (1984). Critical importance of exposure duration for affective discrimination of stimuli that are not recognized. *Journal of Experimental Psychology: Learning, Memory, and Cognition*, 10, 465–469.

Stang, D. J. (1974). Methodological factors in mere exposure research. *Psychological Bulletin*, 81, 1014–1025.

Zajonc, R. B. (1968). Attitudinal effects of mere exposure. *Journal of Personality and Social Psychology Monograph*, 9(2, Pt. 2), 1–27.

Zajonc, R. B. (1980). Feeling and thinking: Preferences need no inferences. *American Psychologist*, 35, 151-175.

Zajonc, R. B. (1984). On the primacy of affect. *American Psychologist*, 39, 117-123.

Zajonc, R. B., & Rajecki, D. W. (1969). Exposure and affect: A field experiment. *Psychonomic Science*, 17, 216–217.

Emotional Organization of Perceptual Memory

Paula M. Niedenthal
Indiana University

Marc B. Setterlund
Concordia College

Douglas E. Jones
The Johns Hopkins University

A number of familiar expressions and truisms have been named in passing as inspiration for psychological research on the interaction between emotion and cognition. People who are happy are said to "look on the bright side" or "see life through rose-colored glasses." Angry people are held to "look for trouble" or "see red." And sad people "look at the dark side" of life. These expressions illustrate, in the current psychological jargon, *emotion congruence*—an agreement between the emotional state of an individual and the affective quality of his or her cognitive responses. Although the verbs in the various expressions (i.e., looking and seeing) seem to refer to *perception*, for the most part they have been conceptualized in terms of higher order cognitive processes. Many researchers have at least implicitly assumed that happy and sad people, as well as fearful, angry, and disgusted people, *see* stimulus events similarly, but *interpret* the events differently (cf. Niedenthal, 1992). As we shall suggest, some models that predict emotion congruence in some memory and judgment processes also predict the phenomenon in

87

perception. In other words, when experiencing different emotions, people may not actually see stimulus events in the same way or see them with equal probability or efficiency. In the present chapter, we describe research from other laboratories as well as our own designed to examine emotional influences in perception. In so doing we evaluate different models of the organization of emotional memory and discuss the implications of such models for the efficiency and the content of perception.

We should make clear at the outset that we are particularly interested in the role of discrete emotions in perception, where emotions are phenomenal states that are associated with distinctive expressive displays, eliciting events, and subjective feeling tone. Emotions can be distinguished from moods in that the latter are more diffuse, often longer lasting, and non-specific in their associated responses (see Isen, 1984; Niedenthal & Showers, 1991). We try to avoid the tendency to use the terms *mood* and *emotion* synonymously, as has been done in much past research, but it is in some cases inevitable. Our strategy is to use mood when discussing research in which that word was employed by the researchers and when there is no basis (e.g., a manipulation check) on which to classify the phenomenon under investigation as an emotion. We sometimes refer to procedures for manipulating the affective state of experimental participants as "mood induction procedure" because they have been so named in the past.

Emotion as Perceptual Hypothesis

One of the earliest experiments to be (re)interpreted as demonstrating emotion congruence in perception (e.g., Bower, 1981) was conducted by Postman and Brown (1952). In the experiment, subjects first participated in a task that was ostensibly designed to measure their "span of apprehension." Subjects saw 15 slides on which there were 12 variously arranged letters and numbers. The slides were presented tachistoscopically for 1 sec and subjects had to immediately recall as many of the symbols as they could. Before each trial, subjects were instructed to publicly announce an "aspiration level," stated in terms of the percentage of previous subjects they thought they were about to outperform. False feedback was supplied following every trial and some of the subjects were consistently told that they had fulfilled their aspirations (success treatment). Others were consistently told that they had fallen short of their aspirations (failure treatment). The remaining subjects did not state an aspiration level or receive feedback (control treatment). Following the apprehension task, subjects performed a different task in which they were exposed to slides of words. Each slide was presented at incrementally increased brightness of exposure until subjects had accurately identified the word.

The stimulus words fell into three categories, labeled "goal words," "deprivation words," and "instrumental words." Goal words were positive words related to the idea of success (*excellent, succeed, perfection, winner*). Deprivation words were negative words related to failure (*failure, unable, obstacle, defect*). Instrumental words were positive words related to agency (*improve, achieve, strive, compete*). Each of the words was matched with a neutral control word. The dependent measure was threshold to recognition. Results indicated that success subjects had the lowest perceptual threshold to goal words, compared to the other subjects. Failure subjects had the lowest threshold to recognition of deprivation words. There was also a tendency for success subjects to show a slightly lower threshold to recognition of instrumental words.

These findings, as well as related findings (McClelland & Liberman, 1949), were interpreted as consistent with the idea that personality factors such as motives and values serve as perceptual hypotheses and that stimulus events are automatically matched against cognitive representations of such hypotheses during perception. Recognition of congruent (*matching*) events was therefore faster than that of incongruent (*mismatching*) events because no alternative perceptual hypothesis had to be compared to the incoming sensation. In this way, hypotheses were held to "organize" perception or to establish "selectivity" in perception (Bruner, 1951; Solley & Murphy, 1960).

An alternative interpretation of this finding invokes emotion. Perhaps the experimental treatment that was designed to instill hypotheses about success and failure primarily influenced the emotions of the subjects. The success treatment may have induced moderate levels of happiness and the failure treatment may have induced sadness or disappointment. That the subjects in the failure condition were more likely to have experienced sadness than anger or annoyance is suggested by examination of the experimental procedure. Subjects in this condition set aspiration levels trial-by-trial but did not, seemingly because of their own personal shortcomings, attain them. Since the experimenter was neither belligerent nor overtly blocked the subjects' goal, it seems unlikely that failure treatment subjects experienced anger (also, D. Brown, personal communication). The words that were used in the word recognition task also differed, as noted, in emotional connotation. Although this was not established empirically, it appears as if the goal words (and the instrumental words to some degree) are related to happiness and the deprivation words are related primarily to sadness. If the procedures and materials are viewed in this light, the results can be taken as evidence of emotion congruence in perception. Specifically, perhaps happy subjects recognized happy-related words with less sensory evidence than sad individuals and sad subjects recognized sad words with less sensory evidence than happy individuals. This post hoc explanation is consistent with recent models of emotion in memory and perception that are reviewed next.

Emotion Network Models

One approach to the cognitive representation and processing of emotion is the associationist position, which endorses some form of a semantic network and spreading activation model of memory (Collins & Loftus, 1975; Anderson & Bower, 1973). Briefly, in such models the unit of mental representation is the node; nodes have also been named concepts, categories, traces, and processors. Generally, nodes are thought to transform and store information in propositional form. These units of representation are linked by connecting pathways that reflect the strength of semantic association among them. A particular idea comes to mind, or enters consciousness, when its node is activated above some critical threshold. A node can be excited by the spread of activation from neighboring nodes, or through direct sensory stimulation. For instance, the idea of a "cat" may come to mind when one sees such an animal, or when one thinks related thoughts (e.g., "pets I have owned") that then spread activation to the node representing "cat."

Bower (1981, 1991) and others (Clark & Isen, 1981; Ingram, 1984; Lang, 1984; Teasdale, 1983) have argued that emotions impose a fundamental organizational structure on information stored in the semantic network. On this view, each emotion is conceptualized as a central organizing node that links together causally related information. For example, nodes that represent beliefs, past events, and physiological patterns associated with *fear* are held to be closely linked (to use the spatial metaphor for associative strength) to the fear node in memory. Likewise, information associated with *happiness* is closely linked to the happy node. Ideas related to "opposite" or incongruent emotions do not share connecting pathways, or may be linked by inhibitory pathways (see Bower, 1991; see Gilligan & Bower, 1984, for elaboration).

The cognitive consequence of an emotional state begins when the relevant emotion node in memory is activated. In time, activation spreads to associated nodes, making those ideas more likely to come to mind or influence subsequent information processing. For example, after being frightened by narrowly missing an automobile accident, the fear node is activated. Activation then spreads to thoughts about things that have frightened one in the past, as well as fears about the future. Many such ideas may have nothing to do with driving, cars, or even death per se. Activation of associated information in the emotion network can also prime the emotion itself. For example, the retrieval of an emotional memory, such as a previous driving accident, can spread activation to the central emotion node and representations of its physiological patterns, thereby instigating the subjective experience of the emotion itself.

Emotion network models make some specific predictions about the encoding and retrieval of affective material in long-term memory during emotional states. One of the central predictions, already illustrated in the above examples, is that of *emotion congruence*. Because an emotion primes a rich context of associated ideas, information that is emotionally congruent should, compared to incongruent information, be more likely to be the focus of attention. Thus, emotion congruence in learning should be observed. The encoding of emotion-congruent stimuli results in a representation that has more links to other cognitive material in the same emotion network. The greater number of links should support enhanced recall of emotion-congruent, compared to other, information during a particular emotional state, because each of these links serves as a potential retrieval pathway. Thus, emotion congruence in retrieval should also be observed. Although the findings are not consistent across emotions of different types, there is empirical support for emotion congruence in both encoding and retrieval (Blaney, 1986; Isen, 1984, 1987; see Singer & Salovey, 1988, for reviews).

Some interactive activation models arguably predict emotion congruence in perception (McClelland & Rumelhart, 1981; see Tanenhaus & Lucas, 1987). Perceptual responses include detection, identification, and classification of words and other stimuli. Such responses may require featural or semantic analysis. In this view, conceptual and other higher order processes can prime lower level representations of graphic features and words. In our discussion of how emotions might influence perception, we concentrate first on perception of words and begin with a overview of ideas shared by interactive activation models of word recognition that are of interest for our purposes.

In word recognition, detectors for specific words, which are here referred to as *semantic codes*, are activated by both top-down (conceptual) and bottom-up (sensory) processes. These sources of activation jointly determine the contents of conscious perception. Conceptual influences include prior knowledge about language as well as transient expectations or goals relevant to a current task (i.e., "context"). An example of interactive activation in word perception is semantic priming. In many studies using lexical decision tasks—tasks in which subjects make speeded judgments as to whether letter strings form words—it has been shown that when a target word is preceded briefly in time by a semantically related word (prime), a subject will make an affirmative lexical decision faster than if the target is preceded by a semantically unrelated prime (Neely, 1977; Meyer & Schvaneveldt, 1971). Apparently, when the prime is semantically related to the target, the code for the target word automatically receives some prior activation. The amount of sensory stimulation by the target word required to raise the activation of its code to threshold is consequently less than if it had been preceded by a semantically unrelated prime, because the semantic code for the target receives no prior activation from an unrelated prime. Summation of activation from conceptual and sensory sources results in faster word recognition as reflected in shorter lexical decision times (Morton, 1969). Results consistent with this interpretation have also been found in experiments using recognition accuracy tasks with degraded words (Meyer & Schvaneveldt, 1976).[1]

If emotions are fundamental organizing categories in an associative network, then the identification of emotion-congruent words during an emotional state should also be more probable, or efficient, than identification of emotion-incongruent (or emotion-unrelated) words. That is, central emotion nodes should spread activation to related concepts and associated semantic codes. Less sensory stimulation should therefore be required to activate the semantic codes for the emotion-congruent words than for the emotion-incongruent words.

Emotional Influences in Perception

Despite the clear and intuitively appealing hypothesis of emotion congruence in *perception*, the phenomenon has not been observed, or has been observed only weakly, in empirical research. Probably the first published set of experiments designed to test the predictions of the emotion network models for perception was conducted by Gerrig and Bower (1982). In the first experiment, highly hypnotizable subjects were induced to feel happiness and anger at different times while experiencing a hypnotic trance. While in each state, subjects were exposed to briefly presented target words that were positive, negative, and neutral in meaning. Following each presentation, subjects tried to recognize the target word from a pair of words. Emotion congruence in recognition accuracy was not observed. That is, subjects were not more accurate at identifying words that were congruent with their current emotional state. In a second experiment, the researchers attempted to replicate Postman and Brown's experiment (1952), which was described earlier. Threshold (operationalized in terms of exposure duration) to recognition of positive, negative, and neutral words was measured when hypnotized subjects were feeling anger and happiness. Emotions were not associated with lower recognition thresholds for emotion-congruent words relative to emotion-incongruent or neutral terms.

Clark, Teasdale, Broadbent, and Martin (1983) had similar lack of success detecting emotion congruence in perception using a lexical decision task. In that study, subjects were induced to feel happy or sad by listening to emotionally evocative music. They then performed a lexical decision task in which the stimulus words were positive, negative, and neutral personality

---

[1]This effect has sometimes been argued to represent intra-lexical priming. See Tanenhaus and Lucas (1987) and Tabossi (1988) for different examples.

attributes. No interaction between emotion condition and word valence was observed when response latencies to lexical decisions were analyzed: happy subjects did not make affirmative lexical decisions about positive words faster than sad subjects, and sad subjects did not make lexical decisions about negative words faster than happy subjects. Sad subjects were merely slower to make lexical decisions about all types of words.

Two other experiments explored the emotion congruence hypothesis with depressed and nondepressed subject samples. MacLeod, Tata, and Mathews (1987) conducted a lexical decision experiment in which word stimuli were positive, negative, and neutral words. Consistent with the findings of Clark et al. (1983), there was no interaction between depression level and word valence in lexical decision times. Powell and Hemsley (1984) found that, compared to nondepressed controls, depressed subjects recognized slightly more negative words at their 50% accuracy threshold, while the same difference between the subject samples was not observed for neutral words. The interaction failed, however, to reach a conventional level of significance.

Only one previous experiment found a reliable emotion congruence effect in perception (Small, 1985). In the experiment, subjects were induced to feel either a depressed or a neutral state by reading a series of sad or bland statements (i.e., the Velten [1968] mood induction procedure). Thresholds to recognition of words related to depression and to the object category, furniture, were then measured. Subjects who received the experimental manipulation of depression showed lowered thresholds to recognition of depression-related terms. There was no difference between depressed and control subjects in threshold to recognition of words denoting types of furniture.

One problem with this experiment is the use of the Velten (1968) procedure. Because the statements used to induce depression contained many depression-related words, it is unclear whether emotion actually mediated word recognition thresholds at all or whether the effect was obtained because depression condition subjects were exposed to graphically and semantically similar stimuli in the Velten procedure. A second problem is that only one type of emotion (depression) and one category of emotion words (depression-related) were used. It is possible that the subjects who received the sad mood manipulation would have recognized all emotion words, including positive ones, with less sensory evidence than the control subjects. Thus, a strong conclusion about emotion congruence cannot be made on the basis of this result.

To summarize, research designed to explore emotional influences in perception has revealed little systematic evidence for changes in the efficiency of word recognition as a function of emotional state. Other null findings are described in Bower (1987). There are two possible conclusions to be drawn. One is that emotions influence high-level cognitive processes involved in stimulus interpretation or response production, but not lower level processes involved in perception. The other is that the experiments did not find support for emotion congruence in perception for conceptual reasons that translated into insensitive tests of the hypothesis. We examine the latter possibility in some detail.

Unidimensional versus Multidimensional Models of Emotion Memory

It seems plausible that the failure of past work to detect emotion congruence in perception is attributable to an erroneous assumption about the way in which emotions organize memory. The model of emotion memory implicitly or explicitly assumed in most extant research is based in a unidimensional model of emotional experience. In this view, all emotions can be located along a single *valence* dimension, and that dimension accounts for the greatest (and perhaps most important) variance in emotional experience. Correspondingly, there might be two superordinate concepts in memory linking together material that is positive and material that is negative.

The valence-organization model has some appeal and seems to find support in much recent research on emotion and judgment (see Clark & Williamson, 1989; Isen, 1987; and Forgas, 1991, for reviews). Results of such studies show that positive and negative moods induced by success or failure experiences, guided imagery, music, flattery or criticism, and so forth, are associated with a tendency to judge as more probable any outcome that carries the same valence as the induced feelings. For example, compared to people in other moods, happy people tend: to see other people and themselves as possessing more positive traits (Adams-Webber & Rodney, 1983; Erber, 1991; Forgas, 1990; Forgas & Bower, 1987; Niedenthal, 1990; Niedenthal & Cantor, 1986); to rate their life and possessions as more satisfactory (Isen, Shalker, Clark, & Karp, 1978; Schwarz & Clore, 1983; Schwarz, Strack, Kommer, & Wagner, 1985); and to judge positive events as more probable (Mayer, Gaschke, Braverman, & Evans, 1992). People who are unhappy tend to overestimate the probability of negative outcomes when making similar kinds of judgments. However, it is not clear that these results reflect the emotional organization of material in memory. Other cognitive processes including the use of the availability heuristic to inform probability estimates (Tversky & Kahneman, 1973), the use of affect as information (Schwarz, 1989), and the mediation of mood regulation strategies (Clark & Isen, 1981) may account for apparent valence congruence in judgment.

Alternative models of emotion memory assume a multidimensional or a categorical structure. Although the valence dimension is typically the primary factor, factor analyses of self-reports of emotional experience often reveal at minimum a two-dimensional bipolar structure. The two dimensions are positivity (valence) and arousal (activity). And anywhere between three and eight dimensions have also been reported (e.g., Abelson & Sermat, 1962; Russell, 1979; 1980; Mayer & Gaschke, 1988; Nowlis, 1965). Emotional memory might therefore be represented in a multidimensional space (e.g., Clark, Milberg, & Ross, 1983).

Bower's (1981) emotion network model actually reflects a categorical model of emotional memory. According to Bower, "The semantic-network approach supposes that each distinct emotion such as joy, depression, or fear has a specific node or unit in memory that collects together many other aspects of the emotion that are connected to it by associative pointers" (p. 135). This statement proposes that each emotion is a separate category in the associative network. Such a view is consistent with differential emotions theories that hold that there is a small set of primary emotions such as fear, anger, disgust, happiness (joy), and sadness (distress), and that each is structurally unique (e.g., Ekman & Friesen, 1975; Ekman, Friesen, & Ancoli, 1980; Izard, 1977; Tomkins, 1962, 1963). These theories are grounded in data on the development of emotional expression, cross-cultural stability of facial expression, self-report of subject feeling, and the analysis of temporal and activation patterns of different emotions. Prototype analyses of emotion words and emotion scripts also provide converging evidence that memory is organized according to primary emotion categories (Fehr & Russell, 1984; Shaver, Schwartz, Kirson, & O'Connor, 1987). In one such study, hierarchical cluster analyses of adults' knowledge of emotions revealed five basic categories of emotion (love, joy, anger, sadness, and fear) (Shaver et al., 1987). With the exception of love, these categories correspond to the primary emotions that are most consistently named in differential theories of emotion.

The valence (unidimensional) and categorical (multidimensional) models of memory organization are not mutually exclusive; both can exist at some level. However, if organization according to valence is assumed in research and there exists a more complex organization, then influences of emotion in perception might not be detected. An examination of the studies described in the previous section reveals that in most investigations of emotion and perception, the experimental manipulation of emotion (or selection of subject sample) was essentially categorical. On the other hand, chosen stimulus words were labeled as congruent or incongruent with the induced emotions only on the basis of valence. Thus positive, negative, and neutral words were presented to subjects in whom feelings of happiness, sadness, or anger were induced.

Table 1 lists the emotion and perception experiments cited above, names the induction procedure and emotions intended, and gives examples of the word stimuli. As can be seen, Gerrig and Bower (1982, Experiment 1), who induced anger and happiness in subjects, used words that they called happy, neutral, and angry. However, the examples of the words listed, which are

***Table* 1   Overview of Recent Research on Emotion and Word Perception**

Source	Mood induction	Word stimuli		
Gerrig & Bower (1982)		"Happy"	"Neutral"	"Angry"
Experiment 1	Hypnotic induction of anger and happiness	glee nice	nine main	pain fail
Experiment 2	Hypnotic induction of anger and happiness	happy joyous ecstatic	style pearl platinum	anger wrath hate
Clark et al. (1983)	Musical induction of sadness and happiness	"Positive" considerate generous loving obliging	"Neutral" bashful firm proud solemn	"Negative" cruel heartless impolite ungrateful
Powell & Hemsley (1984) MacLeod et al. (1987)	Depressed/nondepressed subject samples			
	High frequency	"Good" bed good peace wise	"Neutral" deep long red stop	"Bad" bad fat kill sick
	Low frequency	bath cruise mirth spice	barn crow mode scarf	ache cruel fright stale
Small (1985)	Use of depressing and neutral Velten statements		"Depressed" lonely gloomy worthless	"Furniture" piano mirror lamp

those mentioned in the actual report, are not clearly good instances of those emotion categories. Of course, given the selection criteria for the emotion words (e.g., four letters in length, having a graphically similar neutral control word matched for frequency and length), and the total number of each actually selected (40 happy, 40 angry), it is not at all surprising that many of the words used were not closely related to happiness or anger. In the Clark et al. (1983) study employing a lexical decision task, the trait attributes used were also not categorically related to the happy and sad feeling states of the subjects. The trait terms referred to the tendency to engage in generally desirable, undesirable, or neutral behaviors. Finally, in the two experiments in which depressed and nondepressed subjects participated, stimuli were selected from a list of words published by Broadbent and Gregory (1967). The words were claimed only to have good, neutral, and bad connotations and were not associated with any particular emotional state.

In only two experiments were stimulus words used that were related to the induced emotions in a more specific way. One was the second experiment of Gerrig and Bower (1982). That experiment constituted a failure to show emotion congruence in word recognition using an ascending threshold procedure. The other was the report by Small (1985). Although the experiment contained possible confounds, this was the only one to find evidence of emotion congruence in perception.

When the network model and the spreading activation metaphor are taken seriously, it makes sense that the experience of a particular emotion should not mediate more efficient perception of all information that shares only the same valence. The number of semantic codes in lexical memory is potentially infinite and each word is thought to carry some information about valence (Osgood & Suci, 1955). In the absence of any other cue or contextual information, a primed valence node would presumably spread activation to all words with a common valence, raising the activation level of none of them appreciably. This presents the problem of cue overload or the idea that a perceptual feature or quality that has been associated with a large number of ideas does not serve as a potent retrieval cue to any one idea (Isen, 1984). If we consider only negatively valenced words, it can be appreciated that many negative words are unrelated to a particular emotion, such as fear. When a person is fearful, activation to any given *negative* word may be small or nil. In contrast, activation to fear-related words and representations of other stimuli related to fear should be higher. When a person experiences fear, less activation should be required from sensory input of the categorical type (e.g., fear-related) than sensory input of similar valence (e.g., anger-related), to raise a perceptual or semantic code to threshold.

It may not merely be a question of degree of activation. In the view of differential emotions theories, the experience of one emotion may actually inhibit access to information associated with other emotions. For example, feelings of fear may prevent access to ideas related to anger in order to inhibit inappropriate action (Plutchik, 1984). It is not known whether an emotion such as fear simply activates anger-related information more weakly than fear-related information or actually inhibits access to anger-related information. That is an empirical question. Either way, however, the present analysis suggests that most of the experiments listed in Table 1 constitute relatively insensitive tests of emotion congruence in perception.

Findings from two prior investigations of the influences of induced emotion on memory provide some evidence that emotions are represented in memory in at least a multidimensional way. In one study, subjects heard oral presentations of sentences that reflected each of three negative emotions (anger, sadness, and fear) in both content and vocal quality (Laird, Wagener, Halal, & Szegda, 1982, Study 2). Different randomly constructed sets of the sentences were presented to subjects over three blocks of trials. As they listened to the different sets, subjects adopted the facial expression congruent with one sentence type (anger, sadness, or fear). Facial expression was assumed to induce congruent feelings in the subjects (Duclos, Laird, Schneider, Sexter, Stern, & Van Lighten, 1989; Kraut, 1982; McCaul, Holmes, & Solomon, 1982). Immediately following each block, subjects tried to recall the sentences while maintaining the expression adopted during incidental learning. Despite the (negative) valence common to the three emotions, a categorical effect of emotion on memory was observed. Subjects showed better recall for sentences that matched their emotional expression. These results contrast with findings of many experiments in which negative emotions were experimentally induced and stimulus selection was based on valence, which have failed to observe mood-congruent retrieval or have found only weak evidence of it (see Blaney, 1986; and Singer & Salovey, 1988, for reviews).

Bower (1981) reported a related result. The experimental design was motivated by results of a factor analysis of judgments of similarity between pairs of emotion words (Plutchik, 1980). The analysis revealed eight primary emotions arrayed in an emotion "wheel." Position of the emotions on the circle represented the similarity among emotion terms. Happiness and sadness emerged as opposites (i.e., were separated by 180°) as did anger and fear. The latter two emotions were related at 90° with both of the former two. Bower and his colleague wondered whether these relationships would be corroborated in a test of mood state–dependent memory. In mood state dependency, information learned during one mood state is more easily recalled when the individual is again in that state. In the experiment, hypnotized subjects learned four different lists of neutral words. One list each was learned while subjects experienced happiness, sadness, fear, and anger. Subjects later recalled the items while in moods that were the same, opposite, and related at 90° to the emotion experienced while they learned the list. Subjects' recall was best when their mood during recall was the same as that during learning, and it was worst when they were in an opposite mood. Recall for items retrieved in a mood that was related 90° to learning mood fell somewhere in between. This result provides some support for the categorical implications of the emotion network model. This is suggested in particular by the finding that recall of material learned in an angry state was worst when subjects were feeling fear because these two emotions share common valence.

Emotion Congruence in Perception Revisited

We recently conducted several experiments designed to compare valence and categorical congruence in perception. The valence congruence hypothesis is that stimuli that match the valence of the state of the perceiver will be perceived more efficiently than will other stimuli. The categorical-emotion hypothesis holds that stimuli that match the emotional state of the perceiver in a specific way will be perceived more efficiently than will other stimuli. In this work we did not compare predictions about emotion congruence in perception made by multidimensional versus categorical models of emotion. Thus, we use the term "categorical" to include both notions; that is, to refer to the idea of emotional experience and external stimulus events matched on more dimensions than simply valence. In the first two experiments we examined word perception (Niedenthal & Setterlund, 1993) and in the third we examined face perception. The emotion induction procedure used in all of the experiments, the continuous music technique, was modeled after that described by Eich and Metcalfe (1989). Specifically, in our experiments, subjects heard selections of either happy or sad classical music delivered through headphones for an initial emotion induction period and then continued to hear the music interspersed with instructions throughout the experimental tasks. Subjects in the happy condition heard allegros from *Eine Kleine Nacht Musik, Divertimento #136*, and *Ein Musikalischer Spass*, all by Mozart, and from the concerto for 2 mandolins and strings (in G major, ital r. 532) by Vivaldi. Subjects in the sad condition heard parts of Adagio for Strings by Barber, *Adagietto* (from Symphony no. 5 in C# minor) by Mahler, and the adagio from Piano Concerto no. 2 in C minor by Rachmaninov. These pieces had been shown to induce happiness and sadness, respectively, in prior research, but we also collected self-reports of emotion after the initial induction and prior to the various experimental tasks using an inventory called the Brief Mood Introspection Survey (BMIS, Mayer & Gaschke, 1988). Analysis of self-report data from all of the experiments showed that the classical music was a potent manipulator of happiness and sadness (see also Niedenthal & Setterlund, 1993).

Experiment 1

After the initial musical induction, subjects in the first experiment (N = 36) performed a lexical decision task. There were 60 experimental trials, which included 30 nonword trials and 30 word trials. The stimulus words represented five affect categories, as determined by pretesting. The categories were happy (e.g., joy, cheer, delight), positive (e.g., charm, insight, grace), sad (e.g., hurt, despair, regret), negative (e.g., blame, decay, crime), and neutral (e.g., habit, treaty, code). There were six such words in each category. Average word frequency, length, and concreteness level were roughly equal across word category. The happy words were words that had been previously rated as positive and closely related to the word "happy." The positive words were equally positive but had been rated as relatively unrelated to the word "happy." The sad words had been previously rated as negative and closely related to the word "sad." The negative words were equally negative but unrelated to the word "sad" (see also Niedenthal & Setterlund, 1993).

The data of interest, response latency to lexical decisions to happy, positive, sad, negative, and neutral words were submitted to an analysis of variance (ANOVA), which revealed a significant interaction between induced emotion and word category ($p = .01$, see Figure 1). In order to understand the nature of the interaction we then conducted two additional ANOVAs. The first corresponded to a test of the categorical-emotion congruence hypothesis and involved a 2 (Emotion: happy, sad) × 2 (Word Category: happy, sad) mixed factorial design. The emotion by word category interaction was still significant ($p < .05$). The interaction indicated that happy subjects' lexical decisions about happy words were faster than were those of sad subjects. And sad subjects' lexical decisions about sad words were faster than those of happy subjects. The second ANOVA corresponded to the valence-congruence hypothesis and involved a 2 (Emotion: happy, sad) × 2 (Word Category: positive, negative) design. The emotion by word category interaction did not approach significance in this case ($p > .10$).

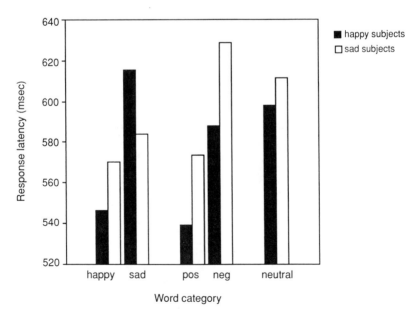

Figure 1   Response latency plotted by word category and emotion induction condition. Experiment 1.

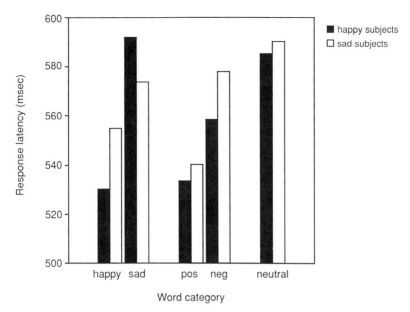

Figure 2   Response latency plotted by word category and emotion induction condition. Experiment 2.

Experiment 2

Because the findings of Experiment 1 were the first clear demonstration of emotion congruence in perception, we conducted a replication with no changes other than in the random order of presentation of the word stimuli (N = 32). The results were consistent with those of Experiment 1 (see Figure 2). In the test of the categorical-congruence hypothesis the interaction between emotion and word category was significant ($p < .01$), whereas this interaction did not reach significance in the test of the valence-congruence hypothesis ($p > .10$).

The results of these two experiments offer some support for categorical-emotion congruence in perception. As the pattern of means in Figures 1 and 2 reveals, however, the categorical interpretation may actually provide a better account of the effects of sadness on perception than of the effects of happiness: sad subjects made lexical decisions about sad words, but not negative words, faster than happy subjects, but happy subjects made lexical decisions about both happy and positive words faster than sad subjects. Thus, it could be argued that valence-congruence characterizes the influence of happiness in perception. Maybe only negative emotions influence perception categorically.

Although an asymmetry in the influence of positive and negative emotions in perception would be interesting and would be consistent with some previous research (e.g., Isen, 1987; Singer & Salovey, 1988), we wanted to conduct a more stringent test of the valence and categorical hypotheses before drawing such a conclusion. To this end, we conducted two repeated measures multiple regressions using the data from the two experiments combined. In the first model the criterion variables were mean response latencies to happy, positive, and neutral words. There were two predictor variables. The first was an estimate of subjects' level of happiness. This score was computed by summing subjects' ratings of the item *happy* on the BMIS with the ratings of the other items that were highly correlated with *happy* (*content* and *lively*). The second predictor variable was an estimate of how sad subjects felt. The sadness score was computed by summing subjects' ratings of *sad* on the BMIS with their ratings of two items that correlated highly with *sad* (*gloomy* and *drowsy*). Note that in these models, emotion induction condition was not a factor; we used level of happiness and sadness, regardless of the experimental treatment (happy or sad music) the subject had received, to predict lexical decision speed. The first regression analysis revealed an interaction only between the repeated measure (word category) and subject happiness ($p < .05$). To explore the nature of the interaction, we conducted separate univariate multiple regressions on the three criterion variables. These analyses revealed a significant negative linear relationship between subject happiness and latency to happy words ($\beta = -.32$, $p < .05$, one-tailed), which indicated that happier subjects made faster lexical decisions about happy words. Happiness was not a reliable predictor of latency to positive or neutral words ($\beta s = -.13$ and $-.07$, respectively), nor was sadness ($\beta s = -.17$ and $-.09$, respectively).

In the second model, mean response latency to sad, negative, and neutral words was regressed on the happiness and sadness scores. In this analysis, only the interaction between the repeated measure and sadness was significant ($p < .01$). Univariate regressions revealed a significant negative linear relationship between sadness and response latency to sad words ($\beta = -.39$, $p < .05$, one-tailed), indicating that greater sadness was associated with faster lexical decisions about sad words. Neither happiness nor sadness was a significant predictor of response latency to negative words ($\beta s = -.14$ and $-.15$, respectively). The results of these regression analyses provided additional support for emotion-congruence in perception. Moreover, it appeared that the categorical hypothesis accounted equally well for both happiness and sadness in the perception of emotional words.

Experiment 3

The third experiment extended the generalizability of the findings of the previous experiments to perception of a different type of stimulus, namely, subjects were exposed to slides of faces of males and females who expressed happiness, sadness, or neutral emotion. Their task was to perform speeded gender discriminations. Similar to a lexical decision (word–nonword) response, the gender (male, female) judgment constituted an implicit measure of the influences of emotion on the perception of faces because subjects did not have to use the facial expression to inform their response; it was irrelevant to the gender judgment. In the task, subjects pressed one button on a response box when they saw the face of a female and another when they saw the face of a male. One-third of the female faces expressed happiness, one-third expressed sadness, and the remainder expressed neutral emotion. The same was true of the male faces. Subjects saw each face only one time during the task.

Based on the results of the other two experiments, we expected that the gender judgments would be mediated by a congruence between the emotion expressed on the target faces and the emotion experienced by the perceiver. This is because the feelings of a perceiver should activate representations of faces that express similar emotion and a holistic perception of the face is required for the gender judgment. Less sensory information should therefore be required to make a decision about an emotion-congruent face than about a face that expressed an incongruent emotion.

Response latencies to discrimination of the male faces conformed to our prediction. The interaction between induced emotion and type of facial expression was marginally significant ($p = .07$) and took the predicted form. The interaction is graphed in Figure 3. There was not a significant interaction

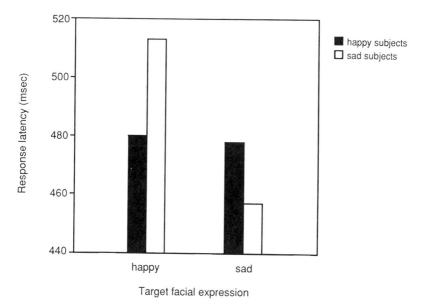

Figure 3 Response latency plotted by target facial expression and emotion induction condition. Experiment 3.

between emotion and facial expression for reaction times to female faces. The response latencies to female faces showed greater variance than reaction times to male faces, possibly because the female targets possessed more variable gender-linked features (e.g., hair length) than did the male targets. It is plausible, therefore, that subjects used a much simpler (i.e., graphic) gender-specific cue to make the judgment. In any event, the results for the male targets are impressive in showing that emotions are associated with greater efficiency at discriminating emotion-consistent and emotion-inconsistent faces on the basis of an affect-unrelated characteristic. This final experiment did not compare the valence- and categorical-congruence hypotheses. However, it did find support for emotion congruence in perception using stimuli that were specifically matched to the felt emotion of the subjects.

Organization of Perceptual Memory

We conducted the experiments just reported to test the hypothesis that emotions influence perception such that emotion-congruent stimuli in the visual field are perceived more efficiently than are emotion-incongruent stimuli. The experimental designs were motivated by the reasoning that previous tests of the emotion-congruence prediction have been insensitive because researchers have induced specific emotions in subjects and then exposed subjects to experimental stimuli, exclusively words, that were matched to the emotions in terms of valence only. The past work was based on an assumption about the manner in which information is organized in memory, namely that it is organized in a unidimensional way. Our findings are more consistent with the idea that the organization of emotion memory is at least multidimensional, if not categorical, in nature.

An interpretation of our findings in terms of memory organization provides one possible explanation for the asymmetry in the mood and memory literature on positive and negative emotions as effective memory retrieval cues (Isen, 1985). Experimentally induced positive emotions have been consistently found to enhance recall of emotion-congruent information in memory (e.g., Isen et al., 1978; Nasby & Yando, 1982; Teasdale & Russell, 1983). However, a complementary effect has not been observed or has been only weakly observed, with experimentally induced negative emotions (e.g., Isen et al., 1978; Mischel, Ebbeson, & Zeiss, 1976; Nasby & Yando, 1982). The same asymmetry between positive and negative emotions has been observed with naturally occurring moods and experimenter-provided stimuli. One explanation of this is that when manipulating positive feelings and developing positive stimulus materials, researchers most often work with happiness (joy). Although surprise, contentment, and love are occasionally named as categorical positive emotions, including happiness and generating words and ideas that are congruent with that emotion seems more easy and more natural. Relatedly, in pretesting stimulus materials, we actually found it difficult to develop lists of words that were positive but not associated with the category happiness. On the other hand, there are numerous negative emotions (e.g., sadness, disgust, anger, fear). In previous experiments, often sadness has been induced, while experimental stimuli have been related to the other negative emotions or to no particular emotion. If emotional memory is organized in emotion categories, it is no wonder that, compared to negative emotions, there is more empirical evidence suggesting that positive emotions serve as retrieval cue function. In those times in which mood-congruent retrieval has been observed with negative emotions, the to-be-retrieved items have been autobiographical memories (e.g., Madigan & Bollenbach, 1982; Salovey & Singer, 1989; Snyder & White, 1982; Teasdale & Taylor, 1981; Teasdale, Taylor, & Fogarty, 1980). These may have been categorically related to the subjects' mood in an idiosyncratic way.

Distinguishing Emotions from Furniture

There are good reasons to conceptualize emotions as phenomena that provide a fundamental organizational basis of memory. Because emotions are ubiquitous and ontologically early qualities of experience, it would make sense that they would serve to provide a structure for the perception, storage, and retrieval of information. Moreover, the arousal component of emotion has an enervating effect on brain activity, which suggests that emotions motivate or direct thought (Buck, 1984; Derryberry & Tucker, this volume; Kitayama, 1990, 1991). The particulars of this view as embedded in semantic network models have, however, met with criticism from different disciplines within psychology (e.g., Isen, 1984; see Leventhal & Tomarken, 1986, for discussion). Consideration of these criticisms suggests ways in which network models are limited in their capacity to conceptualize emotion representation and processing. Such criticisms also suggest possible ways to expand on the associationist idea.

A fairly typical reaction to research that has attempted to integrate emotion within semantic network models of memory is that such models fail to represent the richness of emotional experience and emotional behavior. It is true that in the models, as stated, emotions and emotional ideas are represented in propositional form (code), and processes operating on the representations are conceptualized as logical routines. This, of course, need not be the case (Simon, 1982). As several theorists have reminded us recently, a representation is an internal symbol that stands for a previously experienced internal or external event (Breckler & Wiggins, 1989; Zajonc & Markus, 1984). The way in which the emotional information is transformed and stored cognitively, that is, its *code*, could take different forms. Thus, while some emotion theorists view propositional codes as sufficient for representing emotion stimuli, meaning, and responses (e.g., Lang, 1984; Ortony, Clore, & Collins, 1988), it is possible that other types of code preserve the visual, motor, and somatovisceral aspects of such experience (Buck, 1983, 1984, 1985; Leventhal, 1980, 1984). That we recognize a subjective feeling as "what it is like to be in love" is neither cold nor trivial. Rather, this fact means that there exists a memory representation (or representations) of the bodily feeling of an emotion that has been associated with a verbal label. Thus, the general idea that emotions are stored in and organize memory in an associative way does not have to do away with the "hot" aspects of emotion; an exclusive focus on propositional representation of emotion may do so, however. To explicitly acknowledge this point, we suggest an extension of the associationist position in the sense of adding depth to an emotion network.

To begin with, emotion labels and emotion knowledge refer to subjective states that involve complex physiological processes. This is not true of other concepts, except drives—hunger, thirst and sex—which are closely related to emotion. In contrast, individuals possess semantic codes and conceptual knowledge that do not refer to a subjective feeling (e.g., knowledge about *silverware*), and individuals possess bodily responses about which they have little or no conceptual knowledge (e.g., accommodation to light or temperature). This characterization of emotion knowledge—its representational complexity—is sometimes lost in emotion network models because they contain representations of emotion labels, ideas about emotion, and physiological response patterns of all sorts within a single proposition-based network. Furthermore, these various representations are often connected by bidirectional linkages (Bower, 1981). Bidirectional links are used to indicate the potential activation, or priming, of physiological patterns and a subjective state by associated emotional thoughts, as well as the activation of emotional thoughts by physiological events themselves. Both clinical and personal experience suggest, however, that the activation of words and ideas about emotions do not always activate an emotion. People can reflect on past experiences that brought them to tears, to fits of embarrassment, or to ecstasy without feeling the same emotion or any emotion at all. In fact, it is with surprise and sometimes discomfort that the retrieval of an emotional memory instigates a reexperience of the specific emotion. Sometimes the same type of emotion felt in the past accompanies recall because other factors such as social stimulation, alcohol, fatigue, or stress are also present. This is not to say that emotional memories do not sometimes automatically spread activation to the representation of the emotion, rather that they do not always do so, or perhaps are not sufficient to do so (Lang, 1984).

Given that emotions are not always primed by words or propositions that refer to them, it might make sense to conceptualize emotion knowledge as

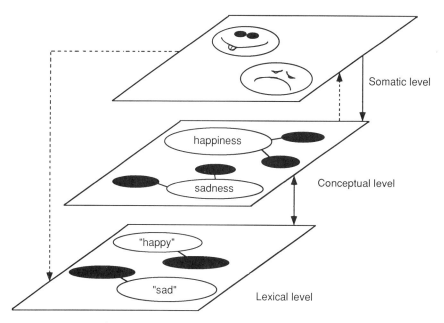

Figure 4   Multiple levels of emotion representation.

existing on (at least) three levels. These are depicted in Figure 4. The first level is the emotion lexicon, which is cognitively represented by semantic codes. Semantic codes are detectors for individual words that refer to emotional experience and they are necessary for the encoding of sensory information from word stimuli. The second representational level is the level of conceptual knowledge. Here, represented in propositional form, are beliefs about emotions and memories of emotional experiences. Finally, at the deepest level, in the sense of being most removed from a verbal representation, is the somatic representation of emotion. We use the word *somatic* not to refer specifically to the somatic nervous system, but because the Latin root *soma* means body. This level includes the neural codes or templates that allow people to recognize feedback from musculature, the autonomic nervous system, the endocrine system, and so forth, as specific emotions.

The links connecting the different types of representation specify possible pathways of interaction between them, pathways along which activation can spread. The solid pathways are suggested by results of past research reviewed in this chapter and elsewhere. The dotted pathways are more speculative. As indicated, activated somatic representations may prime both the emotion lexicon as well as conceptual knowledge. The former link is speculative because it is unclear whether physiological reactions must be interpreted at the conceptual level before activation spreads to semantic codes. In our experiments and others that use musical mood induction, for example, it may be that a process of labeling of emotional state is required to prime the relevant emotion lexicon. We believe that the latter link is not speculative, although others would argue that some experimental results that have been taken to be evidence of somatic priming are, in fact, demonstrations of conceptual priming. For example, in one experiment (Laird, 1984, Experiment 2), subjects who were induced to express a smile through experimenter-guided contraction of the relevant muscles found cartoon stimuli to be more funny than did subjects induced to express a frown. Laird argued that a self-perception process mediated facial feedback and the attribution of funniness of the cartoons. That is, he interpreted the result to mean that there was no direct priming of funniness by feedback from the facial muscles, rather, interpretation of the facial feedback served to prime specific evaluations of the cartoons. Other researchers have suggested, however, that facial feedback effects on cognitive responses are evidence of somatic priming of conceptual information (see Adelmann & Zajonc, 1989, for review).

It seems clear that conceptual priming can activate associated semantic codes for emotion and, perhaps sometimes, somatic representations. This latter link, as mentioned earlier, may only occur under specific conditions (Lang, 1979). Finally, semantic codes should only activate representations at the level of conceptual knowledge; such activation probably does not prime representations of the somatic aspects of an emotion directly. Here we do not mean to suggest that emotion words are not processed with some accompanying affect or arousal (e.g., Kitayama, 1990), rather that the word "happy" does not induce feelings of happiness, but may do so via the priming of relevant conceptual knowledge.

The levels of representation scheme incorporates many of the same components of emotion as those contained, at least in theory, in emotion network models. And it is consistent with models of the emotional response hierarchy (e.g., Buck, 1985; Leventhal, 1984). However, it highlights several conceptual points. One is the fact that memory about different aspects of emotion may be stored in different types of code, that is, that all emotion knowledge may not be propositional in nature. In this respect, it serves to emphasize the possibility that people's memories of an emotion feeling may be functionally independent from what they know about and can communicate about emotion. This idea is obscured somewhat when memory for somatic aspects of emotion is represented with other emotion knowledge in a propositional code. The scheme also highlights the possibility that priming different types of emotion representations may have different effects on cognitive processing of emotional stimuli.

Summary

In this chapter we reported results of recent experiments that provide support for the idea that emotions exert predictable influences on perception of words and human faces. Processes of identification of emotion words appear to be biased by an individual's emotional state such that perception of emotion-congruent words is more efficient, or requires less sensory evidence than does perception of emotion-incongruent words. In addition, individuals appear to be able to make certain (emotion-irrelevant) judgments about faces faster when the faces express an emotion that is congruent with the emotional state of the perceiver. Also revealed by our experiments is the fact that this effect of emotion in perception is categorical in nature: emotions do not influence the efficiency of processing of all stimuli related by valence to the emotion, rather, happy feelings seem to facilitate processing of happy-related stimuli and sadness facilitates processing of sadness-related stimuli.

One implication of this perceptual bias may be that emotion-congruent stimuli are preferentially perceived when there are multiple competing stimuli in the visual field; that is, people may be more likely to see the things that bring them joy rather than those that make them sad when they are in a happy state. Another implication of emotion congruence is that perception of complex, or ambiguous, stimuli might be distorted such that the emotion-congruent elements of the stimulus are visually enhanced, or such that the elements are organized or combined in a manner that is congruent with the perceiver's emotional state (Niedenthal, 1992). These are the topics of ongoing research in this laboratory.

Acknowledgments

Preparation of this chapter and the authors' research were supported by Grants R29 MH44811 from the National Institute of Mental Health and BNS-8919755 and DBS-921019 from the National Science Foundation. We wish to thank Alfonso Caramazza, Asher Cohen, Igor Gavanski, Shinobu Kitayama, and Carolin Showers for their helpful comments on and criticisms of these ideas. Correspondence regarding this chapter should be sent to: Paula M. Niedenthal, Department of Psychology, Indiana University, Bloomington, Indiana, 47405.

References

Abelson, R. P., & Sermat, V. (1962). Multidimensional scaling of facial expressions. *Journal of Experimental Psychology, 63,* 546–554.

Adams-Webber, J., & Rodney, Y. (1983). Relational aspects of temporary changes in construing self and others. *Canadian Journal of Behavioral Science, 15,* 52–59.

Adelmann, P. K., & Zajonc, R. B. (1989). Facial efference and the experience of emotion. *Annual Review of Psychology, 40,* 249–280.

Anderson, J. R., & Bower, G. H. (1973). *Human associative memory.* Washington, D.C.: Winston & Sons.

Blaney, P. (1986). Affect and memory: A review. *Psychological Bulletin, 99,* 229–246.

Bower, G. H. (1981). Mood and memory. *American Psychologist, 36,* 129–148.

Bower, G. H. (1987). Commentary on mood and memory. *Behaviour Therapy and Research, 25,* 443–455.

Bower, G. H. (1991). Mood congruity of social judgments. In J. P. Forgas (ed.), *Emotion and social judgments.* Oxford: Pergamon Press.

Breckler, S. J. & Wiggins, E. C. (1989). On defining attitude and attitude theory: Once more with feeling. In A. R. Pratkanis, S. J. Breckler, & A. G. Greenwald (eds.), *Attitude structure and function* (pp. 407–427). Hillsdale, NJ: Erlbaum.

Broadbent, D. E., & Gregory, M. (1967). Perception of emotionally toned words. *Nature (London), 215,* 581–584.

Bruner, J. S. (1951). Personality dynamics and the process of perceiving. In R. R. Blake & G. V. Ramsey (eds.), *Perception: An approach to personality.* New York: Ronald.

Buck, R. (1983). Emotional development and emotional education. In R. Plutchik and H. Kellerman (eds.) *Emotion: Theory, research and experience.* New York: Academic Press.

Buck, R. (1984). *The communication of emotion.* New York: Guilford.

Buck, R. (1985). Prime theory: An integrated view of motivation and emotion. *Psychological Review, 92,* 389–413.

Clark, D. M., Teasdale, J. D., Broadbent, D. E., & Martin, M. (1983). Effect of mood on lexical decisions. *Bulletin of the Psychonomics Society, 21,* 175-178.

Clark, M. S., & Isen, A. M. (1981). Towards understanding the relationship between feeling states and social behavior. In A. H. Hastorf & A. M. Isen (eds.), *Cognitive social psychology.* New York: Elsevier-North Holland.

Clark, M. S., & Williamson, G. M. (1989). Moods and social judgements. In H. Wagner & A. Manstead (eds.), *Handbook of social psychology.* Chichester: Wiley & Sons.

Clark, M. S., Milberg, S., & Ross, J. (1983). Arousal cues arousal-related material in memory: Implications for understanding effects of mood on memory. *Journal of Verbal Learning and Verbal Behavior, 22,* 633–649.

Collins, A. M., & Loftus, E. F. (1975). A spreading-activation theory of semantic processing. *Psychological Review, 82,* 407–428.

Duclos, S. E., Laird, J. D., Schneider, E., Sexter, M., Stern, L., & Van Lighten, O. (1989). Emotion-specific effects of facial expressions and postures on emotional experience. *Journal of Personality and Social Psychology, 57,* 100–108.

Eich, E., & Metcalfe, J. (1989). Mood dependent memory for internal versus external events. *Journal of Experimental Psychology: Learning, Memory, and Cognition, 15,* 443–455.

Ekman, P., & Friesen, W. V. (1975). *Unmasking the face.* Englewood Cliffs, NJ: Prentice-Hall.

Ekman, P., Friesen, W. V., & Ancoli, S. (1980). Facial signs of emotional experience. *Journal of Personality and Social Psychology, 39,* 1125–1134.

Erber, R. (1991). Affective and semantic priming: Effects of mood on category accessibility and inference. *Journal of Experimental Social Psychology, 27,* 480–498.

Fehr, B., & Russell, J. A. (1984). Concept of emotion viewed from a prototype perspective. *Journal of Experimental Psychology: General, 13,* 464–486.

Forgas, J. P. (1990). Affective influences on individual and group judgments. *European Journal of Social Psychology, 20,* 441–453.

Forgas, J. P. (1991). *Emotion and social judgments.* Oxford: Pergamon Press.

Forgas, J. P., & Bower, G. H. (1987). Mood effects on person-perception judgments. *Journal of Personality and Social Psychology, 53,* 53–60.

Freud, S. (1954). *The origins of psycho-analysis.* New York: Basic Books.

Gerrig, R. J., & Bower, G. H. (1982). Emotional influences on word recognition. *Bulletin of the Psychonomics Society, 19, 197–200.*

Gilligan, S. G., & Bower, G. H. (1984). Cognitive consequences of emotional arousal. In C. E. Izard, J. Kagan, & R. B. Zajonc (eds.), *Emotions, cognition, and behavior* (pp. 547–588). Cambridge: Cambridge University Press.

Hansen, C. H., & Hansen, R. D. (1988). Finding the face in the crowd: An anger superiority effect. *Journal of Personality and Social Psychology, 54, 917–924.*

Ingram, R. E. (1984). Toward an information-processing analysis of depression. *Cognitive Therapy and Research, 8, 443–478.*

Isen, A. M. (1984). Toward understanding the role of affect in cognition. In R. S. Wyer & T. K. Srull (eds.), *Handbook of social cognition* (Vol. 3). Hillsdale, NJ: Erlbaum.

Isen, A. M. (1985). Asymmetry of happiness and sadness in effects on memory in normal college students: Comments on Hasher, Rose, Zacks, Sanft & Doren. *Journal of Experimental Psychology: General, 114, 388–391.*

Isen, A. M. (1987). Positive affect, cognitive processes, and social behavior. In L. Berkowitz (ed.), *Advances in experimental social psychology* (Vol. 20, pp. 203–253).

Isen, A. M., Shalker, T. E., Clark, M., & Karp, L. (1978). Affect, accessibility of material in memory and behavior: A cognitive loop? *Journal of Personality and Social Psychology, 36, 1–12.*

Izard, C. E. (1977). *Human emotions.* New York: Plenum.

Johnson, E., & Tversky, A. (1983). Affect, generalization, and the perception of risk. *Journal of Personality and Social Psychology, 45, 20–31.*

Kitayama, S. (1990). Interaction between affect and cognition in word perception. *Journal of Personality and Social Psychology, 58, 209–217.*

Kitayama, S. (1991). Impairment of perception by positive and negative affect. *Cognition and Emotion, 5, 255–274.*

Kraut, R. E. (1982). Social pressure, facial feedback, and emotion. *Journal of Personality and Social Psychology, 42, 853–863.*

Laird, J. D. (1974). Self-attribution of emotion: The effects of expressive behavior on the quality of emotional experience. *Journal of Personality and Social Psychology, 29, 475–486.*

Laird, J. D. (1984). The real role of facial response in the experience of emotion: A reply to Tourangeau and Ellsworth. *Journal of Personality and Social Psychology, 47, 909–917.*

Laird, J. D., Wagener, J. J., Halal, M., & Szegda, M. (1982). Remembering what you feel: Effects of emotion on memory. *Journal of Personality and Social Psychology, 42, 646–657.*

Lang, P. J. (1979). Language, image, and emotion. In P. Pliner, K. P. Plankstein, & J. M. Spigel (eds.), *Perception of emotion in self and others* (Vol. 3). New York: Plenum.

Lang, P. J. (1984). Cognition in emotion: Concept and action. In C. Izard, J. Kagan, and R. B. Zajonc (eds.), *Emotions, cognition, and behavior.* New York: Cambridge University Press.

Leventhal, H. (1980). Toward a comprehensive theory of emotion. In L. Berkowitz (ed.), *Advances in experimental social psychology* (Vol. 13). New York: Academic Press.

Leventhal, H. (1984). A perceptual motor theory of emotion. In K. S. Scherer & P. Ekman (eds.), *Approaches to emotion.* Hillsdale, NJ: Erlbaum.

Leventhal, H., & Tomarken, A. J. (1986). Emotion: Today's problems. *Annual review of Psychology, 37, 565–610.*

MacLeod, C., Tata, P., & Mathews, A. (1987). Perception of emotionally valenced information in depression. *British Journal of Clinical Psychology, 26, 67–68.*

McCaul, K. D., Holmes, D. S., & Solomon, S. (1982). Voluntary expressive changes and emotion. *Journal of Personality and Social Psychology, 42, 145–152.*

McClelland, D. C., & Liberman, A. M. (1949). The effect of need for achievement on recognition of need-related words. *Journal of Personality, 18, 236–251.*

McClelland, J. L., & Rumelhart, D. E. (1981). An interactive activation model of context effects in letter perception: Part I. An account of basic findings. *Psychological Review,* 88, 375–407.

Madigan, R. J., & Bollenbach, A. K. (1982). Effects of induced mood on retrieval of personal episodic and semantic memories. *Psychological Reports,* 50, 147–158.

Mathews, A., & MacLeod, C. (1985). Selective processing of threat cues in anxiety states. *Behaviour Research and Therapy,* 23, 563–569.

Mayer, J. D., & Gaschke, Y. N. (1988). The experience and meta-experience of mood. *Journal of Personality and Social Psychology,* 55, 102–111.

Mayer, J. D., Gaschke, Y. N., Braverman, D. L., & Evans, T. W. (1992). Mood-congruent judgment is a general effect. *Journal of Personality and Social Psychology,* 63, 119–132.

Mayer, J. L., Mamberg, M., & Volanth, A. J. (1988). Cognitive domains of the mood system. *Journal of Personality,* 56, 453–486.

Meyer, D. E., & Schvaneveldt, R. W. (1971). Facilitation in recognizing pairs of words: Evidence of a dependence between retrieval operations. *Journal of Experimental Psychology,* 90, 227–234.

Meyer, D. E., & Schvaneveldt, R. W. (1976). Meaning, memory structure, and mental processes. *Science,* 192, 27–33.

Mischel, W., Ebbeson, E. B., & Zeiss, A. M. (19976). Selective attention to the self: Situational and dispositional determinants. *Journal of Consulting and Clinical Psychology,* 44, 92–103.

Morton, J. (1969). The interaction of information in word recognition. *Psychological Review,* 76, 165–178.

Murphy, G. (1956). Affect and perceptual learning. *Psychological Review,* 63, 1–15.

Nasby, W., & Yando, R. (1982). Selective encoding and retrieval of affectively valent information. *Journal of Personality and Social Psychology,* 43, 1244–1255.

Neely, J. H. (1977). Semantic priming and retrieval from lexical memory: Evidence for facilitatory and inhibitory processes. *Journal of Experimental Psychology: General,* 106, 226–254.

Niedenthal, P. M. (1990). Implicit perception of affective information. *Journal of Experimental Social Psychology,* 26, 505–527.

Niedenthal, P. M. (1992). Affect and social perception: On the psychological validity of rose-colored glasses. In R. Bornstein & T. Pittman (eds.), *Perception without awareness.* New York: Guilford Press.

Niedenthal, P. M., & Cantor, N. (1986). Affective responses as guides to category-based inferences. *Motivation and Emotion,* 10, 217–332.

Niedenthal, P. M., & Setterlund, M. B. (1993). Emotion congruence in perception. *Personality and Social Psychology Bulletin,* in press.

Niedenthal, P. M., & Showers, C. J. (1991). The perception and processing of affective information and its influence on social judgment. In J. Forgas (eds.), *Affect and social judgment.* Oxford: Pergamon Press.

Nowlis, V. (1965). Research with the mood adjective check list. In S. S. Tomkins & C. E. Izard (eds.), *Affect, cognition, and personality.* New York: Springer Publishing Co.

Ortony, A., Clore, G. L., & Collins, A. (1988). *The cognitive structure of emotions.* New York: Cambridge University Press.

Osgood, C. E., & Suci, G. J. (1955). Factor analysis of meaning. *Journal of Experimental Psychology,* 50, 325–338.

Plutchik, R. (1980). *Emotion: A psychoevolutionary synthesis.* New York: Harper and Row.

Plutchik, R. (1984). Emotions: A general psychoevolutionary theory. In K. S. Scherer & P. Ekman (eds.), *Approaches to emotion.* Hillsdale, NJ: Erlbaum.

Postman, L., & Brown, D. R. (1952). The perceptual consequences of success and failure. *Journal of Abnormal and Social Psychology,* 47, 213–221.

Powell, M., & Hemsley, D. R. (1984). Depression: A breakdown of perceptual defense? *British Journal of Psychiatry,* 145, 358–362.

Pratto, F., & John, O. P. (1991). Automatic vigilance; The attention-grabbing power of negative information. *Journal of Personality and Social Psychology*, 61, 380–391.

Russell, J. A. (1979). Affective space is bipolar. *Journal of Personality and Social Psychology*, 37, 345–356.

Russell, J. A. (1980). A circumplex model of affect. *Journal of Personality and Social Psychology*, 39, 1161–1178.

Salovey, P., & Singer, J. A. (1989). Mood congruency in recall of childhood versus recent memories. *Journal of Social Behavior and Personality*, 4, 99–120.

Schwarz, N. (1989). Feelings as information: Informational and motivational functions of affective states. In E. T. Higgins & R. M. Sorrentino (eds.), *Handbook of motivation and cognition: Foundations of social behavior* (Vol. 2). New York: Guilford Press.

Schwarz, N., & Clore, G. L. (1983). Mood, misattribution, and judgments of well-being: Informative and directive functions of affective states. *Journal of Personality and Social Psychology*, 45, 513–523.

Schwarz, N., Strack, F., Kommer, D., & Wagner, D. (1985). Soccer, rooms and the quality of your life: Mood effects on judgments of satisfaction with life in general and with specific domains. *European Journal of Social Psychology*, 17, 69–79.

Shaver, P., Schwartz, J., Kirson, D., & O'Connor, C. (1987). Emotion knowledge: Further explorations of a prototype approach. *Journal of Personality and Social Psychology*, 52, 1061–1087.

Simon, H. A. (1982). Affect and cognition: Comments. In M. S. Clark & S. T. Fiske (eds.), *Affect and cognition: The seventeenth annual Carnegie symposium on cognition* (p. 333–342). Hillsdale, NJ: Erlbaum.

Singer, J. A., & Salovey, P. (1988). Mood and memory: Evaluating the network theory of affect. *Clinical Psychology Review*, 8, 211–251.

Small, S. A. (1985). The effect of mood on word recognition. *Bulletin of the Psychonomic Society*, 23, 453–455.

Snyder, M., & White, P. (1982). Moods and memories: Elation, depression and the remembering of the events of one's life. *Journal of Personality*, 50, 149–167.

Solley, C. M., & Murphy, G. (1960). *Development of the perceptual world*. New York: Basic Books.

Tabossi, P. (1988). Accessing lexical ambiguity in different types of sentential contexts. *Journal of Memory and Language*, 27, 324–340.

Tanenhaus, M. K. & Lucas, M. M. (1987). Context effects in lexical processing. *Cognition*, 213–234.

Teasdale, J. D. (1983). Negative thinking in depression: Cause, effect, or reciprocal relationship? *Advances in Behaviour Research and Therapy*, 5, 3–25.

Teasdale, J. D., & Russell, M. C. (1983). Differential effects of induced mood on the recall of positive, negative, and neutral words. *British Journal of Clinical Psychology*, 2, 163–171.

Teasdale, J. D., & Taylor, R. (1981). Induced mood and accessibility of memories: An effect of mood state or of mood induction procedure? *British Journal of Social and Clinical Psychology*, 20, 39–48.

Teasdale, J. D., Taylor, R., & Fogarty, S. J. (1980). *Behaviour Research and Therapy*, 18, 339–346.

Tomkins, S. S. (1962). *Affect, imagery, consciousness. Vol. 1. The positive affects*. New York: Springer Verlag.

Tomkins, S. S. (1963). *Affect, imagery, consciousness. Vol. 2. The negative affects*. New York: Springer Verlag.

Tversky, A., & Kahneman, D. (1973). Availability: A heuristic for judging frequency and probability. *Cognitive Psychology*, 5, 207–232.

Velten, E. A. (1968). A laboratory task for induction of mood states. *Behaviour research and Therapy*, 6, 473–482.

Zajonc, R. B., & Markus, H. (1984). Affect and cognition: The hard interface. In C. E. Izard, J. Kagan, & R. B. Zajonc (eds.), *Emotions, cognition, and behavior* (pp. 73–102). Cambridge, England: Cambridge University Press.

Consciousness and Automatic Evaluation

Felicia Pratto
Stanford University

Consciousness has been called the "Mind's Eye"—the seer of mental processes. One old tradition within psychology, from Descartes and Locke to Wundt and Tichener, presumes that all mental activity is "seen" by the Mind's Eye. The fact that we are conscious perhaps led us into this belief. There is something compelling about our conscious experience—it seems to indicate that what we are conscious of at the moment is what our minds are doing at that moment. But there is a more modern tradition in psychology that holds that some of our mental processes are not conscious. Instead, this tradition maintains, we respond to the world in nonconscious ways (see review by Greenwald, 1992). One of the chief ways we respond is by *feeling*, rather than conscious *knowing*. If we can feel things we cannot know, does the "Heart's Eye" see better than the Mind's Eye? Do we understand the sources of our feelings, the process by which we arrive at them, and how they influence us more than we understand our conscious thought processes? If the Mind's Eye has a blind spot, does the Heart's Eye see the missing information?

The Heart's Eye: Emotional Influences in Perception and Attention

Actually, I think the Heart's Eye has the same kind of myopia as does the Mind's Eye. Feelings, like conscious thoughts, are experiential, and our immediate experience of them makes them seem compellingly truthful (Zajonc, 1980). The immediacy of experienced emotions or tastes or distastes can fool us into thinking that we know where these feelings come from. But, if they result partly from nonconscious processes, then they leave us with the same blind spot as consciousness does.

In this chapter I shall describe what is in the blind spot of the Heart's Eye. I argue that we are chronically engaged in ascertaining the goodness or badness of stimuli in our environments, and that this process can occur without our awareness of the process, the outcome of the process, nor even of the stimuli. In other words, we automatically evaluate the environment, or have affective reactions to it that are not amenable to consciousness. Furthermore, it may be that we cannot control automatic evaluations, but they can influence our conscious experiences, including judgments, emotions, and attitudes, in important ways. I shall describe the evidence for evaluative mental activity, which neither the Mind's Eye nor the Heart's Eye sees, and then describe theories of the function of automatic evaluations, including their relationship to learning and emotions.

If conscious experience of ideas or feelings does not allow us to know about our mental processes outside of the view of the "window on the mind," how can we study them? Psychological research has essentially cut another window to our minds, and one which does not peer out onto the stream of consciousness. In this chapter, I describe how psychologists make additional windows on people's minds and what the view through these windows indicates about evaluation outside of consciousness. In other words, there are two views of consciousness: the objective view of the outside researcher, and the subjective view of the subject (e.g., Cheesman & Merikle, 1986). To illustrate both the objective and subjective views, I shall describe the results of the studies from the researcher's point of view: what subjects appeared to do; and also from the subject's point of view: what subjects believed they were doing, and what sort of awareness they had of the processes the researchers observed.

Evidence for Automatic Evaluation

Conscious Apprehension and Automatic Evaluation Are Separate Processes

Perhaps you have had the experience of pulling your hand away from a painful stimulus such as a hot pan before you realized what was causing your pain. If so, you have experienced a sort of evaluation before recognition.

Experientially, you first "knew" (felt) your hand hurt, before you knew (recognized) what hurt you. This example implies that affective responses to stimuli are not contingent on being aware of the stimuli. Let me describe some experimental evidence that affective evaluations of stimuli need not be contingent on awareness of stimuli.

Kunst-Wilson and Zajonc (1980) presented novel stimuli (10 irregular octagons) at exposure durations too short for subjects to see them, and then tested whether subjects could distinguish the old from similar new stimuli. During the presentation phase, subjects looked at a screen on which the 10 shapes were presented for 1 msec, 5 times each. During the test phase, subjects were shown 2 stimuli, 1 from the exposed (old) set, and 1 from an unexposed (new) set, for 1 sec each. Subjects were asked two questions about the pairs, in counterbalanced order between subjects: Which did you see before? Which do you like better? Subjects' recognition of the shapes was at chance levels (48%), but they reported liking the old better than the new shapes 60% of the time. They also expressed more confidence in their liking judgments than in their recognition judgments. Subjects' feelings about the shapes were stronger and a more reliable predictor of prior exposure than was their knowledge of the exposure (see also Matlin, 1971; Zajonc, 1968).

These data suggest that people's affective reaction to the stimuli does not depend on knowing they had seen the stimuli. Further experiments using this paradigm suggest that the evaluative process and whatever process is required for recognition judgments are independent. Seamon, Brody, and Kauff (1983) employed a method similar to the one used by Kunst-Wilson and Zajonc (1980). In Experiment 1, they presented subjects with 10 polygons for 3 msec, 5 times each. In the test phase, subjects discriminated the old from new polygons on both the recognition (66%) and liking (65%) questions. An additional condition was added to reduce subjects' attentional capacity: subjects had to listen to a list of words read at 40 words per minute and repeat the list aloud during the exposure phase. Even in this shadowing condition, subjects were better than chance on the recognition (59%) and liking (65%) questions. Because the subjects performed better than chance on both tasks, the researchers could examine the data to see if either process influenced the other. They computed the contingency between making a correct recognition judgment and making a correct liking judgment for any given polygon. In no case was the contingency coefficient large, suggesting that the processes are independent.

Experiment 2 followed the same procedure as Experiment 1 except that each exposure lasted just 2 msec. The results replicated those of Experiment 1 except that recognition judgments were reduced to chance in the shadowing condition. In other words, at an even shorter exposure duration, liking judgments were influenced by objective familiarity, but recognition was not.

Here again, the contingencies were near zero. Seamon et al. (1983) conducted two additional experiments that demonstrated that different regions of the brain may do the evaluative processing and the processing required for later recognition. (See LeDoux, 1989, for a review of relevant neurophysiological evidence.)

Despite their better-than-chance performance with fast exposures, Seamon et al.'s (1983) subjects did not report having any confidence in or any feeling that they knew what the right answers to the questions were. From an outsider's view, these subjects were making evaluations and "knew" which stimuli they had seen before on this basis. However, from the subjects' views, they did not know that they had seen the stimuli before or that this had increased their liking of them. This is one criterion that has been used to describe processes as automatic: that the perceivers have no awareness of the process. In addition to lack of awareness on the subject's part, automatic processes are also characterized by being unintentional, involuntary, effortless, and autonomous (see reviews by Bargh, 1989; Johnson & Hasher, 1987; Kahneman & Treisman, 1984; Logan & Cowan, 1984; Schneider, Dumais, & Shiffrin, 1984; Zbrodoff & Logan, 1986), although Logan (1989) describes them in process terms, rather than by criteria. In this review, however, I will follow Bargh's (1989) notion that automaticity is conditional, and I will try to establish some conditions that are and are not present in experiments that demonstrate that people automatically evaluate the positivity or negativity of stimuli in their environments.

In the exposure-breeds-liking studies described, one can infer that the subjects had evaluative responses to stimuli during the presentation stage, but the evidence for this comes from the later test stage of the experiments. Evidence that people evaluate stimuli of which they are not aware during the presentation of the stimuli would be even more compelling. To provide this more stringent test we borrowed a method developed by Marcel (1983) to employ subjective subliminal exposures. Marcel used a tachistoscope to present words printed on cards and blank cards to subjects at brief exposures. While presenting the cards to a subject, he decreased the exposure duration until the subject could not accurately guess whether a word had been presented on the card. This exposure duration is called each subject's threshold of apprehension (T). Then Marcel presented words (or blank cards) to subjects at shorter durations than their thresholds and asked them to make various judgments about them. The presence judgment was whether a word was present or absent; the semantic judgment was which of two new words was more similar in meaning to the exposed word, and the graphical judgment was which of two new words had similar graphical features (e.g., tails) to the exposed word. In Experiment 1, subjects were instructed which of these judgments to make before each stimulus was presented. Even though subjects expressed little confidence in their judgments, they performed at better than chance levels on semantic similarity, graphical similarity, and presence/absence judgments when the stimulus duration was (T − 5 msec), (T − 10 msec), or (T − 15 msec). They were better than 70% accurate at the semantic judgment at (T − 20 msec), the shortest duration Marcel used. However, in Experiment 2, in which subjects were not told the question about the stimulus until after it had been shown, performance was not distinguishable from chance. Thus, it is possible that the accuracy of the judgments in Experiment 1 was contingent on the goal to answer the specific question given.

Bargh, Litt, Pratto, and Spielman (1989) tested the hypothesis that people evaluate stimuli without the orientation or intention to do so. On each trial, we presented each stimulus briefly and then instructed subjects to make one of three judgments (Marcel, 1983, Experiment 2). These included a presence judgment, an evaluative judgment ("Did the word you just saw mean something good or bad?"), and a modified semantic judgment. To make the semantic judgment independent of evaluation, both word choices matched the stimulus word's evaluation (e.g., for the stimulus "gentle," the choices were "kind," which is positive and semantically similar, and "intelligent" which is positive but not semantically similar). We employed personality trait adjectives as stimuli whose evaluative values are well known and reliably rated by subjects (e.g., Anderson, 1974). Half the stimuli were blank cards, and half were either positive or negative trait words, which were either extreme or moderate along the positive–negative dimension. We presented the words four times in different orders, blocked on decreasing exposure durations: (T − 5 msec), (T − 15 msec), (T − 25 msec), and (T − 35 msec).

Subjects were able to make the presence/absence judgment at better than chance levels at all four exposure durations. In addition, they were able to answer the semantic question at better than chance levels at (T − 5 msec), but not at shorter durations. However, subjects were able to answer the evaluative question at better than chance levels at both (T − 5 msec) and (T − 15 msec). In other words, subjects were able to make the good/bad judgment with some accuracy at (T − 15 msec), although they could not pick which of two evaluatively matched words was more similar in meaning to the target word. This suggests that apprehending the evaluative meaning of words may occur more readily than apprehending the definition.

We also tested whether performance on any of the three kinds of judgments were dependent on one another by computing contingencies between pairs of judgments (Seamon et al., 1983). For example, if subjects correctly judged presence/absence, were they more likely to make the correct evaluative judgment? Results showed that if subjects answered the presence judgment right, they were more likely to make a correct evaluative judgment. The presence judgments were, however, independent of the semantic judgments, even at (T − 5 msec). The results also showed total independence of the evaluation and the semantic judgments. Thus, correctly ascertaining the evaluative information in the stimuli did not help subjects make the evaluation-controlled semantic judgments.

The results of this experiment support the hypothesis that people automatically evaluate stimuli with little or no other conscious knowledge of the stimuli. In fact, because our subjects could not tell whether they were seeing words or not, some of them saw no point in trying to make the judgments. We had to assure these subjects that they should try to make the judgments, even if it felt like guessing, because previous research had demonstrated that people could make some judgments under this condition. Our subjects' comments about the experiment also indicated that they believed that if they weren't conscious of the stimuli, they could not be evaluating them or ascertaining their meaning.

The apparent contradiction between the objective evidence that people automatically evaluated shape and word stimuli and their subjective lack of awareness of the stimuli and the evaluative process can be resolved if we postulate that there are two somewhat independent processes operating on different time scales. The automatic evaluations happen quickly, with only a few milliseconds of exposure. But for external, visually presented stimuli, people cannot develop conscious expectations in under 500 msec (e.g., Neely, 1977). Thus, the speed of the automatic evaluation process is one reason people may not be able to become conscious of it.

Deliberate Evaluation with Automatic Priming of Valence

Even if the data are quite compelling in demonstrating that people respond affectively to stimuli without intending to, without knowing they do it, and sometimes without awareness of the stimuli, one might well ask, why does it matter? One reason that these nonconscious, unintended affective responses matter is that they may influence conscious, deliberate judgments of other stimuli. Automatic affective responses may be "power behind the throne" of deliberate judgment (Bargh, 1989, p. 38). A priming paradigm is useful for showing that unintended affective responses can carry over to deliberate judgments. In the studies described next, researchers tried to provoke an unintended affective reaction to a prime stimulus, and tested whether that influenced deliberate judgments of a target stimulus.

Fazio, Sanbonmatsu, Powell, and Kardes (1986) proposed that simple, highly accessible attitudes automatically become active on exposure to attitude objects so that attitude objects can be used as primes in an evaluation task. In Experiments 1 and 2, the primes were chosen idiographically for each subject by selecting the primes from a large set of attitude objects (e.g., priest, pizza, toothache) according to each subject's evaluations. In the prime evaluation phase of the study, subjects saw each word on a computer screen and pushed a button indicating whether they felt each word was "good" or "bad." The computer then sorted each subject's responses to this task for good and bad stimuli that had taken the longest or shortest response times in a balanced design (good/bad × fast/slow).

The fast attitude objects were hypothesized to have readily accessible attitudes associated with them, which would serve as valence primes. To test this, the selected attitude objects were used as primes in an evaluation task that subjects performed a few minutes later. On each trial, one of the prime words (or a neutral letter string) was presented and subjects were instructed to remember this word while they evaluated a trait adjective, which was clearly either good or bad. Subjects' response time to evaluate the adjective was recorded and then they recited the prime word aloud. For the fast attitude primes, Fazio et al. (1986) expected the response times to be facilitated (faster) when the attitude object and the trait word had the same valence, and inhibited (slower) when the attitude object and the trait word had the opposite valence; that is, although subjects were not instructed to evaluate the prime words in the second task, their assessments of the primes' evaluations were expected to influence a subsequent deliberate evaluative judgment task. In some conditions, Fazio et al. (1986) used a short interval of time between presentation of the attitude prime and the adjective target (300 msec) called stimulus onset asynchrony (SOA)—one which is so short that conscious expectancies and the ability to stop the priming influence could not develop (see Neely, 1977; Posner & Snyder, 1975). With this prime–target interval for the fast attitudes, subjects did indeed show facilitation on the valence-consistent trials and inhibition on the valence-inconsistent trials, as predicted. Fazio et al. (1986) concluded from these results that highly accessible attitudes automatically become activated on exposure to the attitude objects.

The generalizability of automatic attitude activation was further explored in a series of experiments by Bargh, Chaiken, Govender, and Pratto (1992). Our initial research explored aspects of people's responses to the stimuli not fully explored by Fazio et al. (1986). For example, in Fazio et al.'s Experiment 3, attitude objects that had been responded to rather slowly but which showed much consensus across subjects had also worked as effective valence primes on the trait-evaluation task (when the SOA was 300 msec). This suggests that consistency, and not just speed of initial evaluation, could be a critical determinant of whether the attitudes were automatically activated. First, we conducted a normative study to measure within-subject consistency of prime evaluation by having 30 subjects participate in the prime-evaluation task twice, two days apart. We computed the number of subjects who changed their evaluation of a given stimulus (e.g., from good to bad) across the two days as an index of attitude consistency for the stimulus. Consistency correlated −.74 with evaluation latency, supporting the notion that slowly evaluated stimuli are inconsistently evaluated. We then ran a replication of Fazio et al.'s Experiment 2 (300 msec SOA condition), with an additional consistent prime condition using primes chosen from the most consistently evaluated list (above 93%), but which were among the slowest to be evaluated by subjects. The results of this Experiment 1 replicated the usual prime valence × target valence interaction in both the fast and consistent prime conditions, but not in the slow condition. The evaluation priming effect was shown for attitudes that, in the attitude assessment phase, were evaluated significantly slower than the fastest attitudes, but not as slow as the slowest attitudes. These data indicate that relatively slow attitudes can also be activated, as long as the attitude is consistent (all of the experimental subjects evaluated these objects the same way as the normative study subjects had).

There are two aspects of the procedure Fazio et al. (1986) used that we suspected might heighten attitude accessibility: (1) subjects evaluated the primes just prior to participating in the adjective evaluation task; and (2) subjects were instructed to hold the prime in mind while evaluating the adjective. To eliminate the possibility that these features of the experiment were responsible for the automatic evaluation effect, we eliminated them from several additional experiments. We found automatic attitude evaluation to influence priming in the same way as Fazio et al.'s studies, even: (1) when subjects did not evaluate the prime words just prior to performing the experiment (Experiment 2); (2) when subjects did not hold the prime word in memory while performing the evaluation task (Experiment 3); and (3) whether the subjects had been slow or fast to indicate their attitudes in the attitude assessment phase, as long as the attitudes were consistent (Experiments 1, 2, and 3).

Niedenthal (1990) also used an automatic priming paradigm—one that involved subliminal exposure to affective stimuli during learning and test phases. Rather than word stimuli, Niedenthal used photographs of human faces expressing joy or disgust as affective primes, and novel cartoon characters as the targets to which subjects deliberately attended. In Experiment 1, on a series of trials, subjects saw neutral cartoon characters for 5 seconds each. During the learning phase, each cartoon was immediately preceded by photographs of emotionally expressive faces for 2 msec. For some subjects, the target cartoons were preceded by happy faces and for other subjects the cartoons were preceded by disgusted faces. Following the cartoon-learning phase, subjects were given a recognition test on cartoon characters. Half of the stimuli present on test trials had been presented in the learning phase, and half were new to the subjects. During the recognition test phase, both old and new cartoons were preceded by happy faces on half of the trials and disgusted faces on the other half. Subjects recognized old cartoons faster when they were preceded by the same type of emotional face as the learning phase, compared to when the cartoons were preceded by a face with an inconsistent expression. These results suggest that although subjects were unaware of the face primes, they had implicitly learned the affective association of the cartoon characters.

Moreover, this implicit affective learning carried over onto deliberate judgments. In Experiment 2, subjects were instructed to form an impression of the cartoon character in a similar procedure in which happy, disgusted, or neutral faces were presented. During the test phase, two different kinds of impression measures of the cartoons were taken: endorsement of personality traits, and similarity to person categories such as "nerd." The impression results showed that subjects in the disgusted face condition rated the cartoons less positively on the personality trait ratings, and more similar to the negative person categories, compared with subjects in the neutral and joyful face conditions.

The controllability aspect of evaluation priming results hinges on subjects' awareness of the primes (e.g., Logan, 1989). Niedenthal's (1990) evidence for implicit affective learning occurred without awareness of the primes; detection tasks, the results of which were subjected to procedures of signal detection theory, showed that subjects were unaware of the face primes. With short SOAs in Fazio et al.'s (1986) and Bargh et al.'s (1992) experiments, subjects could not develop a conscious strategy concerning what to do about the prime's influence on the task. With a longer SOA of 1000 msec, Fazio et al.'s (1986, Experiments 2 and 3) subjects did not show the usual priming effects, indicating that with enough time to allow consciousness of the primes, subjects could stop the primes' influence on their subsequent deliberate evaluations. This suggests that the influence that automatic evaluations have over responses can be controlled by editing the influence that automatic evaluations have on one's response (see Logan, 1989).

Automatic Evaluation Interfering with a Primary Task

The priming studies just described imply that people can evaluate emotional stimuli even without being instructed to, or being aware that they are doing so. However, it is possible that these automatic evaluations were goal dependent (see Bargh, 1989), that is, they occurred because the subjects' instructed goal was to evaluate, or form an impression of, the targets. In the exposure-breeds-liking experiments, one might argue that subjects had a similar goal during the exposure phase if one assumes that evaluation is the default deliberate goal. Researchers might then test whether subjects automatically evaluate stimuli by giving subjects an alternative goal that does not involve evaluation. Seamon et al.'s (1983) shadowing task did this in part; it gave subjects an additional attentional goal, but not for the stimuli for which affective responses were tested. This goal reduced recognition performance but not the exposure-breeds-liking effect. Niedenthal's (1990) Experiment 1 subjects had only the goal to recall stimuli, but also showed evidence of automatic evaluations.

An even stronger test of the automatic evaluation hypothesis is to see whether automatic evaluation interferes with a different primary task performed on the same stimuli. For example, Stroop (1935) instructed subjects to name the color of ink in which names of colors were printed. Subjects took longer to name the correct color when the color named did not match the ink color (e.g., when "blue" was written in red ink) compared to when it did (e.g., when "red" was written in red ink). A simple interpretation of this effect is that word recognition occurred automatically and access to the word meaning interfered with the primary color-naming task. (See MacLeod & Dunbar, 1988; Logan, 1980, for explanations of divided attention and automatic processing in Stroop and related tasks.)

This task has also been used with words that do not name colors to examine automatic attention to different kinds of stimuli (e.g., Bargh & Pratto, 1986). For example, we have recently used the task in order to assess attention to automatically evaluated stimuli. Pratto and John (1991) presented words appearing in different colors to subjects whose task was to name the colors in which the stimuli appeared as fast as possible. Interference with the deliberate color-naming task, as measured by longer response latencies, indicates that some other aspect of the stimuli interfered with subjects' accomplishing their deliberate goal. The stimuli were familiar personality trait words that were either desirable (positive) or undesirable (negative). Within the large sets of negative and positive personality traits (40–131 words) the stimuli covered a variety of meanings encompassing every major personality dimension.

In three studies, we found that the valence of the trait adjectives, regardless of extremity of evaluation, word length, word frequency, or expected frequency of the trait, was the best predictor of response times (see left panel of Figure 1). Nearly all subjects took longer to name the colors of negative as compared with positive trait words. The valence effect suggests that subjects' evaluations of the words influenced the color-naming task, especially because other possible influences (e.g., word length) had been controlled.

To examine the possibility that this effect was due to some sort of repression of (or motivated inattention to) negative words, a set of 40 stimuli were presented in different orders in each of two blocks in Experiment 2 so that recall could be assessed. Subjects in this experiment recalled more negative than positive words, so it is probably not the case that they paid less attention to the negative items (see right panel of Figure 1). There was a tendency in the second block for the words that were looked at longer to be

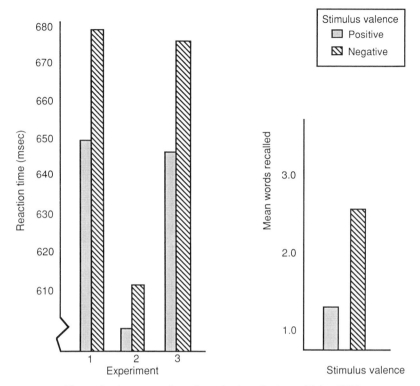

Figure 1   Latency and recall results from Pratto and John (1991).

recalled by more subjects. In fact, given that subjects looked longer at and later recalled more negative words, we interpreted our results as indicating that negative stimuli are automatically attention grabbing. We infer from these results that although subjects did not deliberately attend to evaluative or other aspects of the words' meaning, they automatically evaluated them and the negative evaluations then captured attention.

Although the word frequency of the positive and negative traits was equivalent, it is possible that the valence effect could have been caused by negative traits being more unusual or unexpected than positive traits (e.g., Sears, 1983). To test this alternative explanation, in Experiment 3 we crossed the traits' base rates (common/uncommon) with their valence. The base rate had no main effect or interaction on the color-naming latencies; only the valence effect was obtained.

We performed several analyses to address the possibility that the effect was due to one or two "attention-grabbing" negative traits. We performed trend analyses on the data using each trait word as a case and tested whether the degree to which it was negative or positive predicted mean response latency to that word. We tested for a linear component of desirability, such that the more negative a word was, the longer its response latency, a quadratic component, which should assess extremity of desirability as an influence, and even cubic and tetric components. None of these trends were close to significant in any of the experiments. Instead, the valence contrast between responses to negative and positive words was reliable. This result is rather surprising, given that linear trends are good at describing what are truly categorical differences (e.g., Dawes, 1979). Thus, it appeared that the main evaluation characteristic driving response times to the color-naming task was valence: the negative or positive quality, and not degree of desirability. The failure of degree of desirability to influence responding was also compatible with the Bargh et al. (1989) results, even on an evaluation task. Bargh et al. used both extremely and moderately positive and negative trait words, but found no main effects or interactions with degree of desirability, that is, subjects were not more accurate on the evaluative task for extremely compared to moderately desirable or undesirable words. Bargh et al. (1989) suggested that this should not be surprising; an automatic evaluation process, being fast and requiring no effort or deliberate goal, should not be a fine-grained process.

The findings just reported could also be interpreted as demonstrating that positive traits fail to interfere with color naming, or that they do not automatically capture attention, rather than that negative traits capture attention. In order to test this competing hypothesis, we next compared color-naming latencies of positive and negative stimuli to that of neutral stimuli. We were unable to use personality adjectives for this purpose because there are not enough of them that meet the necessary experimental criteria. These include: (1) unambiguous in connotation, that is, not positive to some subjects or in some ways, and negative to other subjects or in other ways (e.g., aggressive); (2) familiar in meaning to most subjects; and (3) reasonably equal in word length, word frequency, and base rate as the positive and negative stimuli. For this reason, we used objects and activities (nouns and verbs) as stimuli.

Our pilot stimulus list included 10 negative verbs (e.g., mutilating) and 10 negative nouns (e.g., violence) as well as 10 positive nouns (e.g., baby) and 10 positive verbs (e.g., kissing). Both lists were constructed to be equivalent with respect to word length, word frequency, and extremity of evaluation. The "control" stimuli were a set of 10 neutral nouns (e.g., doorstep) and 10 neutral verbs (e.g., administer) that were similar to the valenced stimuli on word frequency and word length and that also had extremely small variance from their neutral evaluations. Forty-eight subjects named the colors in which these 60 randomly ordered words appeared, and their response times to negative, neutral, and positive words were compared.

There was no main effect or interaction for whether the words were nouns or verbs. There was a main effect for valence, F (2,90) = 7.07, p = .001, such that subjects took longer to name the colors of both negative (M = 627 msec) and positive words (M = 626 msec) compared to neutral ones, (M = 614 msec); for negative versus neutral, t(90) = 2.50, p < .02; for positive versus neutral, t(90) = 2.04, p < .05. This pattern also obtained for recall; subjects recalled an average of 1.41 negative, 0.53 neutral, and 1.37 positive words. So it appeared that positive and negative stimuli were both more attention grabbing than neutral stimuli (see also Kitayama, 1991).

Although positivity biases are not uncommon (e.g,. see Taylor, 1991, for a review), we were somewhat surprised that the positive words had been just as attention grabbing as negative items. Upon reexamining our stimulus list, we suspected that the words pertaining to sex or babies might comprise an attention-grabbing category in their own right. (See Johnston & Wang, 1991, for psychophysiological evidence of this in women.) We are currently testing that hypothesis. To reexamine how positive and negative words compare to neutral, we reconstructed our stimulus list, this time excluding words from all valence categories that pertained to sex, romance, or babies. Our second experiment included 30 instances each of negative, neutral, and positive words (with approximately equal numbers of nouns and verbs in each of the valence conditions), but excluded any words that had to do with romance or violent sex or babies. Thirteen subjects named the colors of these words, and they again showed a main effect for valence, F(2,24) = 924, p < .001. This time, however, subjects took longer to name the colors of negative items (M = 673 msec) than of positive items (M = 646 msec); post hoc t(24) = 2.59, p < .01; and than of neutral (M = 652 msec); post hoc t(24) = 2.02, p < .05. It did not take subjects longer to name positive words than neutral words, t < 1.

On recall, there was also a main effect for valence, F(2,24) = 6.10, p < .01, such that subjects recalled more negative (M = 1.92) and positive words (M = 1.38) than neutral words (M = 0.61); t(24) = 3.48, p < .01 for negative; t(24) = 2.03, p = .06 for positive.

The results of these two studies show that valenced stimuli can automatically attract attention away from a primary task more than neutral stimuli. In several studies, negative stimuli attracted more attention than positive stimuli, but it remains to be seen whether special classes of positive stimuli (e.g., "sexy" ones) might also be attention grabbing. This greater attention also contributes to greater incidental learning of the valenced stimuli. In other words, not only is there an automatic evaluation function, but it contributes to automatic attention to negative stimuli—automatic vigilance. This attentional process may influence deliberate judgments as well. For example, in impression formation, negative information is more heavily weighed in overall impressions than is positive information (e.g., Anderson,

1974; Hamilton & Zanna, 1972), and gets more attention during information intake (Fiske, 1980; see Pratto & John, 1991).

Is Automatic Vigilance Amenable to Conscious Control?

We recently conducted an experiment to test the hypothesis that people can control automatic vigilance in the color-naming context. In some cases, when people are told that a particular event might interfere with the color-naming task, they successfully ignore the distraction and show faster, rather than slower, response times (Higgins, Van Hook, & Dorfman, 1988; Pratto, Bargh, & John, 1993). In our experiment, we warned subjects that they might experience interference from the words' evaluation. Thus, in one condition, we warned subjects about the automatic vigilance for negative words effect. Specifically, in a replication of Pratto and John's (1991) Experiment 1, subjects were told that "so far in this experiment, people seem to be taking longer to name the colors of the negative words than the positive words. We'd like you not to do that. Just name the colors as fast as you can." This comprised the True Warning condition. As a comparison, a False Warning condition was included in which subjects were given similar instructions except they were told that "people seem to be taking longer to name the colors of the positive words than the negative words." In the Control condition, subjects were given the usual instructions to name the colors as fast as they could without making mistakes.

If the True Warning condition instructions helped and subjects could control automatic evaluations, we should see a reduction of the automatic vigilance effect compared to the Control condition; that is, there would not be as large a difference (if any) between response times to negative and positive stimuli in the True Warning condition as in the Control condition. Similarly, if the False Warning makes people attend less to the positive words, they should take even less time to name the colors of the positives than the negatives. If, on the other hand, telling people not to commit one of these valence biases makes them all the more likely to do it, we would see an exaggeration of the automatic vigilance effect in the True Warning condition. Likewise, if the False Warning instructions backfire, we might see a reversal of the automatic vigilance to negative words, such that people would take longer to name the colors of positive than negative items. These two sets of predictions are illustrated graphically in the top two panels of Figure 2.

Nineteen subjects participated in the Control condition, 19 participated in the True Warning condition, and 15 participated in the False Warning condition. Either of the two sets of predictions should have resulted in a Warning Condition × Stimulus Valence interaction. However, no such effect emerged. Rather, the main effect of stimulus valence was reliable, $F(1,50) =$

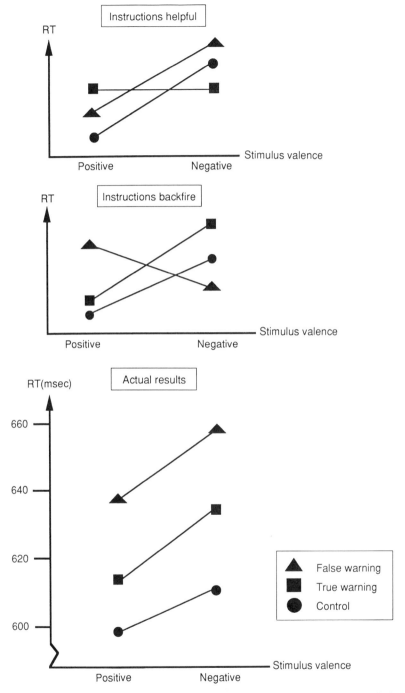

Figure 2 Hypothesized and actual results of a study testing whether being warned about automatic vigilance can help people prevent it.

25.8, $p < .001$, such that subjects in all three conditions took longer to name the colors of negative (M = 633 msec) than positive stimuli (M = 615 msec). An a priori contrast between the two Warning conditions and the Control condition showed that subjects in both Warning conditions were somewhat slower than subjects in the Control condition, but the valence effect held within each of the three conditions, regardless of warnings (see bottom panel of Figure 2). In other words, the warning instructions slowed subjects down (perhaps because they were more deliberately vigilant), but this did not reduce the automatic vigilance effect for negatives. As in Pratto and John's (1991) Experiment 2, subjects also recalled more negative words (M = 2.02) than positive words (M = 1.45); $F(1,50) = 5.20$, $p < .05$, which did not vary as a function of warning condition. So, again, implicit learning was influenced by automatic attention to negative stimuli, and was not changed due to deliberate vigilance against this effect. These results do not unequivocally imply that people cannot stop automatic evaluations. But they do suggest that people will have a hard time stopping them while simultaneously performing another task requiring attention. This experiment does show the failure of control for 4 out of 5 control methods suggested by Logan's (1989) Instance Model of Automaticity. In the experiment, the focus of attention was directed at a nonvalenced aspect of the stimuli (color). The subjects' goal was to name the colors as quickly as possible. The subjects were not in a state that should make valence especially accessible. The RTs in the experimental condition were slower than in the control condition, suggesting that subjects may have attempted to edit their responses, but apparently this editing came after the automatic vigilance response.[1]

The subjects' viewpoints are also informative on this controllability point. In the postexperimental interviews, a significant proportion of the subjects noticed that the stimulus words were valenced: "extreme" or "emotional," unlike in any of our previous experiments with this task. However, subjects did not believe that their response times were influenced by trait valence in any way.

Is Automatic Evaluation a Component of Semantic Priming?

In light of the evaluative priming effects described above, it seems possible that the frequently observed priming effects of word synonyms (e.g., Meyer & Schaneveldt, 1971; see Niedenthal et al., this volume, for review) might be due, in part, to evaluative priming. To explore this possibility, we needed to find stimuli that have an evaluative component (desirability) and semantic (descriptive) component that is separable from the evaluation, so

---

[1]The fifth method, using an algorithm to prevent relying on automatic memory retrieval, was creatively employed by pilot subjects (e.g., they would squint at the stimuli to blur the words). This can prevent the automatic vigilance effect. Therefore, we told our experimental subjects not to squint.

that the amount of priming due to evaluation compared with other semantic aspects could be compared. Personality trait pairs fit such a description (e.g., Peabody, 1968). There exist pairs of traits that match both in evaluation and in terms of the behaviors they describe (true synonyms), that match in neither aspect (true antonyms), and that match in terms of one aspect but not the other. For example, frugal and stingy could describe the same behavior but have opposite valences; calm and excited could hardly describe the same behavior, but both are positive.

We developed a set of 72 personality trait pairs that fit into a 2 × 2 design crossing the descriptive and evaluative similarity or mismatch between each number of the pairs. Pretest subjects rated a large pool of these pairs for similarity of meaning and also rated the degree of desirability of each word. The meaning differences were significantly larger for words in the descriptive mismatch than in the match cell, but the words did not vary significantly in desirability. Likewise, the desirability differences were significantly larger for words in the evaluation mismatch compared to the match cell, but did not vary significantly in meaning. The four conditions were also equivalent in terms of evaluative extremity, word frequency, and word length. Finally, we balanced the design for valence. Half the trait words in each condition were positive and half were negative. Thus, in the conditions in which the valence of the prime and target matched, half the pairs were both negative and half were both positive. In the conditions in which the valence of the prime and target were opposite, half were positive and half were negative, and half of the time the positives were primes.

One word from each pair was randomly chosen as the prime and the other as the target, except that the pairs were adjusted so that the prime set and target set were equivalent with regard to the above-mentioned characteristics. On each trial, the prime word appeared for 350 msec in white letters, followed by a blank screen for 300 msec, at which time the target word appeared in one of five colors. Subjects' task was to name the color of the target word. The color-naming task was used so that subjects would not have the deliberate goals of evaluating or ascertaining the meaning of the stimuli. How should these conditions influence the color-naming latencies?

The logic of priming using an inhibition task is different from the usual priming situation in which semantically related primes facilitate accessibility of the target (see Neill, 1977; Tipper, 1985). In the Stroop (1935) paradigm, the object is to inhibit all possible distractions in order to perform the color-naming task as quickly as possible. I have found that semantic priming with this task speeds up subjects' color-naming latencies. For example, when subjects were primed for either the concepts hostile or kind in a sentence unscrambling task, they named the colors of synonyms of hostile or kind faster in a subsequent Stroop task (Pratto, 1987). In another study similar to Pratto and John's (1991) Experiment 1, subjects who saw a close synonym of a trait word in white letters 300 msec before the target appeared in color named the colors faster, compared to subjects whose prime word was "attention" (Pratto et al., 1993). These results suggest that subjects inhibit the primes and, because the targets are so closely semantically related, the mental representations of the target's meaning are also inhibited before the targets appear. Consequently, the target meaning should not interfere with the primary color-naming task. That is, priming with semantically related information should produce facilitation (faster RTs) with a color-naming task because inhibiting the prime should pre-inhibit the target and make color naming easier (see Neill, 1977, and Tipper, 1985, for a discussion of negative priming).

Thus, in the present research we predicted that subjects would name the color of words faster in the descriptive match conditions than in the descriptive mismatch conditions. Based on previous research (Pratto & John, 1991), we predicted that negative targets would take longer than the positive targets. We also tested for the prime–target valence interaction shown in Fazio et al. (1986) and Bargh et al.'s (1992) studies. It was a main test of this experiment whether the descriptive and evaluative relationships between prime and target would influence response latency and in what way.

Repeated measures analyses were performed on the mean across 9 trait pairs within condition for each subject in a $2 \times 2 \times 2$ design with descriptive match/mismatch, prime valence (positive/negative), and target valence (positive/negative) as within-subjects factors. Results showed that as expected, subjects took longer to name the colors in trials with descriptive mismatches (M = 629 msec) than in those with descriptive matches (M = 619 msec), $F(9,17) = 4.39$, $p < .01$. In addition, conditions that included negative primes (M = 627 msec) took longer than conditions having positive primes (M = 620), $F(9,17) = 8.68$, $p < .001$; the same pattern held for negative targets (M = 626) versus positive targets (M = 622), $F(9, 17) = 5.65$, $p = .001$. The prime and target valence main effects were modified by interactions with descriptive match such that the valence effects were larger in the descriptive mismatch conditions. The prime valence $\times$ target valence interaction was also significant: when both were positive, response times were the fastest (M = 615 msec). In all other conditions, response times were longer (about 627 msec). In other words, the presence of a negative word either as a prime or target slowed down RTs, but this effect was not additive. This shows that automatic attention to negatives can modify the valence-priming effects.

Functions of Automatic Evaluations

Why should we automatically evaluate stimuli, even when we have no particular goal to do so? Why should we evaluate stimuli without even knowing (i.e., being conscious) that we are doing it? A number of independent theorists have recently proposed adaptive models of automatic evaluation. All of these postulate that automatic evaluations serve to orient the organism to the environment. One means of this immediate adaption is readiness of the autonomic nervous system.

Automatic Evaluations Producing Autonomic Responses

Automatic evaluations have been shown to produce autonomic nervous system responses. Corteen and Wood (1972) conducted a divided attention experiment in which the subjects were to attend to a prose passage being presented to one ear and simultaneously recite the passage out loud. (This form of a divided attention task is called dichotic listening.) A list of city names and nouns were presented to the other, nonattended ear. Subjects' skin conductance, a measure of sweating, was recorded along with the nonattended tape. In the control condition, few skin conductances were significantly different than baseline, and these were the same for city names or nouns (5% to 6%, respectively). In the experimental condition, subjects had performed a prior task in which mild electric shocks were associated with three particular city names. In this condition, subjects exhibited significantly more changes in skin conductance just after the shock-associated city names were presented to the unattended ear than when they heard familiar but nonshock-associated nouns (38% vs 12%). Thus, stimuli to which subjects were not deliberately attending provoked autonomic responses. The experimental subjects also exhibited significant changes in skin conductance when unfamiliar city names not previously associated with shock were presented (23%), which did not occur for unfamiliar nouns (9%). Subjects had implicitly "learned" that the category "cities" was painful, and this learning provoked a physiological response associated with emotions and defense.

After the experiment, the experimenter asked the subjects if they had noticed anything in their unattended ears. All 36 subjects said they had heard nothing. Then the experimenter asked the subjects to think carefully, and try to remember if they heard anything, even if they could not remember it now. In answer to this question, five subjects said they remembered some words, but none recalled city names. Then the experimenter explicitly asked them whether they heard any city names. Despite the obvious demand of this question, all the subjects said no. That is, subjects showed autonomic responses to stimuli of which they did not recall being aware. Furthermore, they did so not only in response to shock-associated stimuli, but to stimuli in the same semantic category as the shock-associated stimuli.

The self-reports on awareness of the unattended stimuli were given 1 to 5 minutes after the stimuli were presented, so it is possible that subjects had a momentary awareness of the stimuli, but had forgotten all about it by the end of the tape (see Holender, 1986). To test for momentary awareness, Corteen and Dunn (1974) used the same procedure, but asked the subjects to press a buzzer if they heard a city name in either ear. The results for autonomic responding were virtually the same as in the Corteen and Wood (1972) study. However, out of 114 presentations of city names in the experiment, the buzzer was pressed only once. It seems fair to conclude that people can show autonomic responses to stimuli that have affectively significant consequences, even though they are not subjectively aware of the stimuli.

Automatic Evaluations and Attention Allocation

Pratto and John (1991) proposed that people automatically evaluate information so that attention can be allocated to negatively evaluated stimuli. In other words, automatic evaluations are a form of preconscious filtering that serves the purpose of guiding conscious attention to some stimuli more than to others. We called our negativity effect "automatic vigilance," postulating that its purpose is to make the perceiver aware of things in the environment that may require fast responses. If this mental process was indeed selected, then stimuli requiring attention and fast responses were apparently often negatively valenced during human evolution. If, as more and more theorists believe, the human adaptive environment was (and is) largely a social one (e.g., Brewer & Caporael, 1990), it would not be surprising if these effects are stronger with social stimuli such as person descriptors, social category labels, facial expressions, or even hand gestures.

In fact, Hansen and Hansen (1988; this volume) posited a similar "automatic vigilance" function for facial expressions and hypothesized that attending to faces that could represent threat (angry faces) could be especially adaptive. Hansen and Hansen (1988) predicted that angry facial expressions would show an attentional "pop-out" effect (e.g., Treisman, 1982), whereas happy faces would not. They presented arrays of photographs of faces expressing angry or happy expressions to subjects. Under some conditions, one of the faces expressed a different emotion than the others in the array. Subjects were substantially faster in finding an angry face in a happy "crowd" array than in finding a happy face in an angry crowd. Moreover, the angry face pop-out effect was constant over arrays of 4 or 9 faces, but the happy face effect was not (Experiment 3).

Roskos-Ewoldsen and Fazio (1992) have also posited a visual-attention function to stored evaluations or attitudes. They posited that it would be functional to attend to those objects with potential good or bad hedonic consequences, that is, what one likes and dislikes. They showed that visual attention tended toward drawings of objects that subjects had especially accessible attitudes toward, whether the attitudes were more accessible naturally (Experiment 1) or made so by an experimental procedure (Experiment 2). Moreover, this effect held when subjects were not deliberately attending to attitude-associated stimuli or were actively trying to ignore them (Experiments 3 and 4).

Attention Helps Learning

Attention is not only useful for making decisions about one's actions in the immediate future, but also for the longer term adaptation of learning (e.g., Kentridge & Aggleton, 1990). To understand how automatic vigilance may have come about, we should consider our affective responses to novel stimuli. The exposure-breeds-liking studies are often interpreted to mean that familiarity leads to liking, but the results could just as easily be interpreted as implying that novel stimuli are disliked. Perhaps, then, disliking unknown stimuli is a natural defense when the organism does not yet know how to respond to a stimulus. This interpretation is bolstered by an experiment by Matlin (1971), who showed that conditions under which subjects have several competing responses to a stimulus mimic conditions under which the stimulus is unfamiliar, that is, they produce less liking and less learning.

If novel stimuli evoke competing mental responses, they leave the organism in an ambiguous situation about what to do. That state may not be as adaptive as learning what the stimulus means and how to respond to it. Many experiments have shown that unexpected stimuli, such as a hippopotamus in a barnyard (Friedman, 1979) or an unusual personal characteristic (e.g., Fiske, 1980), capture visual attention. Perhaps, then, the mechanisms giving attention to negative or new stimuli were selected to help organisms learn about the stimuli.

This adaptive theory is supported by neurophysiological evidence. In reviewing a number of studies of monkeys' brains, Kentridge and Aggleton (1990) identify the ventral stream of the striate (visual) cortex, which is involved in stimulus identity, as reaching the TE area of the ventral lobe. In support of the idea that novelty recognition and ascertaining valence are important adaptations for social-living primates, parts of the TE area respond selectively to novelty and to face and hand stimuli.

Automatic Evaluation as Inputs to Emotional Responses

Automatic evaluations may serve another adaptive function as necessary inputs to emotions; Kentridge and Aggleton's (1990), Lazarus's (e.g., 1991), LeDoux's (1989), and others' theories of emotions postulate a primary evaluation mechanism that is outside consciousness, but necessary for emotional experience. (Emotions may also have been selected because they serve hedonic reinforcing functions; see Lazarus, 1991; Rolls, 1990.) The amygdala is thought to do this affective computation on new stimuli, and may be related to the novelty–negative affect link postulated above, because the TE area also has a nervous pathway to the amygdala (LeDoux, 1989; Kentridge & Aggleton, 1990). LeDoux speculates that we can have emotional experiences not only from responses to external stimuli, but also to internal visceral and mental stimuli, such as gut aches, memories, and thoughts, because of pathways from the vagus nerve (which communicates internal information) and the hippocampus (which communicates symbolic informa-tion), respectively, to the amygdala. Kentridge and Aggleton (1990) identify the other part of the loop: because the amygdala projects to a variety of midbrain and brainstem locations, it could influence autonomic and endo-crine functions that could be the physiological basis for emotions (see also Rolls, 1990). LeDoux states that the affective and cognitive systems are neurologically distinct and, although they are connected through nervous pathways, operate somewhat in parallel. Once, however, the amygdala has made a good or bad evaluation, its signals to the midbrain and brainstem could provoke physiological responses associated with emotions. Perhaps, then, awareness of the physiological state, coupled with the current state of consciousness and deliberate information processing (such as interpreta-tion of somatic feelings, the social context) becomes the actual experience of emotions (e.g., Cioffi, 1991; Ellsworth & Smith, 1988; Schachter & Singer, 1962).

In other words, automatic evaluations cannot become emotions without conscious experience of one's feelings. This form of self-awareness of one's present hedonic state need not suppose that an elaborated self-concept exists—rather, simply that one is aware of how one feels. This definition enables us to posit that creatures who might not have elaborate self-concepts (e.g., babies, wolves) can experience emotions. Both the experi-mental and neurophysiological evidence suggest that the aspect of emo-tions that is not amenable to self-awareness is automatic evaluation (see also Spielman, Pratto, & Bargh, 1988). Corteen's work (Corteen & Wood, 1972; Corteen & Dunn, 1974) shows this in humans; Le Doux and his col-leagues have shown a similar dissociation between cortical processing and fear responses in rats. In a typical experiment, rats were exposed to stimuli associated with aversive consequences, such as electric shocks. Both rats with surgical sensory cortex damage and rats without damage showed the usual "fear" responses to the conditioned stimulus. The rats were then exposed to the same stimulus, but this time there was no aversive result associated with the stimulus. The rats who had intact cortices were able to eventually learn that there were no aversive consequences to the stimuli, and their fear responses were gradually extinguished. However, the rats with cortical lesions were less able to unlearn the fear response (see LeDoux, Romanski, & Xagoraris, 1989; LeDoux, 1990). LeDoux (1990) believes that the separate neural pathways for sensory versus consciously integrated input processed in the cortex may account for some of the emotional responding in people that is provoked by the environment for reasons that people cannot understand, nor exhibit much control over.

Implications for Mind–Brain Metaphors

In short, the picture we have been getting of the mind shows that its affective and conscious processes can operate quite separately; the Heart's Eye and the Mind's Eye see different views (Zajonc, 1980). Evaluations of stimuli can be performed without subjective awareness (Bargh et al., 1989; Corteen & Dunn, 1974), objective awareness (Kunst-Wilson & Zajonc, 1980; Niedenthal, 1990; Seamon et al., 1983; Seamon, Marsh, & Brody, 1984), or intention to evaluate (Pratto & John, 1991); and although automatic evaluations can provoke attention (Hansen & Hansen, 1988; Pratto & John, 1991; Roskos-Ewoldsen & Fazio, 1992), deliberate attention to a stimulus is not necessary for them to occur (Roskos-Ewoldsen & Fazio, 1992, Experiments 3 and 4).

How do automatic evaluations and conscious processes such as recognition relate to one another? It appears that there may be a slight time advantage to automatic evaluation (see also Derryberry & Tucker, this volume). For example, in Seamon et al.'s (1983) Experiment 2, subjects discriminated familiar from unfamiliar shapes in the test phase using the liking but not recognition task with 2-msec exposures, but this superiority for liking judgments disappears when the stimuli are presented for 8 msec (Seamon et al., 1984). LeDoux (1989) postulates that such a time precedence for affective responses may sometimes occur because sensory inputs to the amygdala may arrive faster than integrated, representational inputs from the hippocampus to the amygdala. This explains why, if one simultaneously looked at a pot handle and got burned on it, one would feel the burn before one realized "that handle burned me."

The important inputs that automatic evaluations may have for emotions and conscious attention and judgments show that the connections between the parallel affective and conscious processors are important to understand. My description of conscious experience of emotions, when one part of the brain "informs" another part about the output of a process, is the way a number of philosophers have described consciousness (e.g., Armstrong, 1968; Dennet, 1969; Lycan, 1987). Connectionist simulations, then, could be quite informative on this problem as well (see Greenwald, 1992; Rumelhart, Smolensky, McClelland, & Hinton, 1986). In fact, the view of specialized, parallel, and interconnecting brain modules is the one proposed by Gazzaniga (1985), based on research with clinical neurology patients and in experimental psychology. I would merely add that both the experimental evidence and the neurophysiological evidence indicate that automatic evaluation is one of the basic functions that some brain "module" performs.

Consciousness and Automatic Evaluation

In this chapter, I have reviewed much evidence to suggest that people automatically evaluate stimuli—that is, that they ascertain whether stimuli are good or bad, positive or negative for them, without knowing that they do this, without the intention to do it, and sometimes without being aware of the evaluated stimuli. In these senses, automatic evaluation is not a conscious process. Without being conscious of automatic evaluations or their effects, we cannot appreciate their influence on emotional experience and deliberate judgments. We are probably prevented from knowing automatic evaluations experientially by our particular neurophysiology, yet we perform them readily.

There is some clinical evidence about amnesics' evaluations that seems the perfect metaphor for understanding consciousness and automatic evaluations. Johnson, Kim, and Risse (1985) tested evaluations of two new kinds of stimuli in normal subjects, amnesic Korsakoff's patients, and alcoholic (but sober) subjects who were matched to the Korsakoff's subjects on age and education level. In Experiment 1, subjects listened to 32 unfamiliar Korean songs 1, 5, or 10 times each, which they rated as sounding American, "Chinese," or neither. Their liking and recognition for the melodies were tested later. As predicted, the results showed that all the subjects showed the exposure-breeds-liking effect. That is, even Korsakoff's patients liked the songs they had heard more often more than they liked less familiar songs. There was also a tendency for everyone to show better recognition for the melodies they had heard more times, although Korsakoff's patients had poorer recognition than the control subjects. These results showed that when affect depends mainly on perception, Korsakoff's patients were not impaired compared to normal controls.

Johnson et al. (1985), however, postulated that Korsakoff's patients would be impaired when their affective responses to stimuli would depend on what they call the "reflective" system, or the mental system that "involves conscious construction of patterns and relationships" (p. 22). In Experiment 2, the same subjects were shown photographs of two young men, one described as basically good, and one bad. Two hours later, the subjects experienced this procedure again, and rated the two men (time 1). At time 2, which was 2–6 days later, subjects were shown the two photographs and asked which person they preferred. They were also shown two distractor photographs (matched on hair color) and asked which of the four photographs were familiar, whether they recognized the photographs, what they knew about each person pictured, and rated the persons on 20 characteristics. This procedure was repeated at time 3, 10–29 days later.

All of the subjects recognized the faces at time 1 and time 3. All of the control subjects expressed preferences for the "good guy," as did the majority of the Korsakoff's patients at each time period (78% at time 1, 89% at time 2, and 78% at time 3). However, the separation of the conscious consideration processes from the evaluative response is apparent in the subjects' reports of the basis for their affective responses. All the control subjects reported basing their opinions on the descriptions they had heard. However, only one or two (depending on the measure) of the Korsakoff's patients said they had heard anything about the men previously. None of the Korsakoff's patients were able to free recall any information about the men photographed, and even probed recall yielded no memories. The results are consistent with Johnson et al.'s (1985) theory that Korsakoff's patients suffer from a deficit in their "reflection" systems. Without the ability to learn this kind of information, they still have affective responses to new stimuli and can evaluate new information, but they have no awareness of the basis for these evaluations.

Normal people are similar to Korsakoff's patients in being unable to be conscious of automatic evaluations. We can dislike or like people and things, experience emotions, and make deliberate judgments of stimuli, all without knowing the automatic evaluative basis for these judgments and emotions. Normal people, however, have an ability that the Korsakoff's patients did not have: the ability to apply deliberate attention to the stimuli they automatically evaluated (or their memory of the stimuli), and in so doing, to invent reasons for their evaluations.

Qualities of Automatic Evaluations

Further research may indicate further properties and consequences of automatic evaluations, but the research described here shows that automatic evaluations have the following qualities:

1. People ascertain the goodness or badness of stimuli upon exposure, but these automatic evaluations are not fine grained.

2. Automatic evaluations can occur without conscious awareness of the stimuli evaluated or of the process itself.

3. Automatic evaluations occur under a range of conditions and for a variety of stimuli: graphical, faces, and words.

4. Automatic evaluations are not contingent on a deliberate goal to evaluate.

5. People can control the influence that automatic evaluations have on subsequent judgments only when they are aware of the provoking stimuli and its potential influence.

6. Automatic evaluations can cause attention to be guided to valenced, especially negative, stimuli.

7. When the primary task is evaluation, automatic evaluations that are congruent with the deliberate task can help performance.

8. However, if the task requires much attention, automatic evaluation can hurt performance by taking attention (see also Kitayama & Howard, this volume).

Acknowledgments

I am grateful to Bertram Malle, Richard Marsh, John Gabrieli, Dan Levitin, Delia Cioffi, John Bargh, Paula Raymond, Guven Guzeldere, and the editors for their helpful comments on a previous version of this chapter, and to Ileana Perez, Dana Rabois, Candace Tom, Gayatri Taneja, and Gwen Byard for their assistance with some of the research reported herein.

References

Anderson, N. H. (1974). Cognitive algebra: Integration theory applied to social attribution. In L. Berkowitz (ed.), *Advances in experimental social psychology* (Vol. 7, pp. 2–102). San Diego, CA: Academic Press.

Armstrong, D. M. (1968). *A materialist theory of the mind*. London: Routledge & Kegan Paul.

Bargh, J. A. (1989). Conditional automaticity: Varieties of automatic influence in social perception and cognition. In J. Uleman & J. A. Bargh (eds.), *Unintended thought* (pp. 3–51). New York: Guilford.

Bargh, J. A., & Pratto, F. (1986). Individual construct accessibility and perceptual selection. *Journal of Experimental Social Psychology*, 22, 293–311.

Bargh, J. A., Litt, J. E., Pratto, F., & Spielman, L. A. (1989). On the preconscious evaluation of social stimuli. In K. McConkey & A. Bennet (eds.), *Proceedings of the XXIV International Congress of Psychology* (Vol. 3, pp. 357–370). Amsterdam: Elsevier/North Holland.

Bargh, J. A., Chaiken, S., Govender, R., & Pratto, F. (1992). The generality of the automatic attitude activation effect. *Journal of Personality and Social Psychology*, 62, 893–912.

Brewer, M. B., & Caporael, L. R. (1990). Selfish genes vs. selfish people: Sociobiology as origin myth. *Motivation and Emotion*, 14, 237–243.

Cheesman, J., & Merikle, P. M. (1986). Distinguishing conscious from unconscious perceptual processes. *Canadian Journal of Psychology*, 40, 343–367.

Cioffi, D. (1991). Sensory awareness versus sensory impression: Affect and attention interact to produce somatic meaning. *Cognition and Emotion*, 5, 275–294.

Corteen, R. S., & Dunn, D. (1974). Shock-associated words in a non-attended message: A test for momentary awareness. *Journal of Experimental Psychology*, 102, 1143–1144.

Corteen, R. S., & Wood, B. (1972). Autonomic responses to shock-associated words in an unattended channel. *Journal of Experimental Psychology,* 94, 308–313.

Dawes, R. M. (1979). The robust beauty of improper linear models in decision making. *American Psychologist,* 34, 571–582.

Dennet, D. C. (1969). *Content and consciousness.* London: Routledge & Kegan Paul.

Dennet, D. C. (1991). *Consciousness explained.* Boston: Little Brown.

Elssworth, P. C., & Smith, C. A. (1988). From appraisal to emotion: Differences among unpleasant feelings. *Motivation and Emotion,* 12, 271–302.

Fazio, R. H., Sanbonmatsu, D. M., Powell, M. C., & Kardes, F. R. (1986). On the automatic activation of attitudes. *Journal of Personality and Social Psychology,* 50, 299–238.

Fiske, S. T. (1980). Attention and weight in person perception: The impact of negative and extreme behavior. *Journal of Personality and Social Psychology,* 38, 889–906.

Friedman, A. (1979). Framing pictures: The role of knowledge in automatized encoding and memory for gist. *Journal of Experimental Psychology: General,* 108, 316–355.

Gazzaniga, M. S. (1985). *The social brain.* New York: Basic Books.

Greenwald, A. G. (1992). New Look 3: Unconscious cognition reclaimed. *American Psychologist,* 47, 766-779.

Hamilton, D. L., & Zanna, M. (1972). Differential weighing of favorable and unfavorable attributes in impressions of personality. *Journal of Experimental Research in Personality,* 6, 204–212.

Hansen, C. H., & Hansen, R. D. (1988). Finding the face in the crowd: An anger superiority effect. *Journal of Personality and Social Psychology,* 54, 917–924.

Higgins, E. T., Van Hook, E., & Dorfman, D. (1988). Do self-attributes form a cognitive structure? *Social Cognition,* 6, 177–206.

Holender, D. (1986). Semantic activation without conscious identification in dichotic listening, parafoveal vision, and visual masking: A survey and appraisal. *Behavioral and Brain Sciences,* 9, 1–66.

Johnson, M. K., & Hasher, L. (1987). Human learning and memory. *Annual Review of Psychology,* 38, 631–668.

Johnson, M. K., Kim, J. K., & Risse, G. (1985). Do alcoholic Korsakoff's syndrome patients acquire affective reactions? *Journal of Experimental Psychology: Learning, Memory, and Cognition,* 11, 22–36.

Johnston, V. S., & Wang, X. (1991). The relationship between menstrual phase and the P3 Component of ERPs. *Psychophysiology,* 28, 400–409.

Kahneman, D., & Treisman, A. (1984). Changing views of attention and automaticity. In R. Parasuraman & D. R. Davies (eds.), *Varieties of attention* (pp. 29–61). New York: Academic Press.

Kentridge, R. W., & Aggleton, J. P. (1990). Emotion: Sensory representation, reinforcement, and the temporal lobe. *Cognition and Emotion,* 4, 191–208.

Kitayama, S. (1991). Impairment of perception by positive and negative affect. *Cognition and Emotion,* 5, 255–274.

Kunst-Wilson, W. R., & Zajonc, R. B. (1980). Affective discrimination of stimuli that cannot be recognized. *Science,* 207, 557–558.

Lazarus, R. S. (1991). *Emotion and adaptation.* New York: Oxford University Press.

LeDoux, J. E. (1989). Cognitive–emotional interactions in the brain. *Cognition and Emotion,* 3, 267–289.

LeDoux, J. E. (1990). Representation of affect in neural circuits. In L. R. Squire, M. Mishkin, & A. P. Shimamura (eds.), *Learning and memory: Discussions in neuroscience* (pp. 64–68), Amsterdam: Elsevier.

LeDoux, J. E., Romanski, L., & Xagoraris, A. (1989). Indelibility of subcortical emotional memories. *Journal of Cognitive Neuroscience,* 1, 238–243.

Logan, G. D. (1980). Attention and automaticity in Stroop and priming tasks: Theory and data. *Cognitive Psychology, 12,* 523-553.

Logan, G. D. (1989). Automaticity and cognitive control. In J. S. Uleman & J. A. Bargh (eds.), *Unintended thought* (pp. 52–74). New York: Guilford.

Logan, G. D., & Cowan, W. B. (1984). On the ability to inhibit thought and action: A theory of an act of control. *Psychological Review, 91,* 295–327.

Lycan, W. (1987). *Consciousness.* Cambridge, MA: MIT Press.

MacLeod, C. M., & Dunbar, K. (1988). Training and Stroop-like interference: Evidence for a continuum of automaticity. *Journal of Experimental Psychology: Learning, Memory, and Cognition, 14,* 126–135.

Marcel, A. J. (1983). Conscious and unconscious perception: Experiments on visual masking and word recognition. *Cognitive Psychology, 15,* 197–237.

Matlin, M. W. (1971). Response competition, recognition, and affect. *Journal of Personality and Social Psychology, 19,* 295–300.

Meyer, D. E., & Schaneveldt, R. W. (1971). Facilitation in recognizing pairs of words: Evidence of a dependence between retrieval operations. *Journal of Experimental Psychology, 90,* 227–234.

Neely, J. H. (1977). Semantic priming and retrieval from lexical memory: Roles of inhibitionless spreading activation and limited-capacity attention. *Journal of Experimental Psychology: General, 106,* 225–254.

Neill, W. T. (1977). Inhibitory and facilitory processes in selective attention. *Journal of Experimental Psychology: Human Perception and Performance, 3,* 444–450.

Niedenthal, P. M. (1990). Implicit perception of affective information. *Journal of Experimental Social Psychology, 26,* 505–527.

Peabody, D. (1968). Group judgments in the Phillipines: Evaluative and descriptive aspects. *Journal of Personality and Social Psychology, 10,* 290–300.

Posner, M. I., & Snyder, C. R. R. (1975). Attention and cognitive control. In R. L. Solso (ed.), *Information processing and cognition: The Loyola symposium.* Hillsdale, NJ: Erlbaum.

Pratto, F. (1987). On the bipolarity of trait constructs. Unpublished master's thesis. New York University.

Pratto, F., & John, O. P. (1991). Automatic vigilance: The attention-grabbing power of negative social information. *Journal of Personality and Social Psychology, 61,* 380–391.

Pratto, F., Bargh, J. A., & John, O. P. (1993). On the bipolarity of trait constructs: Some priming experiments. Unpublished manuscript. Stanford University.

Rolls, E. T. (1990). A theory of emotion, and its applications to understanding the neural basis of emotion. *Cognition and Emotion, 4,* 161–190.

Roskos-Ewoldsen, D. R., & Fazio, R. H. (1992). On the orienting value of attitudes: Attitude accessibility as a determinant of an object's attraction of visual attention. *Journal of Personality and Social Psychology, 63,* 198–211.

Rumelhart, D. E., Smolensky, P., McClelland, J. L., & Hinton, G. E. (1986). Schemata and sequential thought processes in PDP Models. In J. L. McClelland, D. E. Rumelhart, and the PDP research group (eds.), *Parallel distributed processing: Explorations in the microstructure of cognition* (Vol. 2, pp. 7–57). Cambridge, MA: MIT Press.

Schachter, S., & Singer, J. (1962). Cognitive, social and physiological determinants of emotional state. *Psychological Review, 69,* 379–399.

Schneider, W., Dumais, S. T., & Shiffrin, R. M. (1984). Automatic and control processing and attention. In R. Parasuraman & R. Davies (eds.), *Varieties of attention* (pp. 1–27). New York: Academic Press.

Seamon, J. G., Brody, N., & Kauff, D. M. (1983). Affective discrimination of stimuli that are not recognized: Effects of shadowing, masking, and cerebral laterality. *Journal of Experimental Psychology: Learning, Memory, and Cognition, 9,* 544–555.

Seamon, J. G., Marsh, R. L., & Brody, N. (1984). Critical importance of exposure duration for affective discrimination of stimuli that are not recognized. *Journal of Experimental Psychology: Learning, Memory, and Cognition*, 10, 465-469.

Sears, D. O. (1983). The person-positivity bias. *Journal of Personality and Social Psychology*, 44, 233–250.

Spielman, L. A., Pratto, F., & Bargh, J. A. (1988). Automatic affect: Are one's moods, attitudes, evaluations, and emotions out of control? *American Behavioral Scientist*, 31, 296–311.

Stroop, J. R. (1935). Studies of interference in serial verbal reactions. *Journal of Experimental Psychology*, 18, 643–662.

Taylor, S. E. (1991). Asymmetrical effects of positive and negative events: The mobilization-minimization hypothesis. *Psychological Bulletin*, 110, 67–85.

Tipper, S. P. (1985). The negative priming effect: Inhibitory priming by ignored objects. *The Quarterly Journal of Experimental Psychology*, 37A, 571–590.

Treisman, A. (1982). Perceptual grouping and attention in visual search for features and objects. *Journal of Experimental Psychology: Human Perception and Performance*, 8, 194–214.

Zajonc, R. B. (1968). Attitudinal effects of mere exposure. *Journal of Personality and Social Psychology Monograph*, 9, 1–28.

Zajonc, R. B. (1980). Feeling and thinking: Preferences need no inferences. *American Psychologist*, 35, 151–175.

Zbrodoff, N. J., & Logan, G. D. (1986). On the autonomy of mental processes: A case study of arithmetic. *Journal of Experimental Psychology: General*, 115, 118–130.

Comments on Unconscious Processing: Finding Emotion in the Cognitive Stream

Marcia K. Johnson
Carolyn Weisz
Princeton University

No matter what their domain of research, scholarship, or practice, or their theoretical orientation, most psychologists have at least a closet interest in unconscious processes. In recent years, the question is often framed (some might say "sublimated") as a contrast between automatic and controlled processes, where automatic processes are those that take place outside of conscious awareness, are fast and effortless, and are unlikely to be disturbed by competing task demands. Interest in unconscious processes can be seen in questions such as: Are all meanings of a word simultaneously and automatically activated? Is frequency (or spatial or temporal) information encoded automatically? In what ways does information that we cannot voluntarily recall or recognize nevertheless influence our thought and behavior on priming and other transfer tests? Can emotion arise automatically, unaffected by cognition?

Such questions often turn out to be especially tricky, both conceptually and methodologically. Yet, as the chapters in this volume illustrate, they are central to an understanding of how the mind works. In particular, these chapters explore the extent to which emotion operates at the "front end" of cognition—during a hypothetical, unconscious stage of processing where perception and attention seem to grab stimulus information from the environment. This is sometimes described as an efficient, inflexible, encapsulated, context-free phase of cognition, where "thought" and goals as we phenomenally experience them exert no control. At issue is whether and how emotion affects the detection, identification, and classification of words and nonverbal stimuli such as faces or random shapes, and whether these effects are automatic. Before turning to the studies of emotion and cognition, however, we begin with a tale of a rejected manuscript (Wang & Johnson, 1978). Although the manuscript was about unconscious processing of frequency information, not unconscious processing of emotion, it points out some common themes that arise in work on unconscious processing.

Unconscious Processing of Frequency Information?

Wang and Johnson (1978) explored the intersect of two basic ideas. One was the suggestion that people may have some information about a stimulus even when they cannot tell the specific identity of the stimulus (e.g., Brand, 1971; Jonides & Gleitman, 1972; Postman, Bruner & McGinnies, 1948). The other was the suggestion that processes underlying the monitoring of recurrences, the recording of event frequency, and mechanisms controlling the availability of this information are likely central memory functions (e.g., Hasher & Chromiak, 1977; Johnson, 1977). The question Wang and Johnson (1978) investigated was whether subjects could draw on information reflecting word frequency even if they could not clearly identify a word (a possibility that had been raised, Broadbent, 1967; Brown & Rubenstein, 1961). The two experiments reported were relatively simple: high- or low-frequency four-letter words (e.g., MIND) were presented tachistoscopically and masked, followed by a forced-choice recognition test consisting of the target and a semantically unrelated high- or low-frequency distractor. Performance, measured by errors, response times, and confidence ratings, was better when target and distractor came from different frequency classes than when they came from the same frequency class. This overall pattern was obtained both when the test pairs were orthographically similar, differing in one letter (MIND–MEND) and when they were orthographically dissimilar and shared no letters (MIND–WORK).

The authors suggested that a sensitivity to frequency of occurrence which preceded conscious identification of an item would be a great value as a preattentive screening device for stimuli, allowing the unusual to stand out among the usual or vice versa. The ability to quickly differentiate the familiar from the unfamiliar, even under degraded conditions (e.g., low illumination levels, peripheral vision, noise, etc.) would have obvious evolutionary usefulness. A sensitivity to the frequency with which one has previously experienced an event would permit one to attend selectively to either the familiar or unfamiliar, depending on the goals of the moment.

While the functional importance of a mechanism(s) for detecting familiarity is obvious, the nature of the mechanism is not. Wang and Johnson (1978) suggested that in some situations qualitative or quantitative aspects of *processing* of high- and low-frequency items may differ and people may be sensitive to, though not necessarily conscious of, such characteristics of their own cognitive operations. They considered the possibility that peripheral processing (e.g., the extraction of visual features) of frequent items is faster for high- than for low-frequency items. If subjects were sensitive to the *speed of their own processing*, then this would be a potential discriminative cue on the recognition test. Although this idea seemed plausible (indeed the idea that subjects are sensitive to "perceptual fluency" [Jacoby & Dallas, 1981] now has wide acceptance), it did not exactly fit the particular results obtained. If more visual information were extracted per unit of time for high-frequency words, in addition to the superiority of test pairs differing in frequency, Wang and Johnson should also have obtained at least a small overall advantage for high-frequency targets, which they did not.

Wang and Johnson (1978) favored instead the idea that the amount or degree of dispersion of activation as a consequence of processing a stimulus is positively related to its frequency of occurrence. More activation should typically occur for high-frequency items because meaningfulness, indicated by, for example, the number of the relationships a word enters into (Noble, 1952; Paivio, Yuille, & Madigan, 1968), increases with frequency of occurrence (Noble, 1963; Paivio et al., 1968). If subjects were sensitive to the level of activation generated by an item, then they could potentially use this as a cue; that is, if they were sensitive to the amount of activation generated by the target item, on the forced-choice test between a high- and low-frequency item they could make a match based on the amount of activation of each of the two test items.

The idea that activation spreads based on meaningful (associative or semantic) relations, has had many proponents (e.g., Collins & Lofus, 1975; Meyer & Schvaneveldt, 1971; Osgood, 1953; Morgan & Underwood, 1950; Underwood, 1965). Some word-processing models further proposed that semantic spread to new items *followed* word recognition or detection (see Becker & Killion, 1977; Schvaneveldt, Meyer, & Becker, 1976).

An alternative considered by Wang and Johnson (1978) was that the threshold that is relevant for word identification (and/or conscious awareness or producing a naming response) may not be the same as the threshold that is relevant for initiating the spread of activation to semantically related trace systems. The idea that spreading excitation along semantic associations begins prior to final identification of a word was consistent with other findings suggesting the possibility of subliminal semantic effects (e.g., Dixon, 1971; Erdelyi, 1974) or simultaneous activation of multiple meanings of the same physical stimulus (e.g., Conrad, 1974; Warren & Warren, 1976). In short, if subjects were sensitive to (though not necessarily consciously aware of) the overall degree of activation generated by a subthreshold or incompletely identified stimulus, then this information could be used as a cue to the target's meaningfulness or frequency class.

Wang and Johnson (1978) further speculated that, more generally, attention is attracted by changes, in either direction, in ongoing activation level. Thus, attentional selection could occur not only on the basis of physical or semantic characteristics but on the basis of familiarity as well. Thus, we see a friend stand out in a crowd and yet see a stranger stand out among a group of friends.

The reviewers were not impressed by either the theorizing or the data. They wondered if the effect was somehow specific to the set of items used; maybe the items differed in some way other than word frequency. Maybe the obtained pattern was somehow produced by orthographic frequency letter contingencies at the subword level. The manuscript languished in the "to revise" pile. Perhaps today the same manuscript would get a more receptive set of reviewers, given the general acceptance of ideas such as "perceptual fluency" as a basis for judgment (e.g., Jacoby & Dallas, 1981); activation of semantic information prior to word identification (Marcel, 1983; Fowler, Wolford, Slade, & Tassinary, 1981); and the fundamental importance of frequency information across a range of tasks (Hasher & Zacks, 1979, 1984).

Our goal in recounting the story is not to revive the cause of unconscious processing of frequency. Rather, we want to make two points. First, we empathize with those who toil in the messy field of unconscious processing, and believe that it is healthy to cultivate some theoretical ideas, even if all the rocks have not been removed. Second, and more important, substitute "emotion" for "frequency" in the above discussion, and the argument would be similar to that represented in some of the chapters in this volume. The parallel illustrates something fundamental about unconscious processes: people seem able to unconsciously process many aspects of stimuli such as frequency, perceptual qualities, and affective connotation, and we may unconsciously abstract new relations and contingencies as well (Lewicki, 1986; Niedenthal, 1990; Reber, 1976; but see Perruchet, Gallego, & Savy, 1990).

Is all this information activated automatically and inevitably? Perhaps, but fast, "automatic" processing does not necessarily imply context-free processing that is immune to goals. The stimulus set, cues from instructions, and task demands can create an environment in which subjects show remarkable sensitivity to dimensions, recurrences, and regularities built into a stimulus set by the experimenter. We are inclined to believe that rather than simply reflecting static knowledge structures and inflexible, automatic "modules" or stages of processing, unconscious processes demonstrate some of the same flexibility that conscious processes do: they are sensitive to context, compute information along dimensions that fit current tasks, are opportunistic, and are affected by goals. With this set of assumptions in mind, we will consider some of the findings and ideas in this section of *The Heart's Eye*.

Emotion and "Front-End" Cognition

The chapters in the first section of this volume explore a variety of fundamental issues: Does mood affect not only what we think, but what we see? Do the emotional connotations of words affect perception and thought even before, and perhaps more strongly than, the semantic aspects of words? Can preferences and/or other evaluative responses to stimuli arise before we consciously identify stimuli or become conscious of our evaluations? Does unconscious affect control the deployment of attention? We briefly review some highlights of the chapters in this section, and consider the issues raised in the context of understanding emotion within a broader cognitive framework.

Moods and Spreading Activation

Niedenthal, Setterlund, and Jones (NSJ; this volume) suggest that identification of words whose meanings are congruent with a perceiver's current mood requires less sensory evidence than does identification of words that are not mood congruent. This prediction of perceptual facilitation follows from the idea that information is represented in nodes (or codes) within an interconnected associative network and that identification of a stimulus occurs when the activation in a node exceeds a certain threshold (e.g., Morton, 1969). In such a network, preactivation of a conceptual (or word) node would occur via spreading activation from node(s) that represent the mood or aspects of the mood. A preactivated representation would take less external input to reach its threshold of identification (i.e., conscious awareness). NSJ address a fundamental problem for such a view. Given this clear prediction, why has there been so little good evidence that mood affects perception in the way predicted (e.g., Gerrig & Bower, 1982; Clark, Teasdale, Broadbent, & Martin, 1983)?

NSJ suggest that most studies looking for the effects of mood on perception have been insensitive because they have not taken into account the probable organizational structure of the presumed underlying network. In a structured network, you would not expect activation to spread from a "sad" emotional state equally to any negatively valenced concept, nor from a "happy" emotional state equally to any positively valenced concept. For example, being sad should activate concepts and memories related to *sadness*, but not necessarily concepts and memories related to *fear*. Yet most prior work looked for mood effects on items drawn from a general, valenced (positive or negative) category rather than on items related to the more specific mood that had been invoked. Consistent with this, NSJ then show that the items used in perceptual tasks will determine whether mood effects are found.

NSJ played happy or sad classical music to induce moods (Eich & Metcalfe, 1989) and then had subjects decide whether letter strings were words or nonwords (lexical decision task). The words represented the categories of happy, positive, sad, negative, and neutral and were equated across categories for frequency, length, and immovability (but not, perhaps importantly, for familiarity or interitem associations). Consistent with previous research, the happy and sad subjects did not differ in the time required to make lexical decisions about positively and negatively valenced words that were not specifically related to the induced happy and sad moods. Thus, from these data alone it appears that mood does not affect perception. The intriguing new finding was that happy subjects made lexical decisions about happy words faster than did sad subjects and sad subjects made lexical decisions about sad words faster than did happy subjects. This outcome is clearly consistent with the idea that mood effects in perception and memory may be much more specific than previously assumed.

In another experiment, subjects categorized photographs of faces as male and female as quickly as possible. The faces expressed happiness, sadness, or a neutral emotion. For the male faces only, there was a marginally significant interaction such that sad subjects were slow compared to happy subjects on the happy faces and fast compared to happy subjects on the sad faces. These results were weaker than the lexical decision findings. However, if substantiated with future work, they raise the interesting question of how mood congruence might affect face perception. In a semantic network of concepts represented by words, it is relatively easy to imagine a word becoming preactivated as a consequence of one's mood and hence easier to process. In the case of novel faces that presumably are not already existing nodes in the semantic network, the relevant preactivation that is driven by mood presumably is of component features of various facial expressions or an expression prototype. This feature or prototype preactivation presumably would allow one to process mood-congruent expressive features of new faces more quickly and hence make any identification responses, such as gender, more quickly.

The idea that moods propagate activation through a network in a relatively differentiated or "categorical" way nicely accounts for asymmetrical effects of positive and negative moods reported in the mood and memory literature. Positive emotions more consistently cue emotion-congruent information than do negative emotions (Blaney, 1986; Singer & Salovey, 1988). NSJ suggest that the positive material used in experiments typically more closely matches the induced mood (usually happiness) than does the negative material match the induced mood (usually sadness).

NSJ also discuss the notion that activation spreading from an emotion node such as *sad* may be greater than the activation spreading from a category node such as *furniture* (Gilligan & Bower, 1984). The general idea seems to be that emotional arousal contributes to the spread of excitation, either by producing more activation, longer lasting activation, or activation that spreads further. This provides a potential mechanism for how emotion might disrupt thought processes under certain circumstances. Activation generated from nonemotional concepts (being less strong, briefer, or spreading less far) would not compete effectively with activation generated from emotional concepts. But note, it should be possible to offset such emotional effects with activation generated by ongoing goals or "agendas" (Johnson, 1992; Johnson & Hirst, 1993), which presumably could help keep nonemotional information activated and competitive.

An idea expressed by NSJ that seems problematic to us is that emotion words and emotion knowledge are different than other words and knowledge because they are *felt*, whereas other concepts are not. Consider, for example, ideas like *chair*, *spin*, or *bicycle*, which though not obviously emotional, likely consist of some body knowledge. Conversely, as NSJ point out, activation of words and propositions about emotions do not always activate bodily sensations. Thus, although the somatic aspects of emotion are clearly phenomenally salient and theoretically important, emotional stimuli are unlikely to be unique in their connections with bodily sensations.

A related key idea developed by NSJ is that emotional knowledge exists on at least three basic levels: in a lexicon, as conceptual knowledge, and in somatic representations. However, probably most knowledge includes such levels of information. The main value of emphasizing various "levels" of representation is not to qualitatively distinguish emotion from other categories of experience, but to emphasize the point that not all aspects of emotional knowledge are activated in any particular situation. As NSJ suggest, activation at a given level might sometimes occur with and sometimes without activation at other levels. It seems to us, moreover, in accounting for why activation might sometimes stay within one level and sometimes spread to others, we again enter the domains of context, goals, and control.

Finally, NSJ depict categorical organization at every level of representation (e.g., somatic, conceptual, lexical), implying that interconnections between levels are also organized primarily categorically. But categorical organization may not exist at all levels. Moods may be partially created and maintained because of the activation of certain nonsomatic (e.g., conceptual) representations. Thus, it is possible that the categorical structure of emotional representation resides primarily at conceptual and lexical levels, while representations are less categorical and perhaps only loosely valenced at the somatic level. In order to test the idea that *somatic* representations are themselves categorically organized, one would want to induce moods categorically (e.g., distinguishing between anger and sadness) in ways that do not rely on conceptual and lexical information—a task that seems nearly impossible. For example, sad music probably evokes conceptual associations with sadness as well as instigating somatic affect consistent with a sad mood.

Chronic Evaluation

Pratto (this volume) develops the hypothesis that we chronically *evaluate* stimuli without awareness, and suggests that negative stimuli, especially, attract attention. She advances the argument that chronic evaluation and predisposition toward evolutionarily important stimuli result in a process called "automatic vigilance." As supporting evidence for chronic evaluation, she notes that subjects may show preferences for previously exposed stimuli over new stimuli, even though subjects had not consciously evaluated the stimuli during the preexposure phase (e.g., Seamon, Brody, & Kauff, 1983).

However, as Pratto notes, the fact that these Phase 2 judgments are affected by exposure to the stimuli in Phase 1 does not necessarily mean subjects automatically evaluated the stimuli in Phase 1. One possibility is that subjects have picked up some information in Phase 1 that may be used in making preference judgments in Phase 2 (see also Klinger & Greenwald, this volume). In other tasks, the same information might be used to make nonevaluative judgments when no other basis for decision is readily available (such as lightness or darkness judgments, see Mandler, Nakamura, & Van Zandt, 1987).

Another type of evidence discussed by Pratto is a study by Bargh, Litt, Pratto, and Spielman (1989). Subjects were given brief presentations of personality trait adjectives (e.g., *gentle*). Subjects received semantic probes (choose the word most like the one presented from a pair such as *kind* or *intelligent*) and evaluative probes (was the word *good* or *bad*?). Above-chance performance on the evaluative questions occurred at briefer stimulus presentations compared to the semantic questions. Because people were accurate at the evaluation judgment at such short exposure durations, Pratto suggests that evaluation may occur more readily than the rest of meaning apprehension; that is, people evaluate stimuli preconsciously when a stimulus is presented even though they have no intention to do so.

Similarly, in a study by Fazio, Sanbonmatsu, Powell, and Kardes (1986), subjects were required to evaluate trait adjectives by responding *good* or *bad*. Each item was primed by valenced items such as *priest, pizza,* or *toothache*. Subjects evaluated the adjectives more quickly when the prime (e.g., *pizza*) and the target (e.g., *intelligent*) had the same valence than when the valences of the prime and target were inconsistent. Similar effects were reported by Bargh, Chaiken, Govender, and Pratto (1992). Pratto concludes that attitudes automatically become activated on exposure to the prime stimuli—the facilitation/inhibition presumably reflects this automatic, ongoing evaluation. But, as Pratto notes, the general task context might contribute to such effects. The subject's ongoing and primary task is to evaluate target stimuli; if the responses of "good" and "bad" are highly activated throughout the task, it seems likely they would be applied to the primes as well as the targets in this context. A response to the prime that fits the response appropriate for the target should produce faster times than mismatched responses (i.e., there may be response or motor priming). This does not imply, however, that evaluative responses would be major components of the responses to such items in a nonevaluative context.

More directly to the point that subjects may make evaluative responses when not directed to do so are the Pratto and John (1991) studies. Subjects named the color of the print of personality trait words (e.g., *honest*). Subjects took longer to respond to negative than to positive trait words and remembered the negative words better on a recall test. Furthermore, in a subsequent experiment described by Pratto, subjects took longer on the negative items even when warned (incorrectly) that they might take longer on the positive words. These findings are consistent with the idea that valenced information is activated when not directly relevant to the task, and even when it might interfere with the primary task.

Pratto describes a related experiment in which subjects named print colors of negative (*mutilating, violence*), positive (*kissing, baby*), and neutral (*administer, doorstep*) verbs and nouns. In this case, response times to negative and positive items did not differ and both were slower than to neutral items. However, when items having to do with "romance, violent sex, or babies" were replaced with other items, the negatives again were slower than the positives. (Items were controlled for frequency and word length.) Pratto concludes that negative stimuli and reproductively relevant positive stimuli are particularly "attention grabbing." In short, "simple evaluation as good or bad appears to occur automatically in every sense of the word: effortlessly, uncontrollable, outside of awareness. Yet it signals consciousness by guiding attention to valenced information."

Pratto also makes the interesting suggestion that although evaluation may be chronic, it is not particularly "fine grained" or discriminating. The average response times to name colors of negative traits was longer than the average response times to name colors of positive traits, but the degree of negativity or positivity did not matter.

This rather gross differentiation between negative and positive items in color naming is in contrast to the more categorical mood effects reported by NJS in the lexical decision task. It would be interesting to see if mood-induced subjects would show categorical interference effects in the color-naming task. Such an outcome would suggest that moods can structure spreading activation when reading is incidental to a task (color naming) as well as when it is central to a task (lexical decision). Another possibility is that the word processing that goes on in color naming taps into earlier phases of word processing than does lexical decision. And, as discussed in the next section, there may be even less differentiated affective responses that operate in even earlier stages of word processing. Using a task requiring the perceptual identification of briefly presented words, Kitayama and Howard (this volume) suggest that affective responses discriminate emotional from nonemotional stimuli, but do not differentiate positive from negative stimuli.

Before moving on to consider the Kitayama and Howard chapter, we make one additional comment. Although the results of Pratto and John's (1991) color naming studies present a provocative pattern, they are not entirely persuasive with respect to Pratto's two main points: (1) that evaluation is chronic, regardless of intentions and task demands; and (2) that negative stimuli especially attract attention. The interpretive problem arises, we think, from the possibility of context effects in the color-naming task. As has been noted about semantic priming, estimates of priming vary, depending on the proportion of items of a particular type included in the test list (e.g., Neely, Keefe, & Ross, 1989; Tweedy, Lapinski, & Schvaneveldt, 1977). So, estimates of interference in the color-naming task might be affected by the proportion or items of a particular type. More important, perhaps, the inter-item associations among the words would be expected to affect the extent to which word reading interferes with color naming. If there is semantic priming among items, this would increase activation on particular items, making the reading response easier and consequently increasing the word's potential for competition with color naming. Neither the "expectancy" created by many words of the same type nor the impact of interitem semantic relations on activation level need be "conscious." Furthermore, in the studies described by Pratto, there may be more or stronger interitem relations among the negative (and among a subset of the positive) items than among neutral items. In short, semantic or associative relations among words could increase their activation levels, creating interference in color naming. Such an effect would be expected even when the items are not emotionally loaded. Controlling for word length and frequency among item sets does not control for familiarity and interitem associative relations. The results would more strongly imply chronic evaluation and an advantage for negative items if obtained with only a few unrelated negative and positive target items embedded in many neutral items.

Affect and the Amplification of Attention

Kitayama and Howard (K&H, this volume) assume semantic activation similar to that discussed by NSJ. They also are interested in the attention-grabbing aspects of emotion, as is Pratto. Their notion is that preconscious activation of a *perceptual* code is sufficient to elicit some emotion associated with the code and that this preconscious affect amplifies the attentional processing directed in the region of the perceptual code. According to K&H, whether this "amplified" attention results in enhancement or impairment of conscious perception depends on whether it falls on a relatively isolated target stimulus candidate (producing enhancement), or on a larger set of items including activated competitors (producing impairment).

These ideas were investigated in a study in which trials consisted of a target word flashed at 33 msec, followed by a choice between a pair of words consisting of the target and a distractor with the same valence (Kitayama, 1992). Accuracy of identification did not differ for negative and positive items. Furthermore, whether accuracy was higher or lower for the emotional than for the neutral items depended on word length. For short words, identification of emotional items was worse, and for long words, identification of emotional items was slightly better. K&H suggest this pattern arises because there are fewer likely alternatives for the long than for the short words and thus affect is more likely to amplify the attention given to the correct item relative to its potential competitors in the case of short words. The idea that attention is amplified, however, does not seem to add much to what might follow from a simple notion of spreading activation. If, compared to long words, short words give rise to more alternatives that are more densely connected to other words, any increase in activation would spread more among short words, causing more potential interference.

The particularly interesting idea here is that affect is connected to *perceptual* codes. Thus, a presumably at-one-time neutral perceptual stimulus configuration, such as SEX, comes (presumably through contiguity and other mechanisms) to be affectively charged: emotion is not only attached to the meaning of the message but to the perceptual aspects of the messenger. Because it seems unlikely that affect is connected to individual letter features, the code to which affect is connected must be fairly well developed. But once we start assuming that affect is attached to a high-level perceptual code via learning, it seems to us that we are already in the realm of meaning. The configuration SEX* (the * indicates "important" or "significant" but does not give any evidence of valence) seems to us to constitute a primitive semantics. The fact that activation occurs prior to identification does not necessarily imply it is presemantic (after all, semantic processing occurs prior to identification, Marcel, 1983). Thus, a more general question raised by thinking about Kitayama and Howard's findings is: In what sense are functionally important cues not semantic, especially those that have acquired their functional importance through learning? A related issue is whether the activation of emotional significance occurring prior to conscious identification is valenced or unvalenced. Although K&H describe amplification as an undifferentiated response to emotional stimuli, it is possible that processing of emotional significance is categorical in nature. Codes indicating either positive or negative significance might both trigger attentional processes with the same effect.

Another central consideration raised by K&H is that different aspects of events (e.g., voice quality and verbal content of a spoken message) may carry different affective messages, and the potential for one to interfere with the identification of the affective message of the other depends on the relative ease with which the affective information of each can be extracted. K&H describe a study by Kitayama, Taylor, Brown, and Currier (1992) in which subjects were less accurate and slower to identify the negative semantic content of sentences (e.g., *The house was badly damaged last month*) when the sentences were spoken in a positive tone than when they were spoken in a neutral or negative tone. These kind of "mixed-message" situations are one of life's greater social challenges and constitute a rich domain for research. For example, a subtler (but still conflicting) voice tone might produce less interference, or, given the same voice tone, the degree of interference when tone and message conflict should be related to the semantic complexity of the message or to individual differences in comprehension ability. (We may be particularly likely to give such mixed messages to students who are doing poorly by adopting an especially encouraging voice tone when the feedback is "bad." Those students who are going to find it hardest to comprehend the semantic content of the message are perhaps going to be most influenced, and potentially misled, by the upbeat tone.)

What Gives Rise to Preferences?

Klinger and Greenwald (K&G, this volume) report several experiments by Klinger (1991) patterned after Kunst-Wilson and Zajonc (1980). Klinger presented subjects with five brief (16.7 msec each) exposures to irregular attractive or unattractive (based on other subjects' ratings) octagons in phase one and then in phase two paired these preexposed stimuli with new octagons. Subjects were asked to choose the old item from each pair or to pick the one they liked better. When no mask was used in the preexposure phase (so subjects could clearly see the stimuli) both recognition and preference for old items was above chance. When a mask was used, recognition was at chance, and prior exposure increased preferences for attractive items but decreased it for unattractive items.

A similar pattern was found with attractive or unattractive names drawn from the telephone book. In phase one, subjects judged the number of syllables in each name and in phase two, subjects rated how much they liked items from a list of old and new names that were matched for attractiveness. Subjects preferred the exposed names. In another condition, Klinger attempted to reduce explicit memory for the preexposed items by introducing a distracting task between phase one and phase two. In this case, subjects preferred the preexposed attractive names, but the preexposed unattractive names were slightly less preferred than the new names.

K&G use these results to argue against the notion that exposure increases preference. Their explanation of why liking judgments are mediated by stimulus attractiveness begins with the commonly accepted idea that exposure generates perceptual records that when activated again can give rise to a feeling of familiarity (e.g., Mandler, 1980; Jacoby & Dallas, 1981). K&G note that feelings of familiarity may be attributed to various sources, depending on task demands. They then propose that source attributions account for the mediating effect of attractiveness in the preexposure/ preference paradigm. This last step in the logic is unclear to us. How exactly are source attributions operating (and being mediated by attractiveness) when subjects make liking judgments about polygons and names? (Although we, too, see source monitoring as a fundamental cognitive function [e.g., Johnson, 1988; Johnson, Hashtroudi, & Lindsay, 1993], this is a case where it does not seem central.)[1]

Most previous findings regarding brief preexposure and preference can be explained by assuming that in the absence of any particular preference subjects use differential familiarity responses to choose stimuli in a situation in which they find it difficult to discriminate among stimuli on any other basis. What is especially noteworthy about the results described by K&G is that here preexposure appears to play a role in subjects' computations of attractiveness (as indexed by other subjects' ratings). It is as if preexposure

---

[1]Klinger and Greenwald in fact discuss some other findings that are not directed specifically at affect, but are quite instructive about source monitoring. K&G found the "false fame" effect (Jacoby, Kelley, Brown, & Jasechko, 1989) as a consequence of preexposure of nonfamous names only for previously exposed attractive names, not for previously exposed unattractive names. In another judgment condition, subjects judged that preexposed attractive (but not unattractive) names belonged to a famous senator, and in yet another condition that preexposed unattractive (but not attractive) names belonged to a famous criminal. These studies nicely highlight the fact that the familiarity of stimuli is interpreted in light of task demands, prior beliefs, and so forth to determine the attributions made in a particular situation. Because source attributions are clearly involved in these latter cases, K&G suggest that source attributions must then be involved in the case of liking judgments. However, this connection is not clear to us.

facilitates extracting aspects of a stimulus that affect attractiveness ratings, making the attractiveness of a preexposed attractive stimulus slightly more available than that of its matched distractor and making the unattractiveness of a preexposed unattractive stimulus slightly more available than that of its matched distractor. That is, preexposure may make aspects of the stimulus that are actually relevant to the liking judgment pop out— preexposure may sensitize subjects to aspects of the stimulus that may later be used in a more deliberate way to make attractiveness ratings. This is quite interesting. The fact that the effects of the attractiveness variable wash out when preexposed stimuli are better remembered (not masked originally, or not subject to manipulations to cause forgetting) suggests that feature pop-out effects are subtle and/or fragile and likely not to be noticed or acted upon when stronger, more salient old/new recognition responses occur.

In short, we agree with K&G that there is no evidence that affect was computed unconsciously in the preexposure phase for incompletely processed (unconscious) stimuli, but they have an intriguing demonstration that the information picked up during such preexposures can influence judgments of affect. Furthermore, their results cannot easily be interpreted as an instance of subjects saying to themselves that they do not know which they prefer so they will simply choose on the basis of familiarity. Here, preexposure seems to affect actual evaluative judgments by influencing availability of aspects of the stimulus relevant to evaluative judgments.

General Issues

All of these chapters explore the idea that emotion is a fundamental part of our transaction with the environment. They suggest that emotion may control our attention, even determine the product of earliest perceptual processing. Furthermore, the impact of emotion may be automatic, beyond control. By way of summary, we will consider three questions central to this characterization of cognition and emotion.

What is the nature of the earliest emotional responses generated by stimuli?   Three possibilities are suggested by these chapters: the earliest states of information processing may produce only an unvalenced affective significance (Kitayama & Howard); or, early responses may include valenced affective significance (Pratto); or, early responses may reflect a more categorically differentiated significance (Niedenthal, Setterlund, & Jones). Perhaps one could decide among these possibilities if they were contrasted using the same stimuli in the same paradigm (word identification, color naming, lexical decision, etc.).

Another possibility is that each research program could be tapped into different stages of preidentification processing, perhaps because of processing characteristics of the different tasks used (e.g., color naming of a word string may be affected by earlier stages of word processing than is a lexical decision about it). We might adopt such a serial processing model in which, for any particular stimulus, information specifying emotional significance is generated before information specifying positive or negative valence, which in turn arises before information specifying the categorical nature (e.g., sadness or fear) of the valenced response. Although sequenced, all phases are completed before stimulus identification.

An alternative possibility is that the pattern of activation generated by a stimulus and the time course of the development of the activation are not fixed, but depend on the task environment, the subject's goals, and so forth (an "opportunistic" model). Like the serial model, the opportunistic model assumes that different patterns of activation probably yield information that is differentially useful for different tasks. The difference is that in the opportunistic model, whether this information is likely to affect task performance —or to be quickly processed for that matter—depends on factors in addition to the strength of the preexperimental bond between perceptual features of the stimulus and various semantic and somatic aspects of emotional experience. Thus, whether valenced information is available early may depend on such factors as how many other strongly valenced stimuli have been recently processed (thus having an opportunity to spread activation to the target in question), the subject's activated agendas (e.g., whether there is a current goal or an active set to evaluate), and whether there are other strong, competing cues in the stimulus or goal environment that inhibit or functionally offset activation-yielding affective information.

How should we characterize the relation between emotion and perception?   One possibility is that emotion operates *on* perception. In this view, perception is separate from emotion; emotion serves to energize otherwise activated pathways (K&H), preactivate representations (NJS), or draw attention to particular stimuli (Pratto).

An alternative idea is that emotion does not so much act on perception, rather emotion, like semantics, is an integral part of phenomenal perception; that is, emotion, like meaning, is part of what constitutes perception. In fact, in this view, emotion is part of semantics (e.g., Osgood, Suci, & Tannenbaum, 1957), hence the issue of whether emotion precedes semantics would not make much sense. It would still be interesting if, say, under some particular set of degraded stimulus conditions, valence information was available before, say, taxonomic category information. However, statements about the relative potency of emotion and other semantic relations would have to be based on procedures that fairly equated the potential within sets of items for interitem priming, the perceived goal relevance of the valence and categorical information, and so forth. Unfortunately, if interitem priming itself is context dependent, trying to equate "emotion" and "semantic" sets of items may be an ultimately impossible task. Consequently, rather than contrast the potency of emotion and semantics in a presumed static associative structure, research questions might be rephrased to emphasize the dynamic interactive quality of cognition. For example, we might ask not whether emotion precedes semantics (or stimulus identification, etc.) but instead attempt to characterize the conditions favoring or not favoring the computation of emotion. With this orientation in mind, failures to find "automatic" encoding of affect (e.g., in the second half of the trials in the Kitayama and Ferguson [1992] study described by K&H) are interesting as well.

What is the functional importance of "front-end" emotion in perception and thought?   When emotion does play an early role in processing stimuli, what are the consequences of such affective responses? Consider the case of meaning: even if all meanings of a stimulus are activated simultaneously independent of context, within milliseconds one meaning typically comes to dominate comprehension of the message. Activated information that is not relevant to ongoing schemas seems quite fragile, at least by some measures. The message as comprehended at the idea level is likely to determine what is available for voluntary recall, what further information is sought out, and what inferences seem reasonable and justified. Under some circumstances, the "discarded" meanings seem to play relatively little functional role. When is activated but unattended affective information equally fragile? If I am fleetingly (unconsciously) negatively valenced by something you say, but generally delighted by your message (which fits my own view nicely), under what circumstances does that moment of unconscious negative valence have functional consequences and under what circumstances does it not? In other words, when are we at the mercy of unchecked, perceptually driven, and associative activation and when are we not?

Concluding Remarks

We have focused on aspects of these chapters relevant to clarifying the role of affect in perceptual processing. In addressing issues such as whether affect precedes semantic analysis (or vice versa), we should keep in mind that in dividing significance into categories such as affective and semantic, we have useful categories for conceptualizing the types of information encoded and remembered (e.g., Johnson et al., 1993), but affect and semantics may not arise in fixed temporal order, in a linear information processing stream. The computations involved in both affect and semantics are likely to be influenced by structure within the stimulus array and by goals and motives active at the time. Emotion does not have to be computed "first" to be automatic, or to be independent of goals or context in order to be judged central for our understanding of cognition. Feelings are critical to defining motives and agendas; they signal the potential importance of events, they activate related knowledge, they determine what we ruminate about. Their functional role in perception and thought must be enormous, whether we think of them as "first" or "later," or "immersed" in the cognitive stream. In fact, their profound functional importance may arise not because they come first, but because they act iteratively.

In short, we do not have to settle the issue of which information is "first" or which is more affected by context or agendas to get the main message. As clearly illustrated by the work reported in these chapters, affective connotations of stimuli, like other aspects of meaning (e.g., Marcel, 1983; Treisman, 1960), can be activated without intention or awareness and provide a perhaps underestimated influence on perception, thought, and action. Moreover, taken together, the studies described in these papers are quite consistent with the view that perceptual cues can give rise to affect in the absence of reflection (e.g., Johnson & Multhaup, 1992). At the same time, it becomes increasingly clear that the human cognitive system is capable of responding and/or learning to respond along many different dimensions (e.g., graphemic, phonemic, frequency, semantic, affective) extremely rapidly. This incredible flexibility of rapid "front-end" computations along many dimensions and categories, and not a special capacity for any single one (e.g., frequency/novelty or affective significance), may be the real evolutionary story here.

Acknowledgment

Preparation of this paper was supported by NIA Grants AG09744 and AG09253.

References

Bargh, J. A., Chaiken, S., Govender, R., & Pratto, F. (1992). The generality of the automatic attitude activation effect. *Journal of Personality and Social Psychology, 62,* 893–912.

Bargh, J. A., Litt, J. E., Pratto, F., & Spielman, L. A. (1989). On the preconscious evaluation of social stimuli. In A. F. Bennet & K. M. McConkey (eds.), *International congress of psychology XXIV. Cognition in individual and social contexts* (Vol. 3, pp. 357–370). Amsterdam: Elsevier/North Holland.

Becker, C. A., & Killion, T. H. (1977). Interaction of visual and cognitive effects in word recognition. *Journal of Experimental Psychology: Human Perception and Performance, 3,* 389–401.

Blaney, P. H. (1986). Affect and memory: A review. *Psychological Bulletin, 99,* 229–246.

Brand, J. (1971). Classification without identification in visual search. *Quarterly Journal of Experimental Psychology, 23,* 178–186.

Broadbent, D. E. (1967). Word-frequency effect and response bias. *Psychological Review, 74,* 1–15.

Brown, C. & Rubenstein, H. (1961). Test of response bias explanation of word-frequency effect. *Science*, 133, 280–281.

Clark, D. M., Teasdale, J. D., Broadbent, D. E., & Martin, M. (1983). Effect of mood on lexical decisions. *Bulletin of the Psychonomic Society*, 21(3), 175–178.

Collins, A. M., & Loftus, E. F. (1975). A spreading-activation theory of semantic processing. *Psychological Review*, 82, 407–428.

Conrad, C. (1974). Context effects in sentence comprehension: A study of the subjective lexicon. *Memory and Cognition*, 2, 130–138.

Dixon, N. F. (1971). *Subliminal perception: The nature of a controversy.* London: McGraw-Hill.

Eich, E., & Metcalfe, J. (1989). Mood dependent memory for internal versus external events. *Journal of Experimental Psychology: Learning, Memory, and Cognition*, 15, 443–455.

Erdelyi, M. H. (1974). A new look at the new look: Perceptual defense and vigilance. *Psychological Review*, 81, 1–25.

Fazio, R. H., Sanbonmatsu, D. M., Powell, M. C., & Kardes, F. R. (1986). On the automatic activation of attitudes. *Journal of Personality and Social Psychology*, 50, 229–238.

Fowler, C. A., Wolford, G., Slade, R., & Tassinary, L. (1981). Lexical access with and without awareness. *Journal of Experimental Psychology: General*, 110, 341–362.

Gerrig, R. J., & Bower, G. H. (1982). Emotional influences on word recognition. *Bulletin of the Psychonomic Society*, 19(4), 197–200.

Gilligan, S. G., & Bower, G. H. (1984). Cognitive consequences of emotional arousal. In C. E. Izard, J. Kagan, & R. B. Zajonc (eds.), *Emotions, cognition, and behavior* (pp. 547–588). Cambridge: Cambridge University Press.

Greenwald, A. G., Klinger, M. R., & Liu, T. J. (1989). Unconscious processing of dichoptically masked words. *Memory & Cognition*, 17, 35–47.

Hasher, L., & Chromiak, W. (1977). The processing of frequency information: An automatic mechanism? *Journal of Verbal Learning and Verbal Behavior*, 16, 173–184.

Hasher, L., & Zacks, R. T. (1979). Automatic and effortful processes in memory. *Journal of Experimental Psychology: General*, 108, 356–388.

Hasher, L., & Zacks, R. T. (1984). Automatic processing of fundamental information: The case of frequency of occurrence. *American Psychologist*, 39(12), 1372–1388.

Jacoby, L. L., & Dallas, M. (1981). On the relationship between autobiographical memory and perceptual learning. *Journal of Experimental Psychology: General*, 110, 306–340.

Jacoby, L. L., Kelley, C., Brown, J., & Jasechko, J. (1989). Becoming famous overnight: Limits on the ability to avoid unconscious influences of the past. *Journal of Personality and Social Psychology*, 56, 326–338.

Johnson, M. K. (1977). What is being counted none the less? In I. M. Birnbaum & E. S. Parker (eds.), *Alcohol and human memory* (pp. 43–57). Hillsdale, NJ: Erlbaum.

Johnson, M. K. (1988). Discriminating the origin of information. In T. F. Oltmanns & B. A. Maher (eds.), *Delusional beliefs* (pp. 34–65). New York: Wiley.

Johnson, M. K. (1992). MEM: Mechanisms of recollection. *Journal of Cognitive Neuroscience*, 4, 268–280.

Johnson, M. K., & Hirst, W. (1993). MEM: Memory subsystems as processes. In A. F. Collins, S. E. Gathercole, M. A. Conway, & P. E. Morris (eds.), *Theories of memory* (pp. 241–286). Hove (UK): Erlbaum.

Johnson, M. K., & Multhaup, K. S. (1992). Emotion and MEM. In S.-A. Christianson (ed.), *The handbook of emotion and memory: Research and theory* (pp. 33–66). Hillsdale, NJ: Erlbaum.

Johnson, M. K., & Sherman, S. J. (1990). Constructing and reconstructing the past and the future in the present. In E. T. Higgins & R. M. Sorrentino (eds.), *Handbook of motivation and cognition: Foundations of social behavior* (Vol. 2, pp. 482–526). New York: Guilford Press.

Johnson, M. K., Hashtroudi, S., & Lindsay, D. S. (1993). Source monitoring. *Psychological Bulletin*, 114, 3–28.

Jonides, J., & Gleitman, H. (1972). A conceptual category effect in visual search: O as letter or as digit. *Perception and Psychophysics, 12*, 457–460.

Kitayama, S. (1992). Affect and perception: Some implications of the amplification model. Unpublished manuscript, University of Oregon.

Kitayama, S., & Ferguson, C. M. (1992). Emotional voice quality and emotional verbal content in speech perception: An exploration with a Stroop task. Unpublished manuscript. University or Oregon.

Kitayama, S., Taylor, T., Brown, T., & Currier, J. (1992). The biasing effects of emotional voice tone in sentence comprehension. Unpublished manuscript. University of Oregon.

Klinger, M. R. (1991). Conscious and unconscious processing in the mere exposure effect. Unpublished doctoral dissertation. University of Washington.

Kunst-Wilson, W. R., & Zajonc, R. B. (1980). Affective discrimination of stimuli that cannot be recognized. *Science, 207*, 557–558.

Lewicki, P. (1986). Processing information about covariations that cannot be articulated. *Journal of Experimental Psychology: Learning, Memory, and Cognition, 12*, 135–146.

Mandler, G. (1980). Recognizing: The judgment of previous occurrence. *Psychological Review, 87*, 252–271.

Mandler, G., Nakamura, Y., & Van Zandt, B. J. S. (1987). Nonspecific effects of exposure on stimuli that cannot be recognized. *Journal of Experimental Psychology: Learning, Memory, and Cognition, 13*, 646–648.

Marcel, A. J. (1983). Conscious and unconscious perception: Experiments on visual masking and word recognition. *Cognitive Psychology, 15*, 197–237.

Meyer, D. E., & Schvaneveldt, R. W. (1971). Facilitation in recognizing pairs of words: Evidence of a dependence between retrieval operations. *Journal of Experimental Psychology, 90*, 227–234.

Morgan, R. L., & Underwood, B. J. (1950). Proactive inhibition as a function of response similarity. *Journal of Experimental Psychology, 40*, 592–603.

Morton, J. (1969). Interaction of information in word recognition. *Psychological Review, 76*, 165–178.

Neely, J. H., Keefe, D. E., & Ross, K. L. (1989). Semantic priming in the lexical decision task: Roles of prospective prime-generated expectancies and retrospective semantic matching. *Journal of Experimental Psychology: Learning, Memory, and Cognition, 15*, 1003–1019.

Niedenthal, P. M. (1990). Implicit perception of affective information. *Journal of Experimental Social Psychology, 26*, 505–527.

Noble, C. E. (1952). An analysis of meaning. *Psychological Review, 59*, 421–430.

Noble, C. E. (1963). Meaningfulness and familiarity. In C. N. Cofer & B. S. Musgrave (eds.), *Verbal behavior and learning: Problems and processes* (pp. 76–157). New York: McGraw-Hill.

Osgood, C. E. (1953). *Method and theory in experimental psychology.* New York: Oxford University Press.

Osgood, C. E., Suci, G. J., & Tannenbaum, P. H. (1957). *The measurement of meaning.* Urbana: University of Illinois Press.

Paivio, A., Yuille, J. C., & Madigan, S. A. (1968). Concreteness, imagery, and meaningfulness values for 925 nouns. *Journal of Experimental Psychology Monograph Supplement, 76*, No. 1, Part 2.

Perruchet, P, Gallego, J. & Savy, I. (1990). A critical reappraisal of the evidence for unconscious abstraction of deterministic rules in complex experimental situations. *Cognitive Psychology, 22*, 493–516.

Postman, L., Bruner, J. S., & McGinnies, E. (1948). Personal values as selective factors in perception. *Journal of Abnormal and Social Psychology, 43*, 142–154.

Pratto, F., & John, O. P. (1991). Automatic vigilance: The attention-grabbing power of negative social information. *Journal of Personality and Social Psychology, 61*, 380–391.

Reber, A. S. (1976). Implicit learning of synthetic languages: The role of instructional set. *Journal of Experimental Psychology: Human Learning and Memory, 2*, 88–94.

Schvaneveldt, R. W., Meyer, D. E., & Becker, C. A. (1976). Lexical ambiguity, semantic context, and visual word recognition. *Journal of Experimental Psychology: Human Perception and Performance,* 2, 243–256.

Seamon, J. G., Brody, N., & Kauff, D. M. (1983). Affective discrimination of stimuli that are not recognized: Effects of shadowing, masking, and cerebral laterality. *Journal of Experimental Psychology: Human Learning, Memory, and Cognition,* 9, 544–555.

Singer, J. A., & Salovey, P. (1988). Mood and memory: Evaluating the network theory of affect. *Clinical Psychology Review,* 8, 211–251.

Treisman, A. M. (1960). Contextual cues in selective listening. *Quarterly Journal of Experimental Psychology,* 12, 242–248.

Tweedy, J. R., Lapinski, R. H., & Schvaneveldt, R. W. (1977). Semantic-context effects on word recognition: Influence of varying the proportion of items presented in an appropriate context. *Memory and Cognition,* 5, 84–89.

Underwood, B. J. (1965). False recognition produced by implicit verbal responses. *Journal of Experimental Psychology,* 70, 122–129.

Wang, A. Y., & Johnson, M. K. (1978). Frequency information prior to identification in word recognition. Unpublished manuscript.

Warren, R. E., & Warren, N. T. (1976). Dual semantic encoding of homographs and homophones embedded in context. *Memory & Cognition,* 4, 586–592.

Emotion
and
Attention

Motivating the Focus of Attention

Douglas Derryberry
Oregon State University

Don M. Tucker
University of Oregon

For much of the past thirty years, theorizing within psychology has been dominated by the assumption that cognition is the primary cause of behavior. Although this cognitive paradigm has fostered many advances, it has also led to a relative neglect of "secondary" processes such as emotion and motivation. In recent years, however, research has shown that emotional and motivational processes may at times precede cognition (Zajonc, 1980), and that they often exert important influences on the course of information processing (Blaney, 1986). Thus, psychological theories are moving toward more interactive frameworks, featuring reciprocal influences between cognitive and emotional processes (e.g., Mathews, 1990).

A parallel shift in emphasis is taking place within the fields of the neurosciences. The traditional view has been that the cognitive processes carried out within the cortex function hierarchically to control subcortical circuitry related to motivation and emotion. However, research has accumulated indicating that these subcortical circuits often become active well before the

The Heart's Eye: Emotional Influences in Perception and Attention

cortex (LeDoux, 1987). Perhaps more important, multiple projection systems have been discovered that extend from the subcortical regions to the cortex, projections that appear to modulate processing within the cortex (Saper, 1987). Again, models of brain function are beginning to emphasize reciprocal interactions between cognitive processes within the cortex and motivational processes of subcortical areas (e.g., Edelman, 1989).

The purpose of the present chapter is to explore these complementary perspectives emerging within psychology and the neurosciences. Although they converge around many psychological processes, we will focus on motivation and attention in the present discussion. We will review evidence indicating that motivational processes recruit attentional mechanisms to adaptively regulate perceptual and conceptual processes. More specifically, we will explore the idea that motivational processes involve two separable types of effects on attention. First, they exert a general influence that serves to broaden or narrow the breadth of attention. Second, they exert more specific effects serving to direct attention toward particular sources of information.

Before describing these attentional effects, it is worth clarifying our use of the term "motivation." From a physiological perspective, motivational processes arise from distributed sets of circuits centered on the brain's limbic regions. These circuits receive input from the cortex and other subcortical areas, and respond in terms of the significance or importance of incoming information. When a significant stimulus is detected, the motivational circuits function to adjust and coordinate the body's motor, autonomic, and endocrine systems. This is an active and adaptive regulation aimed at preparing an effective pattern of action. An important consequence is the generation of interoceptive feelings, which may be directly related to the bodily adjustments or centrally generated within the nervous system itself. In either case, we prefer to use the term "emotion" in reference to the experiential, often interoceptive, accompaniments of motivation. For the present discussion, we use the term motivation because it best conveys the regulatory control inherent in these processes.

The chapter's main theme is that this active control is not simply a matter of peripheral bodily regulation. It also involves the modulation of perceptual and conceptual processing, a control aimed at promoting an effective integration of perceptual and response processing. As will be discussed in more detail, this control is exerted through projections from limbic and brainstem regions to the cortex. These projections may mediate psychological processes such as attention, general arousal, and automatic spreading activation, and it is not unreasonable to expect that motivation might influence cognition through all of these mechanisms. However, we will emphasize attention in the present chapter, since attention best captures the specific (rather than general) and capacity-limited (rather than automatic) nature of motivational effects (Posner, 1978).

Attention is often approached as an internal "spotlight" that illuminates the perceptual or conceptual content with which it is aligned. Although obviously a simplification, this spotlight metaphor has generated several important lines of theoretical development. The first views attention in terms of a flexible mechanism whose *direction* can be adjusted by orienting toward discrete sources of information in the external or internal worlds (Posner, Davidson, & Synder, 1980). Information falling within the focus is facilitated, whereas that outside the focus may be suppressed. Although the dynamics of orienting remain controversial, evidence suggests that it consists of three component operations: disengaging from the current location, moving to a new location, and engaging the new location. As discussed below, progress has been made in relating these attentional operations to specific neural systems (Posner, Inhoff, Friedrich, & Cohen, 1987), and in relating these attention systems to other systems involved in motivation (Derryberry & Tucker, 1991).

The second approach emphasizes the idea that the *breadth* of attention can be adjusted in scope. For example, Eriksen and Yeh (1985) have compared attention to a zoom lens, which can constrict to focus on more detailed information, in a sense concentrating its resources on a small set of channels. Conversely, it can broaden in scope to encompass more channels, but with more dilute resources and reduced resolving power. From a neuropsychological perspective, Tucker and Williamson (1984) have suggested that similar effects may arise from brainstem arousal systems that differentially regulate the two cortical hemispheres. States of arousal favoring the left hemisphere contribute to restricted modes of processing that facilitate local at the expense of global information. In contrast, states favoring the right hemisphere promote more expansive processing modes that support global information over local detail. Again, progress has been made in relating these processing modes to the brain's motivational circuitry (Tucker & Williamson, 1984).

Although these two approaches are sometimes viewed as conflicting models of attention, we do not see them as incompatible. As suggested by Posner, Grossenbacher, and Compton (in press), it may be misguided to see the parameters of direction and breadth as in conflict, for these are two aspects of selection that must be coordinated. As reviewed below, psychological studies suggest that motivation regulates both attentional parameters, and physiological evidence indicates that they rely on distinct neural systems. Therefore, our strategy is to approach direction and breadth as potentially separable aspects of attention, to examine their individual effects, and to consider how they might be coordinated.

The first section discusses evidence that motivational states serve to regulate orienting, directing attention toward perceptual information that is important or relevant to the current state. For example, anxious states appear to direct attention toward threats in the external environment (Mathews, 1990). The second section reviews a separate line of research, including semantic as well as perceptual studies, indicating that motivation influences the breadth of attention. Relevant here are findings that anxious states lead to a narrowing of attention (Easterbrook, 1959), whereas positive states support a more expansive focus (Isen & Daubman, 1984). In the third section, we present some preliminary ideas concerning how these two types of effects might work together during motivated thought. We will attempt to illustrate how these combined influences on attentional orienting and focusing are an adaptive function of motivation, but at the same time, how they may lead to unadaptive cognition. Although each section includes brief descriptions of relevant neural mechanisms, we refer the interested reader to more detailed physiological accounts available in Tucker and Derryberry (1992) and Derryberry and Tucker (1991, 1992).

Regulating the Direction of Attention

A motivational approach begins with the assumption that attention will orient to those pathways processing the most important information. One difficulty facing this approach is that there are many types of stimuli that may prove important and thus attract attention. For example, attention is directed to stimuli that are intense (Berlyne, 1971), novel (Johnston, Hawley, Plewe, Elliott, & DeWitt, 1990), abrupt in onset (Yantis & Johnson, 1990), affectively valenced (Pratto & John, 1991), threatening (Mathews, 1990), relevant to current needs (Wise, 1987), high in incentive value (Derryberry, in press; La Berge, Tweedy, & Ricker, 1967), and so forth. Rather than reviewing this literature, we will limit our discussion to motivational states related to anxiety, success, and failure. We will approach orienting as an active component of these states that serves adaptive coping functions.

Anxiety and Attentional Orienting

Anxiety refers to a class of motivational states, elicited by threatening information, involving complex "defensive" patterns of activity across the motor, autonomic, and endocrine systems. Besides these peripheral changes, the anxious state also serves to direct attention to the threatening information itself. This orienting is clearly adaptive, since it facilitates perceptual processing of the threat, and thus promotes more efficient response selection.

Orienting to threatening cues   Much evidence has accumulated in support of such threat-related orienting. Studies using the Stroop task, where subjects name a word's ink color while attempting to ignore its meaning, have found anxious patients to be distracted by words specifically related to their disorder. For example, spider phobics are slow in naming the color of spider-related words (e.g., "web"; Watts, McKenna, Sharrock, & Trezise, 1986), social phobics are delayed when given socially threatening words (e.g., "rejection"; Hope, Rapee, Heimberg, & Dombeck, 1990), and patients with physical concerns or panic disorder are distracted by words conveying physical threat (e.g., "disease"; Mogg, Matthews, & Weinman, 1989). Although these studies are limited to patient populations with chronic anxiety, they are important in suggesting that attention may orient to highly specific types of threats.

Attentional biases are also found during anxious states in nonclinical samples. MacLeod and Mathews (1988) tested subjects under conditions involving low state anxiety (12 weeks before a major exam) and high state anxiety (1 week before the exam). Under the high state anxiety conditions, subjects high in trait anxiety tended to shift attention toward examination-relevant threat words (e.g., "test"), while subjects low in trait anxiety shifted away from these threatening stimuli. Broadbent and Broadbent (1988) also found that individuals high in trait and state anxiety tended to shift attention to the spatial location of a threatening word. In a more recent study, Mogg, Mathews, Bird, and MacGregor-Morris (1990) attempted to produce low state anxiety by means of an easy anagram task and high state anxiety by a difficult anagram task. Under the stressful conditions, both high and low trait-anxious subjects showed biases favoring threatening information. This is again consistent with a state influence on attention, although the analyses failed to show that this bias was mediated by state anxiety rather than some other aspect of the stressful state.

Orienting to relieving cues   In addition to directing attention toward sources of threat, anxious states may exert complementary effects on other information sources. Particularly important from a motivational perspective is orienting toward information useful in coping with the threat. When faced with an approaching predator, for example, the prey animal attends to both the threat (i.e, the predator) and to the means of coping with it (e.g., escape routes and safe places; Toates, 1986). When a human infant becomes anxious around an approaching stranger or in a novel environment, the baby often shifts its visual attention back and forth between the threatening objects and the relieving presence of the mother (Rothbart & Derryberry, 1981). Furthermore, the cognition of some anxious patients, such as some phobics and obsessive–compulsives, is characterized by an excessive concern with coping with the feared object (Shapiro, 1965). As will be discussed in more detail below, the worrisome cognition accompanying normal anxiety is much concerned with coping options (Mathews, 1990; Tucker & Derryberry, 1992). Although research in this area has been limited, these examples are important in emphasizing the active (rather than reactive) influence of motivational states. An adaptive attentional distribution under anxiety would involve anticipatory orienting to both threatening and relieving sources of information.

Also suggestive of active control are findings that attention is sometimes shifted away from threatening stimuli. Many studies have reported impaired recognition of briefly presented threatening compared to neutral words, and this "perceptual defense" has often been viewed as a motivated attentional strategy for coping with anxiety (Dixon, 1981; Erdelyi, 1974). Kitayama (1990) has recently found impaired perception for briefly presented positive as well as negative words. He proposes that the impairment arises because the affective nature of the word causes the attentional searchlight to narrow and intensify, making it more difficult to align with a weakly activated perceptual pathway. With a more strongly activated perceptual code, however, the focused searchlight is less likely to be misdirected, and perceptual enhancement may result.

Although these findings may constrain "defensive" interpretations, other studies using longer stimulus presentations support the notion of avoidant attentional strategies. As mentioned above, MacLeod and Mathews (1988) reported that when faced with the threat of a major exam, subjects low in trait anxiety shifted attention away from relevant threat stimuli (e.g., words such as "failure"). More recently, MacLeod and Rutherford (1992) presented masked and unmasked threat words to subjects varying in trait and state anxiety. Their findings suggested that under conditions of high state anxiety and unmasked exposures, all subjects tended to avoid the threatening content of the words. With masked exposures, this avoidant strategy was evident only in low trait-anxious subjects, with those high in trait anxiety tending to shift toward the threatening content. These findings are consistent with additional research suggesting that individuals differ in their attentional styles of coping with threat. For example, Miller (1987) has investigated two orthogonal dimensions called "monitoring" and "blunting." One dimension, running from low to high monitoring, reflects the tendency to seek out information concerning potential threats, whereas the other, running from low to high blunting, reflects the tendency to seek distraction and avoid threats.

When viewed as a whole, recent research suggests that anxiety exerts multiple effects on attention. Although the core influence may direct attention toward the source of the threat, additional influences appear to be aimed at reducing the anxiety. In some instances, attention may shift toward information relevant to coping with or relieving the threat, and in other cases it may simply shift away from the threat. Evidence so far suggests that this last strategy may be more prevalent in individuals with low trait anxiety, a finding consistent with a role in anxiety reduction.

Orienting Following Success and Failure

Additional examples of the active nature of motivational effects can be found in studies of success and failure (Derryberry, 1988, 1989, in press). These are two motivational states that come into play during virtually all goal-oriented behavior. In these studies, we have found that failure may bias attention toward negative stimuli, but also enhances the holding power of positive incentives. Rather than promoting reflexive attentional shifts, these states appear to function in a more active and anticipatory manner, preparing the processing system for a range of potentially useful information. By exerting complementary effects on contrasting types of information, they set the system so that it can efficiently respond as conditions improve or deteriorate. If these effects can be orchestrated by differentially recruiting components such as the disengage and engage operations, then an intricate and flexible guidance could arise in relation to positive and negative cues.

In these studies, positive and negative feedback signals are presented while subjects are engaged in a simple video game task. The basic trial consists of a target followed after several seconds by a feedback signal. The target stimuli carry either a positive incentive value (i.e., 10 points are gained if the response is fast, but no points are lost if the response is too slow) or a negative value (i.e., 10 points are lost if the response is too slow, and no points are gained if the response is fast). Feedback takes the form of a positive feedback signal (e.g., a "+" presented when the response is faster than the subject's median reaction time [RT]) or a negative signal (e.g., an "**x**" presented when the RT exceeds the subject's median). It is assumed that the feedback signals elicit brief phasic motivational states related to success and failure, and that these states will carry over to influence attention on the subsequent trial. To assess these effects, we examine attention to targets with positive and negative incentive value as a function of the feedback from the previous trial.

Congruent and incongruent feedback effects   Several recent studies have found that when the feedback signal from one trial is followed immediately by the target on the next trial, the feedback exerts a *congruent* effect on the target. In one set of studies (Derryberry, in press), subjects were instructed to press a key with their right hand when the target consisted of an **M**2, **M**5, **W**2, or **W**5, and to press another key with their left hand when some other letter–digit pair appeared. The targets **M**2 and **M**5 carried a positive incentive value of 2 and 5 points, **W**2 and **W**5 carried a negative value of 2 and 5 points, and all other targets were worthless. Each target appeared in the center of the screen approximately 2 sec following the feedback signal from the previous trial. Two studies found that positive feedback decreased RTs to high-valued positive targets (**M**5) on the next trial, whereas negative feedback facilitated high-valued negative targets (**W**5). This congruent feedback influence has recently been replicated in a spatial detection study, where subjects pressed a single key in response to a square target appearing in the right or left visual field. Targets in one visual field were assigned a positive incentive value, whereas those in the other visual field carried a negative value. Again, RTs were faster to targets in positive and negative locations following positive and negative feedback, respectively (Derryberry & Reed, 1993).

These congruent effects arising from success and failure are consistent with findings that mood states facilitate information that matches the mood's valence (e.g., Blaney, 1986). For example, success has been found to decrease perceptual thresholds for success-related words (Postman & Brown, 1952) and to enhance attention to positive information concerning the self (Mischel, Ebbesen, & Zeiss, 1976). However, additional studies have demonstrated that success and failure also elicit *incongruent* effects. What appears to be crucial in producing the incongruent influence is the presentation of a valenced cue before the target. In one set of studies (Derryberry, 1989), detection targets appeared in a location carrying a positive (e.g., left visual field) or negative (e.g., right visual field) incentive value. Either 250 or 500 msec before the target appeared, a spatial cue was presented in order to draw the subject's attention to the positive location, the negative location, or a neutral location at the screen's center. Feedback had an incongruent influence on these cues: negative feedback enhanced the attentional impact of cues in positive locations, whereas positive feedback enhanced the effect of negative cues. Furthermore, analyses of attentional "costs" and "benefits" based on the neutral cues (Posner, 1978) showed that these incongruent effects were limited to the measures of costs. Subjects showed greater costs (i.e., delays) when they had to shift *away from* positive cues following negative feedback and away from negative cues following positive feedback. Feedback had no effect on the RT benefits gained by shifting *toward* positive or negative locations in advance of the target. These results have been replicated using the letter recognition and spatial detection tasks described in the preceding paragraph (Derryberry, in press; Derryberry & Reed, 1993).

Contrasting but adaptive attentional controls   In interpreting the congruent and incongruent effects, two points are worth emphasizing. Although these effects may at first seem conflicting, their opponent nature is actually adaptive. Given failure, for example, the congruent influence is adaptive in that it biases processing in favor of subsequent negative events, and thereby decreases the probability of another loss of points. At the same time, the incongruent effect allows the individual to take advantage of positive cues that may improve the situation. As discussed earlier, similar effects may arise during anxious states when the individual attends to both potential threats and sources of relief. If only the congruent influence were present, the motivational state would tend to lock itself in and behavior would tend to become perseverative. If only the incongruent influence occurred, the state would be weakened and behavior would tend to vacillate. By promoting both kinds of complementary influences, the motivational state can promote more balanced and flexible processing. The individual is prepared for improving as well as deteriorating conditions.

Second, the presence of these effects poses interesting questions concerning the underlying mechanisms. Conflicts could easily arise if the two effects controlled the same mechanism. However, if they influence different component processes, then cooperative regulations become possible. Attentional orienting appears to consist of several component processes, including the disengage, move, and engage operations investigated by Posner et al. (1987). Since the incongruent effect appeared only when attention had to shift from a pretarget cue to a target of contrasting valence, it most likely involves the disengage operation. The locus of the congruent effect most likely involves some other attentional process, such as the move or engage operation, or perhaps a nonattentional process, such as spreading activation. In any event, the important point is that motivation may exert multiple effects on attention by differentially regulating the component operations involved in orienting.

Limbic Regulation of the Neocortex

Additional support for a relationship between motivation and attention can be found in recent studies or brain function. These studies represent a shift from the older notion that the cognitive capacities of the neocortex exert ultimate control over motivational functions of the subcortical limbic system and brainstem. Instead, it appears that the neocortex is itself embedded within an extensive set of regulatory systems that arise from subcortical regions (Derryberry & Tucker, 1991). Before describing these regulatory influences, we will first discuss evidence that the limbic system is the brain region most central to motivational processes.

Limbic response characteristics   The limbic system consists of many parallel subsystems connecting subcortical structures such as the amygdala, hippocampus, and hypothalamus, and also primitive "paralimbic" cortical structures such as the orbital frontal cortex, the insular cortex, and the cingulate cortex. Animal studies have shown that cells in these regions are particularly responsive to motivationally significant stimuli, such as signals related to rewarding outcomes, to aversive outcomes, and to novelty (Rolls, 1987). Neuroimaging studies with humans have also found evidence of activation in the orbital frontal cortex during anxious states (Johanson, Smith, Riesberg, Silfverskiold, & Tucker, 1992) and in the anterior cingulate cortex during painful stimulation (Jones, Friston, and Frackowiak, 1992). Lesions in these regions also suggest a role in motivation. For example, amygdala lesions can reduce anxiety and aggression in animals (Davis, 1992), and orbital frontal lesions were for years an acceptable treatment for human anxiety (Tucker & Derryberry, 1992). Finally, stimulation of the limbic circuits has been found to enhance motivated behavior. Electrical and neurochemical stimulation of the central amygdala enhances behavioral and autonomic components of anxiety in animals (Davis, 1992). In humans, the phenomenon of temporal lobe epilepsy, which often involves an excitatory focus within the amygdala or hippocampus, can generate intense motivated behavior and experience (Bear, 1983). Thus, extensive research using recording, lesion, and stimulation techniques converges on the limbic system as a central component of the brain's motivational systems.

The traditional view has been that the limbic pathways function to recognize the motivational significance of incoming information, after it has been processed within higher level neocortical regions. However, recent anatomical and recording studies indicate that this is not always the case. Anatomically, the limbic circuits do receive information after multistep processing in the neocortex, but they also receive parallel sensory inputs from earlier stages of processing. Incoming sensory information is first processed within the thalamus, from which it branches to form multiple streams. Some of these streams continue to the sensory neocortex, others travel to brainstem cell groups, and others project directly to limbic structures such as the amygdala and hippocampus. Moreover, single unit recordings have found cells within the central nucleus of the amygdala to respond within 50 msec to a threatening auditory tone, a latency well in advance of extensive neocortical processing (LeDoux, 1987). Similar evidence of early activity within the hippocampus (Coburn, Ashford, & Fuster, 1990) and the reticular cell groups (Schultz, 1986) has been found. Together, these anatomical and recording studies suggest that the limbic extraction of motivational significance occurs in parallel with, and in some cases prior to, processing within the neocortex.

Limbic output functions   Upon detecting a significant stimulus, the limbic circuits function to coordinate brainstem cell groups involved in motor, autonomic, and endocrine activity. This establishes a preparatory bodily state that is adaptive, given the significant input and prevailing internal conditions. It is now clear, however, that the limbic circuits also exert wide-ranging effects on the neocortex, setting up a central processing state that is adaptive, given prevailing conditions. This cortical regulation is implemented in three general ways. First, the limbic systems project to the reticular subsystems of the brainstem (Wallace, Magnuson, & Gray, 1992), which in turn send ascending projections to virtually all regions of the neocortex (Saper, 1987). Under the control of limbic inputs, the reticular subsystems employ distinct neuromodulators (e.g., norepinephrine, serotonin, dopamine, acetylcholine) to regulate reactivity across broad expanses of the cortex. Although these reticular influences are relatively general, they exert much more sophisticated effects than those suggested by conventional notions of "nonspecific arousal." As discussed later in the chapter, these influences, particularly those involving the noradrenergic and dopaminergic subsystems, are important in adjusting the overall breadth (i.e., narrow vs broad) of attention (Tucker & Williamson, 1984).

A second type of limbic–cortical influence, and one likely to be involved in attentional orienting, involves limbic projections to thalamic nuclei (e.g., mediodorsal nucleus, medial pulvinar nucleus), which are in turn reciprocally interconnected with relatively precise cortical fields (Gaffan & Murray, 1990). By regulating thalamic activity, limbic circuits may facilitate or sustain processing within localized regions of the cortex, and thus exert more specific effects on attention. The third and perhaps most important influence involves direct limbic projections to the cortex. The amygdala, for example, projects to multiple perceptual regions within the posterior neocortex, including the earliest visual areas within the occipital lobe (Amaral, 1987). Moreover, the amygdala, hippocampus, and orbital frontal regions have strong projections to the anterior cingulate cortex, an important crossroads of the "anterior attention system" described by Posner, Petersen, Fox, and Raichle (1988). Finally, all the paralimbic cortical regions have extensive "backward" projections to the overlying neocortical fields, allowing them to regulate incoming information as it approaches the limbic system (Pandya & Yeterian, 1985). Although the specific functions of these limbic–neocortical pathways remain to be determined, it is clear that the motivational circuitry is well positioned for regulating processing within the neocortex.

An important part of this regulation involves the mechanisms involved in orienting. Posner, Inhoff, Friedrich, and Cohen (1987) have provided evidence that the disengage operation depends on the posterior parietal cortex, the move operation on parts of the brainstem superior colliculus, and the engage operation on the thalamic pulvinar nucleus. Each of these attentional subsystems is accessible by projections emanating from the limbic system. For example, the parietal region crucial for disengaging is extensively interconnected with the paralimbic posterior cingulate cortex. In turn, the cingulate cortex receives massive inputs from the hippocampus and amygdala. Mesulam (1981) suggested that these limbic inputs may help lay out a "motivational map" in the cingulate cortex, within which values are assigned to various spatial locations. Projections from this motivational map to a more purely sensory map within the parietal cortex may then regulate the ease with which attention can be disengaged.

Although our knowledge of the brain remains limited, its general organization appears consistent with recent developments in psychology. The picture that emerges is one in which specialized computational systems, focused within limbic and paralimbic regions, monitor incoming information in terms of its motivational significance. Upon detecting a significant stimulus, these motivational systems function to regulate the state of the nervous system so as to promote adaptive behavior. This regulation establishes a preparatory pattern of readiness across the motor, autonomic, and endocrine subsystems of the body. At the same time, however, it employs ascending reticular, thalamic, and direct cortical projections to set up a state of readiness across multiple neocortical networks. This highly distributed processing state functions adaptively to enhance the highest priority sources of information, thus providing content relevant to maintaining or improving the prevailing motivational conditions.

Much research will be required to characterize the various mechanisms that contribute to this processing state. The psychological evidence reviewed above suggests that the component operations of attentional orienting play a central role. In addition to these effects on the content of processing, however, motivational states also influence the structure of information processing. These effects are not simply perceptual, but extend to include the semantic and episodic representations active within working memory. We turn now to a consideration of these structural effects, examining attentional "focusing" and "expanding" within perceptual and semantic domains.

Regulating the Breadth of Attention

A limiting factor in human cognition is the span of working memory. Although extensive semantic networks may elaborate a given percept or concept, the span of information that can be held in the immediate access of working memory is remarkably limited. This limit may be important both in the perception of environmental data, which may be more complex than can be apprehended in a single perceptual act, and during ongoing cognition, in which only a small fraction of stored information can be accessed at a given time. Because of this limit, a major challenge for effective self-regulation is achieving the optimal tuning of attentional scope. The objective of attentional control in this sense is not selecting certain information contents over others, but regulating the span of information over which scarce attentional resources are spread.

Although the topics of this volume are perception and attention, an analysis of motivational controls must also consider how perceptual information is integrated with the mechanisms of memory. It is in the interface with memory that the costs and benefits of attentional breadth are seen most clearly. When attention is spread too broadly, the immediate mnemonic capacity is strained to the point that representations may become ephemeral and unusable. In contrast, when attention is tightly focused, only a limited range of information is represented in working memory, but the strength of each representation insures its availability, either for further processing or for consolidation into long-term storage. These differing cognitive strategies appear to have evolved in close relation to the motivational states for which they are suited, such that when a state is engaged, it automatically biases the appropriate structure of attention.

We will first describe evidence of structural adjustments during states of failure, anxiety, and elation. We then propose that two forms of arousal, elation and anxiety, apply inherent, and opposite, biases on the scope of attention. We suggest that within this neuropsychological model, the brain's arousal mechanisms represent elementary mechanisms for self-regulating the allocation of limited cognitive resources. By controlling the integration of perceptual information with working memory, these mechanisms may regulate not only the ongoing cognitive strategy, but the structure of immediate perception.

Failure and Attentional Narrowing

Several recent studies in our laboratory indicate that the state of failure, in addition to its effects on orienting, leads to a relative narrowing of attention (Brandt, Derryberry, & Reed, 1992). These studies differ from those described earlier in that all targets were assigned an equal incentive value; subjects simply gained points for each fast response and lost points for each slow response. In addition, the criteria for success and failure were adjusted across alternating blocks of trials, such that on some blocks subjects received roughly 80% positive feedback, while on others they received 80% negative feedback.

An initial study employed a detection task in which targets appeared at varying distances from a central feedback signal. The display consisted of an array of twelve outlined boxes arranged to form an X pattern around a central fixation point, with each box located a close, medium, or far distance from fixation. Each trial began with a positive or negative feedback signal appearing at fixation, followed, after 250 msec, by a square target in one of the twelve boxes. The results showed that RTs for targets in the close and medium locations were similar following the success and failure blocks, but that failure led to a relative delay in detecting targets in the far locations. Thus, failure impaired detection of the peripheral targets, without enhancing that of the more central targets.

A second study attempted to extend this narrowing effect to the domain of object processing (Brandt et al., 1992). The paradigm employed was a variation of a task developed by Navon (1977), in which subjects search for a target within a composite stimulus made up of local elements arranged in a global form. Again, each trial began with a positive or negative feedback signal, followed, after 500 msec, by a target stimulus. The target consisted of a composite form made up of five **T**-shaped elements (local information) arranged into a larger **T**-shaped form (global information). The local elements and global forms were oriented up, down, left, or right. Subjects were instructed to press one key if a **T** oriented up or down was present at either the global or local level, and another key if such forms were absent. The results paralleled those found in the spatial detection task. The success and failure blocks led to similar RTs to targets appearing at the local level. However, the failure blocks led to relative delays, given targets at the global level.

These studies suggest that failure promotes a relative narrowing of attention, impairing detection of peripheral visual targets and global forms. An important issue concerns how this narrowing effect relates to the orienting effects of failure described earlier. Several studies have addressed this issue. The first employed a spatial detection task with targets appearing at either central or peripheral locations (Brandt et al., 1992). At the start of each trial, small arrows cued the incentive value of each location. On some trials, the central locations carried positive value and the peripheral locations were assigned negative value, while on other trials the central locations were negative and the peripheral positive. Feedback gave rise to two independent effects. A "congruent" influence appeared, with failure facilitating targets in negative locations. This was accompanied by a noninteracting "narrowing" effect, with failure delaying RTs to all targets appearing at peripheral locations. The second study was described earlier, in which subjects responded to valuable targets (M2, M5, W2, W5) with one hand, and to worthless targets (some other letter–digit pair) with the other hand (Derryberry, in press). As previously noted, failure led to both congruent and incongruent effects for the valuable targets. In addition, failure delayed responses to the worthless targets, which suggests a general narrowing on the valuable target set. Thus, failure exerted multiple effects, including a tendency to restrict attention to the valuable targets, along with a congruent or incongruent influence on the valuable targets. Although more research is required, these studies are consistent with the notion that failure exerts separable influences on attentional orienting and narrowing.

Restricted Attention in Anxiety

More extensive evidence that motivational states regulate the breadth of attention can be found in studies of anxiety. Visual attention may become overly focused on central targets at the expense of peripheral targets, and object perception may emphasize local rather than global aspects of form. Restricted attention in the semantic domain may lead cognition to become routinized, or fixated on stereotyped themes.

Anxiety and tunnel vision A large and controversial psychological literature has presented evidence that stress or anxiety produces "tunnel vision." Easterbrook (1959) provided a general formulation of this notion, proposing that stress reduces the range of cue utilization, acting both on perception and other cognitive and conceptual skills. In Easterbrook's model, peripheral or less relevant cues are impaired by stress first, whereas central or more relevant cues are affected only by extreme levels of stress or anxiety.

This literature rests on a variety of manipulations included under the rubric of psychological stress. These included drugs or physical discomfort (Callaway & Dembo, 1958), adverse thermal conditions (Bursill, 1958), electric shock (Reeves & Bergum, 1972, Wachtel, 1968), simulated risk of personal or other's injury (Weltman, Smith, & Egstrom, 1971), and participation in dangerous situations, such as ocean driving for unexperienced divers (Weltman & Egstrom, 1966). Other studies involved high versus low trait anxiety (Solso, Johnson, & Schatz, 1968) and a few have reported observations on clinical anxiety disorder (see Easterbrook, 1959). The effect of stress or anxiety in most of these studies was an impairment of accuracy or speed of response to peripheral targets. In most studies the performance on the central task was generally unaffected, or affected to a lesser extent.

It became clear in this research that stress influences the allocation of attention between central and peripheral locations, rather than fixed properties of the visual system itself. Weltman et al. (1971) proposed that there may be either a narrowing of an attentional "beam" under stress, with the peripheral portion disappearing first, or a selective enhancement of central vision, leaving less attentional resources to deploy to the periphery. Peripheral target detection during stress (Bursill, 1958; Weltman & Egstrom, 1966), as well as under nonstressful conditions, decreases markedly when the processing load imposed by the central task is increased (Abernethy & Leibowitz, 1971). Even a slight modification of the central control task, such as changing from steady fixation to require responding to the occasional dimming of a central light (Leibowitz & Appelle, 1969), may lead to a significant increase of thresholds to peripheral detection. Further, peripheral detection, but not central task performance, generally improves with practice, suggesting that subjects may learn to redistribute attentional resources toward the periphery (Abernethy & Leibowitz, 1971).

While the above studies deal primarily with spatial processing, evidence also suggests that anxiety may influence the processing of forms. Tyler and Tucker (1982) examined normals varying in trait anxiety under high and low stress (noise) conditions. They used Navon's (1977) global–local processing task, and titrated the exposure duration so that subjects could attend to either the local or global level, but not to both. Normal subjects in this task show "global precedence," a tendency to attend to the global level first and a tendency for the global level to exert greater interference over local processing than vice versa. Tyler and Tucker found that anxious subjects did not show this pattern, but rather showed a significant bias to attend to the local features.

Anxiety and restricted semantic scope   Although anxiety effects have thus been examined most often in studies of visual attention, there is also evidence that anxiety constricts attention within the verbal cognitive domain as well. In the classic studies of Spence and associates (Spence, 1958), anxious subjects performed well in remembering words that were closely related, but their performance was poorer than that of nonanxious subjects with words that were remotely related. Eysenck (1982) reported that noise-induced stress impairs retrieval of the more remotely associated words in a probed category recall task. Mikulincer, Kedem, and Paz (1990a) applied Rosch's analysis of category organization to examine individual differences in anxiety. Anxious subjects tended to reject nonprototypical exemplars of categories, the breadth of their categories was reduced, and they perceived less relatedness between different categories. In subsequent research, Mikulincer, Paz, and Kedem (1990b) found that anxious subjects categorize objects with less inclusive and more discrete categories, suggesting to these authors that anxiety may lead to conceptual fragmentation.

Thus, both the mild state elicited by failure and the more chronic state of anxiety appear to restrict attention. In anxiety, this narrowing is pervasive, extending across the domains of spatial, object, and conceptual processing. It may seem that this phenomenon is a straightforward effect of higher arousal: with greater arousal there is an impairment of the attentional apparatus, with fewer resources available for more peripheral information sources. However, evidence reviewed below shows that a different state of emotionally significant arousal, elation, also produces a general motivating influence on cognition and behavior, but it produces an opposite—expansive—effect on the scope of attention.

The Expansive Scope of Elation

Pathological positive affect   In clinical settings, the dynamic modulation of attention by emotional state is seen in dramatic form in manic–depressive disorder. Some patients may cycle between the opposite mood states within a few hours, displaying in the course of this mood change a marked change in arousal, activity level, and in the quality of perception and thought. The biases toward positive versus negative cognitive contents are striking. While in the depressed state the patient can find no hope, yet when in the manic state a short time later, life becomes thrilling and glorious.

Changing biases on attentional structure can be seen as well. The mental associations in the depressed state are restricted and unimaginative. A depressive's perceptions, such as those on the Rorschach inkblot test, are bleak and impoverished (Exner, 1979). In the manic state, however, perceptions are richly elaborated, and mental associations may spread so broadly across the semantic network that the thread of continuity may be difficult for the clinician to follow. Yet, unlike a schizophrenic, whose associations are bizarre and fragmented, a manic can usually explain loose associations when challenged by the clinician. The cognitive disorder seems to reflect a state in which working memory has been inflated to span large domains of semantic content, such that the manic sees connections that are not apparent, and often not particularly meaningful when made apparent, to the normal mind.

These clinical observations on manic cognition have been supported by studies using quantitative methods to assess the structure of mental associations. On a categorization task, Andreasen and Powers (1975) observed a tendency toward overinclusive categories in manics that was similar to that seen in creative artists. This finding may be consistent with the frequent occurrence of affective disorder in creative writers.

Other research has shown that changes in attentional scope vary dynamically with the patient's mood state. This research was initiated by the complaints made by many manic patients that a therapeutic regimen of lithium not only normalized their mood swings but impaired their creativity in the workplace. To examine this issue systematically, Shaw, Mann, Stokes, and Manevitz (1986) tested the word associations of manic patients while they were on lithium, then after lithium was discontinued, and finally after it had been readministered. They observed an increase in remote, idiosyncratic associations when lithium was discontinued, but a return to the more restricted pattern of semantic access when it was readministered.

The normal good mood   Evidence with normal subjects suggests that the strong distortions of attentional scope seen in mania may be pathological in degree, but may not be markedly different in kind from the normal influence that an elated state exerts on the breadth of attention. Isen and her associates have observed effects of even mild positive affect, such as that which may be induced by giving the subjects a small bag of candy (Isen, Johnson, Mertz, & Robinson, 1985b; Isen & Daubman, 1984; Isen, Daubman, & Gorgoglione, 1985a). Isen and Daubman (1984) found positive affect subjects to create and use categories more inclusively, to group more stimuli together, and to rate more low-prototypic exemplars as category members than did control subjects. In another study (Isen et al., 1985b), positive affect subjects showed significantly more remote associations to neutral words than did controls. Isen and Daubman (1984) offered a nonattentional account for such expansive conceptual processing, suggesting that positive affect exerts a strong, congruent priming effect on a large and diverse range of information. This extended context may lead to the use of larger or more inclusive categories for processing information.

The notion that the expansive processing is due to a widespread priming is useful, but it remains unclear why the extensive priming should occur during positive states. Isen (1987) has pointed out several limitations of network-based spreading activation accounts of her mood effects. In addition, these approaches are not particularly helpful in explaining the narrowed processing accompanying anxiety, other than to suggest that it arises from restricted priming. It remains unclear why the restricted priming occurs, and moreover, it is difficult to explain impaired perceptual performance in terms of priming. These opposite effects seem best approached in terms of attention, a mechanism that can be utilized across perceptual and conceptual domains, and that may regulate priming within the conceptual domain.

The Inherent Affective Quality of Brain Arousal Mechanisms

In the next section, we will describe a physiological approach to these attentional processes, relating them to primitive brainstem arousal systems. We first consider concepts of arousal in the context of psychometric evidence that relates them to elementary mood states of positive and negative affect. We then describe a model of their neural substrates that may help explain how attention may be qualitatively altered by primitive mechanisms. The main point of this model is that "arousal" has been misunderstood in psychology as being nonspecific in both its affective, subjective qualities and its attentional influences. The major neural mechanisms regulating the brain's level of activity and function, such as the brainstem catecholamine projection systems, produce inherent and qualitative affective as well as attentional changes.

Subjectively felt arousal states   Thayer (1978, 1989) used a psychometric approach to examine subjects' reports of their arousal states, differentiating an "energy" dimension from a "tension" dimension. In Thayer's theorizing, the subjective experience of these arousal states is psychologically important. Unlike earlier cognitive theories of emotion (Mandler, 1985; Schacter & Singer, 1962), arousal in Thayer's model is not an undifferentiated state, available to be transformed into any emotion, depending on the present context and attribution. Rather, the experience of each arousal state provides the person with specific information on the resources available for coping with the situation at hand. Energetic arousal is sensed continuously and is related to decisions on how much effort can be applied to coping demands. Tense arousal is important to dangerous contexts, within which it focuses attention on the danger and, by inhibiting the motor system, engages a vigilant, threat-avoidant posture.

In contrast to the traditional orthogonal valence (pleasant/unpleasant) and intensity dimensions, Thayer (1989) proposes that separating the two dimensions of energetic and tense arousal may be useful in studying the interaction of arousal states. His studies have suggested that the two kinds of arousal may be positively correlated at low levels of engagement, such that in everyday activities a person may feel both energetic and tense. However, at stronger levels of engagement the two dimensions become negatively correlated. A strong state of tense arousal, for example, is likely to be associated with a decrement on the energy dimension.

The argument for rotating the traditional valence and intensity dimensions has also been made in the psychometric studies of Tellegen and associates (Tellegen, 1985; Watson & Tellegen, 1985). In this case the phenomenon in question is not arousal but emotion. In reviewing many self-report studies of mood states, Watson and Tellegen proposed that two underlying dimensions, Positive and Negative Affect, account for the major variance in mood reports. Like Thayer's dimensions, these represent a 45° rotation of the valence and intensity dimensions, such that high Negative Affect bisects the quadrant of negative valence and high intensity (similar to Thayer's "tense" arousal), and high Positive Affect bisects the quadrant of positive valence and high intensity (similar to Thayer's "energetic" arousal).

Qualitative attentional controls   The similarity of the psychometric structures of arousal and mood states suggests that the fundamental basis of motivational states may be formed by elementary arousal mechanisms. Conversely, the arousal mechanisms of the brain may be responsible not only for shifting between drowsiness and motivated alertness, but for engaging subjectively important affect states that may be inseparable from the arousal states.

The affective qualities of brain arousal mechanisms were emphasized by Tucker and Williamson (1984) in their formulation of how elementary controls on neural activity could lead to more complex implications for the structure of attention. In this model, a *tonic activation* system is proposed to have evolved from fight–flight mechanisms. Consistent with its role in maintaining a vigilant posture in the face of threat, a strong engagement of the tonic activation system is proposed to be associated with the subjective experience of anxiety. This system appears to be reflected in the psychometric dimensions of Negative Affect and tense arousal. An inherent lateralization of motor control mechanisms results in the tonic activation system being particularly important to left hemisphere cognition.

A separate neural control system termed by Tucker and Williamson (1984) as the *phasic arousal* system evolved from elementary orienting mechanisms. Variance along the dimension of phasic arousal is proposed to be synonymous with variance on the depression–elation dimension of mood, and thus Positive Affect and energetic arousal. Because of the inherent right-lateralization of perceptual orienting mechanisms, the phasic arousal system is proposed to be particularly important to right hemisphere perception and cognition. Thus, this theoretical framework, although framed in neurophysiological terms, can be seen as paralleling the dimensionality of both arousal (Thayer, 1989) and mood (Tellegen, 1985) in the psychometric studies.

Beginning with the simple differences in the apparent time course of the effects of these systems, one being tonic and the other phasic, Tucker and Williamson (1984) attempted to deduce more complex qualities of attentional control that would be inherent to the operation of these control systems. By tonically maintaining neural activation associated with a given perceptual or mental representation, the tonic activation system applies a *redundancy bias* to ongoing information processing. Whatever information is currently represented tends to be maintained over time. The effect of this simple control is to focus attention and working memory, and in favor of allocating limited representational capacity to a limited range of information. Attention is focused, and working memory is invested conservatively in a thorough representation of limited informational contents. These attentional effects are consistent with the restricted attentional scope observed in anxiety states.

In contrast, the primitive mechanism of the phasic arousal system applies a *habituation bias*. This effect causes the phasic arousal system to decrement its function, and its contribution to information representation, when constancy is maintained in the information channel. Therefore, the brain modulated strongly by this system requires novel perception or cognition to stay awake. This bias toward novel information produces a liberal strategy for investing the resources of working memory. A larger range of information is accessed, but, because capacity is limited, the strength of the representation afforded to any given element is limited. Attentional scope is broad, and working memory is spread thinly. Thus the expansive attentional scope of elation can be understood as reflecting a dominance of the phasic arousal system. The simple mechanism of the habituation bias can explain other features of the manic's psychological process, such as the short attention span and vigorous stimulus seeking.

The tonic activation and phasic arousal systems appear to be grounded in reticular "arousal" systems. Specifically, tonic activation is thought to depend on activity within the dopaminergic systems that ascend from brainstem nuclei (substantia nigra and ventral tegmental area) to regulate the motor circuitry of the basal ganglia, the motivational functions of the limbic system, and the sensory and conceptual functions of the cortex. In contrast, the phasic arousal mechanism depends on the noradrenergic system that arises from the locus coeruleus to regulate processing in most limbic and cortical regions. Although the dopaminergic and noradrenergic nuclei are highly responsive to incoming stimulation, their responsivity appears to be controlled by projections from the limbic system. Thus, the motivational circuitry of the limbic system may adjust the activity of the dopaminergic and nonradrenergic projections systems, and thereby set up a pattern of tonic activation and phasic arousal within the cortex. During states of anxiety, for example, the central nucleus of the amygdala may respond to threatening stimuli by recruiting the dopaminergic system, which in turn promotes tonic activation within its higher level targets. This state of tonic activation is adaptive in the sense that it helps to narrow processing on the most important sources of information, prevents distraction by less important stimuli, and promotes a processing mode that supports the routinized, stereotyped behavioral patterns often involved in defensive behavior.

To better understand these adaptive effects, however, it is necessary to consider more closely their influence on the cortex. Tucker and Williamson (1984) speculated that the elementary attentional controls of tonic activation and phasic arousal differentially regulate the left and right hemispheres. The focused attentional mode of the tonic activation system may be integral to the analytic perception and cognition of the left hemisphere. The expansive attentional control of the phasic arousal system may support the right hemisphere's global perceptual and cognitive processes.

In the case of perceptual processing, substantial evidence suggests that attention to local features requires left hemisphere processing (Robertson, Lamb, & Knight, 1988; Sergent, 1982), whereas attention to global features requires right hemisphere processing (Nebes, 1978). States such as anxiety may preferentially engage dopaminergic and left hemisphere processing systems, leading to attentional biases favoring local at the expense of global information. Conversely, elation would be expected to recruit noradrenergic and right hemisphere systems, thus promoting biases in favor of global aspects of the environment. From this line of reasoning, the key attentional influence of these states may not be attention to central versus peripheral areas of the visual field, but the bias of attention to local versus global features of a stimulus array.

Related hemispheric specializations may contribute to conceptual processing. Studies of language comprehension following brain damage indicate that even for verbal tasks the right hemisphere is important to integrating contextual information (Wapner, Hamby, & Gardner, 1981). Using chronometric methods in normals, Burgess and Simpson (1988) varied the interval between a priming word and a target word in a lexical decision task. With increasing intervals, words presented to the right visual field (left hemisphere) showed enhancement of the word's most frequently used meaning and a decrement in the infrequent meaning. This process would suggest that over time the left hemisphere constrains the scope of primed associates. In contrast, increasing intervals for words presented to the left visual field (right hemisphere) caused the frequent meanings of the words to decline, and the infrequent meanings to increase. This suggests that the right hemisphere accesses semantics in an opposite fashion to the left hemisphere, that is, with increasing scope.

Taken together, the evidence suggests that motivational states may tune semantic structure: anxiety seems to narrow the scope of processing within semantic memory. Conversely, as seen with both mania and normal positive affect, an elated arousal state may broaden the structure of memory access. Although the link between breadth of associations and hemispheric cognition remains controversial, a reasonable hypothesis is that as anxiety and elation alter the scope of semantic access they also shift the balance between right and left hemispheric contributions to the conceptual process.

Although it oversimplifies the relevant neurophysiological mechanisms, the Tucker and Williamson (1984) model provides an exercise in understanding primitive influences on perception. Psychologists often attempt to explain emotional influences on perception through cognitive mediation. In examining the neurophysiological mechanisms, emotional and motivational influences are found to operate directly to shape the scope of attention and perception at the most primitive levels of the vertebrate neural hierarchy. The fight–flight system, for example, requires no attributions to achieve its effects. When engaged by the appropriate internal or external stimuli, it immediately produces the relevant subjective experience, of hostility and/or anxiety, and it immediately and automatically restricts the focus of attention.

Coordinating Attentional Direction and Breadth

A physiological analysis is supportive of the notion that motivation influences both the direction and scope of attention. As described above, motivation-related limbic circuits may preferentially engage the ascending dopaminergic and noradrenergic systems, thereby regulating the general breadth of processing within the cortex. Additional limbic projections to the thalamus and cortex may serve to regulate the component processes involved in orienting, thus directing attention to the most important sources of information. Although these influences appear to depend on separable neural subsystems, his does not mean that they function independently, and research is required to assess their interactions. Indeed, a motivational perspective suggests that a primary function of the limbic systems may be that of coordinating the neural systems involved in orienting and focusing. In this final section, we take a preliminary view of this coordination, considering how it may or may not promote adaptive cognition. We will frame our discussion around the worrisome cognition that often accompanies anxiety.

Attention and Worry

In approaching the topic of worry, it is first important to note that an anxious state can bias attention toward a wide range of threatening material. When faced with a crucial exam, for example, an anxious student may find attention drawn to threat-related objects, such as the textbook lying on the desk or the classroom as it is passed in the hall. The student may also orient to interoceptive sensations, including feelings of fatigue or nervousness that are viewed as threatening because they may impair performance on the exam. Perhaps most important, the anxious student may attend to a range of thoughts of failure and its consequences, thoughts that are tightly interrelated within semantic networks. Thus, the anxious state affords many potential targets for attention, providing a rich source of threatening material to be incorporated into worrisome thought.

Anxiety also promotes biases toward information that may be useful in coping with the threat. When one worries about an impending threat, much of the rumination involves assessing the means and possibilities of coping with it. Mathews (1990) has described worry as similar to problem solving; it allows the individual to rehearse and prepare for dangerous events while searching for a means of preventing them. Along related lines, we have suggested that anxiety promotes cognitive biases that support a process of planning (Tucker & Derryberry, 1992). More specifically, anxiety facilitates anticipatory representations of potential dangers and alternative coping options, which are evaluated and used to set up a plan of action. Rather than a reactive state in which attention is driven by threatening content, worry involves a more active, anticipatory state that may prepare effective coping.

Integral to this process is the redundancy bias applied through the tonic activation mechanism. Attentional narrowing is an adaptive adjustment that serves to limit the processing of less important sources of information and to promote focused, effective responding. In emergency situations, it is essential that the individual avoids distraction by irrelevant input, quickly narrows down the potential avenues of escape, and establishes a tight coupling between threat signals, relief signals, and related responses. When worried about an anticipated threat, the narrowing again limits distraction and helps to constrain the sampling of various threats and coping options. The individual may lose track of daily affairs and other concerns, but the sharpened focus of attention may facilitate an effective plan of coping.

This general description suggests that the combined effects on orienting and focusing help to guide worrisome thought toward an effective solution or plan. Unfortunately, this is not always the case, with normals as well as patients often suffering from painful and inefficient rumination. The present approach suggests that these problems may in part arise from an inadequate coordination of the orienting and focusing processes. Although such coordination is clearly a complex process, an initial view might consider instances in which the focusing component is either too weak or too strong in relation to orienting.

One example would be occasions in which the biases on orienting are underconstrained due to relatively weak focusing. The anxious person may find themselves worrying about many things that might go wrong, and rehearsing numerous ways of dealing with them. But because they consider too many threats and options, or shift too rapidly from one to another, effective evaluation and planning are difficult. This state may arise when tonic activation is not strong enough to restrict less relevant information sources, making it easier for these sources to disengage and attract attention. It may also arise even when focusing is strong, if the additional influences on orienting are particularly potent. In either case, the result will be a distractible and disjointed form of thought, in which the person jumps from idea to idea without constructing an effective plan.

Limitations may also arise when orienting is overconstrained due to strong tonic activation. This may lead to problems when attention focuses on some information sources at the expense of other relevant ones. The person may dwell excessively on the threat itself, leaving little attention to contextual factors or the possibilities for coping. When worrying about an exam, for example, a student may lose sight of the fact that it is worth a small part of the total grade, that it is not scheduled for another month, or that she or he is well prepared to deal with it. As a result, the overall context of the threat is inadequately appraised, effective coping options are not appreciated, and anxiety may intensify. A variant of this vicious circle may be paranoid rumination, in which awareness becomes focused narrowly on the self as the target of others' attention (Fenigstein & Vanable, 1992). The paranoid ignores contextual factors, and weaves the various manifestations of the threat into a tightly integrated logical structure (Shapiro, 1965).

In other instances, attention may focus too narrowly on given coping options. An anxious student may consider different options, such as various ways of studying for an upcoming exam, but without a thorough enough consideration of the exam itself to select an effective strategy. The redundancy bias would favor routine options and select against novel possibilities. With stronger narrowing, an individual may fail to sample adequately the entire set of possible options, perhaps considering only a small subset. The individual may even focus on a single solution, carrying it out in an inflexible and perseverative way. Extreme examples here can be found in obsessive–compulsives, who show excessive concerns with control and prevention along with a relatively general analysis of the threat itself. This tightly focused concern with control expresses itself in a coping strategy (e.g., washing, tidying) executed in a rigid, stereotyped, and perseverative manner (Shapiro, 1965).

Neural mechanisms most relevant to anxious cognition include two parallel sets of circuits that converge on the frontal lobe (Tucker & Derryberry, 1992). These circuits begin in posterior cortical regions, loop through subcortical limbic and basal ganglia regions, and then form "reentrant" projections back upon the frontal cortex. The pathways through the limbic system extract threat-related significance, whereas those through the basal ganglia select and prime potential response components. As they project back to the frontal lobe, anticipatory representations form a general plan integrating the critical cues and response options. These reentrant loops are modulated by dopaminergic systems ascending from the brainstem. By promoting a redundancy bias within their basal ganglia, limbic, and frontal targets, the dopaminergic projections narrow processing on the most relevant threat and coping components. Given continued reentrant processing among the basal ganglia, limbic system, and frontal lobe, the components of the plan (potential sources of threat and coping options) are specified in increasingly effective detail.

Conclusions

For many years psychologists have recognized that selective attention is one of the most central and influential of psychological processes. It plays a crucial role in guiding the course of information processing, in allowing for the entry of information into consciousness, and in facilitating the storage of information in memory. Although much progress has been made in studying these effects of attention, there has been a neglect of the factors controlling attention. Perhaps this has been due to assumptions of cognitive primacy, or perhaps to a reluctance to address issues involving a possible homunculus. In any event, the evidence is now quite strong that attention is in part controlled by motivational processes.

We have reviewed evidence that motivation regulates the attentional parameters of direction and breadth. Direction may be controlled by modulating the disengage, move, and engage components of orienting, while breadth may be regulated by means of the tonic activation and phasic arousal mechanisms. This type of hierarchical control, in which motivational processes can differentially access component attentional processes, provides for a highly specific and flexible tuning of the processing system. This tuning promotes a preparatory processing state that is adaptive, given the prevailing motivational conditions. However, it can also prove unadaptive if the components are inadequately coordinated.

Although we have a long way to go toward understanding motivated thought, the convergence of psychological and physiological models is most encouraging. Researchers studying motivation and attention can now draw upon evidence from many complementary sources across psychology and the neurosciences. These multidisciplinary approaches should support rapid progress in the years ahead.

References

Abernethy, C. N., & Leibowitz, H. W. (1971). The effect of feedback on luminance thresholds for peripherally presented stimuli. *Perception and Psychophysics, 10,* 172–174.

Alheid, G. F., & Heimer, L. (1988). New perspectives in basal forebrain organization of special relevance for neuropsychiatric disorders: The striatopallidal, amygdaloid, and corticopetal components of substantia innominata. *Neuroscience, 27,* 1–39.

Amaral, D. G. (1987). Memory: Anatomical organization of candidate brain regions. In F. Plum (ed.), *Handbook of physiology. Section 1: The nervous system. Volume V. Higher functions of the brain, Part 1.* (pp. 211–294). Bethesda, MD: American Physiological Society.

Andreasen, N. J. C., & Powers, P. S. (1975). Creativity and psychosis: An examination of conceptual style. *Archives of General Psychiatry, 32,* 70–73.

Bear, D. M. (1983). Hemispheric specialization and the neurology of emotion. *Archives of Neurology, 40,* 195–202.

Berlyne, D. E. (1971). *Aesthetics and psychobiology.* New York: Appleton-Century-Crofts.

Blaney, P. H. (1986). Affect and memory: A review. *Psychological Bulletin, 99,* 229–246.

Borod, J. C., Koff, E., & Buck, R. (1986). The neuropsychology of facial expression: Data from normal and brain-damaged adults. In P. D. Blank, R. W. Buck, & R. Rosenthal (eds.), *Nonverbal communication in the clinical context.* University Park, PA: Pennsylvania State University Press.

Brandt, J. L., Derryberry, D., & Reed, M. A. (1992). Failure and attentional narrowing. Unpublished manuscript.

Broadbent, D., & Broadbent, M. (1988). Anxiety and attentional bias: State and trait. *Cognition & Emotion, 2,* 165–183.

Burgess, C., & Simpson, G. B. (1988). Cerebral hemispheric mechanisms in the retrieval of ambiguous word meanings. *Brain & Language, 33,* 86–103.

Bursill, A. E. (1958). The restriction of peripheral vision during exposures to hot and humid conditions. *Quarterly Journal of Experimental Psychology, 10,* 113–129.

Callaway, E. & Dembo, D. (1958). Narrowed attention: A psychological phenomenon that accompanies a certain physiological change. *Archives of Neurology and Psychiatry, 79,* 74–90.

Coburn, K. L., Ashford, J. W., & Fuster, J. M. (1990). Visual response latencies in temporal lobe structures as a function of stimulus information load. *Behavioral Neuroscience, 104,* 62–73.

Davis, M. (1992). The role of the amygdala in fear and anxiety. *Annual Review of Neuroscience*, 15, 353–375.

Derryberry, D. (1988). Emotional influences on evaluative judgments: Roles of arousal, attention, and spreading activation. *Motivation and Emotion*, 12, 23–55.

Derryberry, D. (1989). Effects of goal-related motivational states on the spatial orienting of attention. *Acta Psychologica*, 72, 199–220.

Derryberry, D. (1991). The immediate effects of positive and negative feedback signals. *Journal of Personality and Social Psychology*, 61, 267–278.

Derryberry, D. (in press). Attentional consequences of outcome-related motivational states: Congruent, incongruent, and focusing effects. *Motivation and Emotion*.

Derryberry, D. & Reed, M. A. (1993). Attention and temperament: Orienting toward and away from positive and negative signals. Manuscript submitted for publication.

Derryberry, D., & Tucker, D. M. (1991). The adaptive base of the neural hierarchy: Elementary motivational controls on network function. In R. Dienstbier (ed.), *Nebraska symposium on motivation*, Vol. 38: *Perspectives on motivation* (pp. 289–342). Lincoln, NE: University of Nebraska Press.

Derryberry, D., & Tucker, D. M. (1992). Neural mechanisms of emotion. *Journal of Consulting and Clinical Psychology*, 60, 329–338.

Dixon, N. F. (1981). *Preconscious processing*. New York: Wiley.

Easterbrook, J. A. (1959). The effect of emotion on cue utilization and the organization of behaviour. *Psychological Review*, 66, 183–201.

Edelman, G. M. (1989). *The remembered present: A biological theory of consciousness*. New York: Basic Books.

Erdelyi, M. (1974). A new look at the new look: Perceptual defense and vigilance. *Psychological Review*, 81, 1–25.

Eriksen, C. W., & Yeh, Y. (1985). Allocation of attention in the visual field. *Journal of Experimental Psychology: Human Perception and Performance*, 11, 583–597.

Exner, J. E. (1979). *The Rorschach: A comprehensive system*. New York: Wiley.

Eysenck, M. W. (1982). *Attention and arousal*. New York: Springer-Verlag.

Fenigstein, A., & Vanable, P. A. (1992). Paranoia and self-consciousness. *Journal of Personality and Social Psychology*, 62, 129–138.

Gaffan, D., & Murray, E. A. (1990). Amygdalar interaction with the mediodorsal nucleus of the thalamus and the ventromedial prefrontal cortex in stimulus-reward associative learning in the monkey. *Journal of Neuroscience*, 10, 3479–3493.

Gandelman, R. (1983). Gonadal hormones and sensory function. *Neuroscience & Biobehavioral Reviews*, 7, 1–17.

Hockey, R. (1979). Stress and the cognitive components of skilled performance. In V. Hamilton & D. M. Warburton (eds.), *Human stress and cognition: An information processing approach* (pp. 141–177). New York: Wiley.

Hope, D. A., Rapee, R. M., Heimberg, R. G., & Dombeck, M. J. (1990). Representations of the self in social phobia: vulnerability to social threat. *Cognitive Research and Therapy*, 14, 177–190.

Isen, A. M., Daubman, K. A. (1984). The influence of affect on categorization. *Journal of Personality and Social Psychology*, 47, 1206–1217.

Isen, A. M., Daubman, K. A., & Gorgoglione, J. M. (1985a). The influence of positive affect on cognitive organization. In R. Snow & M. Farr (eds.), *Aptitude, learning and instruction: Affective and conative processes*. Hillsdale, NJ: Erlbaum.

Isen, A., Johnson, M., Mertz, E., & Robinson, G. (1985b). The influence of positive affect on the unusualness of work associations. *Journal of Personality and Social Psychology*, 48, 1413–1426.

Isen, A. M. (1987). Positive affect, cognitive processes, and social behavior. In L. Berkowitz (ed.) *Advances in experimental social psychology*, Vol. 20. New York: Academic Press.

James, W. (1984). What is emotion? *Mind*, 4, 118–204.

Johnston, W. A., Hawley, K. J., Plewe, S. H., Elliott, J. M. G., & DeWitt, M. J. (1990). Attention capture by novel stimuli. *Journal of Experimental Psychology: General*, 119, 397–411.

Jones, A. K. P., Friston, K., & Frackowiak, R. S. J. (1992). Localization of responses to pain in human cerebral cortex. *Science*, 255, 215–216.

Kelly, D. D. (1986). *Stress-induced analgesia*. New York: New York Academy of Sciences.

Kitayama, S. (1990). Interaction between affect and cognition in word perception. *Journal of Personality and Social Psychology*, 58, 209–217.

La Berge, D., Tweedy, J. R., & Ricker, J. (1967). Selective attention: Incentive variables and choice time. *Psychonomic Science*, 8, 341–342.

LeDoux, J. E. (1987). Emotion. In F. Plum (ed.), *Handbook of physiology. Section 1: The nervous system. Volume V. Higher functions of the brain, Part 1* (pp. 419–459). Bethesda, MD: American Physiological Society.

Leibowitz, H. W., & Appelle, S. (1969). The effect of a central task on luminance thresholds for peripherally presented stimuli. *Human Factors*, 11, 387–392.

Livingston, K. E. (1953). Cingulate cortex isolation for the treatment of psychoses and psychoneuroses. *Psychiatric Treatment*, 21, 374–378.

MacLean, P. D. (1958). Contrasting functions of limbic and neocortical systems of the brain and their relation to psychological aspects of medicine. *American Journal of Medicine*, 25, 611–626.

MacLeod, C., & Mathews, A. (1988). Anxiety and the allocation of attention to threat. *Quarterly Journal of Experimental Psychology*, 40, 653–670.

MacLeod, C., & Rutherford, E. M. (1992). Anxiety and the selective processing of emotional information: Mediating roles of awareness, trait and state variables, and personal relevance of stimulus materials. *Behavior Research and Therapy*, 30, 479–491.

Mandler, G. (1985). *Mind and body: Psychology of emotion and stress*. New York: W. W. Norton & Company.

Mathews, A. (1990). Why worry? The cognitive function of anxiety. *Behavioral Research and Therapy*, 28, 455–468.

Mathews, A., May, J., Mogg, K., & Eysenck, M. (1990). Attentional bias in anxiety: Selective search or defective filtering? *Journal of Abnormal Psychology*, 99, 166–173.

Mesulam, M. M. (1981). A cortical network for directed attention and unilateral neglect. *Annals of Neurology*, 10, 309–325.

Mikulincer, M., Kedem, P., & Paz, D. (1990a). Anxiety and categorization - 1. The structure and boundaries of mental categories. *Personality and Individual Differences*, 11, 805–814.

Mikulincer, M., Paz, D., & Kedem, P. (1990b). Anxiety and categorization - 2. Hierarchical levels of mental categories. *Personality and Individual Differences*, 11, 815–821.

Miller, S. M. (1987). Monitoring and blunting: Validation of a questionnaire to assess styles of information seeking under threat. *Journal of Personality and Social Psychology*, 52, 345–353.

Mischel, W., Ebbesen, E., & Zeiss, A. (1976). Determinants of selective memory about the self. *Journal of Consulting and Clinical Psychology*, 44, 92–103.

Mogg, K., Mathews, A., & Weinman, J. (1989). Selective processing of threat cues in anxiety states: A replication. *Behavior Research and Therapy*, 27, 317–323.

Mogg, K., Mathews, A., Bird, C., & MacGregor-Morris, R. (1990). Effects of stress and anxiety on the processing of threat stimuli. *Journal of Personality and Social Psychology*, 59, 1230–1237.

Navon, D. (1977). Forest before trees: The precedence of global features in visual perception. *Cognitive Psychology*, 9, 353–383.

Nebes, R. D. (1978). Direct examination of cognitive function in the left and right hemispheres. In M. Kinsbourne (ed.), *Asymmetrical function of the brain* (pp. 99–140). New York: Cambridge University Press.

Pandya, D. N., & Yeterian, E. H. (1985). Architecture and connections of cortical association areas. In A. Peters & E. G. Jones (eds.), *Cerebral cortex. Volume 4. Association and auditory cortices* (pp. 3–61). New York: Plenum Press.

Panksepp, J. (1981). Brain opioids: A neurochemical substrate for narcotic and social dependence. In S. Cooper (ed.), *Theory in psychopharmacology* (Vol. 1). New York: Academic Press.

Ploog, D. (1981). Neurobiology of primate audio-vocal behavior. *Brain Research Reviews*, 3, 35–61.

Posner, M. I. (1978). *Chronometric explorations of mind*. Hillsdale, NJ: Erlbaum.

Posner, M. I., Davidson, B. J., & Synder, C. R. R. (1980). Attention and the detection of signals. *Journal of Experimental Psychology: General*, 109, 160–174.

Posner, M. I., Inhoff, A. W., Friedrich, F. J., & Cohen, A. (1987). Isolating attentional systems: A cognitive-anatomical analysis. *Psychobiology*, 15, 107–121.

Posner, M. I., Petersen, S. E., Fox, P. T., & Raichle, M. E. (1988). Localization of cognitive operations in the human brain. *Science*, 240, 1627–1631.

Posner, M. I., Grossenbacher, P. G., & Compton, P. E. (in press). Visual attention. In M. Farah & G. Ratcliff (eds.), *The neuropsychology of high-level vision: Collected tutorial essays*. Hillsdale, NJ: Erlbaum.

Postman, L., & Brown, D. R. (1952). The perceptual consequences of success and failure. *Journal of Abnormal and Social Psychology*, 47, 213–227.

Pratto, F., & John, O. P. (1991). Automatic vigilance: The attention-grabbing power of negative social information. *Journal of Personality and Social Psychology*, 61, 380–391.

Rapoport, J. L. (1989). The biology of obsessions and compulsions. *Scientific American*, March, 83–89.

Reeves, F. B., & Bergum, B. O. (1972). Perceptual narrowing as a function of peripheral cue relevance. *Perceptual and Motor Skills*, 35, 719–724.

Robertson, L. C., Lamb, M. R., & Knight, R. T. (1988). Effects of lesions of temporal-parietal junction on perceptual and attentional processing in humans. *Journal of Neuroscience*, 8, 3757–3769.

Rolls, E. T. (1987). Information representation, processing, and storage in the brain: Analysis at the single neuron level. In J. P. Changeaux & M. Konishi (eds.), *The neural and molecular bases of learning* (pp. 503–540). New York: Wiley.

Rolls, E. T. (1990). Functions of neuronal networks in the hippocampus and of backprojections in the cerebral cortex in memory. In J. L. McGaugh, N. M. Weinberger, & G. Lynch (eds.), *Brain organization and memory: Cells, systems, and circuits* (pp. 184–210). New York: Oxford University Press.

Rothbart, M. K., & Derryberry, D. (1981). Development of individual differences in temperament. In M. E. Lamb & A. L. Brown (eds.), *Advances in developmental psychology*, Volume 1 (pp. 37–86). Hillsdale, NJ: Erlbaum.

Saper, C. B. (1987). Diffuse cortical projection systems: Anatomical organization and role in cortical function. In F. Plum (eds.), *Handbook of physiology. Section 1: The nervous system. Volume V. Higher functions of the brain*, Part 1 (pp. 169–210). Bethesda, MD: American Physiological Society.

Schacter, S., & Singer, J. E. (1962). Cognitive, social, and physiological determinants of emotional states. *Psychological Review*, 69, 379–399.

Schultz, W. (1986). Responses of midbrain dopamine neurons to behavioral trigger stimuli in the monkey. *Journal of Neurophysiology*, 56, 1439–1460.

Sergent, J. (1982). The cerebral balance of power: Confrontation or cooperation? *Journal of Experimental Psychology: Human Perception and Performance*, 8, 253–272.

Shapiro, D. (1965). *Neurotic styles*. New York: Basic Books.

Shaw, E. D., Mann, J. J., Stokes, P. E., & Manevitz, Z. (1986). Effects of lithium carbonate on associative productivity and idiosyncracy in bipolar outpatients. *American Journal of Psychiatry*, 143, 1166–1169.

Solso, R. L., Johnson, J. E., & Schatz, G. C. (1968). Perceptual perimeters and generalized drive. *Psychonomic Science*, 13, 71–72.

Spence, K. W. (1958). A theory of emotionally based drive (D) and its relation to performance in simple learning situations. *American Psychologist*, 13, 131–141.

Squire, L. R. (1986). Mechanisms of memory. *Science*, 232, 1612–1619.

Tellegen, A. (1985). Structures of mood and personality and their relevance to assessing anxiety, with an emphasis on self-report. In A. H. Tuma & J. D. Masser (eds.), *Anxiety and the anxiety disorders*. Hillsdale, NJ: Erlbaum.

Thayer, R. E. (1978). Toward a psychological theory of multidimensional activation (arousal). *Motivation and Emotion*, 2, 1–34.

Thayer, R. E. (1989). *The biopsychology of mood and arousal*. New York: Oxford University Press.

Toates, F. (1986). *Motivational systems*. Cambridge, England: Cambridge University Press.

Tucker, D. M. (1991). Development of emotion and cortical networks. In M. Gunnar & C. Nelson (ed.), *Minnesota symposium on child development: Developmental neuroscience*. New York: Oxford.

Tucker, D. M., & Derryberry, D. (1992). Motivated attention: Anxiety and the frontal executive mechanisms. *Neuropsychiatry, Neuropsychology, and Behavioral Neurology*, 5, 233–252.

Tucker, D. M., & Frederich, S. L. (1989). Emotion and brain lateralization. In H. Wagner & T. Manstead (eds.), *Handbook of psychophysiology: Emotion and social behavior*. New York: Wiley.

Tucker, D. M., & Williamson, P. A. (1984). Asymmetric neural control systems in human self-regulation. *Psychological Review*, 91, 185–215.

Tucker, D. M., Roth, R. S., Arneson, B. A., & Buckingham, V. (1978). Right hemispheric activation during stress. *Neuropsychologia*, 15, 697–700.

Tyler, S. K., & Tucker, D. M. (1982). Anxiety and perceptual structure: Individual differences in neuropsychological function. *Journal of Abnormal Psychology*, 91, 210–220.

Wachtel, P. L. (1968). Anxiety, attention, and coping with threat. *Journal of Abnormal Psychology*, 73, 137–143.

Wallace, D. M., Magnuson, D. J., & Gray, T. S. (1992). Organization of amygdaloid projections to brainstem dopaminergic, noradrenergic, and adrenergic cell groups in the rat. *Brain Research Bulletin*, 28, 447–454.

Wapner, W., Hamby, S., & Gardner, H. (1981). The role of the right hemisphere in the apprehension of complex linguistic materials. *Brain and Language*, 14, 15–33.

Watson, D., & Pennebaker, J. W. (1989). Health complaints, stress, and distress: Exploring the central role of negative affectivity. *Psychological Review*, 96, 234–254.

Watson, D., & Tellegen, A. (1985). Toward a consensual structure of mood. *Psychological Bulletin*, 98, 219–235.

Watts, F. N., McKenna, F. T., Sharrock, R., & Trezise, L. (1986). Colour naming of phobic-related words. *British Journal of Psychology*, 77, 97–108.

Weltman, G., & Egstrom, G. H. (1966). Perceptual narrowing in novice divers. *Human Factors*, 8, 499–506.

Weltman, G., Smith, J. E., & Egstrom, G. H. (1971). Perceptual narrowing during simulated pressure-chamber exposure. *Human Factors*, 13, 99–107.

Wise, R. A. (1987). Sensorimotor modulation and the variable action pattern (VAP): Toward a noncircular definition of drive and motivation. *Psychobiology*, 15, 7–20.

Yantis, S., & Johnson, D. N. (1990). Mechanisms of attentional priority. *Journal of Experimental Psychology: Human Perception and Performance*, 16, 812–825.

Zajonc, R. C. (1980). Feeling and thinking: Preferences need no inferences. *American Psychologist*, 35, 151–175.

Attitudes, Perception, and Attention

Russell H. Fazio
Indiana University

David R. Roskos-Ewoldsen
University of Alabama

Martha C. Powell
University of Colorado

Interpretations of an event are determined not only by features of the event itself but also by what the perceiver brings to the situation in terms of relevant knowledge, expectations, and affect. Social psychology has long recognized the constructive nature of perception and judgmental processes (e.g., Asch, 1948; Heider & Simmel, 1944; Kelley, 1950). This perspective formed the essence of the New Look movement (e.g., Bruner, 1957), which viewed perception not as the mere outcome of sensory processes but as an inferential act of categorization. On the basis of featural cues, a perceiver infers that a perceived object belongs to a given identity category.

Included among the many relevant constructs that a perceiver might bring to bear when witnessing an event is his or her attitude toward the object. Attitudes are summary evaluations of an object reflecting one's degree of favorability toward or liking for the object. They may range in nature from a "hot" affect (the attitude object being associated with a strong emotional response) to a "colder" more analytically based judgment of the favorability of the attributes possessed by the object (see Fazio, Sanbonmatsu, Powell, & Kardes, 1986; Fazio, in press; Zanna & Rempel, 1988).

It is well established that attitudes can bias the processing and judgment of information relevant to the attitude object. For example, documenting a phenomenon well known to any sports fan, Hastorf and Cantril (1954) observed varying perceptions of possible infractions committed during the course of a football game as a function of team allegiance. Regan, Straus, and Fazio (1974) found that subjects' attitudes toward a confederate influenced their attributions of the confederate's behavior, such that attitudinally inconsistent behavior was attributed to external forces. Lord, Ross, and Lepper (1979) observed subjects' attitudes toward capital punishment to affect their evaluations of empirical evidence concerning the deterrent efficacy of capital punishment. Fazio and Williams (1986) found individuals' attitudes toward the political candidates to bias their interpretation of the candidates' performances during the presidential debates. Carretta and Moreland (1982) found that Nixon supporters (as identified by earlier voting behavior) were more likely than McGovern supporters to evaluate Nixon's involvement with Watergate as within legal limits and to maintain their positive attitudes toward Nixon through the course of the Watergate hearings.

The studies just mentioned, as well as many others, make it evident that the perceiver's attitude plays an important role in how a stimulus is judged. It is clear that individuals tend to interpret new information regarding an attitude object in a manner that is consistent with their preexisting attitudes. The aim of the present chapter is to consider how far one can extend this reasoning. At what point in the cognitive "stream" do attitudes begin to exert their influence? Attitudes obviously affect judgmental processes. However, do they affect even more fundamental processes such as attention and perception?

In the present chapter, we summarize two empirical projects relevant to this question. The first concerns perception and, in particular, the possibility that attitudes ready the individual to perceive attitude-consistent events. The second section of the chapter concerns visual attention. We will review a series of experiments concerning what we refer to as the orienting value of attitudes—a tendency for attitude-evoking objects to automatically attract attention when they enter the visual field.

Attitudes as Determinants of Perception

As noted earlier, a voluminous literature documents that attitudes bias the processing of information relevant to the attitude object. It is interesting to note that this accumulated evidence typically involves interpretation and judgment in the context of a complex, enriched environment. That is, social psychologists generally have studied biased processing in fairly rich environments that readily allow for multiple interpretations of the target event. If one were to imagine a continuum ranging from sparse to rich environments, it seems quite plausible that the role of the perceiver would be more marked for the richer end of the continuum. The richer the environment and, hence, the more features that are available, the greater the latitude the individual enjoys in terms of the specific features that he or she might notice and consider. The features that receive consideration are likely to vary from perceiver to perceiver (e.g., Massad, Hubbard, & Newtson, 1979). It is not surprising that different samples of information lead to different interpretations.

Newton (1976) discussed biases in attribution processes in precisely this manner. He sought to distinguish between biased attributions due to faulty inference processes (higher order cognitive processes) and biases due to the input process (units of perception). He raised the question of whether it was possible that "both input processes and inference processes may lawfully respond to motivational variables" (p. 245). Thus, Newtson postulated that one factor in biased attribution concerned a bias in feature selection at the perceptual level.

Recent evidence by Sherman, Mackie, and Driscoll (1990) suggests that feature sampling is often an important component of biased processing. Sherman and colleagues provided subjects with a variety of unambiguous information concerning the attributes of two political candidates, including information pertaining to foreign policy affairs and economic matters. They found that a previously activated category (via a passive priming task) influenced which pieces of information subjects used in forming their judgment of the target. Subjects primed with terms related to economics were more likely to base their evaluations on the information relevant to economic matters, whereas those primed with terms related to foreign affairs relied more heavily on the information relevant to foreign policy.

In informationally rich environments, then, attitudinally biased processing may stem from the influence of attitudes on the sampling and weighing of specific features. This raises the question of whether the same attitudinally based bias would be evident even when the situation is stripped of elements that allow for differential feature sampling. Do attitudes bias what people report seeing in an information-sparse environment in which selective attention and weighing of information cannot be occurring? In effect, this question concerns the possibility that attitudes may be influential at a more fundamental perceptual level than suggested by previous research. Instead of focusing on biased interpretations of complex stimulus events occurring in informationally rich environments, our interest concerns potential bias in what an individual reports "seeing." It is the basic perceptual level of "seeing," *not* "interpreting," that differentiates the work we shall summarize from past studies. This notion of "seeing" versus "interpreting" is akin to work by Asch (1940) on conformity, where he posited that, ". . . the process under investigation entails a change in the object of judgment rather than in the judgment of the object" (p. 458).

One goal of the research to be described, then, was to investigate the possibility of biased perception in sparse environments that do not allow for selective attention to attitudinally congruent samples of information. A second goal concerned the existence of an objective, as opposed to a subjective, reality. In essence, past research has involved stimulus events for which there was no objectively correct judgment. The stimulus information allowed for at least two equally valid, or nearly so, subjective interpretations. Even when the stimuli presented in past research were simple, these stimuli have been open to multiple, valid interpretations. For example, Bruner and Minturn (1955) presented subjects with "a broken capital B in which the curved part of the figure was separated from the vertical line . . . [and] could, therefore, be seen either as a B or as a 13" (p. 22). Either interpretation was valid, but the figure presented was not objectively defined as either a "B" or a "13." Do attitudes bias perceptions even when the existence of an objective reality is highlighted for perceivers?

Powell and Fazio (1993) addressed these aims by examining a simple perceptual event. Essentially, subjects saw a flash of light on a computer screen and were required to note its location on the screen. Obviously, this is a much less complex environment than the interactions of participants during a presidential debate. In addition, the judgment that the subject was asked to make also was quite simple. The subject indicated whether the flash was within or beyond a boundary line. This is unlike previous research in which judgments involved making causal attributions or arriving at an overall interpretation of a series of events. The judgment does not require the integration of many pieces of information. Finally, this methodology involves an objective reality against which subjects' responses can be contrasted. The position of the flash of light on the screen was controlled and recorded by the computer. This allowed a comparison of the subject's response to the true position of the flash—a fact that was made salient to the subject.

The subjects' responses were collected in the context of what was described as a computerized "tennis" game that was under development. The flash of light represented the "ball" and the subject decided whether each volley of the ball was in or out of bounds. Biased perception on the part of the subject was examined as a function of the subject's liking or disliking for the target individual who ostensibly was playing against the computer.

Powell and Fazio (1993) reasoned that attitudes, and the expectations and hopes that they generate, operate on one's readiness to perceive in a certain way. That is, one's attitude may lead one to hope that a given event will occur. This enhanced readiness for a particular scenario may increase the likelihood that one does in fact see it that way.

For example, Player A, whom I detest, is involved in a tennis match, for which I am the linesman. Player A hits the ball, and, as I dislike Player A, I hope the ball lands out of bounds. In accord with Bruner's (1957) reasoning regarding the effects of category accessibility, my hope for an out call may both (1) ready me to perceive an event that fits the category, that is, a ball that does land out of bounds, and (2) widen the range of input characteristics that will be accepted as fitting the category, that is, some true in-balls may be perceived as out. The latter implies a greater likelihood of errors that match one's attitudinally driven hopes than errors that are attitudinally inconsistent. The former implies a faster latency in correctly detecting a ball's location when the true location matches one's hopes than when it does not.

The experimental procedure involved Indiana University students' participation in two ostensibly separate pilot studies. The first presumably concerned a series of paper-and-pencil puzzles, but actually provided a context in which subjects' attitudes toward a confederate could be manipulated. When the subject arrived, he or she was informed that a second subject also was scheduled to participate in the study. An entire series of events was then staged so as to induce liking or disliking toward the confederate. In the Like condition, the confederate sported an Indiana University sweatshirt; in the Dislike condition, she was wearing a sweatshirt with the insignia of a rival university. After the experimenter greeted the confederate by name and commented on her tardiness, the confederate replied either by sincerely apologizing and offering the lack of a parking space as an excuse, or by rudely indicating that she could not find a parking place and would like to get on with the experiment. When introduced to the subject, the confederate either smiled, said hello, and shook hands with the subject, or mumbled hello and looked down at her desk. After receiving instructions concerning the puzzles, the confederate asked if it would be okay to eat in the room. When the experimenter gave her consent, the confederate pulled a bag of cookies from her backpack and either offered one to the subject or did not. Finally, the subject either placed her radio and earphones in her backpack or played her radio at an annoyingly high volume. Postexperimental questionnaires revealed this manipulation to have been effective in producing differential liking for the confederate, as well as differential hopes regarding the confederate's winning or losing the computerized game.

After completing the first task, the subject and confederate received an explanation regarding the second study. It was described as a pilot test of a computerized game that was under development, and participants in the study were to help the experimenter test some aspects of the software and hardware. The subject and confederate were then told that one of them would be playing the game, which should serve to provide the experimenter with valuable information about the ease of maneuvering the ball. The other was to observe the game and make some judgments that would allow the experimenter to answer other questions regarding the clarity of the game. Through a rigged drawing, the subject was "randomly" chosen to be the observer and later learned that she was to play a role similar to that of a linesman for the tennis match between the confederate and a computerized opponent. The subject's task was to press a button on a response box to indicate after each and every volley (flash of light) whether the ball landed in or out of bounds. However, the subject was explicitly told she had no control over the game. Her calls would simply provide information for the experimenter on the adequacy of the resolution and contrast of the video display. The computer itself would determine whether a given ball was out of bounds and, if so, would terminate the point. Thus, the subject knew that her responses were to be compared to the true position of the ball as determined by the computer.

The subject then overheard a lengthy conversation in which the experimenter instructed the confederate about how the game was played. Although the subject believed that the confederate was actually playing against the computerized "robot" in the adjacent cubicle, the game was actually "played" solely by the computer. On target trials, the computer randomly selected and executed shots that appeared within 5 pixels of either side of the end line. The computer also executed filler shots that landed near the center of the court or beyond the target positions. The subjects' responses (key presses of IN or OUT) to the target trials, as well as the latencies of those responses, were recorded by the computer.

Simplified here, the analyses involving errors concerned a comparison of two types of errors: (1) errors that showed bias in favor of the confederate (calling a ball hit by the computerized opponent as "out" when it truly was "in" or calling a ball hit by the confederate as "in" when it truly was "out"), and (2) those errors that did not favor the confederate (calling a ball hit by the confederate as "out" when it truly was "in" or calling a ball hit by the opponent as "in" when it actually was "out"). The pattern of errors were indeed attitudinally congruent. Those subjects who were induced to like the confederate made more errors that favored the confederate. Subjects who had been induced to dislike the confederate showed a pattern of errors that favored the confederate's computerized opponent.

The magnitude of these attitudinally congruent biases increased with the closeness of the contest. Which player won any given point and, hence, the eventual game outcome, was randomly determined by the computer software. The error data were especially attitudinally congruent for close contests—ones in which the final score separated the two opponents by three or fewer points. In these close games, attitudinally congruent errors were significantly more numerous than attitudinally incongruent errors. Apparently, when the subject's involvement in the game was maintained as a result of the closeness of the score, the subject's attitudinally driven hopes regarding the game outcome produced a readiness to perceive events as matching the desired category.

The latency data also revealed a significant level of attitude-consistent bias. Subjects who liked the confederate were faster to make correct calls that favored the confederate, whereas subjects who disliked the confederate were faster to make correct calls that favored the computerized player, the confederate's opponent. (This effect was not moderated by the closeness of the game.) Thus, subjects displayed a greater readiness to perceive events that matched their attitudinally based hopes.

The focus of this experiment concerned individuals' reports of what they saw. Although the boundaries between perceptual stages are somewhat nebulous, it may be useful to review the various steps that were taken to ensure that subjects did report what they saw. First, the ostensible purpose of the subjects' participation was to test the equipment, not the subject. That is, subjects were led to believe that various parameters involving levels of contrast and resolution were under examination. In addition, subjects were also aware that the computer was recording their responses and that the experimenter would be comparing subjects' responses to the true positions of the ball. Furthermore, there was no incentive for the subjects to report anything other than what they saw. They had no control over the game and could in no way affect the outcome of the game. Instead, all aspects of the game were under the control of the computer. Finally, feedback was given after each trial, such that if a ball landed in bounds, play continued, regardless of the subjects' call. If a ball landed out of bounds, the play stopped and reset for the next volley, again, regardless of the subjects' call. Taken together, these steps were presumed to diminish any motivation the subject might have had to report anything other than what he or she saw. Despite these precautions, subjects' perceptions of the ball's position were influenced by their attitudinally based hopes regarding the outcome of the game.

The experimental findings attest to the powerful influence of attitudes on perception. Indeed, the results demonstrate the presence of biased processing, due to attitudinally driven hopes, at a basic perceptual level. It is striking that, when such a simple stimulus is presented in so sparse an environment, even subjects instructed to strive for accuracy showed such disparate (and attitudinally congruent) responses. The results imply that attitudes can create expectancies (or wishes) that make one receptive to attitude-consistent perceptual events.

Given that attitudes ready the individual in this way, it is no wonder that attitudes have been found to exert such a biasing influence on the interpretation of complex and rich information. Within a multifaceted event, those elements that are attitudinally congruent (or even somewhat so) enjoy a distinct advantage. The individual is both readier to perceive those elements that truly match the category expected on the basis of the attitude, and quicker to accept elements that only partially share the input characteristics associated with the category as fitting the expected category. Thus, the sample of features that individuals perceive when exposed to a complex event are likely to vary considerably as a function of their attitudes. Given that they have not perceived the same features, individuals with different attitudes are unlikely to judge complex and rich information in the same manner.

Attitudes as Determinants of Attention

The notion of attitudinally based receptivity also was central to a second research endeavor that addressed the potential influence of attitudes on fundamental processes. Individuals interact in a complex social world. As a result, people must select those stimuli, out of the myriad of potential stimuli, that receive attention. Although the cognitive system is capable of processing great quantities of information, the mechanism of selective attention enables the individual to focus on and adequately process specific information within this complex and diverse world. Roskos-Ewoldsen and Fazio (1992) suggested that it would be functional for an individual to direct attention to stimuli that have the potential for some hedonic consequences. In other words, a functional system would, through some mechanism, attend to stimuli that it likes or dislikes—ones that are attitude evoking. Thus, attitudes, or at least certain kinds of attitudes, could serve an orienting function because they direct our attention to attitude-evoking objects.

Although no earlier investigations had directly addressed this orienting value of attitudes, research by Erdelyi and Appelbaum (1973) suggests that attitude-evoking items may influence the allocation of attention. In this study, Jewish subjects were instructed to focus on a fixation point. Then the subjects were briefly exposed to a display of an object at the fixation point (either a swastika, Star of David, or the outline of a window) surrounded by eight other pictures. When the Star of David and swastika were the central items, subjects recalled significantly fewer of the remaining objects. Presumably, the Star of David and the swastika, both attitude-evoking objects for Jewish subjects, attracted attention. However, because the subjects were instructed to focus on the center of the display, their attention already was directed to the critical items (e.g., the swastika or the Star of David), which makes it difficult to ascertain whether the items attracted attention or maintained attention in this location. Thus, rather than attracting attention, a swastika and the Star of David may have disrupted the processing of the other elements of the display (Erdelyi & Blumenthal, 1973; Paulhus & Levitt, 1987).

Renninger and Wozniak (1985) provide additional evidence potentially relevant to the orienting value of attitudes. These investigators measured children's eye gaze. When presented with a number of items simultaneously, children tended to look both initially, and a greater number of times, at toys in which they had greater interest, as measured earlier by playing time. These results suggest that the child's attention was attracted to an attitude-evoking object. However, it is equally possible that the greater familiarity with the "liked" toys guided the allocation of the children's attention.

It is important to consider how attitudes might influence visual processing. Consistent with the hypothesis that affective responses may precede cognitive responses to a stimulus (Wilson, 1979; Zajonc, 1980), an attitude toward an object in the visual field may be activated from memory at an early stage in the processing of visual information. Once evoked, the attitude may orient further attention toward the object, so that, ultimately, the stimulus receives sufficient processing that the individual is able to report having noticed the presence of the object.

This possibility raises an important question concerning whether *all* attitudes serve the orienting function. The reasoning implies that the attitude must be activated from memory upon some coarse, preliminary, and possibly nonconscious identification of the object. Thus, the extent to which an attitude is capable of such automatic activation may be critical. It may be that some kinds of attitudes, namely more accessible ones, would be more likely than other kinds of attitudes to serve an orienting value. The approach to the issue of attitude accessibility was based on a view of attitudes as associations in memory between the attitude object and one's evaluation of the object (see Fazio, in press, for a review). The strength of these object-evaluation associations in memory can vary. This associative strength between the object and the evaluation of the object has been observed to act as a determinant of the likelihood that the evaluation will be automatically activated from memory upon one's encountering the attitude object (Fazio et al., 1986).

This view of varying associative "strength" allows for the consideration of the attitude–nonattitude continuum (Fazio et al., 1986). At the nonattitude end of the continuum is the case of the individual not possessing any a priori evaluation of the object stored in memory. As one moves along the continuum, an evaluation is available in memory and the strength of the association between the object and the evaluation increases. The stronger the association, the greater the likelihood of the attitude being activated upon observation of the attitude object. At the upper end of the continuum is the case of the well-learned association. In this instance, the association between the attitude object and the evaluation of the object is sufficiently strong that the evaluation is capable of being activated automatically from memory upon mere observation of the attitude object. Roskos-Ewoldsen and Fazio (1992) suggested that attitudes at this end of the continuum, those that are likely to be activated from memory upon the mere observation of the attitude object, serve the attention-orienting function.[1] In a series of four experiments, they sought to determine whether such attitude-evoking objects attract attention when presented in an individual's visual field.

Experiments 1 and 2: Do Subjects Notice Attitude-Evoking Objects?

On each trial of Experiments 1 and 2, subjects were briefly presented (1500 msec) a display containing six objects and asked to immediately list as many of the objects as they possibly could. It was reasoned that, if attitude-activating objects do serve an orienting function, then subjects would be more likely to notice and subsequently report those objects toward which they had more accessible attitudes.

The displays consisted of six pictures of common animals and objects arranged in a circle (e.g., bicycle, jet, squirrel, flower, purse, umbrella). The items were taken from Snodgrass and Vanderwart's (1980) standardized set of 260 pictures. In selecting the stimuli, the pictures were restricted to those that were easily identifiable and nameable (above the median on Snodgrass and Vanderwart's name agreement index). Snodgrass and Vanderwart also provide normative data concerning the familiarity of the pictures. These data were used to ensure that the six objects in any given display were equivalently familiar (i.e., the six most familiar items were placed in the same display, the next six most familiar items in the next display, and so forth).

In Experiment 1, attitude accessibility was measured. Prior research has demonstrated that an individual's attitude can be located along the attitude/nonattitude continuum by measuring the latency with which the individual can respond to an inquiry about the attitude (e.g., Powell & Fazio, 1984). The faster the individual can respond, the stronger the object-evaluation association and the more likely the attitude is capable of automatic activation upon observation of the attitude object (Bargh, Chaiken, Govender, & Pratto, 1992; Fazio, 1993; Fazio et al., 1986). To measure attitude

[1]The effect of attitudes on perception, as illustrated by the Powell and Fazio (1993) research, is similarly hypothesized to be dependent on the accessibility of the attitude. It was our presumption that attitudes toward the confederate were relatively accessible for all the subjects in the Powell and Fazio experiment. The various events that led to the confederate's being either liked or disliked transpired immediately before the subject viewed the computerized game. Thus, attitudes toward the confederate were likely to be salient. Theoretically, however, the biasing effects of attitudes on perception should vary directly with attitude accessibility.

accessibility, subjects in Experiment 1 were presented with each object from the stimulus displays one at a time and instructed to indicate whether they liked or disliked the object by pressing the appropriate key. (The order of this task and the noticing task was counterbalanced across subjects.)

Roskos-Ewoldsen and Fazio (1992) anticipated that subjects would be more likely to notice objects that were attitude activating. The extent to which an object was attitude activating was operationally measured via response latency. At an operational level, then, it was predicted that subjects would be more likely to notice those objects about which they could indicate their attitude relatively quickly when asked to do so.

For any given subject and any given display, the three objects associated with the faster latencies were considered the high attitude accessibility items and the three associated with the slower latencies the low attitude accessibility items. The number of items characterized by high and low attitude accessibility that were noticed was then averaged across the displays. As expected, a significantly greater number of objects toward which subjects had more accessible attitudes were noticed than were objects toward which subjects had less accessible attitudes. These results indicate that objects toward which subjects could express their attitudes quickly were more likely to be noticed and subsequently reported.

These results are consistent with the idea that certain attitudes serve an orienting function. More importantly, the experiment demonstrates an association between the accessibility of attitudes toward an object and the likelihood that the object will receive attention. However, the data are correlational in nature. It is possible that other variables increase the accessibility of attitudes from memory and also increase the likelihood that an object will receive attention when presented in a visual display. In Experiment 2, attitude accessibility was manipulated instead of measured, so as to rule out such "third-variable" explanations of the results of Experiment 1.

Earlier research has demonstrated that repeated expression of one's attitude enhances the object-evaluation association and increases the likelihood that the evaluation will be capable of automatic activation upon observation of the object (Fazio et al., 1986; Houston & Fazio, 1989; Powell & Fazio, 1984). In Experiment 2, attitude accessibility was manipulated by inducing subjects to make repeated like/dislike judgments of a randomly selected group of three items from each display of six objects.

Specifically, when subjects arrived for the experiment, they were given booklets and told that the experiment concerned their judgments of a number of objects. For one of these judgment tasks, the subjects were instructed to indicate their attitude toward each of the pictured objects. The response was a dichotomous "like/dislike" judgment. For another set of pictures, subjects were told to judge whether the objects were animate or inanimate. Both tasks were self-paced. The order of these two tasks was counterbalanced across subjects. One-half of the subjects completed the attitude-rehearsal task first, while the remaining subjects completed the control (animate judgment) task initially. In addition, the subjects were warned that, because the experiment concerned whether the judgments became easier with practice, they may see certain items more than once. Subjects were asked to answer each time they saw a picture. After subjects completed each judgment task, they indicated how difficult they found the judgment task and if the judgment task got any easier as they completed it, so as to bolster the cover story.

This manipulation of attitude accessibility resulted in strengthening the object-evaluation association for half of the objects, while holding constant frequency of exposure to all the pictures. Thus, two conditions in which attitudes differ with respect to their position along the attitude–nonattitude continuum could be compared. If our reasoning is correct, and attitude-laden objects do serve an orienting function, then subjects should notice and subsequently report a higher proportion of the objects from the attitude judgment task.

After the attitude judgment task, subjects participated in the noticing task that was employed in Experiment 1. Each visual display was presented for 1500 msec and the subjects listed as many of the items that appeared as they could. Subjects reported having seen a significantly greater proportion of the attitude rehearsal objects than the control objects. Rehearsing one's attitude increased the probability that the subject would notice the object when it was later presented. Thus, when an object was experimentally made more capable of activating an associated evaluation, the object was more likely to receive attention.

The findings from these two experiments demonstrate that objects toward which subjects had accessible attitudes were more likely to have been noticed in a visual display. This held true regardless of whether attitude accessibility was measured, as in Experiment 1, or manipulated, as in Experiment 2. Apparently, then, attitude-evoking stimuli do receive attention when presented in a visual field. As argued earlier, it is functional for an organism to be able to selectively detect and attend to those items in the environment that have the potential for hedonic consequences.

Nevertheless, the goal of the research was to demonstrate that attitude-evoking objects *attract* attention. Experiments 1 and 2 indicate that attitude-evoking items *receive* attention. Unfortunately, the results do not unambiguously demonstrate that such objects attract attention. The subjects' very task involved their noticing as many items as possible. Thus, an important question concerns whether attitude-laden items attract attention when subjects are not actively searching a visual display. In other words, do attitude-evoking objects only receive attention when an individual is actually searching the environment, or do such objects attract attention in more general circumstances as well?

Experiment 3: Do Attitude-Evoking Objects Attract Attention Incidentally?

If attitude-eliciting items were to receive attention even when subjects were performing a task for which it was functional to ignore the attitude-evoking items, then one could be more confident that actively searching and encoding the environment is not a necessary condition for the observed effect. Evidence of subjects' having attended to attitude-activating objects, when doing so was counter to the task at hand, would constitute stronger support for the orienting value of accessible attitudes.

Experiment 3 utilized an incidental learning paradigm to examine this question. Specifically, subjects were involved in a number–letter discrimination task. In the critical phase of the experiment, the to-be-discriminated items were surrounded by six "distracter" items. Subjects were instructed to ignore these distractor items and perform the number–letter judgment as quickly as possible. The accessibility of subjects' attitudes toward three of the six distractor items was enhanced experimentally. To the extent that attitude-evoking objects attract attention, subjects were expected to notice and subsequently report those distractor items toward which they had made repeated attitudinal judgments—despite the fact that it was functional for the subjects to ignore these distractor items.

There were three stages to the experiment. The first stage involved manipulating the accessibility of subjects' attitudes toward the various objects. Just as in Experiment 2, subjects made repeated like/dislike judgments of half of the objects and repeated animate/inanimate judgments of the remaining objects. Following the manipulation, the subjects received instructions for a second task—a number–letter discrimination task, which was simple to perform. In the middle of the subject's screen, a number or a letter appeared on each trial. The subject simply pressed one key if the stimulus was a number, another if it was a letter. The subjects were told to respond as quickly as possible. After a series of trials like this, the subject was informed that the aim of the final task was to see how well they could do at number–letter discrimination when some potential distractors were also presented. On these trials, the number or letter was to be surrounded by six pictures. The subject was to ignore the pictures. In fact, the subject was told to try to respond just as quickly as before.

At the end of a series of such trials, the subjects were asked to list any distractors that they could remember. This came as quite a surprise to the subjects. In fact, some of them expressed some anger toward the experimenter, feeling that the contract had been violated. After all, they had been told to try to ignore the distractors. In fact, the subjects did not do well. They recalled on average only about 4 of the 54 pictures that had been shown as distractors. However, they were more likely to have incidentally noticed those objects toward which they had earlier rehearsed their attitudes, that is, the attitude-evoking ones. A subsequent recognition test yielded similar results. Thus, subjects were more likely to notice those distractors that were attitude evoking, even though it was not functional for subjects to attend to the pictures given the nature of the task they were performing.

Experiment 4: Do Attitude-Evoking Distractors Interfere with Search Performance?

The results of Experiment 3 provide further support for the hypothesis that attitude-evoking objects attract attention. However, the experiment relied on incidental learning as an indirect measure of attention. Experiment 4 employed a traditional visual search task in order to examine attention more directly. The subject's task was to determine as quickly as possible whether either of two target objects was present in the display. On each trial, the subject was presented with the names of two target objects, for example, dog and banana, followed by the presentation of a display of 6 pictures. If either one of the target objects was in the display, the subject was to answer yes.

However, the task had a little wrinkle in it—one modeled after Shiffrin and Schneider's (1977) "diagonal" study in which subjects were to search for a target letter in displays presenting 4 letters. In the Shiffrin and Schneider study, the target letter for any given trial was restricted to appearing in the upper left or lower right corner of the display, if it was to appear at all. Given appropriate earlier training, items in the irrelevant positions interfered with the subjects' visual search, indicating that these distractor items were automatically attracting the subject's attention.

A similar procedure was followed in the present experiment. Subjects were told that the task was difficult and that to make it easier the stimuli had been arranged in a particular way. If the target was present, it would be in one of three positions of the display. No target would ever be in the other three positions. So, the subjects could effectively ignore these positions. In order to train subjects to trust this rule, the subjects then undertook a series of 30 practice trials in which the rule was never violated.

Following this training, the actual experimental trials began. Of major interest was the latency with which subjects could perform the visual search task. How quickly could they indicate that a target was or was not present? These trials varied in terms of what the subjects had done at the beginning of the experiment with respect to those objects that were located in the distractor positions. For some of the trials, all the distractors were ones for which the subjects had earlier performed attitude rehearsal. For other trials, the distractors were items about which the subjects had made animate/inanimate judgments. If objects toward which one has a strongly associated evaluation automatically attract attention, then distractors from the attitude rehearsal set should interfere with visual search performance. That is, subjects should be slower to respond that a target object was or was not present when the distractors were from the attitude rehearsal set than when they were from the control set.

As predicted, when subjects had highly accessible attitudes toward the distractors, they took significantly longer to determine whether the target was present than if their attitudes toward the distractors were relatively less accessible from memory. This held true whether the target was or was not present in the display. Apparently, the presence of attitude-evoking distractors interfered with subjects' ability to efficiently search the display, indicating that such objects attracted subjects' attention, even though subjects were told to ignore those positions.

By virtue of its involving a much more direct measure of attention, Experiment 4 is distinct from the earlier experiments. In one way or another, memory for the objects was involved in all three of the earlier experiments. In Experiments 1 and 2, even though subjects immediately reported the objects they had noticed in the display, they had to briefly rely on their memory for the displays. In Experiment 3 there was a clear memory component because subjects were asked to recall and recognize objects from displays they had seen several minutes earlier. The results of the first three experiments may reflect the fact that subjects can remember attitude-evoking objects better or longer. This was not the case in the present experiment. Even if attitude-evoking items may be easier to remember, it is difficult to understand how the ease of remembering attitude-evoking objects could explain the results regarding interference on the visual search task. Instead, Experiment 4 lends further credence to the attentional explanation of Experiments 1, 2, and 3.

The findings from this series of four experiments provide evidence that objects toward which individuals have accessible attitudes automatically attract attention when they enter the visual field. Like earlier experimental work (Fazio et al., 1986), the results indicate that attitudes involving relatively strong object-evaluation associations in memory may be automatically activated from memory upon the individual's encountering the attitude object. However, these four experiments go beyond the earlier findings in establishing that attitudes can exert an influence at an early stage in an individual's processing of visual information. Apparently, preattentive identification of a visual stimulus can be sufficient to activate an associated evaluation of the object from memory. Such activation serves to direct further attention to the visual stimulus, increasing the likelihood that the stimulus receives sufficient processing for it to be consciously noticed and reported.

Supplementary analyses of the recall and recognition data from Experiment 3 examined the role of attitude extremity (deviation from the neutral point of an attitude scale) in the allocation of attention (see Roskos-Ewoldsen & Fazio, 1992, for details). These analyses revealed main effects of both the attitude accessibility manipulation and attitude extremity, with no interaction. Thus, the effect of attitude extremity was independent of the effect of attitude rehearsal. Given that more extreme attitudes tend to be more accessible from memory (Fazio & Williams, 1986; Houston & Fazio, 1989; Powell & Fazio, 1984), they are more likely to meet what we theorize to be the prerequisite condition for an attitude to influence visual attention— namely, that it be capable of automatic activation. However, once activated, extreme attitudes also are apt to more powerfully draw attention to the objects; such objects are, by virtue of their strongly associated extreme evaluations, more hedonically relevant than attitude objects associated with more mild evaluations.

Regardless of whether the evaluation is mild or extreme in its degree of polarization, the accessibility of the attitude plays an important role in the attentional process. Some attitudes, those that involve relatively strong object-evaluation associations in memory, are more likely to be activated in response to the attitude object and, hence, are more likely to orient attention toward the object.

This conclusion is consistent with an emerging body of literature suggesting that affect is preattentively "extracted" and influences subsequent perception. For example, a number of studies have found the presentation of undetectable affective stimuli to have consequences for subsequent perception and judgment (e.g., Greenwald, Klinger, & Liu, 1989; Niedenthal, 1990). Kitayama (1990) has observed that, under certain conditions, briefly displayed words that are affectively charged can be identified more accurately than neutral words. Hansen and Hansen (1988) have obtained evidence suggesting a preattentive processing of faces for features of facial threat (see also Hampton, Purcell, Bersine, Hansen, & Hansen, 1989), and Pratto and John (1991) have provided evidence indicating that attention is automatically directed toward undesirable trait terms. All of these findings point to an important role of affect in attention, perception, and judgment processes. The experiments summarized here indicate that the preattentive activation of the affect associated with an object influences the extent to which the object attracts additional attention.

In some of the research mentioned above, as well as Taylor's (1991) recent review, the specific focus has involved a comparison of positive and negative affect. The major interest has been in testing the possibility that negative stimuli attract attention more so than positive stimuli, presumably because attending to negative stimuli is relatively more adaptive and more critical to the individual's well-being. For example, the research by Hansen and Hansen (1988) found that angry faces attracted more attention than did happy faces. Similarly, the work of Pratto and John (1991) revealed that undesirable trait terms attracted more attention than did desirable ones. In this context, it is interesting to note that our experiments failed to detect any such asymmetry favoring negative objects. Regardless of whether the object was positively or negatively valued, the more accessible the subject's attitude toward the object, the greater the likelihood that the object automatically attracted attention. However, as Roskos-Ewoldsen and Fazio (1992) emphasized, the stimuli for these experiments were not selected with the specific comparison of positive to negative stimuli in mind. A more systematic examination involving carefully equated positive and negative objects may reveal a tendency for individuals to be particularly attentive to negative objects.

It also is possible, however, that our failure to detect the advantage for negative stimuli that others have observed reflects a difference between person and object domains. The person domain may constitute a rather special case. Negative information about the social characteristics of other people is relatively unexpected (Kanouse & Hanson, 1972; Kanazawa, 1992) and highly diagnostic (Skowronski & Carlston, 1989). As a result, we may have learned to be especially sensitive to the general class of features suggestive of a person who is to be avoided. Being extravigilant for, and directing attention to, negative-stimulus persons, such as those with threatening facial gestures or those described by negative traits, may prove adaptive.

In the object domain, on the other hand, the likelihood of encountering positive and negative stimuli may not be as disproportionate as it is for the person domain. It may prove just as functional to have attention drawn to those objects from which one can attain desirable outcomes as it is to have attention drawn to those objects that pose the potential for some form of dissatisfaction. In our view, the influence that accessible attitudes—positive or negative—have on attention is enormously functional for the individual. If a strongly associated evaluation of the object exists in memory, then that object attracts attention. Hence, we are likely to notice those objects that we have personally defined as likable—those that can help us, that can provide some reward or satisfaction, those that we wish to approach. Likewise, we are likely to notice those objects toward which we have a strongly associated negative evaluation—those that can hurt us, those that we wish to avoid. This receptivity for noticing affectively laden objects can set the stage for an individual to maximize positive outcomes and minimize negative ones.

The Power of Attitudes

The research summarized here illustrates the power that attitudes can exert. Just as suggested by Smith, Bruner, and White (1956), attitudes provide the individual with "a ready aid in 'sizing up' objects and events in the environment" (p. 51). This sizing up is not limited to higher order cognitive processes that involve the selection, interpretation, judgment, and/or integration of attributes possessed or displayed by the object. Instead, attitudes also have the potential to influence more basic processes of perception and attention. They can ready the individual to perceive events that are attitudinally congruent. They also can ready the individual to attend to those objects in the visual field that are hedonically consequential.

Acknowledgments

Preparation of this chapter was supported by Research Scientist Development Award MH00452 and Grant MH38832 from the National Institute of Mental Health. The authors thank Paula Niedenthal for her helpful comments on an earlier draft.

References

Asch, S. E. (1940). Studies in the principles of judgments and attitudes: II. Determination of judgments by groups and by ego standards. The Journal of Social Psychology, 12, 433–465.
Asch, S. E. (1948). The doctrine of suggestion, prestige, and imitation in social psychology. Psychological Review, 55, 250–276.
Bargh, J. A., Chaiken, S., Govender, R., & Pratto, F. (1992). The generality of the automatic attitude activation effect. Journal of Personality and Social Psychology, 62, 893–912.
Bruner, J. S. (1957). On perceptual readiness. Psychological Review, 64, 123–152.
Bruner, J. S., & Minturn, A. L. (1955). Perceptual identification and perceptual organization. The Journal of General Psychology, 53, 21–28.
Carretta, T. R., & Moreland, R. L. (1982). Nixon and Watergate: A field demonstration of belief perseverance. Personality and Social Psychology Bulletin, 8, 446–453.
Erdelyi, M. H., & Appelbaum, A. G. (1973). Cognitive masking: The disruptive effect of an emotional stimulus upon the perception of contiguous neutral items. Bulletin of the Psychonomic Society, 1, 59–61.
Erdelyi, M. H., & Blumenthal, D. G. (1973). Cognitive masking in rapid sequential processing: The effect of emotional picture on preceding and succeeding pictures. Memory and Cognition, 1, 201–204.
Fazio, R. H. (1993). Variability in the likelihood of automatic attitude activation: Data re-analysis and commentary on Bargh, Chaiken, Govender, & Pratto (1992). Journal of Personality and Social Psychology, 64, 753–758.
Fazio, R. H. (in press). Attitudes as object-evaluation associations: Determinants, consequences, and correlates of attitude accessibility. In R. E. Petty & J. A. Krosnick (eds.), Attitude strength: Antecedents and consequences. Hillsdale, NJ: Erlbaum.
Fazio, R. H., & Williams, C. J. (1986). Attitude accessibility as a moderator of the attitude-

perception and attitude-behavior relations: An investigation of the 1984 presidential election. *Journal of Personality and Social Psychology, 51,* 505–514.

Fazio, R. H., Sanbonmatsu, D. M., Powell, M. C., & Kardes, F. R. (1986). On the automatic activation of attitudes. *Journal of Personality and Social Psychology, 50,* 229–238.

Greenwald, A. G., Klinger, M. R., & Liu, T. J. (1989). Unconscious processing of dichoptically masked words. *Memory and Cognition, 17,* 35–47.

Hampton, C., Purcell, D. G., Bersine, L., Hansen, C. H., & Hansen, R. D. (1989). Probing "pop out": Another look at the face-in-the-crowd effect. *Bulletin of the Psychonomic Society, 27,* 563–566.

Hansen, C. F., & Hansen, R. D. (1988). Finding the face in the crowd: An anger superiority effect. *Journal of Personality and Social Psychology, 54,* 917–924.

Hastorf, A. H., & Cantril, H. (1954). They saw a game: A case study. *Journal of Abnormal and Social Psychology, 49,* 129–134.

Heider, F., & Simmel, M. R. (1944). An experimental study of apparent behavior. *American Journal of Psychology, 57,* 243–259.

Houston, D. A., & Fazio, R. H. (1989). Biased processing as a function of attitude accessibility: Making objective judgments subjectively. *Social Cognition, 7,* 51–66.

Kanazawa, S. (1992). Outcome or expectancy? Antecedent of spontaneous causal attribution. *Personality and Social Psychology Bulletin, 18,* 659–668.

Kanouse, D. E., & Hanson, L. R. (1972). Negativity in evaluations. In E. E. Jones, D. E. Kanouse, H. H. Kelley, R. E. Nisbett, S. Valins, & B. Weiner (eds.), *Attribution: Perceiving the causes of behavior* (pp. 47–62). Morristown, NJ: General Learning.

Kelley, H. H. (1950). The warm-cold variable in first impressions of persons. *Journal of Personality, 18,* 431–439.

Kitayama, S. (1990). Interaction between affect and cognition in word perception. *Journal of Personality and Social Psychology, 58,* 209–217.

Lord, C. G., Ross, L., & Lepper, M. R. (1979). Biased assimilation and attitude polarization: The effects of prior theories on subsequently considered evidence. *Journal of Personality and Social Psychology, 37,* 2098–2109.

Massad, C. M., Hubbard, M., & Newtson, D. (1979). Selective perception of events. *Journal of Experimental Social Psychology, 15,* 513–532.

Newtson, D. (1976). Foundations of attribution: The perception of ongoing behavior. In J. H. Harvey, W. J. Ickes, & R. F. Kidd (eds.), *New directions in attribution research* (pp. 223–247). Hillsdale, NJ: Erlbaum.

Niedenthal, P. M. (1990). Implicit perception of affective information. *Journal of Experimental Social Psychology, 26,* 505–527.

Paulhus, D. L., & Levitt, K. (1987). Desirable responding triggered by affect: Automatic egotism? *Journal of Personality and Social Psychology, 52,* 245–259.

Powell, M. C., & Fazio, R. H. (1984). Attitude accessibility as a function of repeated attitudinal expression. *Personality and Social Psychology Bulletin, 10,* 139–148.

Powell, M. C., & Fazio, R. H. (1993). Unpublished raw data. Indiana University.

Pratto, F., & John, O. P. (1991). Automatic vigilance: The attention-grabbing power of negative social information. *Journal of Personality and Social Psychology, 61,* 380–391.

Regan, D. T., Straus, E., & Fazio, R. H. (1974). Liking and the attribution process. *Journal of Experimental Social Psychology, 10,* 385–397.

Renninger, K. A., & Wozniak, R. H. (1985). Effects of interest on attentional shift, recognition, and recall in young children. *Developmental Psychology, 21,* 624–632.

Roskos-Ewoldsen, D. R., & Fazio, R. H. (1992). On the orienting value of attitudes: Attitude accessibility as a determinant of an object's attraction of visual attention. *Journal of Personality and Social Psychology, 63,* 198–211.

Sherman, S. J., Mackie, D. M., & Driscoll, D. M. (1990). Priming and the differential use of dimensions in evaluation. *Personality and Social Psychology Bulletin, 16,* 405–418.

Shiffrin, R. M., & Schneider, W. (1977). Controlled and automatic human information processing: II. Perceptual learning, automatic attending, and a general theory. *Psychological Review*, 84, 127–190.

Skowronski, J. J., & Carlston, D. E. (1989). Negativity and extremity biases in impression formation: A review of explanations. *Psychological Bulletin*, 105, 131–142.

Smith, M. B., Bruner, J. S., & White, R. W. (1956). *Opinions and personality*. New York: John Wiley & Sons.

Snodgrass, J. G., & Vanderwart, M. (1980). A standardized set of 280 pictures: Norms for name agreement, image agreement, familiarity, and visual complexity. *Journal of Experimental Psychology: Human Learning and Memory*, 6, 174–215.

Taylor, S. E. (1991). Asymmetrical effects of positive and negative events: The mobilization-minimization hypothesis. *Psychological Bulletin*, 110, 67–85.

Wilson, W. R. (1979). Feeling more than we can know: Exposure effects without learning. *Journal of Personality and Social Psychology*, 37, 811–821.

Zajonc, R. B. (1980). Preferences need no inferences. *American Psychologist*, 35, 160–171.

Zanna, M. P., & Rempel, J. K. (1988). Attitudes: A new look at an old concept. In D. Bar-Tal & A. W. Kruglanski (eds.), *The social psychology of knowledge* (pp. 315–354). New York: Cambridge University Press.

Automatic Emotion: Attention and Facial Efference

Christine H. Hansen
Ranald D. Hansen
Oakland University

Davidson and Cacioppo (1992) have characterized emotion as "a self-organizing, integrative state that is coherent across several response systems" (p. 21). In defining the function of emotions, many theorists have embraced the concept that emotions, or at least a set of primitive emotions, have survival value—that they serve as prototypic, primitive but rapid, responses to biologically significant stimuli (Ekman, 1992; Izard, 1977; Öhman, 1986; Plutchik, 1980; Tomkins, 1962; Zajonc, 1985). If so, it seems reasonable to hypothesize that the mere presence of biologically significant stimuli instigates automatic processes and that the consequences of these automatic processes will be evident across response systems. In this chapter, we will present the results of research testing this hypothesis with one stimulus whose features display biologically significant information, the human face. We begin where this program of research began: with an amazingly large body of research indicating that humans should have the capacity to automatically process facial displays of emotion, but surprisingly little direct evidence that they actually possess it.

Facial Displays of Emotion: Efficiently Processed, Available, Constant

If one were searching for stimuli whose features were both capable of carrying biologically significant information and capable of being automatically processed, facial displays of emotion would be good candidates. First, a great deal of research indicates that primitive processing of faces is both sufficiently efficient that it may be automatic and appears early enough in development to be potentially innate. Second, a substantial body of research suggests that facial displays of emotion possess the properties requisite for the development of automatic processing, even if it is not innate.

Primitive processing of facial displays of emotion is highly efficient—efficient enough to suggest that it is automatic. Findings reported by a number of researchers indicate that the human perceptual system is particularly well suited for detecting human faces (Homa, Haver, & Schwartz, 1976; van Santen & Jonides, 1978). Further, although it is controversial, there is some evidence that common facial feature configurations can be processed holistically as perceptual units rather than as a conjunction of features (Intons-Peterson, 1981, 1984). Other research hints at the possibility that this capacity may be innate. For example, many researchers have reported that infants, even early in development, are capable of recognizing and discriminating among facial displays of emotion (Barrera & Maurer, 1981; LaBarbera, Izard, Vietze, & Parisi, 1976; Schwartz, Izard, & Ansul, 1985; Wilcox & Clayton, 1968). In addition, many theorists have argued that the universality of emotional facial displays implies the operation of innate mechanisms (cf. Adelmann & Zajonc, 1989; Darwin, 1872/1965; Ekman, 1972; Ekman Levenson, & Friesen, 1983; Izard, 1977; Mineka & Sutton, 1992; Öhman, 1986; Öhman, Dimberg, & Öst, 1985; Tomkins, 1962, 1981; Zajonc, 1985; Zajonc, Murphy, & Inglehart, 1989). Similar claims can be made from data indicating that neonates and infants show evidence of organized facial displays (Ekman & Oster, 1979), which appear to be facial expressions of emotion (Fox & Davidson, 1988). Whether these findings are interpreted as evidence for the operation of innate mechanisms or not (Hager & Ekman, 1983; Mineka & Sutton, 1992; Zajonc & McIntosh, 1992), they nevertheless indicate that facial displays of emotion satisfy an important prerequisite for the development of automaticity.

The results of an extensive series of experiments conducted by Shiffrin, Schneider, and their colleagues have documented the properties of stimuli that enable the development of automatic processing (Schneider, Dumais, &

Shiffrin, 1984; Schneider & Fisk, 1982; Schneider & Shiffrin, 1977a,b; Shiffrin & Schneider, 1977). Their research clearly demonstrated that automaticity evolves when stimuli are repeatedly available, and their features are "consistently mapped" to their significance. For example, subjects given the task of processing an array of stimuli in search of a target among distractors developed the capacity to automatically detect a stimulus only after many trials and, then, only when the stimulus consistently appeared as a target, not as a distractor. When the stimulus was "variably mapped" to significance (on some trials the stimulus was the target and on others it appeared as a distractor), the development of automaticity was directly linked to consistency—the proportion of trials on which it appeared as the target (Schneider & Fisk, 1982).

Facial displays of emotion clearly have the necessary properties for the development of automatic processing: displays are available and consistently associated with specific emotions across individuals and cultures. This is amply demonstrated in a substantial body of research accumulated primarily through the efforts of Ekman and his associates (Ekman, 1972; Ekman, Davidson, & Friesen, 1990; Ekman & Friesen, 1975, 1978; Ekman, Friesen, & Ancoli, 1980; Ekman, Friesen, & Ellsworth, 1972; Ekman, Friesen, & O'Sullivan, 1988; Ekman et al., 1983; Ekman, Sorenson, & Friesen, 1969; Izard, 1971). Across all of the cultures investigated, unique configurations of facial features have been consistently mapped to happiness, sadness, anger, fear, and disgust. Individuals can readily identify these emotions even when posed by an individual from an anthropologically distant culture. Analyses of facial feature distortions, using an anatomically based coding system for groupings of facial muscles (Ekman & Friesen, 1978), indicate that facial displays of emotion are quite consistent across cultures. And, while there is some evidence to the contrary (cf. Bruner & Tagiuri, 1954), the majority of the research supports the conclusion that unique facial displays are consistently associated with each of these emotions and demonstrates that these facial displays are meaningful to other human beings (Ekman, 1989; Ekman et al., 1988, 1990). There are times, of course, when facial displays do not match emotions. Dissociation between facial displays and emotions can occur because of "display rules" (Ekman, 1972), because the displayer is masking an emotion (Ekman & Freisen, 1982), or because the displayer is engaging in "facial deceit" (Ekman & Friesen, 1974). But, such deviations from consistency from time to time may not preclude the development of automaticity. Schneider and Fisk (1982) found that automaticity can develop, although it requires more practice, even at fifty percent consistency. In summary, the case for humans' capacity to automatically process facial emotions is circumstantial, but strong. A great deal of evidence suggests that humans should have this capacity, but little direct evidence indicates that they do.

Automatic Processing: Distinctions and Potential Capabilities

Before discussing the research we have conducted to test automatic processing of facial displays of emotion, we need to make a few careful distinctions (cf. Bargh, 1989). Most theorists would agree that automatic processes are simple, efficient, nonflexible, and stimulus-controlled processes, which are unaffected by capacity limitations on controlled cognition (Bargh, 1982, 1984, 1989; Posner & Snyder, 1975; Treisman, 1982; Treisman & Souther, 1985). Some would argue that automatic processes cannot be suppressed by controlled processes (e.g., Schneider et al., 1984; Shiffrin & Schneider, 1977). Others would disagree, arguing that automatic processes can be suppressed when they conflict with controlled processes, but that the suppression will consume controlled processing resources (Bargh, 1982, 1984, 1989; Bargh & Pratto, 1986). Finally, a recent analysis of cognitive automaticity (Bargh, 1989) highlighted the importance of avoiding the conceptual confounding of automatic with nonconscious processes. Bargh notes that automatic processes can be categorized as preconscious or postconscious, depending on whether the occurrence of the automatic effect requires conscious awareness of the stimulus instigating the automatic process.

What can be accomplished with facial displays of emotion at the level of automatic processing? Research and theory suggest a number of functions that might be accomplished at the nonconscious level. First, automatic processes might be capable of influencing the affective content of controlled processes. Indeed, some research indicates that this might occur at the preconscious level (Bargh, Litt, Pratto, & Spielman, 1988; Kunst-Wilson & Zajonc, 1980; Seamon, Brody, & Kauff, 1983; Seamon, Marsh, & Brody, 1984). Second, automatic processes could be capable of altering the accessibility of memorial representations available for controlled processing, thus impinging on the content of controlled processes (Bower, 1981; Bower & Cohen, 1982; Clark, 1982; Clark & Isen, 1982; Isen, 1984; Isen, Shalker, Clark, & Karp, 1978). Third, automatic processes may be capable of instigating activity in noncognitive response systems, such as facial feature distortions (e.g., Cacioppo & Petty, 1979; Cacioppo, Petty, Losch, & Kim, 1986; Schwartz, Ahern, & Brown, 1979; Schwartz, Fair, Salt, Mandel, & Klerman, 1976; Tassinary & Cacioppo, 1992) or patterns of autonomic activity (Ekman, 1992; Ekman et al., 1983; Levenson, 1992). Finally, automatic processes may be capable of influencing the allocation of controlled processing resources by orienting or restricting conscious attention (Fiske, 1980; Posner, 1992; Pratto & John, 1991; Roskos-Ewoldsen & Fazio, 1992; Shiffrin & Schneider, 1977).

Automatic Processes and Conscious Affect

A number of researchers have attempted to demonstrate that automatic processing of stimuli can alter the affective content of conscious processes even though the stimuli fail to achieve conscious awareness (Adelmann & Zajonc, 1989; Greenwald, Klinger, & Lui, 1989; Kihlstrom, 1987; Kunst-Wilson & Zajonc, 1980; Niedenthal, 1990; Tassinary, Orr, Wolford, Napps, & Lanzetta, 1984; Zajonc, 1980; Zajonc et al., 1989). Zajonc (1980) captured the essence of the research—"preferences need no inferences" (p. 151). A number of researchers have reported data indicating that subjects had predictable emotional responses to stimuli to which they had been exposed but did not consciously recognize (Bargh et al., 1988; Greenwald et al., 1989; Kunst-Wilson & Zajonc, 1980; Seamon et al., 1983, 1984).

There is some controversy surrounding the nature of the processing that occurs in many of these experiments (Cheesman & Merikle, 1984, 1985, 1986; Fowler, Wolford, Slade, & Tassinary, 1981; Greenwald, 1992; Marcel, 1983a,b). For example, the criterion for testing the operationalization of nonconscious processes (stimulus detection, awareness, discrimination, recognition) has varied across experiments. Although the findings supported the hypothesis that automatic processes can influence conscious affect, some doubt exists about whether these effects occur at the nonconscious level. The strongest support for nonconscious automaticity occurs when the researcher adopts the subject's phenomenological definition of conscious awareness, and the weakest support is obtained when an objective threshold definition of conscious awareness is used (Cheesman & Merikle, 1986; Greenwald, 1992).

Automatic Processes and Emotive Accessibility

A number of theorists have contended that most, or all, stimuli receive some automatic processing (Bargh, 1982, 1984; Bruner, 1957; Neisser, 1967). Some research has indicated that the emotive meaning of stimuli is a likely target of this automatic processing (Stangor & Duan, 1991). This could have an interesting consequence for controlled processing if the accessibility of a memorial representation is a function of its total activation by both controlled and automatic processes (cf. Bargh, 1982, 1984; Bargh & Pietromonaco, 1982). If, as many contend, memory is emotionally structured, one consequence of automatic processing might be priming of the accessibility of memorial representations available to controlled processing (Bower, 1981; Bower & Cohen, 1982; Clark, 1982; Clark & Isen, 1982; Isen, 1975; Isen et al., 1978).

Much of the support for this hypothesis rests on research demonstrating that controlled processing of stimuli is susceptible to emotive priming effects resulting from the prior controlled processing of another stimulus, even though the goal of the prior processing was unrelated to the goal of the subsequent processing (e.g., Isen, 1975; Isen et al., 1978; Stangor & Duan, 1991). Hansen (Hansen, 1992; Hansen & Shantz, 1992), for example, found that positive and negative mood states influenced the accessibility of emotionally valenced stereotypic schemas used by subjects in an impression formation task. Subjects were incidentally exposed to instrumental music, which had been pilot tested to induce either a positive or a negative mood. After this exposure, they performed an impression formation task in which they were instructed to form an accurate impression based on a presented list of traits. In a subsequent memory test, subjects in a positive mood failed to recognize negative traits to which they had been exposed and reported recognizing positive traits to which they had not been exposed. Conversely, subjects in a negative mood failed to recognize positive traits to which they had been exposed and reported recognizing negative traits to which they had not been exposed. The findings suggested that the mood induction stimulus had primed emotively congruent memorial representations (Bargh, 1984; Bargh & Pratto, 1986; Bargh & Thein, 1985). In short, encoding of the impression was influenced by the prior activation of memorial representations in an unrelated task. The effect was neither controlled nor intended, a category of effect Bargh (1989) labeled context-dependent automaticity.

One other domain of theory and research may produce findings supportive of preconscious automatic influences on the emotive accessibility of memorial representations available for controlled conscious processing: repression. As noted by Davis (Davis, 1987; Davis & Schwartz, 1987), the essence of repression (Freud, 1915/1957) is the inaccessibility of memorial representations associated with negative emotions, particularly threat. Some evidence is beginning to accumulate in this area that nonconscious automatic processes may be involved in maintaining the repressive inaccessibility of memorial representations associated with threat and, hence, in defending controlled conscious processing from threatening cognitions (Wexler, Michaelis, Warrenburg, & Schwartz, 1989a; Wexler, Schwartz, Warrenburg, Cervis, & Terlatzis, 1986; Wexler, Schwartz, Warrenburg, & Jamner, 1989b). Although these findings are consistent with theoretical accounts of the potential role of perceptual defense in repression (Erdelyi, 1974, 1985; Erdelyi & Goldberg, 1979; Hansen, Hansen, & Shantz, 1992) and are promising, they are not conclusive. It is not at all clear that subjects' postexposure reports of being unaware of the presence of stimuli should be taken as prima facie evidence that the stimuli failed to achieve conscious awareness. This might be particularly true of repressors who may wish to avoid more extensive processing of any threatening stimuli of which they had become aware.

Automatic Processes and Noncognitive Response Systems

Evidence for automatic innervation of activity in noncognitive response systems comes from two sources. First, researchers using facial electromyography have demonstrated that facial muscle movements, reliably discriminated by the valence of the eliciting stimuli, marked the occurrence of valenced emotional information processing. These facial muscle movements are micromomentary and covert and have a sufficiently short latency from stimulus onset that it is unlikely that they are the result of controlled processes (Cacioppo, Losch, Tassinary, & Petty, 1986; Cacioppo, Martzke, Petty, & Tassinary, 1988; Cacioppo & Petty, 1979; Dimberg, 1990; Tassinary & Cacioppo, 1992). In addition, a recent experiment indicated that these facial muscle movements elicited by emotional stimuli could not be suppressed or altered by controlled processes (Cacioppo, Bush, & Tassinary, 1992). Together, these properties suggest that these micromomentary facial displays of (valenced) emotion are innervated by automatic processes.

The second source of evidence comes from researchers investigating the effects of directed facial activity (e.g., Ekman, 1992; Ekman et al., 1990; Levenson, 1992; Levenson, Ekman, & Friesen, 1990). Here, there are two categories of data suggestive of automatic processes. First, when subjects are directed to configure their faces into facial displays of emotion, measures of autonomic activity yield discriminable patterns (Ekman, 1992; Levenson, 1992; Levenson et al., 1990). Although subjects may or may not have been consciously aware of the facial displays of emotion produced by the directed facial action task (Torangeau & Ellsworth, 1979; Izard, 1981; Tomkins, 1981), the production of patterned automatic activity was not intended, and there is some evidence that it cannot be regulated by controlled processing (Schwartz, 1990). Second, a number of experiments indicate that facial displays of emotion directed by controlled processes are *not* equivalent to spontaneous facial displays of emotion, such as facial expressions generated in response to external emotional stimuli or facial displays that occur during mimicry (e.g., Dimberg, 1982, 1986, 1990; McHugo, Lanzetta, Sullivan, Masters, & Englis, 1985; Öhman, 1986). Further, recent research (Ekman et al., 1990) indicates that brain physiology coincident with spontaneous facial emotion differs from that coincident with facial emotions directed by controlled processing. Although not conclusive, the data from these psychophysiological investigations are supportive of the hypothesis that facial displays of emotion as well as autonomic patterns can be regulated by automatic processes. This interpretation is particularly tantalizing because it yields the prediction that the operation of automatic processes will be marked by a broad spectrum of effects including facial efference.

Automatic Processes and the Allocation of Controlled Attentional Resources

Finally, we turn our attention to a powerful resource for coping with a biologically significant stimulus, controlled attentional processing. Most cognitive theorists contend that controlled attentional processing is highly flexible, serial in nature, under conscious control, and capacity limited

(Bargh, 1984, 1989; Broadbent, 1958; Posner & Snyder, 1975; Shiffrin & Dumais, 1981; Shiffrin & Schneider, 1977; Treisman, 1982; Treisman & Souther, 1985). Because of its limitations in speed and capacity, control over the deployment of controlled processing resources is a critical function. Automatic processes, then, would have to be construed as rather powerful if they could impinge on the allocation of these resources. And, a number of theorists have proposed that automatic processes serve just such a function (Bargh, 1982, 1984, 1989; Bargh & Pietromonaco, 1982; Bruner, 1957; Neisser, 1967; Kitayama, 1990, 1991; Shiffrin & Schneider, 1977; Srull & Wyer, 1989; Treisman, 1982; Treisman & Gelade, 1980; Treisman & Paterson, 1984; Treisman & Souther, 1985; Wyer & Gordon, 1982). Nonconscious processing may be capable of orienting conscious attention to a particular stimulus in an array (Bargh, 1982; Posner, 1992; Roskos-Ewoldsen & Fazio, 1992; Shiffrin & Schneider, 1977) and restricting (Posner, 1992) or amplifying (Kitayama, 1990, 1991) the controlled processing resources allocated to that stimulus or some aspect of the stimulus (cf. Bargh, 1984; Bruner, 1957; Neisser, 1967; Stangor & Duan, 1991; Srull & Wyer, 1989).

Ample research exists to assert that some stimuli can be automatically detected (Schneider et al., 1984; Schneider & Fish, 1982; Schneider & Shiffrin, 1977a,b; Shiffrin & Schneider, 1977; Treisman, 1982; Treisman & Gelade, 1980; Treisman & Paterson, 1984; Treisman & Souther, 1985). In numerous experiments, these researchers have demonstrated that the detection of target stimuli was not influenced by the size of the array of distractors in which it appears. This finding was important because it implied that targets were not being detected as a result of controlled processing. Controlled processing is serial. Detection of a stimulus would require a sequential search of the stimulus array and, hence, detection of the target using controlled processing resources would be sensitive to the number of distractors in the array. The absence of this effect indicated that stimuli were being detected through automatic processes. Other researchers have reported evidence suggesting that some stimuli automatically attract attention and that this attraction is difficult, if not impossible, to suppress (e.g., Roskos-Ewoldsen & Fazio, 1992; Pratto & John, 1991). The research reported by Pratto and John (1991) and by Roskos-Ewoldsen and Fazio (1992) was particularly interesting because it extended this line of inquiry directly to automatic processing of emotion. Ewoldsen and Fazio reported evidence indicating that objects associated with highly accessible attitudes (i.e., the objects were hedonically significant) consumed controlled processing resources even though subjects were attempting to ignore them or the objects appeared as distractors in an array. Pratto and John reported similar results but found the effort stronger for negative than for positive stimuli. In a Stroop-type task, stimulus words with a negative connotation interfered with subjects' naming of the color in which the word was printed. They also found that subjects' recall was better for negative than for positive words. These results indicated that more extensive controlled processing resources had been devoted to negative than to positive words. Pratto and John argued that this resulted from "automatic vigilance" for negative stimuli that cannot be suppressed by controlled processing.

Again, we must carefully delineate the nature of the automatic and controlled processes being described. For example, Roskos-Ewoldsen and Fazio (1992) argued that their results reflected preattentive automatic detection (cf. Treisman & Souther, 1985) because the influence of attention-attractive distractors was not inhibited by controlled processing goals. If this influence on attentional orientation had been suppressed, even at a cost to controlled processing, it would have been more difficult to contend that their influence derived from preattentive automatic processes (Posner & Snyder, 1975). In that case, it could be argued that all distractors received minimal attentional processing and that automatic processes increased the probability that hedonic distractors became the focus of attention and achieved conscious awareness. With this in mind, we turn to our research on automatic and controlled processing of facial emotions.

Automatic Processing of Emotional Faces

Our theoretical perspective is built on the assumption that facial displays of emotion are prototypic, biologically significant, social stimuli. Obviously, automatic processing of facial displays of other individuals would be adaptively advantageous. These automatic processes would be simple, fast, nonflexible, and their operation would be opaque to conscious awareness. We think it probable that these automatic processes will turn out to be innate, but we do not wish to argue that position here. It is our presumption that automatic processes devoted to emotional faces serve an important function and that its function will be manifest in the capabilities of these processes.

In particular, it seems to us that evolution would be particularly likely to favor the capacity to efficiently process and respond to threat. Certainly there is ample evidence that negative stimuli exert an exceptionally strong force on a number of psychological processes (Heider, 1958; Lang, Bradley, & Cuthbert, 1992; Kahneman & Tversky, 1984; Pratto & John, 1991). Given this function of coping with threat, what could we anticipate about the capabilities of automatic processes devoted to facial displays of emotion? First, we hypothesized that the capacity to efficiently detect the presence of threat and to orient controlled processing resources to that threat would be advantageous. We predicted that as a result of automatic processes, facial displays connoting threat (anger and fear) would attract conscious attention. Second, it also seemed reasonable to hypothesize that automatic processes would facilitate controlled processing of facial displays of threat by either amplifying controlled processing (e.g., increasing the accessibility of threat-relevant memorial representations) or restricting its focus to threat (e.g., suppressing distraction). Third, we hypothesized that the ability to instigate incipient coping activity in noncognitive systems also would be biologically advantageous. We expected, then, that facial feature distortions and autonomic nervous system activity could be innervated as a consequence of the automatic processing of facial displays of emotion. Let us now turn to the research conducted in our own laboratory that bears on these hypotheses.

Face in the Crowd

The first experiments that we conducted were designed to test a "face-in-the-crowd" hypothesis (Hansen & Hansen, 1988). In three experiments, subjects were given the task of reporting the presence (Hansen & Hansen, 1988, Experiments 1 and 3) or the location (Experiment 2) of a happy face in an angry crowd or of an angry face in a happy crowd. We predicted that an angry face in a happy crowd would be found faster than a happy face in a crowd of angry faces. We based this prediction on the hypothesis that angry faces could be preattentively detected. At the preattentive level, we construed automatic processing as a filtering process. As a result of filtering, some faces in an array (a crowd) are "passed through" and others are "filtered out" (Hansen & Hansen, 1988); a face passed through is more likely to be the target of attention and to receive controlled processing. From the perspective of the individual, it would seem that a passed-through face commanded attention—it would appear to "pop out" of the crowd (Treisman, 1982; Treisman & Gelade, 1980; Treisman & Paterson, 1984; Treisman & Souther, 1985).

The anticipated face-in-the-crowd effect emerged from the reaction time data in all three experiments. The third experiment was modeled after the research reported by Treisman demonstrating the "pop-out" phenomenon, a diagnostic for preattentive parallel detection. Results from Experiment 3 seemed to support the hypothesis that angry faces could be automatically detected at the level of preattentive processing. It took substantially more time to find a happy face in a crowd of eight than of three angry distractors, whereas the time to find an angry face was not appreciably influenced by the size of the crowd. This was the kind of asymmetry that would be expected if angry faces could be preattentively detected.

However, the emotional expressions on the faces used in this experiment (Hansen & Hansen, 1988, Experiment 3) were found to be confounded with light and dark areas (Hampton, Purcell, Bersine, Hansen, & Hansen, 1989). The face-in-the-crowd effect was obtained in two experiments using unconfounded faces (Hampton et al., 1989, Experiments 1 and 3), but the times to find both a happy face in an angry crowd and, significantly, an angry face in a happy crowd were influenced by the position of the face in the crowd. This would not have occurred if angry faces popped out of happy crowds as a result of preattentive, parallel detection. Consistent with this conclusion, pop out has not appeared in replications of our original experiment (Hansen & Hansen, 1988, Experiment 3) using unconfounded faces (Stewart, Purcell, & Skov, 1993) and appears with the confounded faces only when subjects are aware of the confound (Purcell, Stewart, & Skov, 1993). In short, it is quite clear now that angry faces do not pop out of happy crowds as the result of the preattentive, parallel detection of angry faces.

Controlled anger inferiority and automatic anger superiority The evidence indicates that facial emotions do not seem to have signal value at the level of preattentive parallel processing. Finding a face in a crowd displaying a discrepant emotion requires a sequential, attentional search of the crowd, and the face-in-the-crowd effect reflects an asymmetry in that sequential search. It takes more time to serially search a crowd of angry than of happy faces. When crowds of nine faces had to be searched, scanning differences were quite evident (Hampton et al., 1989, Experiments 1 and 3; Hansen & Hansen, 1988, Experiment 1; Stewart et al., 1993, Experiment 2; but see Stewart et al., 1993, Experiment 3 for an exception); but, when only four faces had to be scanned, the effect was unreliable (Hampton et al., 1989, Experiment 2; Stewart et al., 1993, Experiment 3). There are at least two factors that could have contributed to the less rapid sequential search of angry than of happy crowds.

First, if multiple faces receive minimal attentional processing when attention is being intentionally shifted from one face to the next, they may disrupt the controlled search of the crowd directed by the individual's conscious processing strategy or goal. These faces would be insufficient to attract attention and achieve conscious awareness but sufficient to serve as a distraction. Controlled processing resources, then, would have to be devoted to suppressing the distraction (Bargh, 1984, 1989; Bargh & Pietromonaco, 1982; Roskos-Ewoldsen & Fazio, 1992). Because controlled processing has a limited capacity, allocation of a portion of these limited resources to the suppression of distraction would reduce the residual capacity available for the controlled search of the faces in the crowd (Bargh, 1984, 1989; Bargh & Pratto, 1986). If automatic processes are capable of maintaining vigilance for threat, as suggested by the findings reported by Pratto and John (1991), angry faces should have greater distracting power than happy faces. As a result, more controlled processing resources would have to be devoted to suppressing the attractive influence of angry than of happy faces, and the controlled search of an angry crowd would be less efficient than the controlled search of a happy crowd. Seemingly, these automatic processes operate above the level of preattentive parallel processes but below the level at which conscious awareness of the distractor emotions could serve as an input to controlled search (cf. Pratto & John, 1991, p. 390). However, the superiority of angry faces as distractors resulting from automatic vigilance for threat is only one factor that may have contributed to the less efficient search of angry crowds. Perhaps the most obvious potential explanation for the face-in-the-crowd effect is the inferiority of the controlled processing of each sequentially searched angry face (Hampton et al., 1989).

Indeed, the research literature on processing facial emotions seemed to offer almost unqualified support for the position that angry faces are more difficult to process than are happy faces (e.g., Kirouac & Doré, 1984, 1985; Mandal & Palchoudhury, 1985; McAndrew, 1986; Stalans & Wedding, 1985). More careful examination, however, reveals that this literature is problematic. Many researchers have not been rigorous when defining the processing operations required by their experimental tasks. Distinctions have not been consistently made among detection, recognition, and discrimination. The problems are made more accute by poorly conceived operationalizations. For example, Stalans and Wedding (1985) reported that positive emotions were discriminated more rapidly than were negative emotions. But, for some reason, these researchers considered surprise to be a positive emotion. In short, although an anger inferiority effect in controlled processing seems well documented, the research is sufficiently troublesome that our acceptance should be tempered by caution.

Alternative explanations   Before proceeding, a few points should be considered. Most important, compelling evidence in favor of the inferior controlled processing of each angry face in the crowd would not necessarily falsify the contribution of automatic vigilance to the face-in-the-crowd effect as described above. It may have been overwhelmed by any postattentive, controlled processing effects. Second, even if one were to accept the position that the face-in-the-crowd effect derived solely from inferior controlled processing of angry faces, the question of why angry faces require more extensive controlled processing must be addressed. On one hand, the results were strikingly similar to the automatic vigilance effects by Pratto and John (1991). The longer controlled processing times absorbed by angry faces may have been the inevitable consequence of these faces automatically engaging controlled processing resources. That is, anger inferiority at the level of controlled processing may have resulted from anger superiority at the level of automatic processing. Alternatively, angry faces simply may be more difficult to process.

Two explanations have been offered in defense of this last position. First, the facial feature distortions resulting in displays of some emotions may be more confusable or less distinct than those involved in other displays (cf. Hampton et al., 1989; Stalans & Wedding, 1985). The facial feature distortions yielding a display of happiness, for example, might be particularly distinctive; those yielding a display of anger might have considerable overlap with those involved in fear or sadness. But, this does not yield a completely satisfying account in the case of the face-in-the-crowd findings reported earlier. The emotion displayed on each face in every crowd of the experiments was either happiness or anger. Unless one proposes that conscious processing of facial features is rather extensive and necessarily driven to the point of recognition (i.e., anger/not anger vs happy/not happy), discriminating anger from happiness would seem to be about as difficult as discriminating happiness from anger.

A second explanation depends on the frequency with which facial displays of various emotions are encountered and processed (Hampton et al., 1989; McAndrew, 1986). More controlled processing resources must be devoted to less frequently encountered stimulus features because the memorial representations that must be activated in order to process these stimuli are less accessible (Bargh, 1984; Bargh, Bond, Lombardi, & Tota, 1986). If angry faces are encountered less frequently than happy faces, which seems probable, an anger inferiority effect might emerge. This, in one sense, is quite compatible with the hypothesis that automatic processes orient attention to threatening stimuli. Research indicates that attention is drawn to unexpected or less frequent stimulus features (Bargh, 1989) and, perhaps because they *cannot* be automatically processed, these features require more controlled processing (Bargh, 1984; Hastie & Kumar, 1979; Srull & Wyer, 1989; Stangor & Duan, 1991). Here, however, we encounter an apparent theoretical dilemma. The position described here suggests that attention is drawn to stimuli that cannot be encoded with the activation of inaccessible memorial representations. Roskos-Ewoldsen and Fazio (1992), on the other hand, argued from their data that attention is drawn to stimuli whose processing can be achieved by the activation of highly accessible memorial representations. Perhaps the simplest resolution is to argue that the representations that must be activated for encoding facial emotions are highly accessible, but in the context of these representations, angry faces are unexpected. In any case, both positions would maintain that facial emotions that attract attention as the result of automatic processing also would absorb more controlled processing capacity once attention has been engaged. Clearly, a more definitive test of the hypothesis that angry faces attract attention as the result of automatic processes was needed.

Automatic and Controlled Processing of Facial Emotion: Focus of Attention

The first experiment we conducted in our next series (Hansen & Hansen, 1992) was designed to test this hypothesis. We sought to construct an experimental paradigm that would allow for a clear test of the hypothesis. Our goal was to design a stimulus array and a controlled processing task that would allow us to use saccadic eye movements as a meaningful marker of the operation of automatic processes. On each trial of the experiment, subjects were exposed to two faces. One was on the left and the other was on the right, equidistant at a visual angle of 8.1° from a central fixation point. The faces used on each trial were photographs of the same person (Ekman & Friesen, 1976) and subtended a visual angle of 4.94° vertically and 3.75° horizontally.

Subjects were exposed to two blocks of trials, each having a different processing task. In one block, subjects were given the conscious processing task of detecting an angry face. In the other block, subjects were given the task of detecting a happy face. Subjects were instructed to respond as rapidly as possible without sacrificing accuracy. They were forewarned that saccading from the central fixation point to the target they were seeking was the preferred strategy for maximizing performance. The faces were displayed only after subjects focused on the central fixation point. The distance of the faces from the fixation point was selected so that subjects could not perform the task without shifting their attention away from the fixation point. Preliminary research had shown that subjects could not reliably shift their attention to the target they were seeking under these circumstances.

On each trial, the face on the right displayed either happiness or anger. The face on the left displayed either happiness or anger. In other words, on one-half of the trials, the same emotion was displayed on both faces; on the remaining half of the trials, the faces displayed different emotions. The same-emotion trials precluded adoption of an arbitrary one-face search strategy, because the emotion displayed on one face was not diagnostic of the emotion displayed on the other.

The primary data acquired during each trial were electrooculographic (EOG) signals used to measure the saccadic eye movements marking shifts of conscious attention. Because psychophysiological measures are relatively uncommon, we will explain the methods for treating these data more fully (see Oster & Stern, 1980, and Pivik, 1986, for more detailed descriptions). Horizontal saccadic eye movements were recorded from .25-cm Ag-Ag/Cl surface electrodes in bipolar placement at the outer canthi of the subject's eyes. EOG signals were amplified with a Grass 7P122 Low-Level DC amplifier, passed through a Metrabyte A–D converter, and sampled by a microprocessor at a rate of 1 kHz. A sequence of calibration trials was conducted at the beginning of each trial block. On the first calibration trial, subjects focused their attention on the central fixation point. On the second, they focused their attention on the point where the left face would appear. On the third, they focused their attention where the right face would appear. These callibration trials allowed the transformation of acquired experimental data into meaningful points in horizontal space designating the orientation of the subject's conscious attention. The calibration data were also used by the microprocessor to trigger the onset of the face displays. Faces were not presented until the subject's attention was focused on the central fixation point.

Two parameters were extracted from the EOG data acquired during each of the experimental trials. The first was the direction of the subject's initial saccade from the fixation point—to the left or the right facial display. The second parameter was the latency of the initial saccade from the time of stimulus display onset. These parameters were transformed into the direction and the latency of saccades toward and away from happy and angry faces. These transformed parameters were submitted to multivariate analyses of variance and planned contrasts.

Controlled processing and attention The results indicated that the initial saccade was *not* influenced by controlled processing of the stimulus faces. Subjects had been given the task of detecting the presence of an angry face in one block and the presence of a happy face in the other. If subjects could process the facial displays of emotion prior to a shift in attention, they would reliably shift their attention to the target: a happy face in one block, an angry face in the other block. Yet, subjects were about as likely to shift their eyes to a happy face as to an angry face. The manipulation of the processing task across blocks had no effects. They were no more likely to shift their attention to a happy face when they were searching for a happy face than when they were searching for an angry face. Likewise, they were no more likely to shift their attention to an angry face when they were attempting to detect an angry face than when they were attempting to detect a happy face. Similarly, the task manipulation failed to produce any effects on the latency of their initial saccades from the fixation point. They shifted their attention toward an angry face equally fast whether they were searching for an angry face or a happy face. And, their attention shifted to a happy face with about the same latency when they were searching for a happy or an angry face. In other words, the facial displays of emotion appeared to be refractory to controlled processing without a shift of attention. If any processing occurred prior to a shift of attention, it was probably automatic.

Automatic processing and attention The second and most important question the data could answer was whether there was any evidence that threatening faces attracted attention as a result of automatic processes. The answer was yes. The latency of saccades toward angry faces was shorter than the latency of saccades toward happy faces. Conversely, the latency of saccades away from angry faces was longer than the latency of saccades toward happy faces. The shortest latencies were observed when subjects saccaded away from happy faces toward angry faces. The longest latencies were observed when subjects saccaded away from angry faces toward happy faces. Finally, the latency of saccades was longer when both faces were angry than when both faces were happy. Planned contrasts indicated that these effects were significant in both task conditions and not qualified by an interaction with task.

These findings were consistent with the hypothesis. It appeared that facial displays of threat attracted attention. The latency of attentional shifts away from angry faces was retarded, and the latency of attentional shifts toward angry faces was accelerated. Further, the data clearly suggested that angry faces attracted attention as the result of automatic processes. Under the present circumstances, controlled processing of the facial displays did not occur prior to an attentional shift. In addition, it should be noted that even though the attraction of threatening displays was not sufficient to reorient attention, the failure of angry faces to force reorientation was probably induced by the distance of the facial displays from the fixation point. With sufficient tuning, it is likely that a distance could be found at which controlled processing of the facial displays would remain negligible, but the attraction of angry faces would be adequate to reorient attention.

Whether automatic processes and the power of threatening facial displays to attract attention actually played a role in the face-in-the-crowd effect remains unclear. Relative to the power of flexible controlled processing to suppress distraction, automatic vigilance for threatening faces may be fairly weak. In that sense, finding any trace of its influence on controlled processing is rather remarkable.

Anger superiority of automatic processing and anger inferiority of controlled processing   These findings implied an anger superiority effect at the level of automatic processes, but the face-in-the-crowd effects we reported earlier and the results of previous research indicated that we could anticipate an anger inferiority effect at the level of controlling processing. That is, controlled processing of angry faces may require more time than controlled processing of happy faces. We thought we had better find out, so we conducted an additional experiment using the paradigm described above for measuring the focus of attention.

The design of this second experiment was similar to the first. Only task and the parameters extracted from the EOG data were changed. The trial displays and procedures were identical to the first experiment. As in the first experiment, there were two blocks of trials, each with a different processing task. In one block, subjects were given the task of identifying the emotions displayed on the faces. In this block they were instructed to appraise the emotions displayed on both faces and to name the emotions on the faces in the order in which they surveyed them. They were told that their responses could be recorded only if they focused their attention on the fixation point. Thus, subjects were required to saccade from the fixation point to one face and appraise it, saccade to the second face and appraise it, and then saccade back to the fixation point and name the emotions. They were told that once they appraised a face they could not return to it. The task in the remaining block also required this pattern of attentional orientations. However, rather than naming the emotions, they had to merely report whether the emotions displayed on the two faces were the same or different. We incorporated both tasks because subjects in the face-in-the-crowd experiment could have been engaging in either operation in pursuit of the discrepant face.

The parameters extracted from the EOG data were the direction of the initial saccade from the fixation point and the first intersaccade interval (i.e., the time from the initial saccade to a face and the subsequent saccade away from that face or, in other words, the time on the first target). The intersaccade interval data were transformed into controlled processing for angry and happy faces and submitted to analyses. Preliminary analyses revealed that, as in the first experiment, subjects were no more likely to saccade to an angry face than to a happy face. Task produced no effect on the direction of the initial saccade, but, as predicted, it did produce a main effect on controlled processing times. Controlled processing times were significantly longer when subjects had to appraise and name the emotions than when they had to merely report if the facial displays were the same or different. Finally, task was not involved in any significant interactions. The effect of facial emotions on controlled processes was fairly consistent across recognition and discrimination tasks.

We now turn to the effects of particular interest. Intersaccade times were longer when subjects' attention was focused on angry than on happy faces. More time was devoted to the controlled processing of angry faces than to that of happy faces. The effect was significant within both trial blocks and was not influenced by the emotion displayed on the other face. Once again, however, two categories of explanations for this effect seem plausible. First, by its nature, facial threat may be more difficult to process, either because the configuration of facial features that constitute a threat display are uniquely complex or as a result of the accessibility of memorial representations. Second, facial threat may receive more extensive controlled processing by virtue of its power to maintain itself as the focus of attention (cf. Posner, 1992). A stimulus that attracts attention at the level of automatic processing may well also engage more extensive resources at the level of controlled processing. Automatic vigilance may introduce effects at both the automatic and controlled level; once attention is attracted to a threatening face, it may be difficult to suppress its hold.

Automatic Processing of Facial Emotion and Noncognitive Response: Facial Efference

If facial displays of emotion can exert an automatic influence on the orientation of conscious attention, they also might be capable of automatically eliciting incipient facial muscle responses. Two considerations led us to believe that this was plausible (Hansen & Hansen, 1992). First, a number of theorists and researchers have argued that the emotive activity of the facial muscles has afferent significance (Ekman, 1992; Levenson et al., 1990; Izard, 1977; Laird, 1974; Leventhal, 1980; Levenson, 1992; Matsumoto, 1987; Tomkins, 1962; Zajonc, 1985; Zajonc & Markus, 1984). These theories cast the face in the pivotal role of instigating specific patterns of activity in the autonomic nervous system (e.g., Levenson et al., 1990) and of impinging on core cognitive processes involved in memory (e.g., Zajonc & Markus, 1984) and feeling (e.g., Laird, 1974; Ekman et al., 1990; Zajonc, 1985).

Our second consideration was an accumulating body of research suggesting that the facial muscle system engages in activity that cannot be explained parsimoniously in terms of its function as an interindividual social signal (cf. Ekman et al., 1988, 1990; Zajonc, 1985). Emotional stimuli elicit short latency, micromomentary, covert facial muscle movements that correspond to the valence of the stimulus (Cacioppo et al., 1986, 1988; Cacioppo & Petty, 1979; Dimberg, 1990; Tassinary & Cacioppo, 1992), which apparently cannot be suppressed or altered by controlled processes (Cacioppo, Bush, & Tassinary, 1992). One interpretation of these findings is that the facial muscle system functions to trigger emotions. In addition, facial displays of emotion voluntarily directed by controlled processes are *not* equivalent to the consequences of spontaneous facial displays of emotion (Ekman et al., 1988, 1990). This suggests that they may be innervated by different processes. It seems reasonable to hypothesize that spontaneously generated facial muscle activity can be innervated without reliance on conscious cognitive processes. This interpretation of the literature led us to conduct an experiment in the hope of finding nonconscious facial efference.

Facial activity   The experiment was conducted much like the first experiment in this series. The trial displays and instructions were the same. As in the first experiment, in one block of trials subjects were given the task of detecting the presence of a happy face. In the other block, they sought an angry face. Again, EOG was used to measure the direction of the subject's initial saccade from the central fixation point. The goal of the present experiment, however, was to measure automatic facial muscle activity—activity that occurred before the initial saccade to a facial display. We used facial electromyography (EMG) to measure this activity.

Facial muscle activity was recorded using surface electrodes in bipolar placement over three muscle regions of the face (refer to Fridlund & Cacioppo, 1986, for a discussion of these procedures). The first was the left *corrogator supercilii*, the muscle involved in pulling the eyebrows down and inward. The second was the left *orbicularis oculi*, the muscle involved in closing the eye fissure and drawing the tissue of the face toward that fissure. The last placement was over the region of the *zygomaticus major*, the muscle involved in drawing the angle of the lips up and backward. Previous research has associated increased activity in the *corrogator* with negative emotion and increased activity in the latter two with positive emotion (e.g., Fridlund & Izard, 1983; Ekman et al., 1990). The raw facial EMG data were amplified using Grass P511 AC amplifiers, rectified, and then smoothed using contour-following integrators (Fridlund, 1979) with a time constant of 10 msec. The rectified IEMG data were passed through a Metrabyte high-speed A–D converter and sampled at a rate of 1 kHz by the microprocessor.

As in the previous experiments, the EOG data were used to identify the location of the subject's initial saccade away from the fixation point and the time of that initial saccade. The results of the first experiment implied that any facial muscle activity elicited by the emotional faces during this presaccade period would probably be the result of automatic processes. The electromyograms obtained during this presaccade period were the data of interest.

Evidence of automatic facial efference   Before turning to the analyses of these data, we should note that the EOG data were analyzed. As in the earlier experiment, these analyses indicated the task produced no effect on saccade direction. Subjects shifted their attention in the direction of a happy face about as often as toward an angry face no matter which facial emotion they were attempting to detect.

The rectified IEMG data was averaged over the entire presaccade period for each of the three muscle sites. Only the data from trials on which both faces displayed the same emotion were entered into a multivariate analysis of variance. This analysis produced the anticipated results. First, the conscious processing task produced no significant effects. The emotional display, angry or happy, that subjects were consciously attempting to detect had no effect on presaccadic facial muscle activity. However, the facial displays to which subjects were exposed on these trials did have an effect. Presaccadic *corrogator* activity was significantly higher when the faces were angry than when the faces were happy. Presaccadic activity of the *zygomaticus* and particularly the *orbicularis oculi* region was significantly higher when the faces displayed happiness than when they displayed anger. In short, it appeared that the facial displays of emotion elicited facial efference in the absence of conscious processing—nonconscious facial efference. Currently, we are continuing this investigation and extending the data analyses.

Conclusions and Implications

In the findings we have described above, we believe we are beginning to see emotion, as it was characterized by Davidson and Cacioppo (1992), at the level of automatic processing. The results suggested that automatic processes can both impinge on the orientation of attention and innervate patterns of activity in the facial muscle system, and we suspect that automatic processes can do more.

It is our belief that automatic emotions are best seen as primitive mechanisms of adaptive response, instigated by the detection of stimuli whose presence have implications for the survival of the organism. Human facial displays of emotion—universally available and constant in meaning—certainly fit this definition of biologically significant stimuli. So, we began there. In this context, it was not surprising to discover that facial displays of threat attract attention. Controlled cognitive processing, after all, is a powerful and flexible invention for coping with threat. Endowing automatic processing with the capability of orienting this resource to facial displays of threat has an adaptive advantage. What, however, is the significance of automatic facial responses?

Facial afference theorists maintain that facial afference influences the memorial representations available for controlled cognitive processing (cf. Tomkins, 1962, 1980; Zajonc, 1985; Zajonc & Markus, 1984), and research indicates that facial afference impinges on the activity of the autonomic nervous system (cf. Ekman, 1992; Levenson, 1992). Within this view, facial displays of emotion have intraindividual effects on controlled cognition and the autonomic nervous system, two systems at the core of emotion. Facial afference theorists, however, must contend with the central question of why the facial muscle system would evolve into this critical role. Why would the face be involved in instigating emotions in the first place?

One answer may involve mimicry. When one individual's facial display of emotion is mimicked by another, the afferent influence of the facial efference, or reafference (Zajonc & Markus, 1984), yields an emotion in the mimicker parallel to that of the displayer (cf. Dimberg, 1982; Öhman, 1986). In this context, the significance of automatic emotion can be more fully appreciated. If one individual's facial emotion can instigate automatic facial efference in another, as the data imply, automatic reafference seems probable. In other words, emotion can be instigated without the intervention of controlled cognition. This is not just an elegant solution to the question of why facial displays of emotion elicit automatic facial efference. It is a possibility that dramatically underscores the fundamental importance of human facial displays of emotion as unconditioned stimuli (Englis, Vaughan, & Lanzetta, 1982; Lanzetta & Orr, 1980; Vaughan & Lanzetta, 1980, 1981). We believe emotional faces are prototypic emotional stimuli and that automatic emotion offers an important clue to defining their full adaptive significance.

Acknowledgments

This manuscript was prepared as part of a continuing research program funded by a grant from the National Institute of Mental Health (1RO1MH45388).

References

Adelmann, P. K., & Zajonc, R. B. (1989). Facial efference and the experience of emotion. *Annual Review of Psychology*, 90, 249–280.

Bargh, J. A. (1982). Attention and automaticity in the processing of self-relevant information. *Journal of Personality and Social Psychology*, 43, 425–436.

Bargh, J. A. (1984). Automatic and conscious processing of social information. In R. S. Wyer & T. K. Srull (eds.), *Handbook of social cognition* (Vol. 3, pp. 1–43). Hillsdale, NJ: Erlbaum.

Bargh, J. A. (1989). Conditional automaticity: Varieties of automatic influence in social perception and cognition. In J. S. Uleman & J. A. Bargh (eds.), *Unintended thought* (pp. 3–51). New York: Guilford Press.

Bargh, J. A., & Pietromonaco, P. (1982). Automatic information processing and social perception: The influence of trait information presented outside of conscious awareness on impression formation. *Journal of Personality and Social Psychology*, 43, 437–449.

Bargh, J. A., & Pratto, F. (1986). Individual construct accessibility and perceptual selection. *Journal of Experimental Social Psychology*, 22, 293–311.

Bargh, J. A., & Thein, D. (1985). Individual construct accessibility, person memory, and the recall-judgment link: The case of information overload. *Journal of Personality and Social Psychology*, 49, 1129–1146.

Bargh, J. A., Bond, R. N., Lombardi, W. J., & Tota, M. E. (1986). The additive nature of chronic and temporary sources of construct accessibility. *Journal of Personality and Social Psychology*, 50, 869–878.

Bargh, J. A., Litt, J. E., Pratto, F., & Spielman, L. A. (1988). On the preconscious evaluation of social stimuli. In K. McConkey & A. Bennet (eds.), *Proceedings of the XXIV International Congress of Psychology* (Vol. 3, pp. 1–57). Amsterdam: Elsevier/North-Holland.

Barrera, M. E., & Maurer, D. (1981). The perception of facial expressions by the three-month old. *Child Development*, 52, 203–206.

Bower, G. H. (1981). Mood and memory. *American Psychologist*, 36, 129–148.

Bower, G. H., & Cohen, P. R. (1982). Emotional influences in memory and thinking: Data and theory. In M. S. Clark & S. T. Fiske (eds.), *Affect and cognition* (pp. 291–331). Hillsdale, NJ: Erlbaum.

Broadbent, D. E. (1958). *Perception and communication*. London: Pergamon Press.

Bruner, J. S. (1957). On perceptual readiness. *Psychological Review*, 64, 123–152.

Bruner, J. S., & Tagiuri, R. (1954). The perception of people. In G. Lindzey (ed.), *Handbook of social psychology* (Vol. 2, pp. 634–654). Reading, MA: Addison-Wesley.

Cacioppo, J. T., & Petty, R. E. (1979). Attitudes and cognitive response: An electrophysiological approach. *Journal of Personality and Social Psychology*, 37, 2181–2199.

Cacioppo, J. T., Losch, M. L., Tassinary, L. G., & Petty, R. E. (1986). Properties of affect and affect-laden information processing as viewed through the facial response system. In R. A. Peterson, W. D. Hoyer, & W. R. Wilson (eds.), *The role of affect in consumer behavior: Emerging theories and applications* (pp. 87–118). Lexington, MA: D.C. Heath.

Cacioppo, J. T., Petty, R. E., Losch, M. E., & Kim, H. S. (1986). Electromyographic activity over facial muscle regions can differentiate the valence and intensity of affective reactions. *Journal of Personality and Social Psychology*, 50, 260–268.

Cacioppo, J. T., Martzke, J. S., Petty, R. E., & Tassinary, L. G. (1988). Specific forms of facial EMG response index emotions during an interview: From Darwin to the continuous flow hypothesis of affect-laden information processing. *Journal of Personality and Social Psychology*, 54, 592–604.

Cacioppo, J. T., Bush, L. K., & Tassinary, L. G. (1992). Microexpressive facial actions as a function of affective stimuli: Replication and extension. *Personality and Social Psychology Bulletin*, 18, 515–526.

Cheesman, J., & Merikle, P. M. (1984). Priming with and without awareness. *Perception and Psychophysics*, 36, 387–395.

Cheesman, J., & Merikle, P. M. (1985). Word recognition and consciousness. In D. Besner, T. G., Waller, & G. E. MacKinnon (eds.), *Reading research: Advances in theory and practice* (Vol. 5, pp. 311–352). New York: Academic Press.

Cheesman, J., & Merikle, P. M. (1986). Distinguishing conscious from unconscious perceptual processes. *Canadian Journal of Psychology,* 40, 343–367.

Clark, M. S. (1982). A role for arousal in the link between feeling states, judgments, and behavior. In M. S. Clark & S. T. Fiske (eds.), *Affect and cognition* (pp. 263–289). Hillsdale, NJ: Erlbaum.

Clark, M. S., & Isen, A. M. (1982). Toward understanding the relationship between feeling states and social behavior. In M. S. Clark & S. T. Fiske (eds.), *Affect and cognition* (pp. 73–108). Hillsdale, NJ: Erlbaum.

Darwin, C. (1872/1965). *The expression of the emotions in man and animals.* Chicago, IL: University of Chicago Press.

Davidson, R. J., & Cacioppo, J. T. (1992). New developments in the scientific study of emotion: An introduction to the special section. *Psychological Science,* 3, 21–22.

Davis, P. J. (1987). Repression and the inaccessibility of affective memories. *Journal of Personality and Social Psychology,* 53, 585–593.

Davis, P. J., & Schwartz, G. E. (1987). Repression and the inaccessibility of affective memories. *Journal of Personality and Social Psychology,* 52, 155–162.

Dimberg, U. (1982). Facial reactions to facial expressions. *Psychophysiology,* 19, 643–647.

Dimberg, U. (1986). Facial expression as excitatory and inhibitory stimuli for conditioned autonomic responses. *Biological Psychology,* 22, 37–57.

Dimberg, U. (1990). Facial electromyography and emotional reactions. *Psychophysiology,* 27, 481–494.

Ekman, P. (1972). Universals and cultural differences in facial expressions of emotions. In J. Cole (ed.), *Nebraska symposium on motivation.* Lincoln, NE: University of Nebraska Press.

Ekman, P. (1989). The argument and evidence about universals in facial expressions of emotion. In H. Wagner & A. Manstead (eds.), *Handbook of psychophysiology: The biological psychology of emotions and social processes* (pp. 143–164). London: Wiley.

Ekman, P. (1992). Facial expressions of emotion: New findings, new questions. *Psychological Science,* 3, 34–38.

Ekman, P., & Friesen, W. V. (1974). Detecting deception from body or face. *Journal of Personality and Social Psychology,* 29, 288–298.

Ekman, P., & Friesen, W. V. (1975). *Unmasking the face: A guide to recognizing emotions from facial cues.* Englewood Cliffs, NJ: Prentice-Hall.

Ekman, P., & Friesen, W. V. (1976). *Pictures of facial affect.* Palo Alto, CA: Consulting Psychologists Press.

Ekman, P., & Friesen, W. V. (1978). *The facial action coding system.* Palo Alto, CA: Consulting Psychologists Press.

Ekman, P., & Friesen, W. V. (1982). Felt, false, and miserable smiles. *Journal of Nonverbal Behavior,* 6, 238–252.

Ekman, P., & Oster, H. (1979). Facial expression of emotion. In M. R. Rosenzweig & L. W. Porter (eds.), *Annual Review of Psychology,* 30, 527–554.

Ekman, P., Sorenson, E. R., & Friesen, W. V. (1969). Pan-cultural elements in facial displays of emotion. *Science,* 164, 86–88.

Ekman, P., Friesen, W. V., & Ellsworth, P. E. (1972). *Emotion in the human face: Guidelines for research and an integration of findings.* New York: Pergamon Press.

Ekman, P., Friesen, W. V., & Ancoli, S. (1980). Facial signs of emotional experience. *Journal of Personality and Social Psychology,* 39, 1125–1134.

Ekman, P., Levenson, R. W., & Friesen, W. V. (1983). Autonomic nervous system activity distinguishes between emotions. *Science,* 221, 1208–1210.

Ekman, P., Friesen, W. V., O'Sullivan, M., Diacoyanni-Tarlatzis, I., Krause, R., Pitcairn, T., Scherer, K.,

Chan, A., Heider, K., LeCompte, W. A., Ricci-Bitti, P. E., & Tomota, M. (1987). Universals and cultural differences in the judgments of facial expressions of emotions. *Journal of Personality and Social Psychology*, 53, 712–717.

Ekman, P., Friesen, W. V., & O'Sullivan, M. (1988). Smiles when lying. *Journal of Personality and Social Psychology*, 54, 414–420.

Ekman, P., Davidson, R. J., & Friesen, W. V. (1990). The Duchenne smile: Emotional expression and brain physiology II. *Journal of Personality and Social Psychology*, 58, 342–353.

Englis, B. G., Vaughan, K. B., & Lanzetta, J. T. (1982). Conditioning of counterempathetic emotional responses. *Journal of Experimental Social Psychology*, 18, 375–391.

Erdelyi, M. H. (1974). A new look at the New Look: Perceptual defense and vigilance. *Psychological Review*, 81, 1–25.

Erdelyi, M. H. (1985). *Psychoanalysis: Freud's cognitive psychology*. New York: W. H. Freeman.

Erdelyi, M. H., & Goldberg, B. (1979). Let's not sweep repression under the rug: Toward a cognitive psychology of repression. In J. Kihlstrom & F. Evans (eds.), *Functional disorders of memory* (pp. 355–402). Hillsdale, NJ: Erlbaum.

Fiske, S. T. (1980). Attention and weight in person perception: The impact of negative and extreme behavior. *Journal of Personality and Social Psychology*, 38, 889–906.

Fowler, C. A., Wolford, G., Slade, R., & Tassinary, L. G. (1981). Lexical access with and without awareness. *Journal of Experimental Psychology: General*, 110, 341–362.

Fox, N. A., & Davidson, R. J. (1988). Patterns of brain electrical activity during facial signs of emotion in 10-month old infants. *Developmental Psychology*, 24, 230–236.

Freud, S. (1915/1957). Repression. In J. Strachey (ed. and trans.), *The standard edition of the complete psychological works of Sigmund Freud* (Vol. 14). London: Hogarth Press.

Fridlund, A. J. (1979). Contour-following integrator for dynamic tracking of electromyographic data. *Psychophysiology*, 16, 491–493.

Fridlund, A. J., & Cacioppo, J. T. (1986). Guidelines for human electromyographic research. *Psychophysiology*, 23, 567–589.

Fridlund, A. J., & Izard, C. E. (1983). Electromyographic studies of facial expressions of emotions and pattern of emotions. In J. T. Cacioppo & R. E. Petty (eds.), *Social psychophysiology: A sourcebook* (pp. 243–286). New York: Guilford.

Greenwald, A. G. (1992). New Look 3: Unconscious cognition reclaimed. *American Psychologist*, 47, 766–779.

Greenwald, A. G., Klinger, M. R., & Lui, T. J. (1989). Unconscious processing of dichoptically masked words. *Memory and Cognition*, 17, 35–47.

Hager, J. C., & Ekman, P. (1983). The inner and outer meanings of facial expression. In J. T. Cacioppo & R. E. Petty (eds.), *Social psychophysiology: A sourcebook* (pp. 287–306). New York: Guilford.

Hampton, C., Purcell, D. G., Bersine, L., Hansen, C. H., & Hansen, R. D. (1989). Probing "pop-out": Another look at the face-in-the-crowd effect. *Bulletin of the Psychonomic Society*, 27, 563–566.

Hansen, C. H. (1992). The effects of arousal and mood on schematic and controlled processing. Unpublished manuscript. Oakland University.

Hansen, C. H., & Hansen, R. D. (1988). Finding the face in the crowd: An anger superiority effect. *Journal of Personality and Social Psychology*, 54, 917–924.

Hansen, R. D., & Hansen, C. H. (1992). The automatic influence of facial emotion: Attention and facial efference. Unpublished manuscript. Oakland University.

Hansen, C. H., Hansen, R. D., & Shantz, D. W. (1992). Repression at encoding: Discrete appraisals of emotional stimuli. *Journal of Personality and Social Psychology*, 63, 1026–1035.

Hansen, C. H., & Shantz, C. (1992). Arousal effects schema-triggered affect but not schematicity. Unpublished manuscript. Oakland University.

Hastie, R., & Kumar, P. (1979). Person memory: Personality traits as organizing principles in memory for behaviors. *Journal of Personality and Social Psychology*, 37, 25–38.

Heider, F. (1958). *The psychology of interpersonal relations*. New York: Wiley.

Homa, D., Haver, B., & Schwartz, T. (1976). Perceptibility of schematic face stimuli: Evidence for a perceptual gestalt. *Memory and Cognition, 4,* 176–185.

Intons-Peterson, M. J. (1981). Constructing and using unusual and common images. *Journal of Experimental Psychology: Human Learning and Memory, 7,* 133–144.

Intons-Peterson, M. J. (1984). Faces, rabbits, skunks, and ducks: Imaginal comparisons of similar and dissimilar items. *Journal of Experimental Psychology: Learning, Memory, and Cognition, 10,* 699–715.

Isen, A. M. (1975, April). Positive affect, accessibility of cognitions and helping. In J. Piliavin (chair), *Current directions in theory on helping behavior.* Symposium conducted at the meeting of the Eastern Psychological Association, New York.

Isen, A. M. (1984). Toward understanding the role of affect in cognition. In R. S. Wyer & T. K. Srull (eds.), *Handbook of social cognition* (Vol. 3). Hillsdale, NJ: Erlbaum.

Isen, A. M., Shalker, T. E., Clark, M. S., & Karp, L. (1978). Affect, accessibility of material in memory, and behavior: A cognitive loop. *Journal of Personality and Social Psychology, 36,* 1–12.

Izard, C. E. (1971). *The face of emotion.* New York: Appleton-Century-Crofts.

Izard, C. E. (1977). *Human emotions.* New York: Plenum.

Izard, C. E. (1981). Differential emotions theory and the facial feedback hypothesis of emotion activation: Comments on Tourangeau and Ellsworth's "The role of facial response in the experience of emotion." *Journal of Personality and Social Psychology, 40,* 350–354.

Kahneman, D., & Tversky, A. (1984). Choices, values, and frames. *American Psychologist, 39,* 341–350.

Kihlstrom, J. F. (1987). The cognitive unconscious. *Science, 237,* 1445–1452.

Kirouac, G., & Doré, F. Y. (1984). Judgment of facial expressions of emotion as a function of exposure time. *Perceptual and Motor Skills, 59,* 147–150.

Kirouac, G., & Doré, F. Y. (1985). Accuracy of the judgment of facial expression of emotions as a function of sex and level of education. *Journal of Nonverbal Behavior, 9,* 3–7.

Kitayama, S. (1990). Interaction between affect and cognition in word perception. *Journal of Personality and Social Psychology, 58,* 209–217.

Kitayama, S. (1991). Impairment of perception by affect. *Cognition and Emotion, 5,* 255–274.

Kunst-Wilson, W. R., & Zajonc, R. B. (1980). Affective discrimination of stimuli that cannot be recognized. *Science, 207,* 557–558.

LaBarbera, J. D., Izard, C. E., Vietze, P., & Parisi, S. A. (1976). Four- and six-month-old infants' visual responses to joy, anger, and neutral expressions. *Child Development, 47,* 535–538.

Laird, J. D. (1974). Self-attribution of emotion: The effects of expressive behavior on the quality of emotional experience. *Journal of Personality and Social Psychology, 29,* 475–486.

Lang, P. J., Bradley, M. M., & Cuthbert, B. N. (1992). A motivational analysis of emotion: Reflex-cortex connections. *Psychological Science, 3,* 44–49.

Lanzetta, J. T., & Orr, S. P. (1980). Influence of facial expressions on the classical conditioning of fear. *Journal of Personality and Social Psychology, 39,* 1081–1087.

Levenson, R. W. (1992). Autonomic nervous system differences among emotions. *Psychological Science, 3,* 23–27.

Levenson, R. W., Ekman, P., & Friesen, W. V. (1990). Voluntary facial action generates emotion-specific autonomic nervous system activity. *Psychophysiology, 27,* 363–384.

Leventhal, H. (1980). Toward a comprehensive theory of emotion. In L. Berkowitz (ed.), *Advances in Experimental Social Psychology, 13,* 139–207.

McAndrew, F. T. (1986). A cross-cultural study of recognition thresholds for facial expressions of emotion. *Journal of Cross-Cultural Psychology, 17,* 211–224.

McHugo, G. J., Lanzetta, J. T., Sullivan, D. G., Masters, R. D., & Englis, B. G. (1985). Emotional reactions to a political leader's expressive displays. *Journal of Personality and Social Psychology, 49,* 1513–1529.

Mandal, M. K., & Palchoudhury, S. (1985). Perceptual skill in decoding facial affect. *Perceptual and Motor Skills*, 60, 96–98.

Marcel, A. J. (1983a). Conscious and unconscious perception: Experiments in visual masking and word recognition. *Cognitive Psychology*, 15, 197–237.

Marcel, A. J. (1983b). Conscious and unconscious perception: An approach to the relation between phenomenal experience and perceptual processes. *Cognitive Psychology*, 15, 238–300.

Matsumoto, D. (1987). The role of facial response in the experience of emotion: More methodological problems and a meta-analysis. *Journal of Personality and Social Psychology*, 52, 769–774.

Mineka, S., & Sutton, S. K. (1992). Cognitive biases and the emotional disorders. *Psychological Science*, 3, 65–69.

Neisser, U. (1967). *Cognitive psychology*. New York: Appleton-Century-Crofts.

Niedenthal, P. M. (1990). Implicit perception of affective information. *Journal of Experimental Social Psychology*, 26, 505–527.

Öhman, A. (1986). Face the beast and fear the face: Animal and social fears as prototypes for evolutionary analyses of emotion. *Psychophysiology*, 23, 123–145.

Öhman, A., Dimberg, U., & Öst, L. G. (1985). Animal and social phobias: Biological constraints on learned fear responses. In S. Reiss & R. R. Bootzin (eds.), *Theoretical issues in behavior therapy* (pp. 123–145). New York: Academic Press.

Oster, P. J., & Stern, J. A. (1980). Measurement of eye movement. In I. Martin & P. H. Venables (eds.), *Techniques in psychophysiology*. New York: Wiley.

Pivik, R. T. (1986). Sleep: Physiology and psychophysiology. In G. H. Coles, E. Donchin, & S. W. Porges (eds.), *Psychophysiology* (pp. 378–406). New York: Guilford Press.

Plutchik, R. (1980). A general psychoevolutionary theory of emotion. In R. Plutchik & H. Kellerman (eds.), *Emotion: Theory, research, and experience* (Vol. 1, pp. 3–33). New York: Academic Press.

Posner, M. J. (1992). Attention as a cognitive and neural system. *Current Directions in Psychological Science*, 1, 11–14.

Posner, M. J., & Snyder, C. R. R. (1975). Attention and cognitive control. In R. L. Solso (ed.), *Information processing and cognition: The Loyola symposium*. Hillsdale, NJ: Erlbaum.

Pratto, F., & John, O. P. (1991). Automatic vigilance: The attention-grabbing power of negative social information. *Journal of Personality and Social Psychology*, 61, 380–391.

Purcell, D. G., Stewart, A. L., & Skov, R. (1993). *The face in the crowd: An effect of a confounding variable*. Paper presented at the meeting of the American Psychological Society, Chicago, IL.

Roskos-Ewoldsen, D. R., & Fazio, R. H. (1992). On the orienting value of attitudes: Attitude accessibility as a determinant of an object's attraction of visual attention. *Journal of Personality and Social Psychology*, 63, 198–211.

Schneider, W., & Fisk, A. D. (1982). Degree of consistent training: Improvements in search performance and automatic process development. *Perception and Psychophysics*, 31, 160–168.

Schneider, W., & Shiffrin, R. M. (1977a). Automatic and controlled information processing in vision. In D. LaBerge & S. J. Samuels (eds.), *Basic processes in reading: Perception and comprehension* (pp. 127–154). Hillsdale, NJ: Erlbaum.

Schneider, W., & Shiffrin, R. M. (1977b). Controlled and automatic human information processing: I. Detection, search, and attention. *Psychological Review*, 84, 1–66.

Schneider, W., Dumais, S. T., & Shiffrin, R. M. (1984). Automatic and control processing and attention. In S. Kornblum & J. Requin (eds), *Preparatory states and processes* (pp. 1–27). Hillsdale, NJ: Erlbaum.

Schwartz, G. E. (1990). Psychobiology of repression and health: A systems approach. In J. L. Singer (ed.), *Repression and dissociation* (pp. 405–434). Chicago: The University of Chicago Press.

Schwartz, G. E., Fair, P. L., Salt, P., Mandel, M. R., & Klerman, G. L. (1976). Facial muscle patterning to affective imagery in depressed and nondepressed subjects. *Science, 192,* 489–491.

Schwartz, G. E., Ahern, G. L., & Brown, S. L. (1979). Lateralized facial muscle response to positive and negative emotional stimuli. *Psychophysiology, 16,* 561–571.

Schwartz, G. E., Izard, C. E., & Ansul, S. E. (1985). The five-month-old's ability to discriminate facial expressions of emotion. *Infant Behavior and Development, 8,* 65–77.

Seamon, J. G., Brody, N., & Kauff, D. M. (1983). Affective discrimination of stimuli that are not recognized: Effects of shadowing, masking, and cerebral laterality. *Journal of Experimental Psychology: Learning, Memory, and Cognition, 9,* 544–555.

Seamon, J. G., Marsh, R. L., & Brody, N. (1984). Critical importance of exposure duration for affective discrimination of stimuli that are not recognized. *Journal of Experimental Psychology: Learning, Memory, and Cognition, 10,* 465–469.

Shiffrin, R. M., & Dumais, S. T. (1981). The development of automatism. In J. R. Anderson (ed.), *Cognitive skills and their acquisition.* Hillsdale, NJ: Erlbaum.

Shiffrin, R. M., & Schneider, W. (1977). Controlled and automatic human information processing II. Detection, search, and attention. *Psychological Review, 84,* 127–190.

Srull, T. K., & Wyer, R. S. (1989). Person memory and judgment. *Psychological Review, 96,* 58–83.

Stalans, L., & Wedding, D. (1985). Superiority of the left hemisphere in the recognition of emotional faces. *International Journal of Neuroscience, 25,* 219–223.

Stangor, C., & Duan, C. (1991). Effects of multiple task demands upon memory for information about social groups. *Journal of Experimental Social Psychology, 27,* 357–378.

Stewart, A. L., Purcell, D. G., & Skov, R. (1993). *Another look at the face in the crowd: An anger inferiority effect.* Paper presented at the meeting of the American Psychological Society, Chicago, IL.

Tassinary, L. G., & Cacioppo, J. T. (1992). Unobservable facial actions and emotion. *Psychological Science, 3,* 28–33.

Tassinary, L. G., Orr, S. P., Wolford, G., Napps, S. E., & Lanzetta, J. T. (1984). The role of awareness in affective information processing: An exploration of Zajonc' hypothesis. *Bulletin of the Psychonomic Society, 22,* 489–492.

Tomkins, S. S. (1962). *Affect, image, consciousness: Volume 1. The positive affects.* New York: Springer.

Tomkins, S. S. (1980). Affect as amplification: Some modifications in theory. In R. Plutchik & H. Kellerman (eds.), *Emotion: Theory, research and experience* (Vol. 1, pp. 141–164). New York: Academic Press.

Tomkins, S. S. (1981). The role of facial response in the experience of emotion: A reply to Tourangeau and Ellsworth. *Journal of Personality and Social Psychology, 40,* 355–357.

Torangeau, R., & Ellsworth, P. C. (1979). The role of facial response in the experience of emotion. *Journal of Personality and Social Psychology, 37,* 1519–1531.

Treisman, A. (1982). Perceptual grouping and attention in visual search for features and for objects. *Journal of Experimental Psychology: Human Perception and Performance, 8,* 194–214.

Treisman, A., & Gelade, G. (1980). A feature-integration theory of attention. *Cognitive Psychology, 12,* 97–136.

Treisman, A., & Paterson, R. (1984). Emergent features, attention and object perception. *Journal of Experimental Psychology: Human Perception and Performance, 10,* 12–31.

Treisman, A., & Souther, J. (1985). Search asymmetry: A diagnostic for preattentive processing of separable features. *Journal of Experimental Psychology: General, 114,* 285–310.

van Santen, J. P. H., & Jonides, J. (1978). A replication of the face-superiority effect. *Bulletin of the Psychonomic Society, 12,* 378–380.

Vaughan, K. B., & Lanzetta, J. T. (1980). Vicarious instigation and conditioning of facial expressive and autonomic responses to a model's expressive display of pain. *Journal of Personality and Social Psychology, 38,* 909–923.

Vaughan, K. B., & Lanzetta, J. T. (1981). The effect of expressive displays on vicarious emotional arousal. *Journal of Experimental Social Psychology, 17,* 16–30.

Wexler, B. E., Schwartz, G. E., Warrenburg, S., Cervis, M., & Terlatzis, I. (1986). Effects of emotion on perceptual asymmetry: Interactions with personality. *Neuropsychologia*, 24, 699–710.

Wexler, B. E., Michaelis, J., Warrenburg, S., & Schwartz, G. E. (1989a). Heartrate acceleration secondary to unconsciously processed negative emotion-evoking stimuli. Unpublished manuscript. Yale University.

Wexler, B. E., Schwartz, G. E., Warrenburg, S., & Jamner, L. D. (1989b). Corrugator muscle response to unconsciously processed negative emotion-evoking stimuli: Differences between repressors and true low anxious subjects. Unpublished manuscript. Yale University.

Wilcox, B. M., & Clayton, F. L. (1968). Infant visual fixation on motion pictures of the human face. *Journal of Experimental Child Psychology*, 6, 22, 32.

Wyer, R. S., & Gordon, S. E. (1982). The recall of information about persons and groups. *Journal of Experimental Social Psychology*, 18, 128–164.

Zajonc, R. B. (1965). Social facilitation. *Science*, 149, 269–274.

Zajonc, R. B. (1980). Feeling and thinking: Preferences need no inferences *American Psychologist*, 35, 151–175.

Zajonc, R. B. (1985). Emotion and facial efference: A theory reclaimed. *Science*, 228, 15–21.

Zajonc, R. B., & McIntosh, D. N. (1992). Emotions research: Some promising questions and some questionable promises. *Psychological Science*, 3(1), 70–74.

Zajonc, R. B., & Markus, H. (1984). Affect and cognition: The hard interface. In C. E. Izard, J. Kagan, & R. B. Zajonc (eds.), *Emotions, cognition, and behavior*. London: Cambridge University Press.

Zajonc, R. B., Murphy, S. T., & Inglehart, M. (1989). Feeling and facial efference: Implications of the vascular theory of emotion. *Psychological Review*, 96(3), 395–416.

Emotion
and
the
Eyewitness

Howard Egeth
The Johns Hopkins University

When I was asked to contribute to this volume on emotion and perception I was intrigued by the possibility of using this occasion to reexamine some thoughts I had expressed ten years ago on some closely related subjects.

Back in 1983 Mike McCloskey and I entered into a debate on the validity of expert testimony by psychologists about eyewitness identification (Egeth & McCloskey, 1984; McCloskey & Egeth, 1983; McCloskey, Egeth, & McKenna, 1986). In short, we argued that psychologists did not know enough about the factors determining eyewitness accuracy to be able to say much that would be helpful to jurors involved in a particular case. We said that there might be some things that were well established scientifically though little known by the general public that might well be discussed by psychologists in court. The example we gave was the achromatic nature of scotopic vision. However, that was not the sort of factor that eyewitness experts tended to talk about. They focused on things such as cross-race identification, weapon focus, and the effect of arousal on performance. It was our contention back in 1983 that scientific knowledge about those topics had not advanced to the stage where they could serve as the basis for courtroom testimony.

In this chapter I assess the current state of knowledge about two of the topics touched on in our original review: the effects of arousal and of the presence of a weapon on the accuracy of eyewitness testimony. For other recent reviews of the effects of arousal see Christianson (1992a) and several of the chapters in Christianson (1992b). Steblay (1992) presents a meta-analytic review of the literature on weapon focus. Discussions of some of the other factors addressed by eyewitness experts are provided by Ebbesen and Konecni (1989) and Egeth (1993a,b).

Arousal

Many crimes involve emotional stress to the victims and witnesses; this is perhaps the factor that is most frequently discussed in the courtroom by eyewitness experts. The argument is that a crime is a stressful situation, and this is likely to result in impairment of perception and/or memory. Thus, jurors should be skeptical of the accuracy of reports and identifications made by a witness undergoing stress. How justified is this argument?

According to a recent survey of experts in the area of eyewitness testimony, the argument may well be justified. Kassin, Ellsworth, and Smith (1989) asked a group of 119 psychologists working in the area of eyewitness testimony to indicate their opinions about various issues associated with the accuracy of eyewitness identification; 63 of these experts responded. With regard to arousal, the following statement was presented: "Very high levels of stress impair the accuracy of eyewitness testimony." Of the 63 respondents, 79% agreed with the statement and 71% thought this phenomenon was reliable enough for psychologists to present it in courtroom testimony.

Now, it seems quite reasonable, a priori, that emotion could influence eyewitness identification. This entire volume is a testament to the fact that emotion has widespread effects on human mental processes. However, to recognize this is not to say that stress necessarily impairs eyewitness performance. I shall argue below that the 71% majority was quite wrong; the relation between stress and accuracy is too complex to be captured by the simple statement offered by Kassin et al. (1989).[1] Indeed, if one were, for

---

[1] It is interesting to speculate on possible reasons for what I claim to be an incorrect assessment of the literature. One possibility that comes to mind is that many investigators who come into contact with the justice system find professionals (e.g., prosecutors) who argue that high stress affects memory by "burning in" details in a way that makes them unforgettable (cf. Kramer, Buckhout, Fox, Widman, and Tusche, 1991, p. 483). Perhaps the experts find this lay opinion to be so outrageous an overstatement as to need some sort of counterbalancing corrective, even if it is not supported (yet) by empirical research.

some reason, intent on capturing the relation with a(n) (overly) simple statement, one might be well advised to consider endorsing the opposite of the one chosen by the majority: "high levels of stress improve the accuracy of eyewitness testimony."

Literature Review

The literature on the effect of stress[2] on eyewitness accuracy was equivocal at the time of the McCloskey and Egeth (1983) review. We cited a review of 21 studies (Deffenbacher, 1983); 11 of the studies showed that eyewitness memory declines with increasing stress while 10 showed either no effect or an improvement of memory with increasing stress. Deffenbacher attempted to fit these facts to the inverted U-shaped function of the Yerkes–Dodson Law by fiat; that is, a study that showed increasing performance with increasing arousal was simply assumed to fall on the left-hand, or rising, limb of the inverted U, and a study that showed decreasing performance with increasing arousal was simply assumed to fall on the right-hand, or decreasing, limb of the function. In the absence of a metric of arousal that can be applied across studies this is unjustifiable. The lack of justification of Deffenbacher's (1983) treatment notwithstanding, the Yerkes–Dodson Law still serves as the motivating principle for most of the research in this area. Thus, further discussion is well justified.

The Yerkes–Dodson Law was originally proposed to account for the performance of mice who were motivated via exposure to electric shock (Yerkes & Dodson, 1908). The idea is that as motivation/arousal/stress increases, performance at first increases, then reaches a peak, and finally decreases (the shape of the function is described as an inverted U.) Further, the level of arousal at the peak of the curve is a function of task complexity; the peak occurs at lesser levels of motivation for more complex tasks. This is, obviously, a "law" that covers a lot of territory; it is used far beyond the realm of eyewitness performance.

Easterbrook (1959) proposed a hypothesis to account for the Yerkes–Dodson Law in terms of the range of cue utilization. The idea is that performance in a given task requires the use of a certain range of environmental cues. When arousal is low, the organism is not selective with respect to cue usage; both relevant and irrelevant cues are perceived and used. When arousal is increased somewhat, fewer cues can be utilized. To the extent that the organism can selectively utilize relevant cues (and ignore irrelevant cues) performance should improve in this circumstance. When arousal is

---

[2]In this chapter I shall not make any effort to distinguish between *stress* and *arousal* but shall use the terms more or less interchangeably. For that matter, I am not much more discriminating about the use of the word *emotion*. Given the negative nature of the stimuli used in much of the reviewed research, I do not think this casualness with respect to terminology is a likely source of confusion.

increased still further the range of utilizable cues shrinks even more. To the extent that some of the cues that the organism can no longer use are task relevant, performance will deteriorate. If we assume further that less complex tasks require a narrower range of cues, we have a model that can account for the finding that optimal arousal decreases with task complexity.

Although there is a substantial amount of support for this hypothesis in a variety of domains (see, e.g., Kahneman, 1973, for a review), it would not appear to be a complete account of the effects of arousal. For example, as Kahneman points out, Easterbrook's hypothesis ". . . implies the unlikely idea that the difficulties of the under-aroused, drowsy subject result from an excessive openness to experience" (p. 40). Problems notwithstanding, as we shall see below, some recent investigations have been motivated by Easterbrook's hypothesis.

In recent years some have attempted to justify the continued use of the Yerkes–Dodson Law (e.g., Anderson, 1990). However, others have argued that it is an outmoded and invalid concept (e.g., Neiss, 1988, 1990). In part, the argument against the Yerkes–Dodson Law is that arousal, motivation, stress, or whatever one might place on the x-axis of the graph that portrays the Law is not a unitary concept. Thus, it is an oversimplification to try to account for behavior in terms of a single concept such as arousal without considering other cognitive and emotional factors.

To give an example of why it may be problematic to consider the x-axis to be unitary, Neiss (1990) considered a study by Anderson and her colleagues in which it was assumed that when college students are put into a situation in which they are given a mock Graduate Record Exam, they will experience uniform arousal, specifically, heightened test anxiety. However, there is much evidence that college students in such situations show a variety of psychobiological responses "from virtual immobilization in the face of potential criticism to exhilaration at the prospect of receiving accolades" (Sarason, 1978, p. 193). It is tempting to consider an analogous argument concerning eyewitness testimony. Some witnesses may perform more poorly because of stress. Others may be motivated by a desire to be able to make an accurate identification and thus "get" the perpetrator. It is certainly thinkable that the latter motivation might result in enhanced performance. We are not yet in a position to make broad pronouncements about the effects of arousal; more detailed knowledge of the effects of individual differences and situational determinants of performance are needed. Research on the effects of arousal on eyewitness performance has not changed materially in nature since the time of the McCloskey and Egeth review in 1983. In part, this is due to ethical restraints on the kinds of stressors that subjects can be exposed to in the laboratory (see, e.g., Christianson, Goodman, & Loftus, 1992). As investigators freely admit in their publications, experimental stressors probably differ in both quality and quantity from the stressors experienced in a real crime.

What does this recent research tell us? As the following capsule summaries of some recent studies make clear, the picture is still mixed. It is still the case that some studies show that arousal impairs performance, while others show no effect, or even an improvement in performance. Some studies have shown improvement for some sorts of information and impairment for other sorts; pursuing such differential effects provides hope that the confusion and inconsistency in this literature may some day be resolved.

Case Studies

A provocative place to begin is with a report of responses to an actual crime. Yuille and Cutshall (1986) interviewed 13 witnesses to a shooting. The criminal was killed at the scene of the crime and there was an abundance of forensic evidence. Thus the accuracy of eyewitness descriptions could be assessed. With respect to the factor of stress, subjects differed in the degree to which they were stressed or upset by the event. The five witnesses who had contact with the thief, the store owner, or a weapon reported the greatest amount of stress. On a 7-point scale they rated their stress levels as 5, 7,7,7, and 8(!). The mean accuracy score for this group was 93% in the police interview immediately after the crime and 88% in the research interview 5 months later. Seven of the remaining 8 witnesses reported stress levels ranging from 1 to 5, and the final subject reported no stress at all. The overall accuracy for these witnesses was 75% correct in the police interview and 76% correct in the later research interview.

Yuille and Cutshall's (1986) results are most likely not a fluke, as other tests of memory for emotionally arousing real-life events have also shown that arousing events may be well remembered. Several studies are concerned with so-called flashbulb memories (Brown & Kulik, 1977); this refers to the sort of memory that may be involved in answering a question such as, Where were you when you heard that Kennedy had been assassinated? Responses are often made confidently and suggest a vivid and accurate memory. While the vividness is not in doubt, there has been some debate about the accuracy of such memories and whether they are the result of some special psychobiological process. The preponderance of the evidence suggests that subjects remember the details surrounding their learning of shocking national news events better than they remember similar information for ordinary events, even though memory for shocking events is not completely accurate (McCloskey, Wible, & Cohen, 1988; Neisser, 1982). In some of these studies, subjects have been asked to rate how aroused they were at the time when they heard the arousing news; the results suggest that higher levels of arousal are associated with greater accuracy (Bohannon, 1992; Christianson, 1989; Pillemer, 1984).

The above findings suggest that stress may be *positively* related to recall of details about crimes and other events experienced in real life. It is important to understand that the data do not make this case unambiguously. In the case of the Yuille and Cutshall (1986) study, the witnesses who were most stressed were also those more deeply involved with or central to the criminal event and thus may have had a better opportunity to observe the events. In the case of the flashbulb memory studies, it is often difficult to establish objectively what subjects really were doing when they heard calamitous news. In any event, however, the results certainly provide no support for the view that stress/arousal automatically leads to poor performance. Because of the difficulty of interpreting such uncontrolled nonlaboratory studies, we shall move on to several more traditional experimental investigations. There are, of course, some problems with doing this; some of the better controlled laboratory studies tend to lack verisimilitude and forensic relevance. However, when independent variables are under the control of the researcher, it is easier to draw conclusions about cause and effect from such studies. In addition, under laboratory conditions it is possible to attempt to asses arousal in various ways, including physiologically. Before continuing with the review of the literature I shall comment briefly on the measurement issue.

In some of the following studies in which arousal level has been manipulated, an effort has been made to assess the efficacy of the manipulation either by subjective report or by physiological measure (e.g., GSR). In other cases a stimulus set has been pretested for arousing effects in a previous study. In a few cases the effect of, say, viewing a picture of a disfigured body has simply been assumed.

One might think that the more objective physiological measures are superior to subjective reports. However, it is not obvious that this is the case. To quote two well-known workers in this field, "Given the long history of arousal in psychological theory, it would seem that the measurement of arousal would be straightforward. Unfortunately, this is not the case. Rather the failure of different measures of arousal to agree with one another is perhaps the greatest source of dissatisfaction with the use of arousal as a unifying theoretical construct" (Revelle and Loftus, 1992, p. 117). They go on to say (p. 122), "when measures are taken within subjects, self-reports of arousal correlate more highly with each of the separate physiological measures than the measures do with each other." Given this situation, it hardly seems reasonable to criticize an individual study on the grounds that it did not include a physiological assessment of subjects' arousal levels.

Laboratory Studies

Negative effect of arousal   There are several experiments that show that arousal can have a deleterious impact on eyewitness accuracy. One widely cited example is Loftus and Burns's (1982) attempt to demonstrate that "mental shock" (an emotionally upsetting picture) can produce retrograde amnesia, that is, that it can lead to forgetting of material encountered just before the shocking event. They presented a 2-min film that depicted a bank robbery that ended with either a violent episode (a boy who is an innocent bystander is shot in the face) or a nonviolent episode. The efficacy of the violence manipulation was confirmed by responses to two questionnaire items asking about the degree to which the videotape was interesting and upsetting. For "upsetting," on a 5-point scale, the violent version earned a mean of 3.30 compared with 1.77 for the nonviolent version, $p < .001$. For "interesting," the scores were 3.77 and 3.50, respectively, $p < .03$.[3] The viewers were asked a series of questions about details from the film. One particular detail, the number on the boy's jersey, was deemed critical by the investigators. They found reduced performance on this item for subjects who had viewed the violent episode (4% correct recalls) compared to those who had viewed the nonviolent episode (28%). This result is taken to support the possibility that arousal can affect eyewitness performance in a retrograde fashion.

In trying to understand what this result means it should be borne in mind that the investigators also examined recall of other items of information. On these items the average percentage of recall was 80% when the episode was violent and 84% when it was nonviolent. This is a small difference; one wonders why the effect is so different for the critical item and the other items. Does mental shock affect only trivial details? Does it affect only items that occur a few seconds before the violent episode? From this study we cannot tell.

The authors would like us to believe that the difference between the violent and nonviolent versions of the story are captured by the notions of stress and arousal. However, the two versions may differ in other ways as well (e.g., how unusual or distinctive they are). Is it reasonable to attribute the obtained difference to emotion? We return to this point later.

In a study by Kramer, Buckhout, Fox, Widman, and Tusche (1991), subjects were shown a sequence of 19 unrelated slides (generally, easily named travel scenes). The tenth item was critical. In the high-stress condition the tenth slide showed the face of a deceased man who had been mutilated with a claw hammer; the slide had a label that read "Courtesy of N. Y. Police Department." In the medium stress condition the same picture was shown but the label said "Courtesy of MGM Studios." The control (low stress) condition showed a woman tourist posing in a travel slide. The subjects' task was to recall the pictures.

There were two chief findings. First, and in direct contrast to Loftus and Burns (1982), there was no retrograde "amnesia" for items presented prior to

---

[3]I have gone into some detail about the assessment of arousal in this first experiment chiefly to give the flavor of the methodology. In general, for the following studies I shall not say much about the assessment of an arousal manipulation unless it is important.

the critical slide. Second, there was a significant anterograde effect; recall of items following the critical slide was significantly worse in the high-stress condition than in the low-stress condition.

Other studies have also found that arousal impairs facial identification. To present just one example, Brigham, Maass, Martinez, and Whittenberger (1983) used electric shock to induce arousal. Subjects saw sequences of slides of faces. In the moderate-arousal condition the first face was followed by a moderate shock, the remaining 24 faces were accompanied by no shock. In the high-arousal condition a low, medium, or high intensity shock was delivered on 12 of the 24 trials. A check indicated that this manipulation worked only for female subjects, thus only the data for the female subjects were analyzed further.

A recognition test was given 7 minutes after the last face was shown. Subjects were shown 68 slides including the 24 shown earlier and asked to indicate via an "old"/"new" judgment which ones they had seen before. Recognition performance was significantly worse for subjects in the high-arousal condition than in the moderate-arousal conditions. The design of this experiment prompts a methodological note. The arousal in this experiment was imposed on the subjects by means of a manipulation that was independent of the content of the stimuli. This should be distinguished from cases in which emotionally arousing materials are to be remembered. This is a general distinction that needs to be kept in mind as one reads studies in this area, as intrinsically and extrinsically generated emotion may have different effects on performance (e.g., Christianson & Mjorndal, 1985; Christianson, Nilsson, Mjorndal, Perris, & Tjellden, 1986).

No effect of arousal   In an ambitious effort to involve subjects directly in a "crime," Hosch and Bothwell (1990) randomly assigned subjects to be either victims of, or bystanders to, a staged purse snatching. In one of the two experiments reported in this paper control subjects were also included in a no-crime condition. Arousal was monitored via skin impedance. There was no significant correlation between identification accuracy and arousal. To the extent that there was a correlation ($p < .10$) it was in the direction of higher arousal being associated with more accurate identification. (Incidentally, reminiscent of Yuille and Cutshall's, 1986, findings in the case of a real crime, victims were more accurate than bystanders.)

In another effort to involve subjects directly in the experimental situation, Maass and Kohnken (1989) investigated arousal in the context of a study of weapon focus. Subjects were studied in a room that contained medical and physiological recording equipment. They were approached by an experimenter who was either holding a syringe or a pen and who either did or did not threaten to give the subject an injection. Threat of an injection did not affect recognition performance on a seven-person target-absent lineup; however, viewing a hypodermic syringe did have such an effect. So, there may be some support here for the notion of weapon focus (this is discussed further below), but not for the importance of threat per se.

Cutler, Penrod, and Martens (1987), had half of their subjects view a videotape of a violent version of a staged crime and the other half view a relatively calm version. Violence of the crime had no effect on identification performance; if anything, identification of the target from a videotaped line-up was slightly but not significantly better in the high-violence condition. If it can be assumed that violence of the crime affected the arousal level of the witness, then we have here an example of a null effect of arousal.

Tooley, Brigham, Maass, and Bothwell (1987) gave half of their subjects noise feedback for "errors" in a photo recognition task and also threatened them with electric shock (this study is described more fully in the section on weapon focus). The effect found here was that hit rate was *higher* for the high-arousal condition. However, when d', the measure of discriminability from signal detection theory, was calculated, that effect disappeared, leaving no difference between arousal conditions.

Positive effect of arousal Earlier, it was pointed out that prominent and emotionally arousing material may interfere with recall, although there is some dispute about whether the effect is anterograde or retrograde (e.g., Kramer et al., 1991; Loftus and Burns, 1982). However, it is important to understand that such material may, itself, stand out in memory. For example, in the study by Kramer et al. (1991), all of the subjects in all conditions recalled the critical tenth slide. Similarly, Ellis, Detterman, Runcie, McCarver, and Craig (1971) studied free recall of names of pictures of unrelated common objects. On one list the eighth (middle) item was a human nude. Recall of this item was near 100%, compared to about 30% for the comparable item in a control list. (In addition, recall of items following the nude was depressed compared to control, and there was a slight diminution of performance on the item immediately preceding the nude.) Of course, this was a test of memory for the name of the slide. Thus, it tests knowledge *that* a nude picture was presented, but does not test whether subjects can tell *which* nude was presented. It would have been interesting to put the face of the nude into a photospread to see if identification was affected by this procedure. The authors might have discovered "genitalia focus" a possible counterpart to weapon focus, which is discussed later.

Loftus and Burns (1982) found that memory for a specific incidental detail was impaired in the arousal condition. In another study in the same vein (Christianson & Loftus, 1987) tests of memory for both trivial and important aspects of a scenario were included. Two groups of subjects each saw a different episode portrayed in a slide show consisting of 15 slides. The two episodes were identical over the first 5 and last 5 slides; only the middle

5 slides differed. In one episode, the middle 5 slides showed a traumatic event (a personal-injury auto accident), while in the other episode the middle 5 slides were emotionally neutral. Slides were presented at the slow rate of 1 every 10 sec to give the subjects time to write down the most salient characteristic of each slide. After a retention interval (20 min or two weeks) subjects were asked to recall in writing all of the features of the slides that they had previously written down. Because these were salient characteristics, this was considered to be a test of central aspects of the event. Finally, they were given a 4-alternative, forced-choice recognition test. One of the four choices in each set was a slide previously shown; the other three were variants that differed in viewpoint. This was considered to be a test of memory for peripheral detail. (Note that there is a confounding between type of information—central vs. peripheral—and type of test—recall vs. recognition).

The chief result was that recall was better for the central events in the traumatic condition than in the neutral condition, but that recognition of details was poorer in the traumatic than in the neutral condition. These effects were limited to the middle 5 slides of the sequences.

The implications of this study for eyewitness situations is a bit unclear. The fact that recall is enhanced by trauma goes against what many experts would like to say about the effects of arousal on performance. The fact that recognition is impaired is interesting but forensically irrelevant because the alternatives were simply different camera shots of the same central objects. Note that facial identification was not tested in this study.

Mixed results: some crucial complications   The finding that memory for details is impaired by arousal is potentially important. However, this result is not inevitable. Heuer and Reisberg (1990) used a paradigm similar to that of Christianson and Loftus (1987). Subjects watched a sequence of 12 slides accompanied by a taped narration that portrayed a story about a mother who takes her son to visit his father at work. The sequences were identical except for the middle group of 5 slides. In the neutral version the father is an auto mechanic and the son watches him repair a car. In the arousal version the father is a surgeon and the son watches him operate on a badly injured accident victim. Two weeks after subjects viewed one of these sequences they were brought back to the laboratory and given unexpected memory tests. Both central and peripheral details were tested via both recall and recognition.

There are some important differences between the Christianson and Loftus (1987) study and the Heuer and Reisberg (1990) study. For one thing, Heuer and Reisberg (1990) defined central and peripheral differently from Christianson and Loftus (1987). In the earlier paper, central information was defined to include any detail pertinent to central characters in the story (e.g., the color of the main character's coat). In the later paper, central information was construed to be any fact or element that could not be changed or excluded without changing the basic story line. Thus, whether the boy was carrying a lunchbox or soccer ball was peripheral, while whether he watched the surgery (or repair) or played in a back room was central. The later paper did not include the forensically useless test of memory for viewpoint (i.e., camera angle).

The chief finding of the Heuer and Reisberg (1990) study was that memory for both central and peripheral details was better in the traumatic than in the neutral condition. The advantage for the arousal subjects was clear and significant for the recognition test. Their advantage was significant in the recall test only for central information. The advantage of the arousal subjects was not just for those slides that were designed to be arousing, but also for the final slides in the story that were identical in the arousal and neutral conditions. Heuer and Reisberg (1990) explicitly make the point that their data are contrary to the Easterbrook (1959) hypothesis; ". . . emotional arousal seems actually to have enhanced the subjects' range of attention, and to have produced fuller, more detailed memory" (p. 504).

Finally, Heuer and Reisberg (1990) point out some interesting and statistically significant differences in the error patterns of their subjects. In examining the recall protocols, they noted that neutral subjects tended to err about the plot, often importing events that had not actually occurred. For example, a subject might recall that the mother went grocery shopping after she left the garage. In contrast, arousal subjects made few plot errors; instead they confabulated about subjects' emotional reactions and motives. "For example, one subject reported vivid recollections of hearing that the mother was upset that the child saw the operation. . . ." (p. 503).

In a recent and rather complex study, Burke, Heuer, and Reisberg (1992) tried to resolve the discrepancy between those studies showing that arousal impairs performance on peripheral details and those that show emotion improves memory for those details. They distinguished among four kinds of to-be-remembered information. What Heuer and Reisberg (1990) had called central information (plot relevant) was now divided into gist and basic-level visual information. Gist refers to a fact or element that one would include when narrating the story, for examples, the fact that the father is a surgeon rather than a pediatrician. Basic-level visual information refers to a basic-level (e.g., Rosch, 1975) answer to the question, What does this slide show? That the slide showed the mother hailing a cab rather than walking was considered basic-level visual information. What Heuer and Reisberg (1990) had called peripheral information (plot irrelevant) was now divided into central details and background details. Central details included plot-irrelevant information associated with the main characters, for example, the color of the mother's sweater. Background details included any detail not associated with the central characters (e.g., whether a slide showing a centrally important damaged car also showed other cars in the background).

Using the same sort of paradigm used earlier by Christianson and Loftus (1987) and Heuer and Reisberg (1990), they found that emotion had markedly different effects on different kinds of material. Arousal improved memory for the gist of a story and for basic-level visual information. It also improved memory for plot-irrelevant details that were associated with the event's center. However, arousal impaired memory for details not associated with the event's center, that is, background details. The interaction between arousal condition and type of event is important, but it by no means captures the full complexity of the reported results. The findings above were moderated by retention interval, by whether they were obtained on a first or a second test of retention, and by story phase (i.e., the first few slides, the critical middle slides, or the final few slides). For the sake of simplicity I shall not attempt a full description of the result, and shall mention just two of the highlights.

With respect to retention interval they found support, albeit weak, for the claim that the effect of emotion is moderated by retention interval (cf. Kleinsmith & Kaplan, 1963, 1964). More specifically, the observed effects suggest that arousal slows the rate of forgetting (see Heuer & Reisberg, 1992, for a fuller discussion).

They also found an effect that is likely to be of forensic relevance, because witnesses to a crime are typically questioned more than once. They found that subjects retested after a week performed better than those tested for the first time at that delay. Further, the repeated testing changed the pattern of the results; the effects of arousal at a one-week second test were more like the effect found at the immediate test rather than that found at the one-week first test. If nothing else, this result serves as an important methodological caution.

At this point I would like to return to a question raised earlier. In the experiments involving stories depicted in film, is it reasonable to attribute the observed effects to emotion rather than some other factor such as distinctiveness, incongruity, or surprise? Several of the investigators have addressed this issue; for an interesting discussion see Burke et al. (1992). The basic answer is that we cannot totally eliminate the possibility of a story/arousal confound; however, with ingenuity and effort investigators can make specific alternative explanations increasingly unlikely. As an example of this process, consider an experiment by Christianson and Loftus (1991). Memory for an unexpected emotional event was compared to memory for an unexpected unusual event; in one case a woman with a bloody head was lying in the street next to a bicycle, and in the other case a woman was walking in the street carrying a bicycle on her shoulder. In the two cases background details were the same. As one would expect from the discussion above, memory for central details was better for the emotional condition. It could be argued that the unusual slide was less distinctive and attention grabbing than the emotional slide. However, it was surely more distinctive and attention grabbing than a control slide, which showed a woman riding her bicycle, and yet performance in the unusual and control slides was comparable. Thus unusualness per se is unlikely to be the crucial factor.

Mechanisms

The effects of emotion on eyewitness testimony are, at present, too complex to be encompassed by any single, simple theory. I certainly do not want to either propose or endorse any specific theoretical account at this time. However, to provide a sense of what is needed in such a theory I shall describe Heuer and Reisberg's (1992) account of emotion's effects.

They propose first that subjects attend differently to emotional materials, and, in particular, attend closely to the central aspects of an emotional scene. On the (plausible) assumption of limited attentional capacity this means less capacity is available to be devoted to peripheral aspects of the scene. They argue that emotionality may also distract subjects at the time of the memory test if it is given after a short retention interval. Over longer retention intervals other factors come into play. They speculate that, "thanks to arousal, and distinctiveness, and increased rehearsal emotional events will be forgotten more slowly than neutral events. In addition the passage of time may sharpen the selectivity of subjects' memories of emotional events . . . as subjects continue to think about the specifics of the emotional episode, rather than the episode's more general features" (p. 175). Together, these factors suggest that the effects of emotion will shift over time, as indeed is indicated in the available data. This account provides a promising start for contemporary theorizing.

Summary and Recommendations

This review suggests that it is still too soon to tell juries anything useful about the effects of arousal on the accuracy of eyewitness testimony.

With respect to forensic relevance there are several problems with research on the effects of arousal on eyewitness performance. For one thing, no single clear pattern has emerged. Studies show a negative, zero, or even positive effect of arousal on performance. There is no way yet to predict with accuracy and confidence which outcome will occur in a given circumstance. However, to the extent that a consensus may be developing on the basis of some of the more ambitious recent studies, it seems to be that arousal improves rather than impairs performance on central information. This flies in the face of what most eyewitness experts now tell juries. It will be important for future studies to address the following issues.

1. As will be evident from the foregoing review, many otherwise interesting and important studies have not tested face recognition (much less in a forensically relevant paradigm). It is not clear at this point to what extent the face of a perpetrator is better characterized as a "central" or as a "peripheral" detail. In any event, it is obviously important to determine whether arousal improves or impairs facial recognition.

2. The story in the laboratory is not yet completely clear, and we do not know how well laboratory-based studies approximate reality. The ability to generalize from the laboratory to the field will require a better theoretical understanding of the underlying processes than we currently have available.

3. The role of individual differences in the response to stress has been relatively neglected. A clear hint of the importance of such considerations comes from an observation mentioned in passing earlier. Brigham et al. (1983) used electric shock to induce arousal; this manipulation worked only for female subjects. More generally, there are some well-established effects of personality characteristics on perception and/or memory. For example, Eysenck, MacLeod, and Mathews (1987) presented homophones auditorily that had both a threat-related and a neutral meaning (e.g., *die* and *dye*, *guilt* and *gilt*). Subjects simply wrote down the spelling of each word as they heard it. Those subjects who were high in trait anxiety wrote down significantly more threat-related interpretations than did those who were low in trait anxiety. In a subsequent study, Eysenck, Mogg, May, Richards, and Mathews (1991) showed a similar effect with ambiguous sentences in a design that suggests the effect is not just a response bias. Research on the effects of arousal on eyewitness behavior would benefit greatly from an increased emphasis on individual differences.

Weapon Focus

The basic idea is that a weapon attracts attention. Time spent attending to a weapon is time not spent processing the face of the weapon holder. Thus, ability to identify the perpetrator should be impaired by weapon presence.

Theoretically, weapon focus would seem to be an entirely reasonable thing to hypothesize. It trades on the notion that attention has a limited capacity and thus the more one attends to one stimulus, the less capacity is available for processing other stimuli (cf. Kahneman, 1973). Roughly analogous phenomena have been documented. For example, Roskos-Ewoldsen and Fazio (1992) have shown that the presence of attitude-evoking objects in the visual field interferes with subjects' performance on a visual search task, and Hansen and Hansen (1988) have shown that angry faces "pop out" of a crowd of other faces in a search task. In both of these studies it seems reasonable to think that the emotion-evoking stimuli were less potent than a weapon.

Literature Review

There is a relatively small literature that pertains directly to the issue of weapon focus. At the time of our earlier review (Egeth & McCloskey, 1984), weapon focus was cited by defense experts at trial, but the data on which their conclusions were based were virtually nonexistent. Since then additional (and improved) studies have been conducted. Twelve studies permitting a total of nineteen tests of the weapon-focus effect were recently subjected to a meta-analysis (Steblay, 1992). Six of these tests showed significant impairment in identification in weapon-present as compared to weapon-absent conditions; thirteen of the tests showed no significant difference. Overall, the meta-analysis showed that the size of the weapon-focus effect was small (.13) for the crucial dependent variable of accuracy of identification in a lineup. For the dependent variable of accuracy of featural description the effect was moderate (.55). Meta-analysis notwithstanding, it will probably be worthwhile to describe some of the individual studies.

Perhaps the most imaginative is the aforementioned study by Maass and Kohnken (1989) in which a weapon was simulated with a hypodermic syringe. These authors examined all combinations of visual exposure to a syringe versus a pen (used as a nonthreatening control) and threat of injection versus no threat. Subjects were brought into a quasi-medical experimental situation and were greeted by a confederate of the experimenters (also referred to below as the target) who was holding either a syringe or a pen. She then said that the injection was either for the subject or for someone else. (In fact, no injections were given.)

Manipulation checks (questionnaires) indicated that subjects were made tense and uneasy by exposure to the syringe but not by mere threat of injection. Recognition accuracy was assessed by means of a seven-person, target-absent lineup with foils similar to the target who had held the syringe. Recognition performance was affected substantially by presence versus absence of the syringe, and affected somewhat, but not reliably, by threat of injection.

Recall of information was also assessed. The results here were not clear-cut for recall of facial details, but they did suggest that recall of information about the hands was better after exposure to the syringe than to the pen, and also after receiving the threat of an injection.

The authors take their findings to be supportive of the notion of weapon focus. The presence of the simulated weapon (the syringe) made subjects more likely to incorrectly choose someone from a lineup that did not contain the actual confederate who had held the syringe.

The applicability of this research to the real world is limited in several ways. On one hand, a syringe is not really a weapon. It is not clear in what direction the results would change if a weapon were used. It is possible that the results would be even more supportive of weapon focus. However, it is also possible that they would be less so. There are no solid a priori principles for deciding this in the absence of additional research.

In addition, the lineup appears to have been presented as a forced-choice procedure; witnesses did not have the option, as far as I can tell, of saying "none of the above." This is a serious problem; many of the false alarms might have been avoided if this option had been available.

Despite the limitations mentioned here this experiment deserves high marks for the effort it represents to move beyond slides and videotaping to a more realistic scenario in which the witnesses have some personal involvement in the situation. Most research on weapon focus uses those more traditional media. Following are some recent examples.

Tooley et al. (1987) investigated the hypothesis that the presence of a weapon can interfere with the encoding of the weapon holder's facial features. White female college students played a visual discrimination "game." They saw a series of 24 slides, each of a man standing in a convenience store. The slides were projected life size. They were to look at each slide and then try to press the "correct" one of four buttons. In fact, there was no correct button; this was merely a cover task to get the subjects (i.e., witnesses) to pay attention to the slides.

There were 24 life-size full-body views; 12 of the slides were of a man holding a gun, 12 were of a man holding an object other than a gun. Each slide was presented for 10 sec and then an additional 5 sec was allowed for the subject to make her choice.

Following the presentation of the slides, subjects viewed 72 color Polaroid photos (including the 24 target persons in different clothing than before, and in a different setting) plus 48 distractors. Each picture was shown for 10 sec, and subjects had to indicate if the person in the photo was a target (i.e., had been shown in a slide earlier).

With respect to weapon focus there was a small but significant effect on accuracy of recognition. Scores (d') were .35 versus .31 for weapon-absent versus weapon-present conditions. To give a feel for the numerical values involved here, note that the following approximate equivalence holds: if the test had required a choice between two alternatives (one target and one distractor) for each target person shown in a slide, the proportion correct would have been approximately .60 in the weapon-absent condition and .59 in the weapon-present condition (estimated from tables by Hacker & Ratcliff, 1979). The effect of weapon presence is small in that it accounts for only 1.6% of the variance.

The design of this study is similar to that of classical laboratory investigations of perception and memory. It lacks forensic relevance. For one thing, subjects saw many targets in a rapidly presented series (10 sec viewing time each). For another, the recognition test required a standard old–new judgment, rather than a photospread or lineup format. (The latter presumably would include a statement that "none of the above" is a reasonable response.) In addition, the numerical results show a small difference between weapon presence and absence. It would be easy for jurors to be misled by simple emphasis on the fact that the results were significantly different.

Kramer, Buckhout, and Eugenio (1990) conducted a two-part investigation into weapon focus. In their first experiment they used slides with an accompanying sound track to expose subjects to a simulated crime that took 70 sec to play out. The event had the complexity and messiness of everyday life. In one condition the assailant held the weapon (a bottle) in such a way that it was visible for 12 sec; in the control condition it was visible for only 4 sec. Subjects were asked questions about features of the assailant (height, weight, age, hair color, etc.). In addition, subjects were shown a six-picture target-present photospread.

A manipulation check showed that the subjects felt more aroused in the experimental condition than in the control condition. The chief finding was that descriptions of the assailant were less accurate for the subjects who had seen the bottle for 12 sec rather than for 4 sec. Not surprisingly, those with a longer exposure were also more accurate in identifying the weapon as a bottle. Performance on the photospread was so poor overall that no difference emerged between the two groups.

In the second part, consisting of four experiments, Kramer et al. (1990) drastically simplified the situation in an attempt to study weapon focus in the absence of emotional arousal; there was just a single person walking in a stark environment. The individual carried either a news magazine (neutral object) or a bloody meat cleaver (weapon). Across the four experiments there was also a manipulation of the exposure durations of the object being carried and of the face of the individual.

As before, there were lower feature-identification scores for those subjects who saw the weapon rather than the magazine. There was also an effect of exposure duration; it was not until the weapon was visible for a fairly small fraction of the total time that the weapon-focus effect was eliminated.

This study is important in that it shows that a weapon-focus effect can be obtained in the absence of heightened arousal. With respect to forensic relevance, however, it is worth keeping in mind that in none of the five experiments reported was there a significant effect on recognition in the photospread.

Loftus, Loftus, and Messo (1987) conducted a test of the weapon-focus hypothesis and directly tested a possible mechanism—differential eye fixations—that might produce the effect. They showed a sequence of slides depicting an event in a fast-food restaurant. Half of the subjects saw a customer point a gun at the cashier, the other half saw the customer hand the cashier a check. In the first experiment, eye movements were recorded while subjects viewed the slides. Results showed that subjects made more eye fixations on the weapon than on the check, and the fixations on the gun were longer in duration than those on the check.

Memory for the events depicted in the slide sequence was assessed 15 min after the end of the slide show. Subjects were given a 20-item, multiple-choice questionnaire. Seven of the items pertained to the target (the customer who held either a gun or a check, depending on the condition). They were then given a photospread with a set of 12 photos.

Subjects in the weapon-present condition were not significantly better than those in the weapon-absent condition on the questionnaire. In the lineup test 7 of the 18 subjects in the weapon-absent condition chose the correct person and 2 of the 18 subjects in the weapon-present condition did so. This difference was significant between the .05 and .06 levels.

Presumably because the results of Experiment 1 did not reach a conventional level of statistical significance, Experiment 2 was conducted with 80 subjects, 40 in the weapon-present condition, and 40 in the weapon-absent condition. No eye movement recording was made.

On the questionnaire (7 items pertaining to the target) there was a significant effect (.05 level) of weapon presence. Weapon subjects were correct on 56% of the items, while control subjects were correct on 67%. On the 12-person lineup, weapon subjects were correct 15% of the time, while control subjects were correct 35% of the time ($p < .05$).

This study provides support for the weapon-focus hypothesis. It also provides support for an obvious mechanism, namely, viewers tend to look at the weapon. Why? Is it the inherent threat that is important or is it that any novel or unexpected object would have the same effect? One cannot tell in the absence of further research.

Given a limited amount of time, it seems reasonable that subjects confronted with a gun may spend some of the available viewing time on the gun rather than on the perpetrator's face. This may reduce the viewer's ability to later remember the face. Such an explanation seems especially appropriate for the present study in which a total of 18 slides were presented for 1.5 sec each, for a total of about 27 sec. The weapon/check was in view for 4 slides, or 6 sec. (It was not indicated how long the target person was in view.) In a crime lasting longer than this it may still be the case that the viewer spends some proportion of the available time looking at the gun (or looking for an escape route). However, this may not matter for later identification if enough time has been spent looking at the face. What is enough time? This is not clear. One possible hint comes from a study by Cutler et al. (1987). One of the factors they manipulated in a large-scale study was exposure duration. Subjects viewed a crime in which the robber was visible for either 30 or 75 sec. There was no significant difference between these conditions (if anything, the shorter exposure led to better performance). Thus, it is at least possible that asymptotically good performance may result with something less than 30 sec of viewing time. This means that beyond some unspecified duration, weapon focus may prove to be relatively unimportant. (This conclusion is not tested by the data of Kramer et al., 1990, as the total exposure duration in each of their second series of experiments was just 18 sec).

One additional article provides some pertinent information. In the aforementioned article by Cutler et al. (1987) there was also a manipulation of weapon visibility. In this study a gun was either brandished throughout the duration of the crime (30 or 75 sec), or was kept hidden most of the time under the robber's coat. Identification of the criminal was better ($p < .01$) in the concealed-weapon condition than in the brandished-weapon condition. The mean scores were .46 and .26, respectively (these means are derived from scoring correct identifications and correct rejections as 1 and misses and false alarms as 0).

In view of the discussion above, it would be useful to know whether the effect of weapon presence differs as a function of exposure duration. This was not reported in the paper, and the data are not shown individually for the four relevant conditions. Instead, it was pointed out that only 4 of the 78 possible two-way interactions in this large, multifactor study were significant at the .05 level, which is about what one would expect on the basis of chance.

Why is this important? I argued above that weapon focus may be more important when the face is exposed for a short rather than a long time. But this seemingly plausible conclusion is not consistent with the implication that there is no interaction between weapon visibility and exposure duration of the assailant's face with an exposure up to 75 sec. This is a puzzling situation. It would be best to design a study to explicitly focus on the possible interaction of target and weapon exposure duration.

Summary and Recommendations

Since McCloskey and Egeth's (1983) critique, several studies have been published that suggest presence of a weapon may influence identification accuracy and may cause foils to be incorrectly selected from target-absent lineups. None of the studies individually tells an entirely convincing story. It is tempting in such circumstances to conclude that en masse the studies correct one another's shortcomings and lead to a supportable conclusion.

That is a plausible but not a necessary outcome. It will be important for further research to address the following issues.

1. The effect of weapon focus has not been found consistently in identification tasks using photospreads or lineups, but it is precisely identification, rather than accuracy of verbal descriptors, that juries are most concerned with.

2. The forensic relevance of weapon-focus studies would be enhanced if the effect were demonstrated with target-absent lineups, as this is the kind of lineup that can lead to an innocent person's conviction.

3. Individual differences in susceptibility to the weapon-focus effect need to be assessed.

4. The theoretical explanation of the weapon-focus effect needs to be clarified and rigorously tested. This includes clarification of the temporal factors associated with weapon focus (e.g., the factors that affect the proportion of time spent viewing an assailant's weapon rather than his or her face).

5. As part of the theoretical development called for in 4., a particular point is worth mentioning, given the focus of this volume. Kramer et al. (1990) argued that emotional arousal was not crucial, as weapon focus was obtained even in a stark environment. This claim needs to be examined carefully. It is possible that it is the emotion-evoking properties of the weapon that are important in creating the weapon-focus effect, even if the arousal is not sufficient to cause a significant change in self-rating of arousal on a seven-point scale.

We clearly know more about weapon focus than we did ten years ago. However, until the above issues are addressed in a satisfactory fashion I would have to conclude that it is still too early for psychologists to testify about weapon focus in front of juries.

Acknowledgments

Support for this research was provided in part by the Air Force Office of Scientific Research (AFOSR-ISSA-92-0041) and by the National Science Foundation (BNS-8919554).

References

Anderson, K. J. (1990). Arousal and the inverted-U hypothesis: A critique of Neiss' "Reconceptualizing arousal." *Psychological Bulletin*, 107, 96–100.

Bohannon, J. N. (1992). Arousal and memory: Quantity and consistency over the years. In E. Winograd & U. Neisser (eds.), *Affect and accuracy in recall: The problem of "flashbulb" memories* (pp. 65–91). New York: Cambridge University Press.

Brigham, J. C., Maass, A., Martinez, D., & Whittenberger, G. (1983). The effect of arousal on facial recognition. *Basic and Applied Social Psychology,* 4, 279–293.

Brown, R., & Kulik, J. (1977). Flashbulb memories. *Cognition,* 5, 73–99.

Burke, A., Heuer, F., & Reisberg, D. (1992). Remembering emotional events. *Memory & Cognition,* 20, 277–290.

Christianson, S. A. (1989). Flashbulb memories: Special, but not so special. *Memory & Cognition,* 17, 435–443.

Christianson, S. A. (1992a). Emotional stress and eyewitness memory: A critical review. *Psychological Bulletin,* 112, 284–309.

Christianson, S. A. (1992b). *The handbook of emotion and memory: Research and theory.* Hillsdale, NJ: Erlbaum.

Christianson, S. A., & Loftus, E. F. (1987). Memory for traumatic events. *Applied Cognitive Psychology,* 1, 225–239.

Christianson, S. A. & Loftus, E. F. (1991). Remembering emotional events: The fate of detailed information. *Cognition & Emotion,* 5, 81–108.

Christianson, S. A., & Mjorndal, T. (1985). Adrenalin, emotional arousal, and memory. *Scandinavian Journal of Psychology,* 26, 237–248.

Christianson, S. A., Nilsson, L. G., Mjorndal, T., Perris, C., & Tjellden, G. (1986). Psychological versus physiological determinants of emotional arousal and its relationship to laboratory amnesia. *Scandinavian Journal of Psychology,* 27, 302–312.

Christianson, S. A., Goodman, J., & Loftus, E. F. (1992). Eyewitness memory for stressful events: Methodological quandaries and ethical dilemmas. In S. A. Christianson (ed.), *The handbook of emotion and memory: Research and theory* (pp. 217–241). Hillsdale, NJ: Erlbaum.

Cutler, B. L., Penrod, S. D., & Martens, T. K. (1987). The reliability of eyewitness identification: The role of system and estimator variables. *Law and Human Behavior,* 11, 233–258.

Deffenbacher, K. (1983). The influence of arousal on reliability of testimony. In S. M. A. Loyd-Bostock & B. R. Clifford (eds.). *Evaluating witness evidence* (pp. 235–251). Chichester: Wiley.

Easterbrook, J. A. (1959). The effect of emotion on cue utilization and the organization of behavior. *Psychological Review,* 66, 183–201.

Ebbesen, E. B. & Konecni, V. J. (1989). Eyewitness memory research: Probative v. prejudicial value. Unpublished manuscript, University of California, Department of Psychology, San Diego.

Egeth, H. E. (1993a). What do we *not* know about eyewitness identification. *American Psychologist,* 48, 577–580.

Egeth, H. E. (1993b). Expert psychological testimony about eyewitnesses: An update. In F. Kessel (ed.), *Psychology, science, and human affairs: Essays in honor of William Bevan.* Boulder, CO: Westview (in press).

Egeth, H. E., & McCloskey, M. (1984). Expert testimony about eyewitness behavior: Is it safe and effective? In G. L. Wells & E. F. Loftus (eds.), *Eyewitness testimony: Psychological perspectives.* Cambridge: Cambridge University Press.

Ellis, N. R., Detterman, D. K., Runcie, D., McCarver, R. B., & Craig, E. M. (1971). Amnesic effects in short-term memory. *Journal of Experimental Psychology,* 89, 357–361.

Eysenck, M. W., MacLeod, C., & Mathews, A. (1987). Cognitive functioning and anxiety. *Psychological Research,* 49, 189–195.

Eysenck, M. W., Mogg, K., May, J., Richards, A., & Mathews, A. (1991). Bias in interpretation of ambiguous sentences related to threat in anxiety. *Journal of Abnormal Psychology,* 100, 144–150.

Hacker, M. J., & Ratcliff, R. (1979). A revised table of d′ for M-alternative forced choice. *Perception & Psychophysics,* 26, 168–170.

Hansen, C. H., & Hansen, R. D. (1988). Finding the face in the crowd: An anger superiority effect. *Journal of Personality and Social Psychology, 54,* 917–924.

Heuer, F., & Reisberg, D. (1990). Vivid memories of emotional events: The accuracy of remembered minutiae. *Memory & Cognition, 18,* 496–506.

Heuer, F., & Reisberg, D. (1992). Emotion, arousal and memory for detail. In S. A. Christianson (ed.), *The handbook of emotion and memory: Research and theory* (pp. 151–180). Hillsdale, NJ: Erlbaum.

Hosch, H. M., & Bothwell, R. K. (1990). Arousal, description, and identification accuracy of victims and bystanders. *Journal of Social Behavior and Personality, 5,* 481–488.

Kahneman, D. (1973). *Attention and effort.* Englewood Cliffs, NJ: Prentice-Hall.

Kassin, S. M., Ellsworth, P. C., & Smith, V. L. (1989). The "general acceptance" of psychological research on eyewitness testimony. *American Psychologist, 44,* 1089–1098.

Kleinsmith, L. J., & Kaplan, S. (1963). Paired-associative learning as a function of arousal and interpolated interval. *Journal of Experimental Psychology, 65,* 190–193.

Kleinsmith, L. J., & Kaplan, S. (1964). The interaction of arousal and recall interval in nonsense syllable paired-associate learning. *Journal of Experimental Psychology, 67,* 124–126.

Kramer, T. H., Buckhout, R., & Eugenio, P. (1990). Weapon focus, arousal, and eyewitness memory: Attention must be paid. *Law and Human Behavior, 14,* 167–184.

Kramer, T. H., Buckhout, R., Fox, P., E., Widman, & Tusche, B. (1991). Effects of stress on recall. *Applied Cognitive Psychology, 5,* 483–488.

Loftus, E. F., & Burns, T. E. (1982). Mental shock can cause retrograde amnesia. *Memory and Cognition, 10*(4), 318–323.

Loftus, E. F., Loftus, G. R., & Messo, J. (1987). Some facts about "weapon focus." *Law and Human Behavior, 11,* 55–62.

Maass, A., & Kohnken, G. (1989). Eyewitness identification: Simulating the "weapon effect." *Law and Human Behavior, 13,* 397–408.

McCloskey, M., & Egeth, H. (1983). Eyewitness identification: What can a psychologist tell a jury? *American Psychologist, 38,* 550–563.

McCloskey, M., Egeth, H., & McKenna, J. (1986). The experimental psychologist in court: The ethics of expert testimony. *Law and Human Behavior, 10,* 1–13.

McCloskey, M., Wible, C. G., & Cohen, N. J. (1988). Is there a special flashbulb-memory mechanism? *Journal of Experimental Psychology: General, 117,* 171–181.

Neiss, R. (1988). Reconceptualizing arousal: Psychobiological states in motor performance. *Psychological Bulletin, 103,* 345–366.

Neiss, R. (1990). Ending arousal's reign of error: A reply to Anderson. *Psychological Bulletin, 107*(1), 101–105.

Neisser, U. (1982). Snapshots or benchmarks? In U. Neisser (ed.), *Memory observed* (pp. 43–48). New York: W. H. Freeman.

Pillemer, D. B. (1984). Flashbulb memories of the assassination attempt on President Reagan. *Cognition, 16,* 63–80.

Revelle, W., & Loftus, D. A. (1992). The implications of arousal effects for the study of affect and memory. In S. A. Christianson (Ed.), *The handbook of emotion and memory: Research and theory* (pp. 113–149). Hillsdale, NJ: Erlbaum.

Rosch, E. (1975). Cognitive reference points. *Cognitive Psychology, 7,* 532–547.

Roskos-Ewoldsen, D. R., & Fazio, R. H. (1992). On the orienting value of attitudes: Attitude accessibility as a determinant of an object's attraction of visual attention. *Journal of Personality and Social Psychology, 63,* 198–211.

Sarason, I. G. (1978). The test anxiety scale: Concept and research. In C. D. Speilberger & I. G. Sarason (eds.), *Stress and anxiety,* (Vol. 5, pp. 193–216). Washington, D.C.: Hemisphere.

Steblay, N. M. (1992). A meta-analytic review of the weapon focus effect. *Law and Human Behavior, 16,* 413–424.

Tooley, V., Brigham, J. C., Maass, A., & Bothwell, R. K. (1987). Facial recognition: Weapon effect and attentional focus. *Journal of Applied Social Psychology, 17*(10), 845–859.

Yerkes, R. M., & Dodson, J. D. (1908). The relation of strength of stimulus to rapidity of habit-formation. *Journal of Comparative and Neurological Psychology, 18*, 459–482.

Yuille, J. C., & Cutshall, J. L. (1986). A case study of eyewitness memory of a crime. *Journal of Applied Psychology, 71*(2), 291–301.

The View from the Heart's Eye: A Commentary

Jerome Bruner
New York University

I

Before commenting on particular chapters in this volume, first I need to discuss some historical, philosophical, and even autobiographical issues in order to make clearer the perspective from which I want to approach my task.

Let me begin with a historical note. There are not many enduring "mental" dichotomies (in contrast to "moral" ones) to be found in our culture's folk psychology—dichotomies that show up again and again in folktales, fiction, and folk maxims. One of them is the ancient contrast between "emotion" and "cognition"—classically referred to as "the passions" versus "reason" and more latterly captured by the distinction, say, between "ego" and "id." This distinction, at the very heart of the present volume, is a puzzling one, for it is concerned with a contrast that, anomalously, seems at once to be intuitively obvious, though in fact it is conceptually elusive, as we shall soon see. Yet, it may well be its very anomalousness that makes the distinc-

The Heart's Eye: Emotional Influences in Perception and Attention

tion as attractive to the "new" scientific psychology of the last two centuries as it had been to the folk psychology that preceded it. Both folk psychology and its upscale scientific cousin seem more susceptible to the provocations of anomaly than to the seemingly humdrum and self-evident—more stirred to "explain" visual illusions, say, than the visual constancies.

One might even innocently suppose that the distinction between emotion and cognition, given its ancient origin and stubborn persistence, must correspond to some clear-cut distinction in human phenomenology: that we *experience* "the passions" in one way and "reason" in some distinguishably different way, just as, say, we experience "hearing" differently from we experience "seeing." Everybody appreciates the sensory difference between the two senses, even though it is astonishingly difficult to explain it to anybody who is not already able to appreciate it. Yet, we would have to conclude after some reflection that the cognition–emotion dichotomy could not possibly be based on such a self-evident phenomenological marking. If it were, there would never have been such an everlasting human dilemma as to whether at any given moment we were, ourselves, under the control of reason or of some passion. Humankind (at least since the Greeks) has, after all, been constantly occupied with devising technologies (like logic, mathematics, and science) to "check up" on whether we have kept to the straight and narrow path of reason or have gone astray. We, in our own times, have even constructed our share of such technologies, ranging from psychoanalysis for sorting ego from id to logic machines for sorting out the computable from the uncomputable. The two examples, indeed, suggest a deeper truth: that the distinction itself could not be founded on "immediate phenomenology," but must instead be based on one's conceptual position about how the mind "works"—upon an implicit or explicit "theory of mind." And theories of mind differ, as we all know, in astonishing degree: in their notions about the mind's access to an "external world," in conceptions of mental architecture, even in claims about the "substance" of which mind is composed.

In spite of all that, however, the contending theories continue to agree in differentiating mental operations driven by "emotional" states of mind from ones guided by "reason." This leads one to suspect that the distinction, rather than being based upon a phenomenological foundation, must rest instead on a pragmatic assessment of the *results* or consequences of various mental activities. Reason guides mental activities that end up with "right results"; passions drive mental activities into getting "wrong" ones. But the "wrong results" are not simply random in nature; they are also systematic in their own way. The systematic ways in which the passions presumably "get it wrong" come eventually to be labeled in terms of a morphology of the passions whose categories even become conventionalized (Mesquita & Frijda, 1992). Mental processes are said to fall systematically under the control of particular "passions" under particular circumstances, like jealousy, or envy, or fear, or greed, each producing a recognizable set of "mental errors" in contrast with the "right results" forthcoming under the sway of reason.

Note that in this cool dispensation, passions are *many*, reason *one*. There is presumed to be a singular set of principles of "right reason" but many routes to error. And philosophers from the Sophists to Boole and contemporary AI theorists have all believed (or hoped) that *the* principles of right reason could finally be set down in a kind of rule book. But nobody (or at least nobody in his or her right mind) ever dreamed that all the roads leading to the errors of passion could be mapped. The wrong roads, rather, were to be found in the unfinished and unfinishable atlas of narrative, story, drama, allegory that tell about human failings. And during the Age of Positivism (out of which we are only now emerging), the two domains—right reasoning and storytelling—were to be kept strictly segregated.

It is tempting to imagine that the distinction between the passions and reason dates back to an earlier evolutionary period when our ancestors, as Whiten (1991) has proposed, were first constructing a "theory of mind" to help construe whether their conspecifics were "really" in an agonistic, cooperative, or mating frame of mind, or only pretending so for ulterior reasons. Insofar as our primate ancestors can be supposed to have used and recognized deceit in interacting with each other, they must already have been making a distinction between actions guided by particular passions (or drives) and action guided by a "rational" assessment of its consequences. In any case, following Whiten's argument, it is easier to imagine that the distinction first rose in assessing the results of action in the social sphere rather than in the sensorimotor one.

It is probably an evolutionary legacy of that early primate adjustment that has made *Homo sapiens* so sensitive, swift, and precocious in recognizing emotional expressive states in our conspecifics—in their facial expression, gesture, voice tone, and so on. From this legacy might also come the capacity to recognize such emotional states even without the intervention of elaborate inferential activity (Zajonc, 1984). What happens, however, as human culture becomes elaborate and our conspecifics come to rely on an increasingly semiotic system for expressing their intentional states? Preadapted recognition mechanisms no longer suffice for recognizing threat gestures or signs of fear or sexual arousal in others and, by the same token, the process of conventional semiotization may even make our own states of internal arousal less recognizable to us (if the James–Lange theory is to be believed). Perforce, inferences and calculation come into play, and we may even depend finally on such institutions as law courts to decide whether somebody was being "really" unfriendly or operating with a cooly fraudulent intent.

Therefore, with semiotic conventionalization, the distinction between the purely cognitive and the emotional becomes more contingent, more context sensitive, more culturally imbedded. The "stimuli" that were supposed "naturally" to evoke emotional reactions must now be judged in the light of taboos, normative expectations, conventions of situational appropriateness, felicity conditions, and the like. The "sexiness" of a potential partner is no longer just a matter of physique or bodily gesture alone, but depends as well on classificatory kinship, social class, appropriate dress, and even the "right accent."

It becomes even more involved than that. In any developed culture, folk psychology, custom, and even the code of law "packages" acceptable links between how one is supposed to feel and think and the situation one is supposed to be in for these states to be appropriate: what conditions should conventionally produce envy, or fear, or rage, or even feelings of guilt, and how one is supposed to operate mentally in those states and under those conditions. The law is full of such prescriptive packages. It cannot be first degree murder if the accused's arousal was "tonic": that makes it second degree murder or manslaughter. There has to be "phasic" malice afore-thought; even at that, under the doctrine of *mens rea*, it is not first degree murder, whatever the emotional arousal, unless the accused party can be shown to understand the difference between "right" and "wrong." Murder, by law and by folk psychology, requires an element of rationality.

What I have said up to now is, of course, distorted, for it is only one side of the coin—the world from a rationalistic perspective. Both our tradition and the history of human culture tell us that "emotion" has surely *not* always been awarded lower marks than "reason" in guiding human activity, even mental activity. This rationalistic bias has, in fact, never spread much beyond science and mathematics, and it hardly held sway in science before Des-cartes (Toulmin, 1990). Descartes's powerful but chilling notion was that issues of truth could be decided in the light of reason alone, and to do so one had only to examine the consistency of the formal propositions in which truth claims were couched and then evaluate them against the empirical evidence on which such claims were based. Rhetoric—appeals to the heart, as it were—had no place in Cartesian science. However, in the ordinary conduct of life, on the contrary, we have always honored "faith," "love," "loyalty," "righteous indignation," and so on as indispensable to "knowing" the everyday world. We teach our children to be sensitive to suffering and need, to recognize the affection of others, to give the benefit of doubt to kin and friends with respect to their "intentions," and none of these by posterior reflection alone, but in the way we experience things directly. Those who depend on afterthought to see the world in a kindly or "human" light are soon classified, like Brutus, as having a "lean and hungry look." If the sci-ences idealize the power and virtues of cool, unclouded reason in the "ratio-nal domain," then literature, morality, and the arts celebrate the other side of the story in the "human" one.

So, the people whom we study in our experiments and case studies come to us like Hamlets, unwilling to live "sicklied o'er with the palid cast of thought," but uneasy when heeding only "the still small voice of reason." As I have tried to point out elsewhere (Bruner, 1986, 1991), they develop modes of thought, of reckoning, and of perceiving that correspond to the two ideals: the paradigmatic one of rational science and logic, and the narrative one of literature and myth—the first concerned with "truth" and explanation, the second with "lifelikeness" and understanding; one aimed at achieving cool context independence, the other at increasing sympathy and sensitivity to cultural or "human" contexts. It is not surprising, then, that we have difficulty understanding our subjects' reactions when we "run them through" our experiments. (The very expression, "run them through" probably reflects our wish to turn them into neutral creatures with a psychological pH of 7.0!) Indeed, the debate about "direct" versus "inferential" perception of emotions is a reflection of that perplexity. Are they inferring or experiencing emotional arousal directly and without intervening inference? Why need it be one *or* the other? There is surely enough evidence in this volume alone to suggest that the two kinds of processes constantly interact with each other in everyday life.

The deeper question is *how* they interact, not whether one can devise clever experiments to isolate them from each other. Nor does it seem to me to be theoretically necessary for Zajonc (1984), or Lazarus (1982), or Derryberry and Tucker (this volume) to make claims for or against such autonomy. The more fruitful questions, rather, are about the constituent processes in emotional arousal, how they are triggered, and how they find a final common path in perceiving, thinking, and remembering. Everybody agrees, I think, that there is both evidence for as well as adaptive advantages to fast, direct affective arousal that can preadapt and then steer subsequent cognitive processing. Everybody also agrees that too much or too preemptive such preattentive triggering risks biasing attendant cognitive processing into maladaptive error and psychological tunnel vision.

That the capacity for interaction between "ordinary" and "emotionally driven" perceptual processes is available is not doubted any longer, thanks to three decades of reliable research. We have a solid body of evidence that extends well beyond the rebellious wave of early New Look research: the well-known priming procedure has demonstrated the link between the two again and again, to take just one example of experimental findings. Meaningful priming stimuli, for example, facilitate the subsequent recognition of semantically related stimuli, even when the primes have been shown to have gone undetected and even have been visually masked out for good measure, as well (Marcel, 1983a,b). Eagle (1959) showed that judgments of the "perceived character" of a pictured boy are significantly influenced by whether the judging task was preceded by a subthreshold presentation of the boy engaged in a kindly or in a hostile activity. In addition, if priming studies were not enough to pin down forever the interaction of emotion and perception, there is the evidence of quite deep preattentive processing available from studies of blindsight (Weiskrantz, 1986). To bring the catalog to an end, there is ample evidence that "switching" in dichotic listening is triggered by the nonconscious processing of meaning and personal relevance through the "tuned-out" ear. Granted that one can find instances of nonreplication of some of these results, I am now inclined to interpret them as suggesting that it is not easy to control emotional states in a laboratory setting—a matter to which I shall revert later. In any case, we no longer need to feel compelled to "explain away" these effects in support of a positivist sense-data theory of perception, but need rather to make sense of them in terms of a general theory that gets us beyond the old positivism—even if the theory at the start does little more than implicate different processing loci in the brain, like the amygdala and hippocampus, or the right cortex and the left.

II

Here, I must drag in some autobiography to make my own biases clearer. I have long been puzzled about how perception manages to be sensitive both to the stimulus geography of the impinging world while at the same time serving as a selector and/or filter in helping us sort out adaptively "relevant" features of input. Balancing these two requirements for a perceptual system—representational accuracy and selective filtering—poses an adaptive problem of the first order, one that is by no means solved just by postulating an intervening buffer store that holds a denser representation of the world in short-term memory, from which longer term processes can then "select" a more situationally and motivationally relevant sample for conscious recognition. Wherever this filter-attenuator may be, at a buffer store or in the "heart's eye," it still needs to resolve the problem of balancing representativeness and relevance in its selection (Bruner, 1957a).

Little of this balancing act ever gets into consciousness: it seems wholly or principally "preattentive," which suggests it is affected by some sort of modular architecture, as many have pointed out (e.g., Johnson-Laird, 1983). I once suggested (Bruner, 1957c), more in the interest of finding a working metaphor than of offering an explanation, that such a system resembles a connected set of unconscious hypotheses, each of which could be preactivated by cuing. The more preactivated a hypothesis, the less input necessary for its confirmation. Particular hypotheses could then be cued by their serial position in larger scale hypotheses about the expected order of events in the world (e.g., Miller, Bruner, & Postman, 1954). Such higher order, serially ordered hypotheses were only one of many kinds of "hypothetical strate-gies." They could be serially ordered in many ways. In reading ordinary text, for example, expected order might be determined by learned rules of gram-mar (Miller, Heise, & Lichten, 1951), or they could be governed by narrative expectancies, as in the classic experiment of Heider and Simmel (1944). One might even characterize hypothesis strategies in terms of personal "styles": cautious and daring (Bruner, 1957c), defensive or vigilant (Bruner & Post-man, 1947), leveling and assimilating (Klein, 1964), even pessimistic or not (Cantor & Kihlstrom, 1987).

Whatever the rules governing such a system, whatever its "strategy," it had to balance the requirements imposed by the twin criteria of "representative-ness" and "relevance." The first serves to minimize surprise, to represent perceptually what is "there" in the world of objects and spaces, and this function is of course greatly facilitated by such innate or "autochthonous" perceptual processing as figure–ground formation, contour and gradient resolution, and so on. However, such processing also relies heavily on learn-ing as well, learning where things are to be found, and under what circum-stances what might be expected to go with what else. It must be a system highly sensitized to the slightest deviations from canonical contingencies; so, like Sokolov (1963), I even speculated that this sensitivity to deviation might be neurally mediated by the Ascending Reticular System's fast trans-mission of deviations to the cerebral cortex, with consequent arousal of corrective exploratory scanning (Bruner, 1957b). I was greatly taken in those days by George Miller's compelling metaphor: once equipped with such a system, he argued, we were in possession of a representation of the world that could be "spun" forward a little faster than the world went in order to anticipate coming world states, or spun backward in order to discover errors and make corrections.[1]

The second objective, "relevance," had as its principal function to keep us tuned to what we needed, wanted, feared, were searching for. It was the "hot" side of the perceptual system, or as Karl Pribram (1971) insisted, the "amyg-dala" side. Indeed, it is this side of things that the present volume is about, the "heart's eye" view of perception. It is the more difficult, the "passions" side.

Mary McCarthy (1992) quotes George Orwell's maxim that an autobiogra-phy is no good unless it tells something awful about its author. The awful thing I have now to report is that this darker side of perception made me lose my nerve, or, to put it in a more kindly (but undeserved) light, I fell victim to frustration.

I fell victim to what must have been the most powerful positivist percep-

---

[1]This was a position that Miller put forward in a General Education course, "Conceptions of Man," that the two of us taught jointly at Harvard in the 1960s.

tual dogma in existence in the dark days before the cognitive revolution: that perception (that is to say, *real* perception) is simply registering or not registering on sense-based stimulus input, a matter of stimuli "out there" getting above the threshold of consciousness. Percepts, on this view, were not constituted by organizational processes, such as those under the control of emotional arousal, but were simply there, to be registered in awareness only when they jumped over the threshold barrier. It seemed to me in my state of frustration, that the best way of unseating this positivist dogma was to outflank it rather than to attack it frontally. Otherwise, the opposition would continue to interpret any emotional effects on perception as yet another demonstration that you could raise or lower thresholds by altering the "set" of the observer ("set" usually being rendered as *Einstellung* to indicate its hallowed origins), just like Helmholtz's "unconscious inference" sorting out cues in depth perception. It was this positivist view that stoked the Judas Eye outcry: how could a perceiver "know" that a stimulus "was" and yet not "see" it? Not until the early studies of semantically guided dichotic switching, followed by Broadbent's (1958) masterful dual-process proposal of a Short-Term Memory with a buffer store plus a Long-Term Memory, did the Judas Eye outcry begin to abate. My attempt (Bruner, 1957b) to invoke the "wet" machinery of the extrapyramidal Ascending Reticular System as a vehicle of preattentive priming (as it would later be called) never got off the ground in psychology, though it was already textbook fodder in neurophysiology (e.g., Adrian, 1954).

What particularly baffled me at that time were the curious *categorical* findings that kept reappearing in the data we were collecting, categorical findings plainly related to the operation of "emotional" or motivational factors. The prerecognition "guesses" of our subjects in tachistoscopic experiments illustrate the problem. Subjects seemed to be picking up affectively and motivationally related information from stimulus inputs before they could properly recognize what was "really there." Exposed at subthreshold durations to tachistoscopically presented words representing their high value preferences, for example, subjects often produced "covaluant" synonyms (Postman, Bruner, & McGinnies, 1948). This simply could not be response suppression to "dirty words," which was an alternative, more behaviorist version of the Judas Eye argument. I began getting much more interested in the idea of perceptual recognition as involving, *inter alia*, early recognition of category membership even before the stimulus words we were using could be processed for their particular meanings. I began to wonder whether such preattentive category placement might lay at the heart of emotionally mediated perceptual selectivity.

I got caught by the nature of categorization itself—what was involved in recognizing something as an instance of a wider category. Soon enough I began detouring out of perception into the study of conceptual processes where categorization is the very name of the game. That was also a good way to get away from the barking of the dogmatic positivists. It was not particularly courageous, but those years of research with Goodnow and Austin (Bruner, Goodnow, & Austin, 1956) were wonderfully diverting. In any case, the New Look, or New Look 1, as it is now called, gradually dimmed, though a New Look 2 soon emerged (more cognitively oriented [cf. Bruner, 1992]), and now we are in the midst of what is plainly New Look 3, of which this book is a sterling example.

III

Now to some comments on this volume, and I want to begin by noting what seem to me to be its principal features. Virtually all the foregoing chapters show what I can only refer to as a renewed respect for a rather classical form of functionalism, one that tries to situate perception in a broader functional picture of human adaptation. Some of this functionalist emphasis grows out of hypotheses about presumed constraints imposed by humans' evolutionary history, some from hypotheses about what living in social groups might require of perceptual processing, and some from assumptions about what it takes particularly to deal with threat and anxiety. I shall return to details presently, but here I only want to remark on the fact that this new functionalism situates perception more firmly in general psychological theory. By doing so, moreover, it manages to steer clear of ancestral tendencies to lean too heavily on psychoanalytic metaphors, on ones drawn from learning theory, or on some unearthly combination of the two. Several authors (Kitayama & Howard; Niedenthal, Setterlund, & Jones; and Derryberry and Tucker, all in this volume), for example, even argue explicitly against old-style "dynamic" metaphors that have perceptual selectivity serving only in behalf of ego defenses, as in the tired 1950s dichotomy between perceptual vigilance and defense. However, the authors in question are certainly not lacking in a sense of the adaptive dynamics of selectivity: their views are simply subtler than the old psychoanalytic dogmas.

Let me try to construct a kind of composite picture of how these investigators go about their business, hoping that in doing so I can avoid doing violence to the differences between them. It can start with the process referred to by Kitayama and Howard (this volume) as "amplification." Amplification in perception is effected by just enough initial preconscious "previewing" of stimulus input to yield a minimal "sense of understanding." This may be something like "category placement." Output from this previewing then shunts subsequent processing into a narrower categorical domain, and activates memory traces and processing strategies relevant to that narrower domain. The initial previewing process may (but need not) be mediated by direct (noninferential) priming of the kind found by Hansen and Hansen (this volume) who show by electromyography, for example, that perceivers mimic the facial gestures of a target face at prerecognition exposure durations. The Hansens' findings suggest that a quick-triggered mimetic reaction might not only facilitate affective bonding with a putative partner, but could also send reafferent signals back into the system to assure arousal-appropriate perceptual processing of that partner.

What happens next depends on what emotional state is aroused by the perceived stimulus, since each aroused state may access distinctive processing programs. Further arousal will also depend, of course, on situational and ontogenetic factors that may be concurrently at work; but whatever situational and ontogenetic factors may operate, they can only operate within the narrowed domain initially activated (accessing, e.g., only domain-relevant memory traces).

Initial preattentive priming, however, does not determine everything that happens downstream of it. Take the preactivation of threat as an example. It does not determine everything that follows. However fast the initial and automatic preattentive response, adaptational reasons may still require that a subsequently recognized threatening stimulus input be more carefully or "deeply" processed than a neutral stimulus. Even when threatening stimuli evoke hair-trigger preattentive priming, later processing may still be slow. We know this from Hansen and Hansen's (1988) work, inspired by Treisman and Souther's (1985) "pop-out" paradigm. Hansen and Hansen, using a "face-in-the-crowd" recognition task, found that a happy face in an angry crowd takes longer to spot than an angry face among happy ones—which makes its own adaptive sense, for it takes more time and effort to process angry faces that "matter" sociobiologically than to process simply "pleasant" ones. Presumably, we cannot as easily "let go" perceptually of angry faces while searching for a happy one as we can happy ones while searching for an angry one. In this interesting example, then, preattentive "amplification" and subsequent processing may have their own requirements and seem able, then, to function independent of each other.

My composite example serves well to illustrate how far beyond the "top-down" style of invoking vigilance-defense the new work has come. What strikes me about the new approach is not only its flexibility, but the sheer range of empirical phenomena that it can encompass. By comparison, the ad hoc predictions drawn from top-down psychoanalytic metaphors seem wooden and contrived. Let it be said, by the way, that even psychoanalytic researchers, like Donald Spence (1993), for example, are turning to more general principles of cognitive functioning under motivated conditions to guide psychoanalytic thinking rather than following the reverse route.

One final point about the new functionalism. Under its sway, even the old "common sense" assumption that threat was the only source of preattentive vigilance has fared poorly. The burden of research now seems to indicate that *any* emotionally or motivationally relevant stimulus input, whatever its valence, has an alerting prerecognition effect. But the valence of a priming input may nonetheless have differential effects on subsequent processing, as we can infer from the face-in-the-crowd research just described. Therefore, it is to be expected that perceptual processing as an extended activity will not yield stereotyped effects that can be predicted from the valence of a stimulus alone.

Indeed, the impact of threat, anxiety, and stress on perception figures often in the chapters of this volume. Let me go back to an older study to illustrate some additional changes in interpretation that distinguish the newer work from the older. In an early experiment by Postman and myself (Postman & Bruner, 1948), for example, stress was induced in our subjects by hassling them for "doing so badly" during a standard tachistoscopic recognition task on which they were engaged. In fact, they were doing fine until we "got to them." After a while they began to perform less cumulatively and to concentrate on tiny details of the word displays being presented. Not surprisingly, their recognition thresholds were raised.

Now, traditionally, one would invoke the Yerkes–Dodson Law to account for the decrement in performance: the stress presumably raised motivation beyond the optimum peak of the Yerkes–Dodson function. But the Yerkes–Dodson Law really has nothing to say about the processes leading to such a decrement in performance. It is not about process at all, and it certainly says nothing about excessive motivation *narrowing* perceptual processing. I should have known that from an earlier rat study (of all things!) indicating that if animals are too hungry, they pick up fewer surplus cues in a maze-learning task (Bruner, Matter, & Papanek, 1955). The hungrier rats also showed less Vicarious Trial and Error ("looking back and forth" at choice points in the maze), as behaviorally compelling an indication of "perceptual narrowing" as you can find. Thus, rather than anybody invoking the vacuous Yerkes–Dodson Law (Yerkes & Dodson, 1908) to account for a performance decrement in that old Postman–Bruner (1948) study, one would do far better to consider the instrumental consequences of forcing our subjects to get "quick results" in order to please the tormenting experimenters.[2]

That kind of functional interpretation, it seems to me, comes much closer to the spirit of the newer work on the perceptual effects of stress. As in all cognitive activity, and in perception under emotion, one looks for particular and appropriate strategies that affect how people pick up and transform information about the world. It is not enough to invoke the great global processes like the Yerkes–Dodson Law, reinforcement, vigilance, or whatever—

---

[2]In fact, we did not invoke the Yerkes–Dodson Law to account for our results, but some of our learning theory colleagues did.

not because the age is against Grand Theory, but simply because Grand Theory gets nowhere unless you can specify little rules that convert it into Particular Performance, like showing how "deep structure" grammar affects the particulars of "surface structure" speech.

Now, with a steady enough diet of particular forms of arousal, our modes of processing may even become habitual or traitlike. A tendency toward narrowing, for example, may even generalize. Evidence in this volume even suggests how this might occur. Narrowing, we have known for some time, is a consequence of emotional arousal, no matter what its valence, for example, Worthington (1969) and Erdelyi and Appelbaum (1973). Narrowing, however, has some curious supplemental effects. Emotion-inducing words are, for example, perceived as brighter than their neutral pair-mates, even though both are still below recognition threshold in a tachistoscopic presentation. An emotion-arousing central target, we learn from the above studies, also impairs the perception of visually peripheral cues, even when it is at sub-threshold level. This is all in addition to the narrowing effects of "amplification." It seems to lead to accentuation, to "peripheral" inhibition, and to the usual narrowing of subsequent processing.

Take a further step. Is it not reasonable to suppose that some people ("typologically," as it were) tend toward more ready emotional arousal? Might they not be more susceptible, given more practice in arousal, to more extreme amplification—more vivid accentuation, more tunnel vision when aroused, more "locked-in" subsequent processing of input, or, conversely, less so, by way of a self-protective adaptation to their own tendencies? Indeed, George Klein (e.g., 1964) devoted his later life trying to derive (unsuccessfully, I believe) just such kinds of perceptual orientations from psychoanalytic theory—"sharpening" in contrast to "leveling." What do our authors in this volume have to say about such matters?

Suppose we agree at the outset with Derryberry and Tucker that "it is clear that orienting is regulated not only by properties of a given stimulus in itself, but also by an analysis of the stimulus in relation to current needs and goals" (Derryberry & Tucker, this volume). To this general summary, however, some complications need to be added. Take the matter of "analysis . . . in relation to current needs and goals" just mentioned. These authors themselves speak of the "incentive" properties of a display—features of it that are sensed to be goal relevant or not (Derryberry & Tucker, this volume). May there not be some chronic difference in the "sensing" of putative relevance by different subjects? May this not be an aspect of "emotionalism"?

Some chapters in this volume speak to such issues. Take Thayer's proposed two-dimensional scheme contrasting the "energetic" dimension of arousal with its "tenseness" (Derryberry & Tucker, this volume). The former distinguishes between an arousal that is "alert" from one that is "sleepy"; the other between a "steady" in contrast to a "jittery" arousal. Let me come back to these in a moment. The second suggestion is Tucker and Williamson's distinction between "tonic" and "phasic" arousal, the first more occasion linked, the other more chronic. In Thayer's account, subjects can be highly energized yet jumpy (like the stressed subjects in the Postman–Bruner [1948] study cited earlier), or they can be alert and steady, and so on. The "tenseness" of arousal is more chronic and more likely to characterize some-body's arousal pattern over time. Thayer suggests, interestingly, that too high a level of tenseness may lead eventually to a decrement in sheer arousal level, for it may be difficult to sustain. Such long-range and middle-range effects on arousal (though still untested hypotheses) are highly sug-gestive of the forms that emotionality may take.

The Tucker–Williamson tonic–phasic proposals are suggestive in a com-plementary way. The tonic activation system is presumed to have its origins in fight–flight mechanisms, closely related to the arousal and regulation of the motor neurosystem. It is presumed, accordingly, to be related to threat and alarm and to responses appropriate to them, and because motor con-trol implicates cognitive processing in the left hemisphere, the tonic system is presumed to be lateralized on that side. In Tucker's view, this system specializes processing to deal with redundant features of input. Phasic arousal, on the other hand, is related to the depression–elation dimension of mood. Rather than responding to redundant features of the stimulus world, it is sensitive to novelty and habituation. In tonic arousal, attention is more focused on the longer term features of input in order to be able to register on redundancy—and is consequently negligent of novelty. The re-verse tendency is present in phasic arousal, and because mood seems more dependent on right-brain functioning, phasic arousal is assumed to be lat-eralized on that side.

What I like particularly about both approaches, the energy–tenseness and the tonic–phasic distinction as well, is that they begin to yield hypotheses about "perceptual styles" and such cognitively related dispositions as intro-version, extraversion, and the like. However, what is needed, I think, is more effort to tie such ideas back into specific perceptual theories, like the ideas about "amplification" discussed earlier. By combining the two approaches, we might be able to form some closer union between the findings of specific "occasion related" experiments and those that derive from more persono-logical research—the kind of union that motivated George Klein (1964), and that seems to be a feature of New Look 3 as well (e.g., Erdelyi, 1992).

Indeed, perhaps such a union may be further encouraged by neuropsy-chological research, which is also a feature of much of the work reported in this volume. Here is an example: if tonic anxiety arousal tends to focus attention on local rather than global features of a stimulus array (for which there is good evidence), it is of considerable additional interest that this sort of "local focusing" is also associated with left-hemisphere functioning. Might we not also expect from these findings some predictions about the further effects of left and right hemisphere stimulation or injury—or, to revert to an earlier point, some predictions as well about amygdala and hippocampal activation or injury?

As for particular methodological "procedures" that impress me in the chapters of this volume, my favorite is priming. It provides a powerful tool, not only for investigating preattentive perceptual functioning, but also, by permitting localization of stimulus presentation on the retina, allows for exploration of the locus of neural mediation. As in the Marcel (1983a,b) studies already mentioned, the priming procedure also permits the use of masking input as a means for interfering differentially with the iconic storage of primes, and while this technique was introduced a decade ago, it has not yet been exploited to its full. And priming can be used not only to study the facilitation (or inhibition) of subsequent *recognition* of related stimuli, but also for its effects on judgment, as in Eagle's (1959) old study cited earlier. I rather suspect that if Rip Van Winkle had fallen asleep during New Look 1 and come awake today, what would most likely light up his amygdala would be the still unexploited possibilities of the priming tool. In fact, this volume would have been impossible without it, all of which is hardly to hail it as the first "all purpose" procedure, a matter to which I come next.

With respect to promising changes in research design reflected in this volume, I am most struck by the addition of a new "naturalism," both in stimulus materials and in perceptual tasks used. There has always been a risk that perceptual theories would be squeezed down to a scope that fit only the stimulus variable we traditionally had worked with (word frequencies, text redundancy, grammaticality, etc.) plus a last little codicil about "other effects," including emotional arousal. Now, however, we are getting studies of the perception of real faces or of real voices in real states of emotion, paired with referentially conflicting verbal labels, as in Stroop-like designs. All of this casts into some doubt what I said directly above about the priming paradigm, which, on the whole, has been restricted to verbally encoded stimulus material, though it surely need not be. If I had to choose a particularly interesting example of the "new naturalism," I would single out again the Hansen and Hansen study in this volume. It employs faces as stimuli, looks to resulting innervation of the subject's own facial musculature as both an interpersonal mediator and as a reafference booster, and could even examine what happens when ambiguous faces (let us not forget the Mona Lisa!) are employed, or when the subject's own facial musculature is concealed, say, by a mask that would make it invisible to a putative partner. However, I do not mean to push the issue of naturalism. Psychological experiments, like any other kinds of experiments, are designed with the eventual aim of "taking things apart" with a view to testing a theory. I have it in mind only that if the object of the exercise is to study emotions, one should not stint in arousing them and in trying to do so with a view to representative design.

I certainly hope that the movement toward greater naturalism will go even further, for, in fact, we know much too little about aroused perception in "real life," and we have little idea whether our laboratory procedures properly capture it. There was that emotionally upsetting Princeton–Dartmouth football game that Hastorf and Cantril (1954) studied, or the case study of those people scared out of their wits by the infamous Orson Welles' broadcast of "The War of the Worlds" (Cantril, 1940). However, neither of them studied the perceptual details, nor do we quite know how to go about it. There is also "eye-witness testimony" (see Egeth's chapter, this volume), but it is mostly linked to studies of "accuracy of report," and that is only a small part of the perceptual puzzle. What of the perceptual overspill of such phenomena as attribution, apparent locus of control, categorization, apparent causality, and intention? Do they require perceptually determined sympathetic weather? I even have a cranky little theory about why we do not study such matters more, aside from the sheer technical difficulty of doing so. Let me end this chapter with it, for it will also serve to bring us back to the point where we started.

For at least a decade now, there has been a lively movement for a new "cultural psychology" (Shweder & LeVine, 1984; Cole, 1993; Bruner, 1990; Shweder, 1991; Markus & Kitayama, 1991). It is mostly centered on the processes through which human beings construct meaning, and on the "prosthetic devices" that a culture provides for doing so. One of the most powerful means we have for making meaning is our narrative capacity: our power to create and to use stories as means for bringing order and sense into experience. Stories are not "after the fact": we *perceive* stories in progress—we *see* or *hear* people as heroes, recognize situations as dangerous or benign in terms of an encompassing plot.

In addition, of course, stories are about the "passions"—about the many different ways in which (from a paradigmatic-logical perspective) we fail to get "right results." As many writers on the technical properties of narrative have pointed out (Labov, 1981; Bruner, 1991), stories revolve around departures from expectancy, how these came about, and what people do about them. I suspect that when we take our subjects into our laboratories, we are giving them some sort of clear signal to stop acting in the narrative mode. We make it seem that we want them to tell us the "naked untruth" about what they see or hear (to borrow the playwright Christopher Fry's telling phrase).

Suppose, instead, we switched on their narrative mode when we led them to the tachistoscope or put on their impedance-matched earphones. Suppose we told them they were about to see or hear scenes from a story and that their job was to figure out what was happening now and what would happen next. After all, that is what we do ourselves when we walk into a department meeting or come home after work or go visit a friend, enemy, or lover. To what extent and in what manner, under those circumstances, would "amplification," with its sequencing, accentuation, and the rest, operate differently? Would they enhance narrative structure? Will the "rules" of narrative processing differ in major ways from what we find when we tell our subjects to tell us straight out what they really "see" or "hear"—even though we tell them to "guess" when they are not sure?

Ever since first reading Bartlett's *Remembering* (1932), I've wondered what he meant when he said that the schematic elaboration of memory provided "sympathetic weather" for events being recalled. Surely "eye witness" research makes plain that "sympathetic weather" does not brew up in memory alone, for whenever we have allowed ourselves to find out, we also discover that perception is as richly schematic as memory; it is in the provision of sympathetic weather, I suspect, that emotion provides its biggest assist in the organization of perceptual life.

Many of our most emotionally evocative encounters with the world are produced not so much by particular events in the world but by how we constitute these events into a form that allows them to function in stories, as constituents of narrative structures. We perform these feats so rapidly, so automatically, and so without awareness, that the ensuing awareness is like naked consciousness itself. If, as Nisbett and Wilson (1977) say, the unconscious knows more than you can tell, then what it knows is most often how something fits into a particular kind of story—and such a "fit" (or "misfit") is surely one of the most powerful activators of emotion. There is nothing intrinsically enraging about a white jury in a middle-class California suburb acquitting some Los Angeles police officers of a charge of violent assault against a Black. The enraged emotion in the Rodney King cases comes from a narrative sense of what the events meant. Much of the priming in everyday behavior comes not from the subthreshold flash of a stimulus, but from chronic expectancies that hair-trigger our stored narrative structures. Are those tonic arousal patterns to which Derryberry and Tucker (this volume) refer organized around the narratives that organize our expectations about fight and flight activities?

To sum it all up, finally, the state of play in the study of emotion and perception is surely bubbling. Those who thought the New Look had bogged down were plainly wrong. The *new* New Look (cf. *American Psychologist*, June, 1992) seems to have given a new life to the study of emotion-and-perception. At last, it has finally liberated us from the positivist sense-data dogma—that perception is just a matter of physical input getting up over the threshold, and the rest is trivial. *That* is progress!

References

Adrian, E. D. (1954). The physiological basis of perception. In E. D. Adrian (ed), *Brain mechanisms and consciousness*. Oxford: Blackwell.

Bartlett, F. C. (1932). *Remembering*. Cambridge: Cambridge University Press.

Broadbent, D. E. (1958). *Perception and communication*. Oxford: Pergamon.

Bruner, J. S. (1957a). Going beyond the information given. In J. S. Bruner, E. Brunswik, L. Festinger, F. Heider, K. Muenzinger, C. E. Osgood, & D. Rapaport, (eds.), *Contemporary approaches to cognition*. Cambridge: Harvard University Press.

Bruner, J. S. (1957b). Neural mechanisms in perception. *Psychological Review*, 64, 340–358.

Bruner, J. (1957c). On perceptual readiness. *Psychological Review*, 64, 123–152.

Bruner, J. S. (1986). *Actual minds, possible worlds*. Cambridge: Harvard University Press.

Bruner, J. S. (1990). *Acts of meaning*. Cambridge: Harvard University Press.

Bruner, J. S. (1991). The narrative construction of reality. *Critical Inquiry* (Autumn Issue), 1–21.

Bruner, J. (1992). Another look at New Look I. *American Psychologist*, 47, 780–783.

Bruner, J. S., & Postman, L. (1947). Emotional selectivity in perception and reaction. *Journal of Personality*, 16, 69–77.

Bruner, J. S., Matter, J., & Papanek, M. L. (1955). Breadth of learning as a function of drive level and mechanization. *Psychological Review*, 62, 1–10.

Bruner, J. S., Matter, J., & Papanek, M. L. (1958). Breadth of learning as a function of drive level and mechanization. *Psychological Review*, 62, 1–10.

Bruner, J. S., Goodnow, J. J., & Austin, G. A. (1956). *A study of thinking*. New York: Wiley.

Cantor, N., & Kihlstrom, J. F. (1987). *Personality and social intelligence*. Englewood Cliffs, NJ: Prentice-Hall.

Cantril, H. (1940). *The Invasion from Mars*. Princeton, Princeton University Press.

Cole, M. (1993). Culture and mind. In G. Harman (ed.). *Conceptions of the Mind: Essays in Honor of George A. Miller*. Hillsdale, NJ: Erlbaum.

Eagle, M. (1959). The effects of subliminal stimuli of aggressive content upon conscious cognition. *Journal of Personality*, 27, 578–600.

Erdelyi, M. H. (1992). Psychodynamics and the unconscious. *American Psychologist*, 47, 784–787.

Erdelyi, M. H., & Appelbaum, G. A. (1973). Cognitive masking: The disruption effect of an emotional stimulus on the perception of contiguous neutral items. *Bulletin of the Psychonomic Society*, 1, 59–61.

Hansen, C. H., & Hansen, R. D. (1988). Finding the face in the crowd: An anger superiority effect. *Journal of Personality and Social Psychology*, 54, 917–924.

Hastorf, A., & Cantril, H. (1954). They saw a game: A case study. *Journal of Abnormal and Social Psychology*, 97, 399–401.

Heider, F., & Simmel, M. (1944). An experimental study of apparent behavior. *American Journal of Psychology*, 57, 243–259.

Johnson-Laird, P. N. (1983). *Mental models*. Cambridge: Harvard University Press.

Klein, G. S. (1964). Need and regulation. In M. R. Jones (ed.), *Nebraska symposium on motivation*. Lincoln: University of Nebraska Press.

Labov, W. (1981). Speech actions and reactions in personal narrative. *Georgetown University Round-table on Language and Linguistics*, 219–247.

Lazarus, R. S. (1982). Thoughts on the relation between emotion and cognition. *American Psychologist*, 37, 1019–1024.

McCarthy, M. (1992). *Intellectual memoirs: New York 1936–1938*. New York: Harcourt Brace Jovanovich.

Marcel, A. J. (1983a). Conscious and unconscious perception: Experiments on visual masking and word recognition. *Cognitive Psychology*, 15, 197–237.

Marcel, A. J. (1983b). Conscious and unconscious perception: An approach to the relations between phenomenal experience and perceptual processes. *Cognitive Psychology,* 15, 238–300.

Markus, H., & Kitayama, S. (1991). Culture and the self: Implications for cognition, emotion, and motivation, *Psychological Review,* 98, 224–253.

Mesquita, B., & Frijda, N. H. (1992). Cultural variations in emotions: A review. *Psychological Bulletin,* 112, 179–204.

Miller, G. A., Heise, G. A., & Lichten, W. (1951). The intelligibility of speech as a function of the context of the test materials. *Journal of Experimental Psychology,* 41, 329–335.

Miller, G. A., Bruner, J. S., & Postman, L. (1954). Familiarity of letter sequences and tachistoscopic identification. *Journal of General Psychology,* 50, 129–139.

Nisbett, R. E., & Wilson, T. D. (1977). Telling more than we can know: Verbal reports on mental processes. *Psychological Review,* 84, 231–259.

Postman, L. & Bruner, J. S. (1948). Perception under stress. *Psychological Review,* 55, 314–323.

Postman, L., Bruner, J. S., & McGinnies, E. (1948). Personal values as selective factors in perception. *Journal of Abnormal and Social Psychology,* 43, 142–154.

Pribram, K. (1971). *Languages of the brain: Experimental paradoxes and principles of neuropsychology.* Englewood Cliffs, NJ: Prentice-Hall.

Shweder, R. (1991). *Thinking through cultures: Expeditions in cultural psychology.* Cambridge: Harvard University Press.

Shweder, R., & Levine R. A. (eds.). (1984). *Culture theory: Essays on mind, self, and emotion.* Cambridge: Cambridge University Press.

Sokolov, Y. N. (1963). *Perception and the conditioned reflex.* Oxford: Pergamon Press.

Spence, D. (1993). The hermeneutic turn: Soft science or loyal opposition? *Psychoanalytic Discourse,* 3, 1–10.

Toulmin, S. (1990). *Cosmopolis: The hidden agenda of modernity.* Chicago: University of Chicago Press.

Treisman, A. M., and Souther, J. (1985). Search asymmetry: A diagnostic of preattentive processing of separable features. *Journal of Experimental Psychology: General,* 114, 285–310.

Weiskrantz, L. (1986). *Blindsight: A case study and implications.* Oxford: Clarendon Press.

Whiten, A. (ed.). (1991). *Natural theories of mind: Evolution, simulation, and development of everyday mindreading.* Oxford: Basil Blackwell.

Worthington, A. G. (1969). Paired comparison scaling of brightness judgments: A method for the measurement of perceptual defense. *British Journal of Psychology,* 60, 363–368.

Yerkes, R. M., and Dodson, J. D. (1908). The relation of strength of stimulus to rapidity of habit formation. *Journal of Comparative and Neurological Psychology,* 18, 459–482.

Zajonc, R. (1984). On the primacy of affect. *American Psychologist,* 39, 117–123.

Index